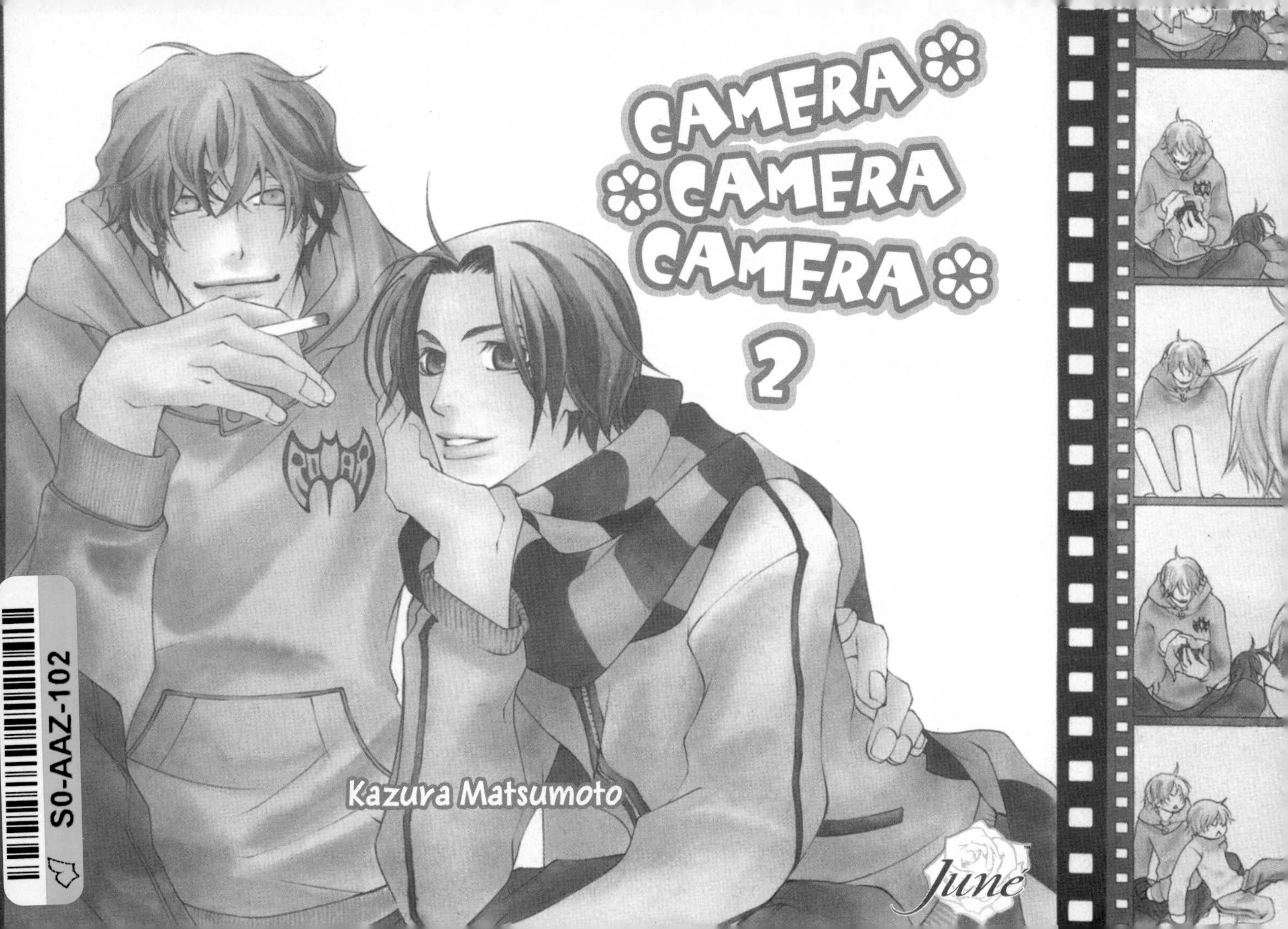
CAMERA CAMERA CAMERA
2
Kazura Matsumoto
Juné

❀ CAMERA CAMERA CAMERA ❀

2

Translation	Sachiko Sato
Lettering	Samantha Yamanaka
Graphic Design	Fred Lui / Wendy Lee
Editing	Samantha Yamanaka
Editor in Chief	Fred Lui
Publisher	Hikaru Sasahara

English Edition Published by
DIGITAL MANGA PUBLISHING
A division of DIGITAL MANGA, Inc.
1487 W 178th Street, Suite 300
Gardena, CA 90248

www.dmpbooks.com

First Edition: February 2008
ISBN: 1-56970-758-8
ISBN-13: 978-1-56970-758-6

1 3 5 7 9 10 8 6 4 2

Printed in China

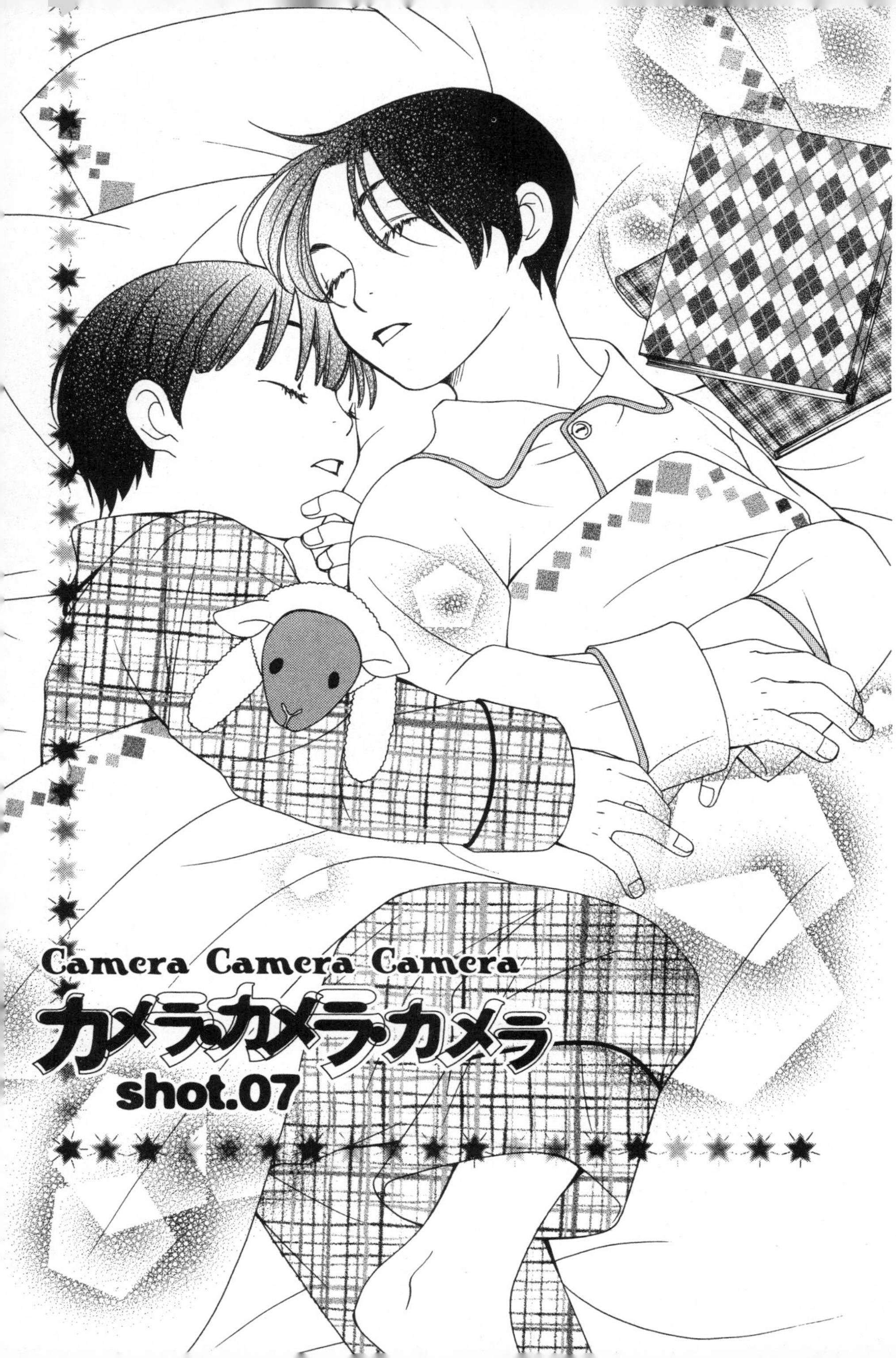
Camera Camera Camera
カメラ・カメラ・カメラ
shot.07

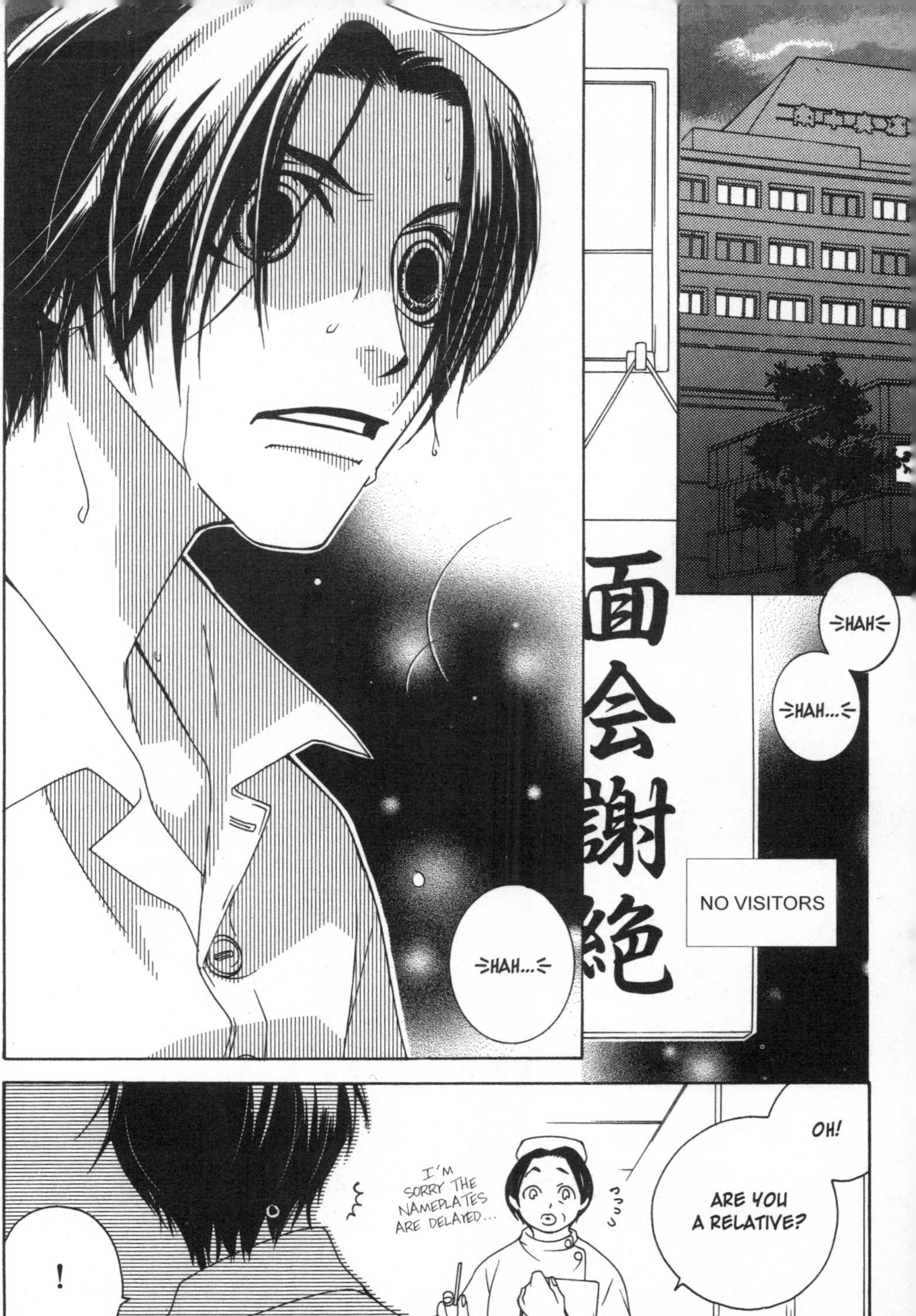

HAH
HAH...
面会謝絶
NO VISITORS
HAH...
OH!
ARE YOU A RELATIVE?
I'M SORRY THE NAMEPLATES ARE DELAYED...
!

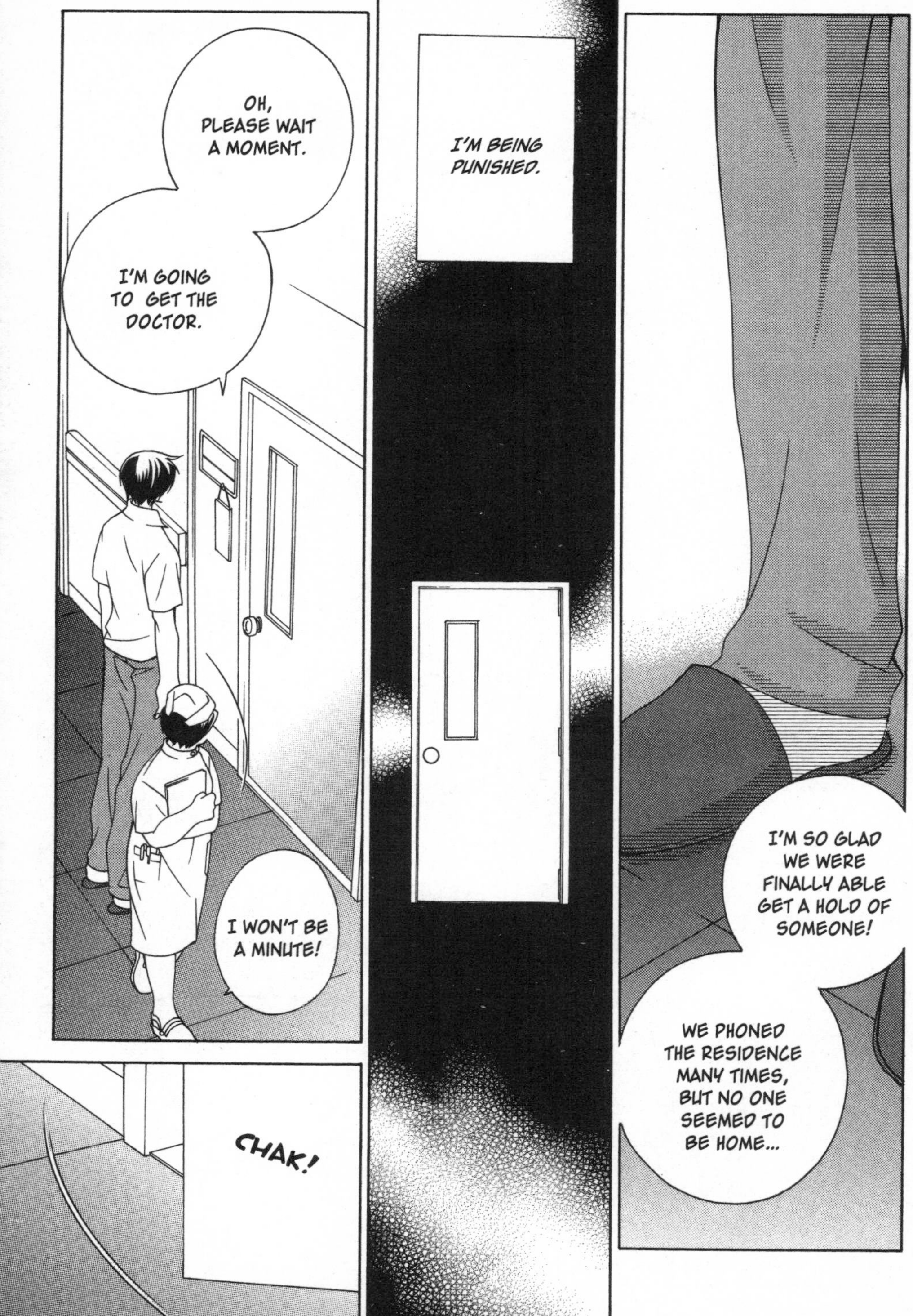
I'M SO GLAD WE WERE FINALLY ABLE GET A HOLD OF SOMEONE!
WE PHONED THE RESIDENCE MANY TIMES, BUT NO ONE SEEMED TO BE HOME...
I'M BEING PUNISHED.
OH, PLEASE WAIT A MOMENT.
I'M GOING TO GET THE DOCTOR.
I WON'T BE A MINUTE!
CHAK!

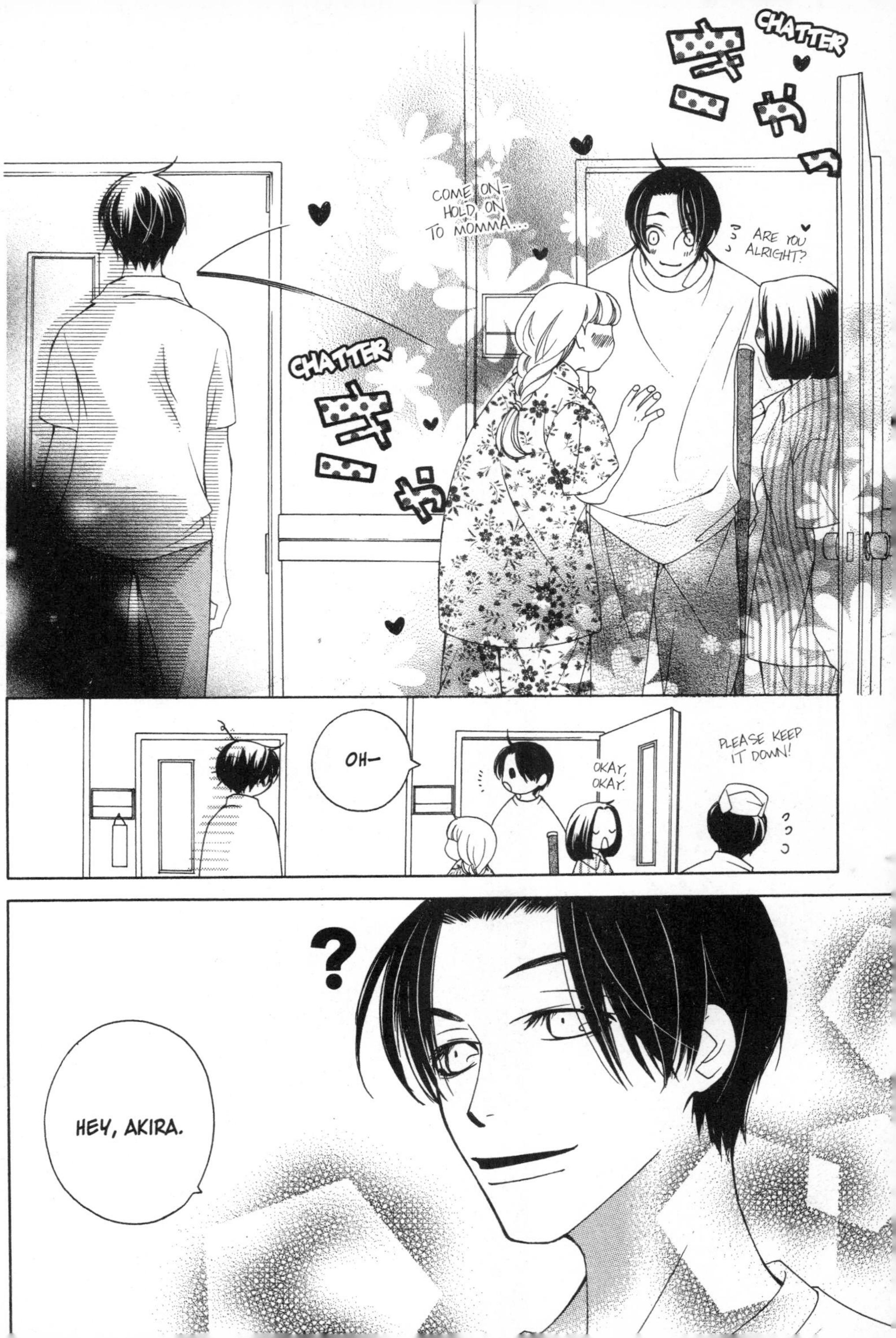
CHATTER
ARE YOU ALRIGHT?
COME ON— HOLD ON TO MOMMA...
CHATTER
PLEASE KEEP IT DOWN!
OKAY, OKAY.
OH—
HEY, AKIRA.

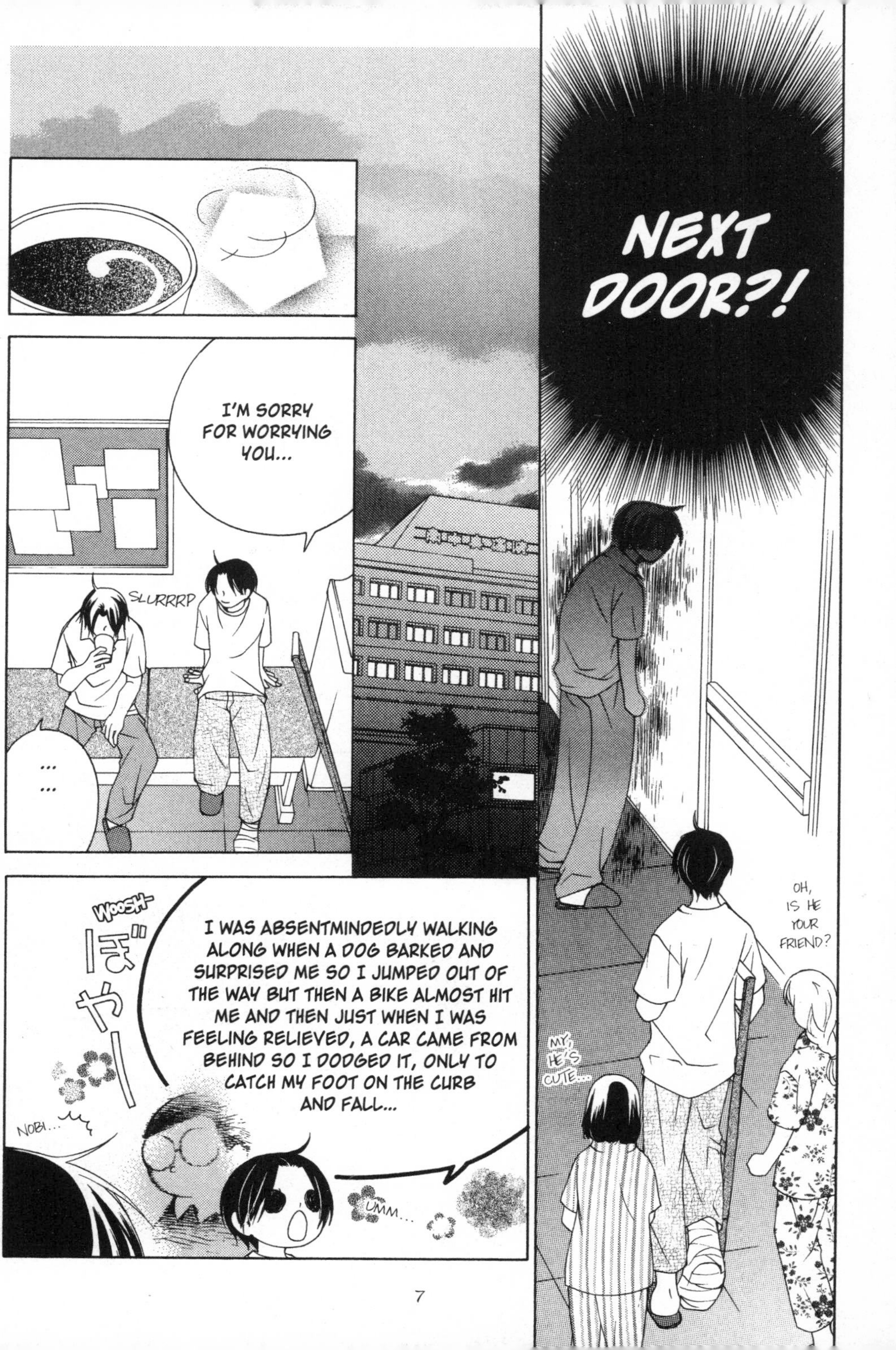
NEXT DOOR?!
OH, IS HE YOUR FRIEND?
MY, HE'S CUTE...
I'M SORRY FOR WORRYING YOU...
SLURRRP
... ...
WOOSH-
ぼやー
I WAS ABSENTMINDEDLY WALKING ALONG WHEN A DOG BARKED AND SURPRISED ME SO I JUMPED OUT OF THE WAY BUT THEN A BIKE ALMOST HIT ME AND THEN JUST WHEN I WAS FEELING RELIEVED, A CAR CAME FROM BEHIND SO I DODGED IT, ONLY TO CATCH MY FOOT ON THE CURB AND FALL...
NOBI...
UMM...

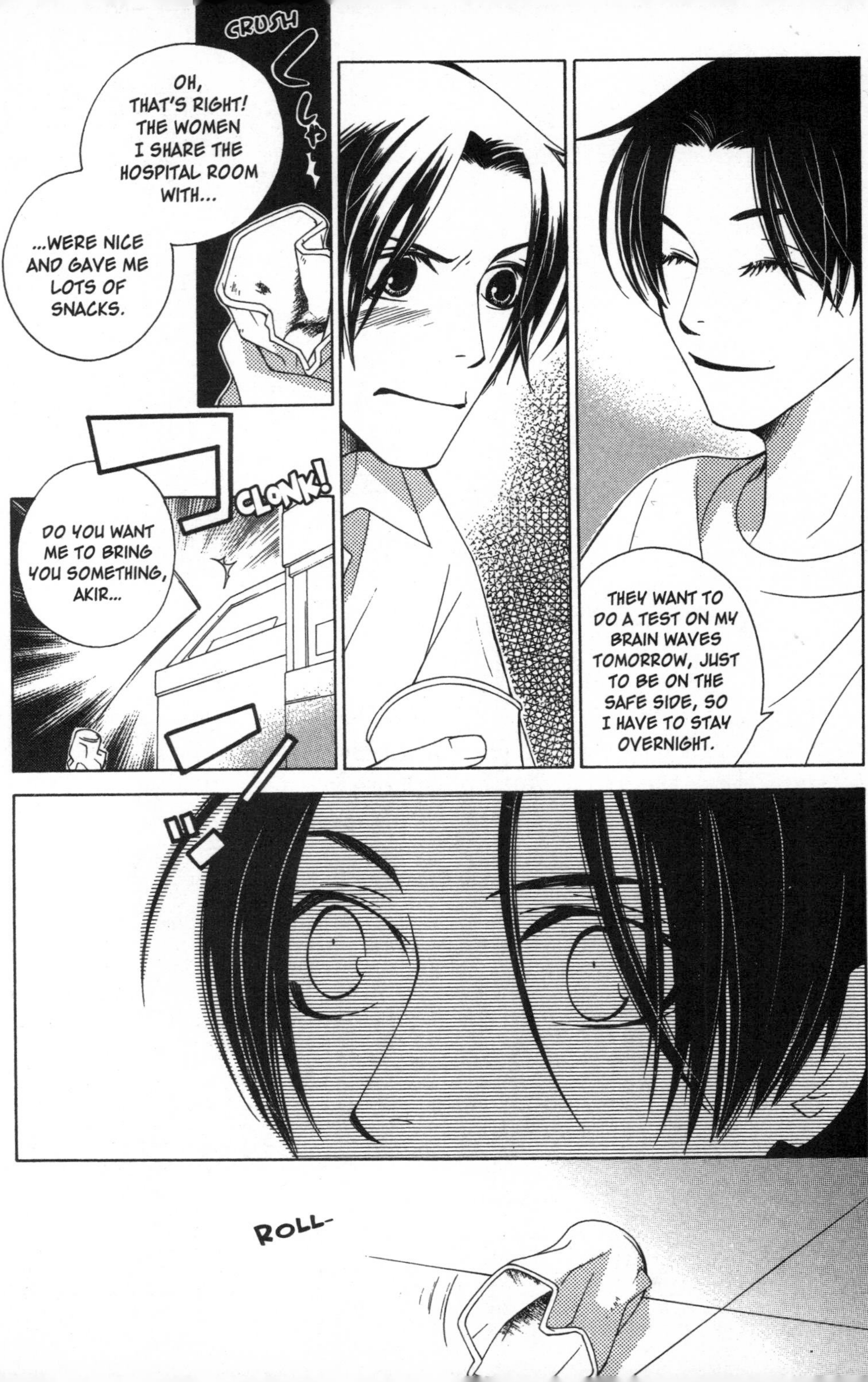
THEY WANT TO DO A TEST ON MY BRAIN WAVES TOMORROW, JUST TO BE ON THE SAFE SIDE, SO I HAVE TO STAY OVERNIGHT.
CRUSH
OH, THAT'S RIGHT! THE WOMEN I SHARE THE HOSPITAL ROOM WITH...
...WERE NICE AND GAVE ME LOTS OF SNACKS.
CLONK!
DO YOU WANT ME TO BRING YOU SOMETHING, AKIR...
ROLL-

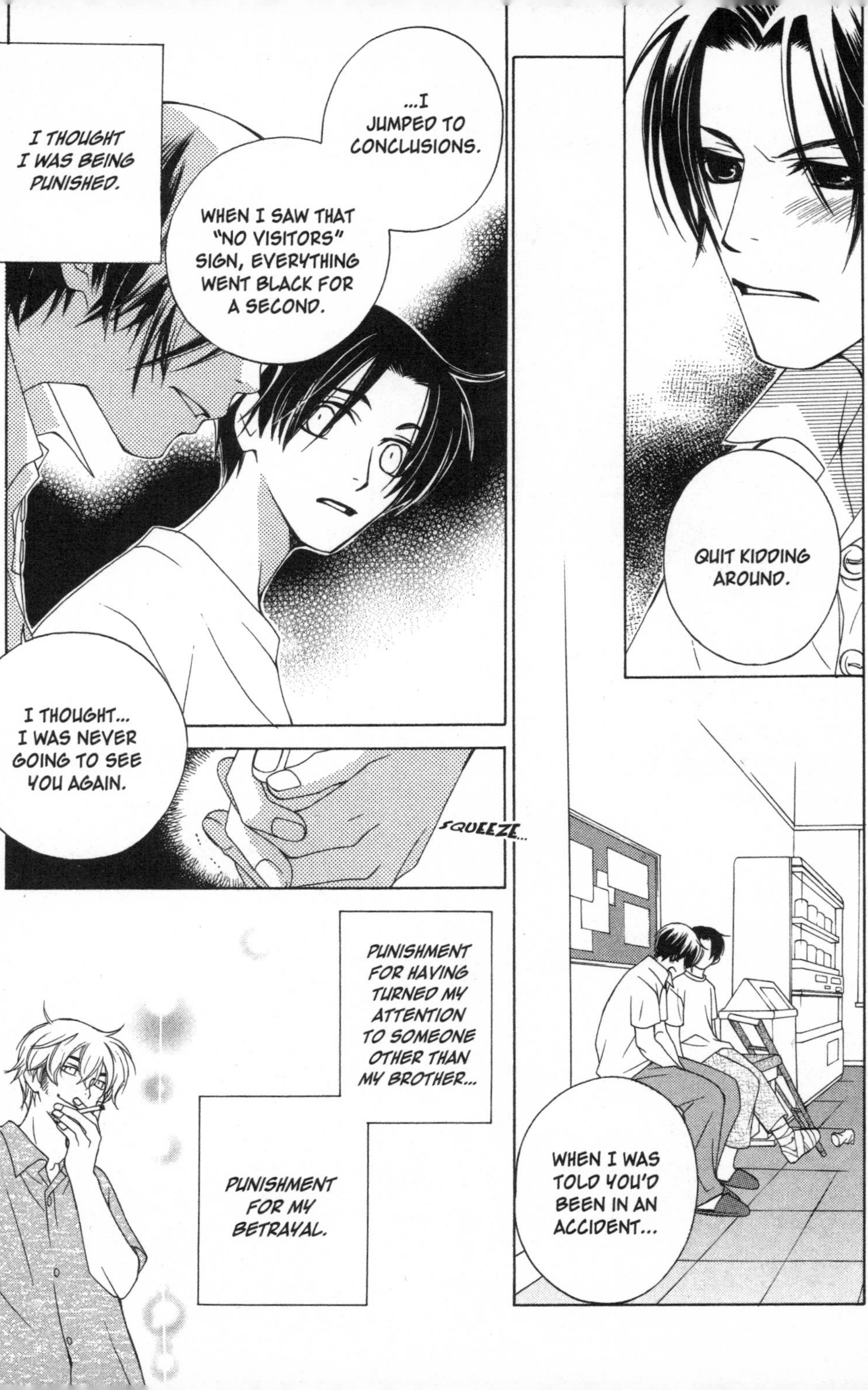
QUIT KIDDING AROUND.
...I JUMPED TO CONCLUSIONS.
WHEN I SAW THAT "NO VISITORS" SIGN, EVERYTHING WENT BLACK FOR A SECOND.
I THOUGHT I WAS BEING PUNISHED.
I THOUGHT... I WAS NEVER GOING TO SEE YOU AGAIN.
SQUEEZE...
WHEN I WAS TOLD YOU'D BEEN IN AN ACCIDENT...
PUNISHMENT FOR HAVING TURNED MY ATTENTION TO SOMEONE OTHER THAN MY BROTHER...
PUNISHMENT FOR MY BETRAYAL.

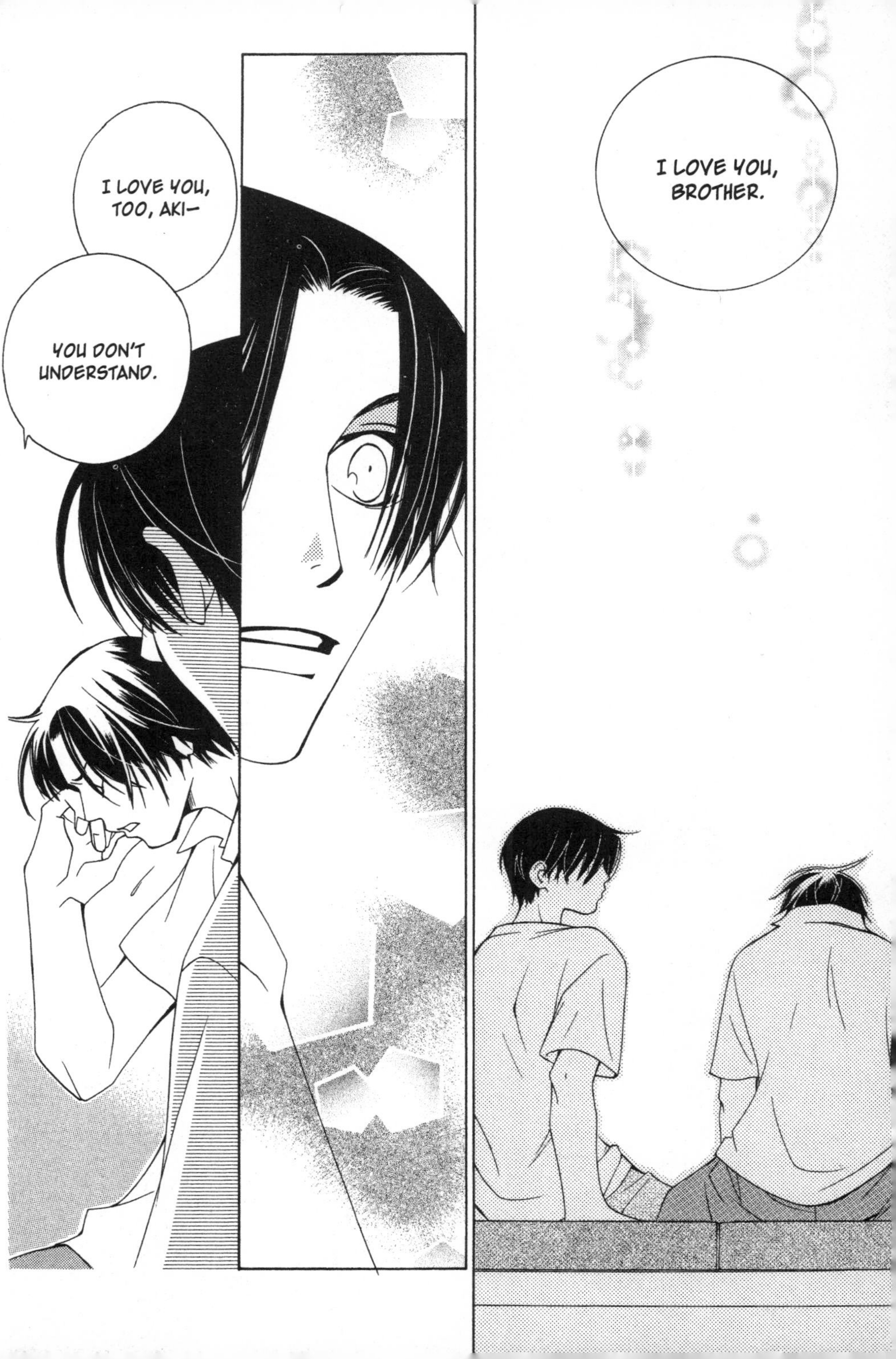
I LOVE YOU, BROTHER.
I LOVE YOU, TOO, AKI—
YOU DON'T UNDERSTAND.

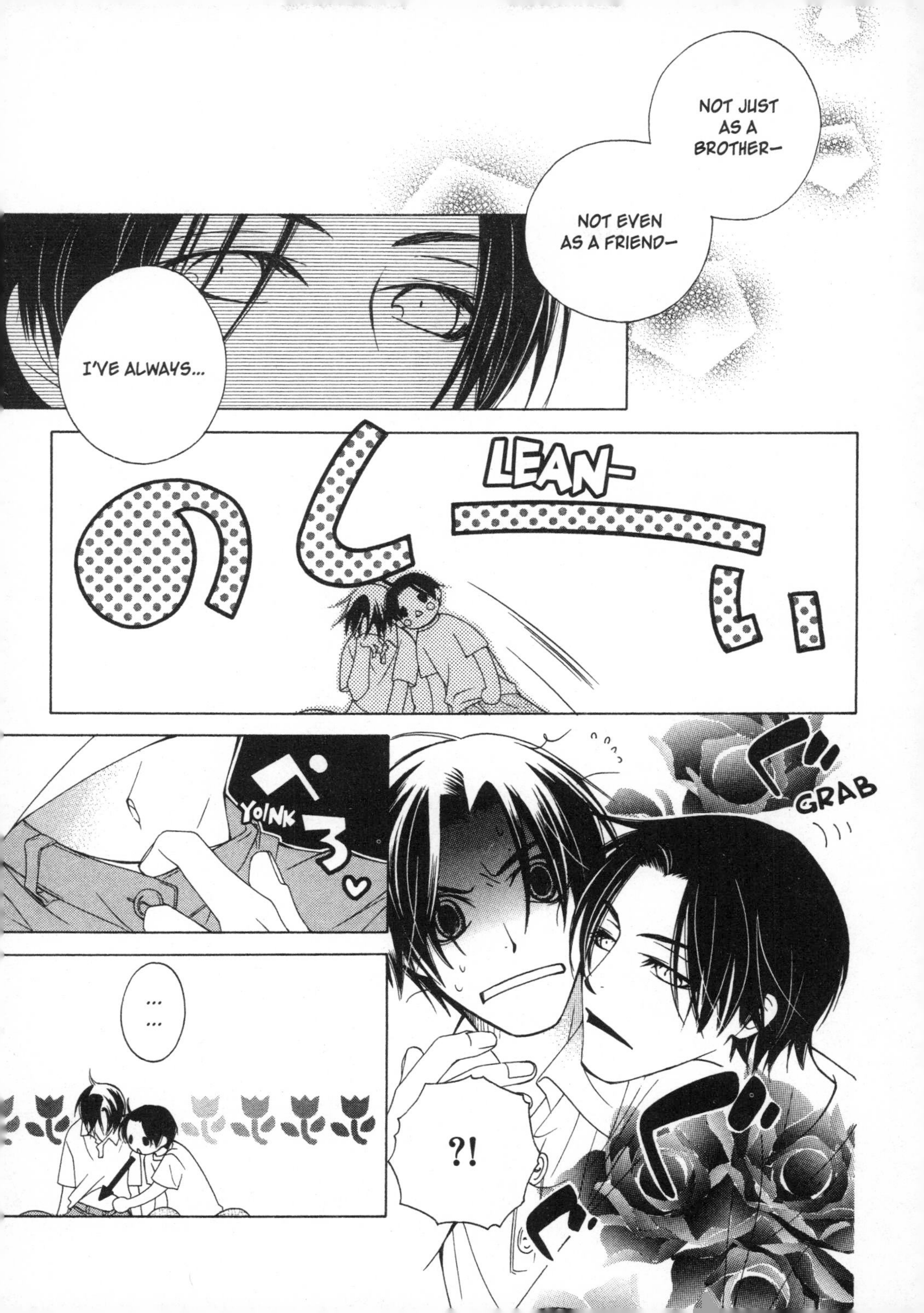
NOT JUST AS A BROTHER—
NOT EVEN AS A FRIEND—
I'VE ALWAYS...
LEAN-
GRAB
?!
YOINK
...
...

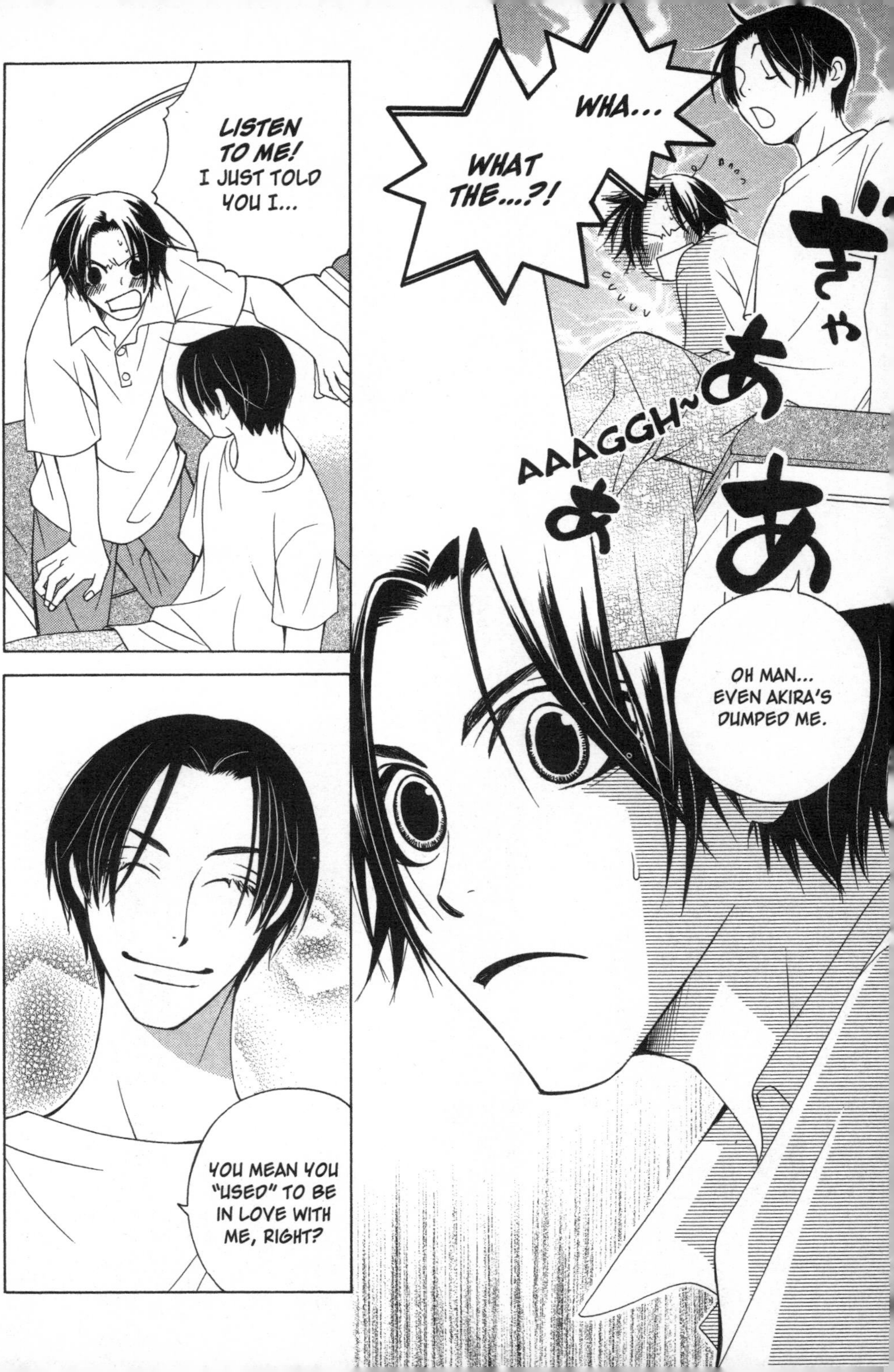
WHA... WHAT THE...?!
ぎゃあああ
AAAGGH~
OH MAN... EVEN AKIRA'S DUMPED ME.
LISTEN TO ME! I JUST TOLD YOU I...
YOU MEAN YOU "USED" TO BE IN LOVE WITH ME, RIGHT?

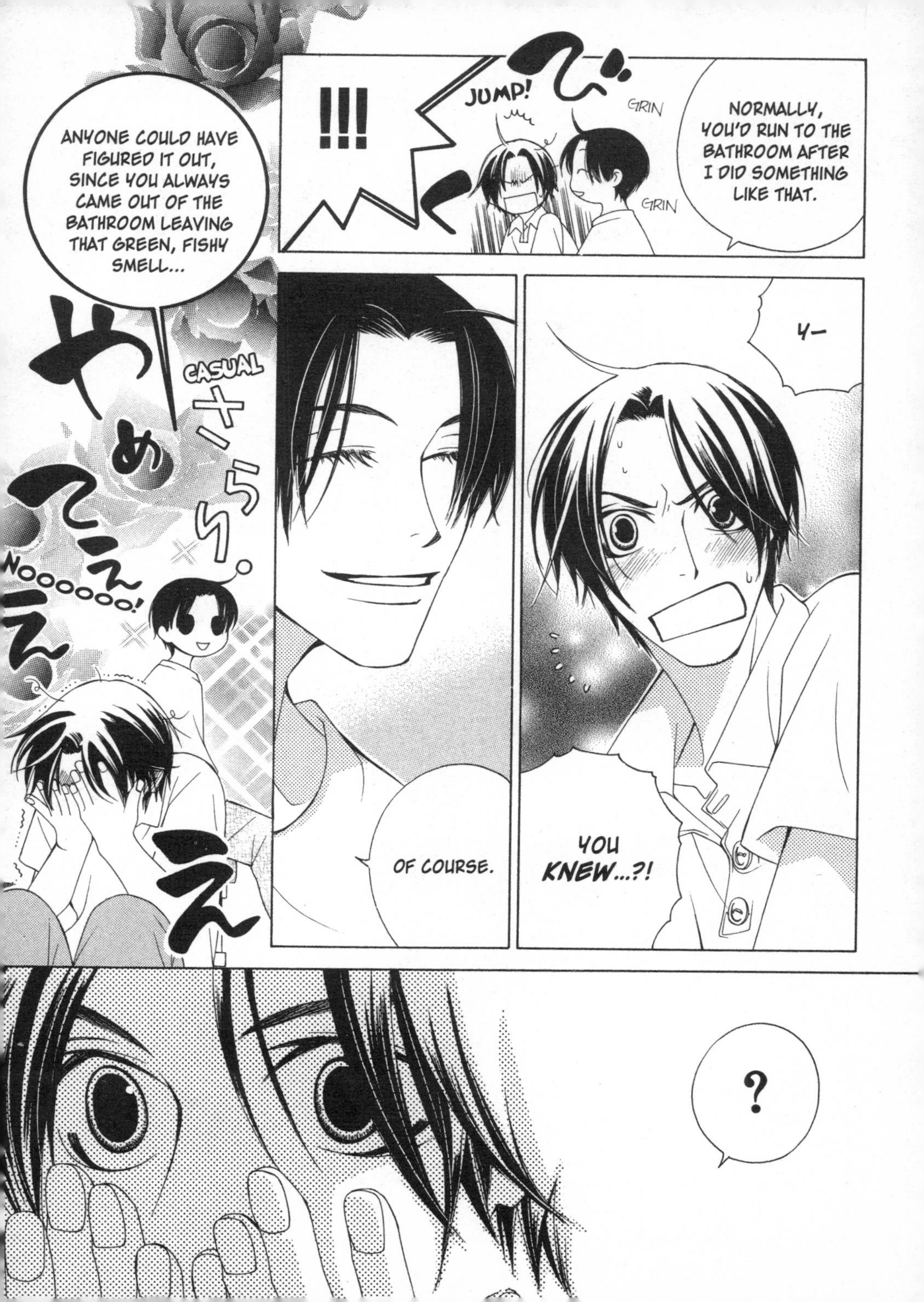

NORMALLY, YOU'D RUN TO THE BATHROOM AFTER I DID SOMETHING LIKE THAT.
GRIN
GRIN
JUMP!
!!!
Y—
YOU KNEW...?!
OF COURSE.
ANYONE COULD HAVE FIGURED IT OUT, SINCE YOU ALWAYS CAME OUT OF THE BATHROOM LEAVING THAT GREEN, FISHY SMELL...
CASUAL
さらり
NOOOOOOO!
?

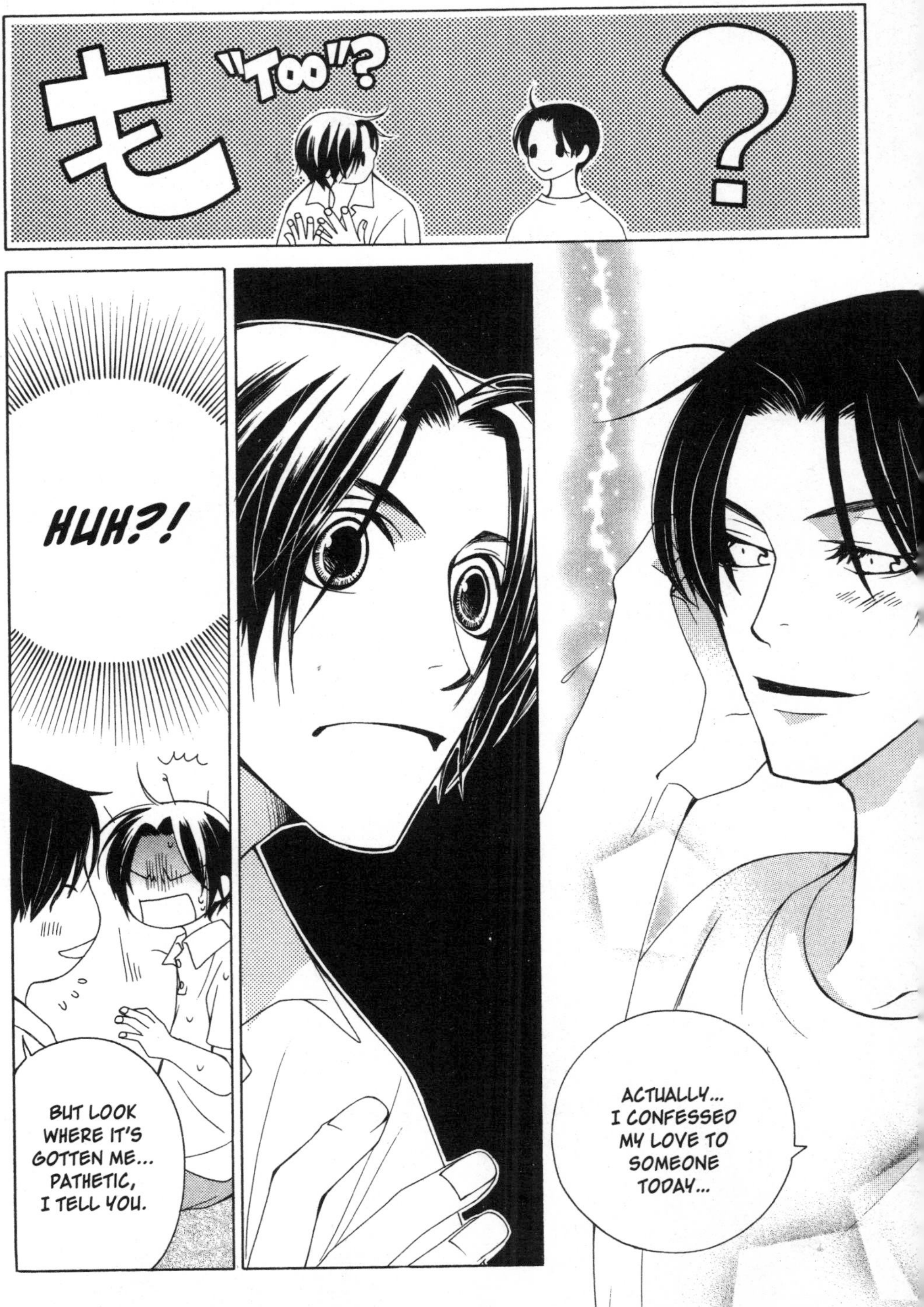
も
"TOO"?
?
ACTUALLY... I CONFESSED MY LOVE TO SOMEONE TODAY...
HUH?!
BUT LOOK WHERE IT'S GOTTEN ME... PATHETIC, I TELL YOU.

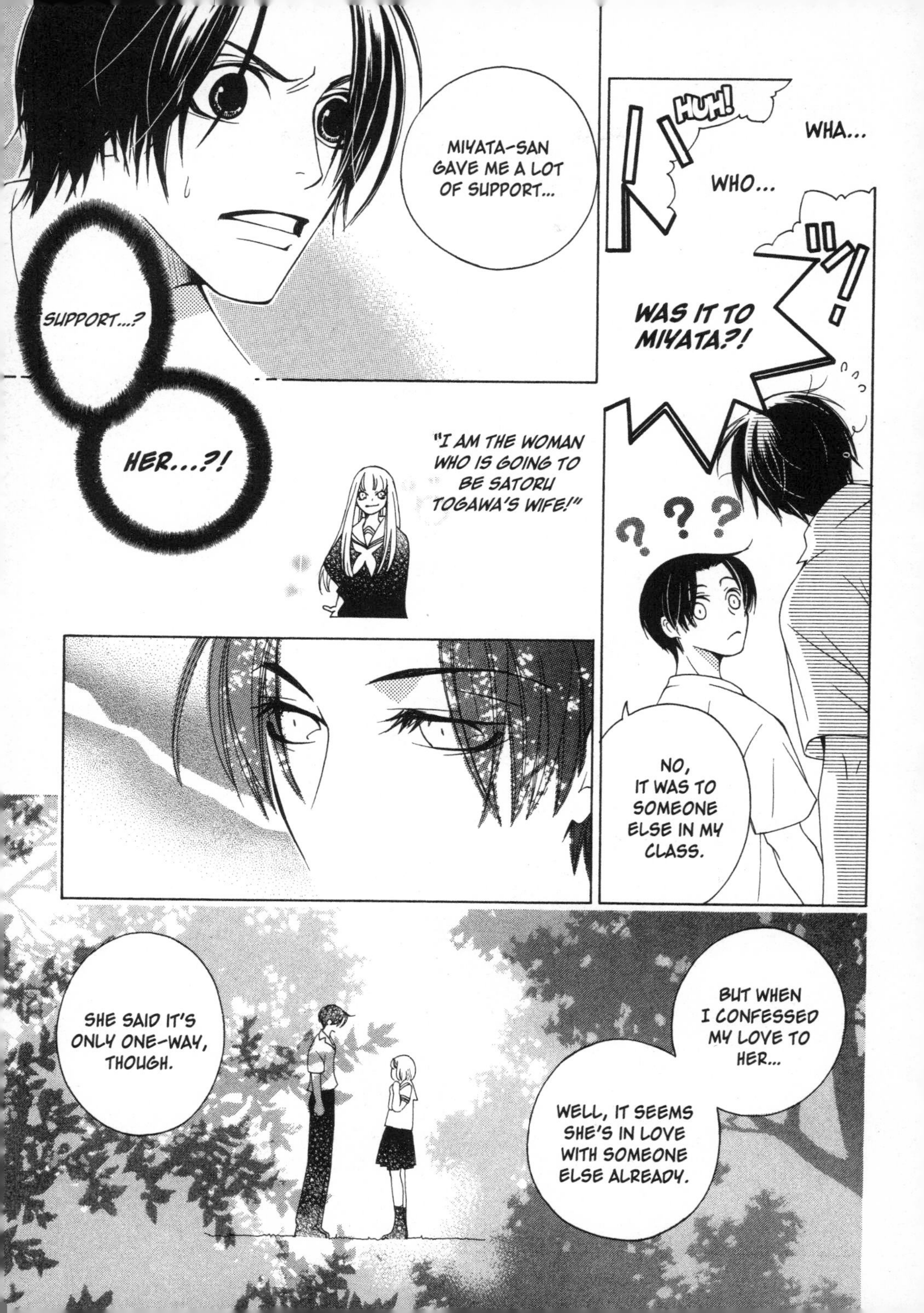
WHA...
HUH!
WHO...
WAS IT TO MIYATA?!
NO, IT WAS TO SOMEONE ELSE IN MY CLASS.
MIYATA-SAN GAVE ME A LOT OF SUPPORT...
SUPPORT...?
HER...?!
"I AM THE WOMAN WHO IS GOING TO BE SATORU TOGAWA'S WIFE!"
BUT WHEN I CONFESSED MY LOVE TO HER...
WELL, IT SEEMS SHE'S IN LOVE WITH SOMEONE ELSE ALREADY.
SHE SAID IT'S ONLY ONE-WAY, THOUGH.

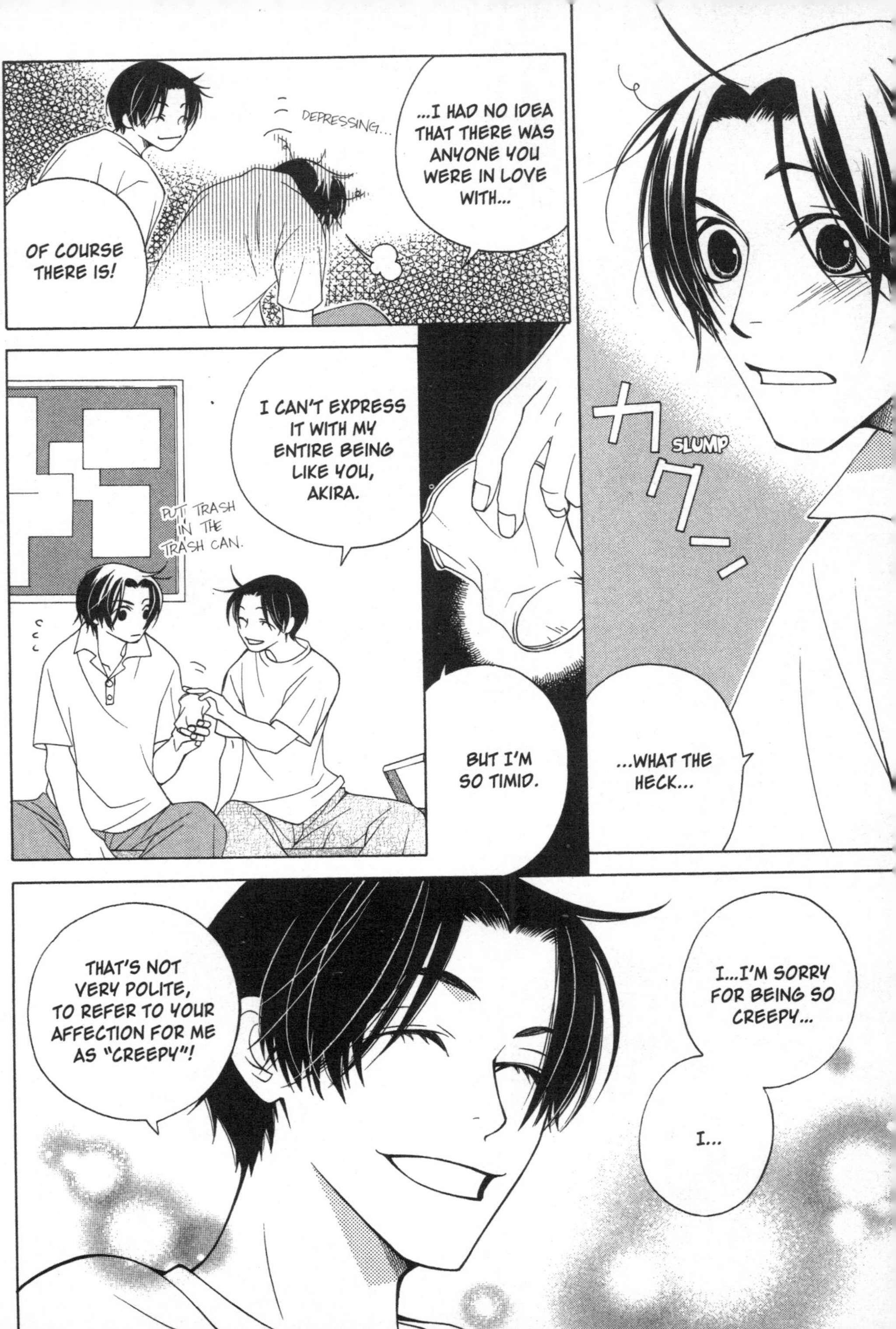

SLUMP
...WHAT THE HECK...
...I HAD NO IDEA THAT THERE WAS ANYONE YOU WERE IN LOVE WITH...
DEPRESSING...
OF COURSE THERE IS!
BUT I'M SO TIMID.
I CAN'T EXPRESS IT WITH MY ENTIRE BEING LIKE YOU, AKIRA.
PUT TRASH IN THE TRASH CAN.
I...I'M SORRY FOR BEING SO CREEPY...
I...
THAT'S NOT VERY POLITE, TO REFER TO YOUR AFFECTION FOR ME AS "CREEPY"!

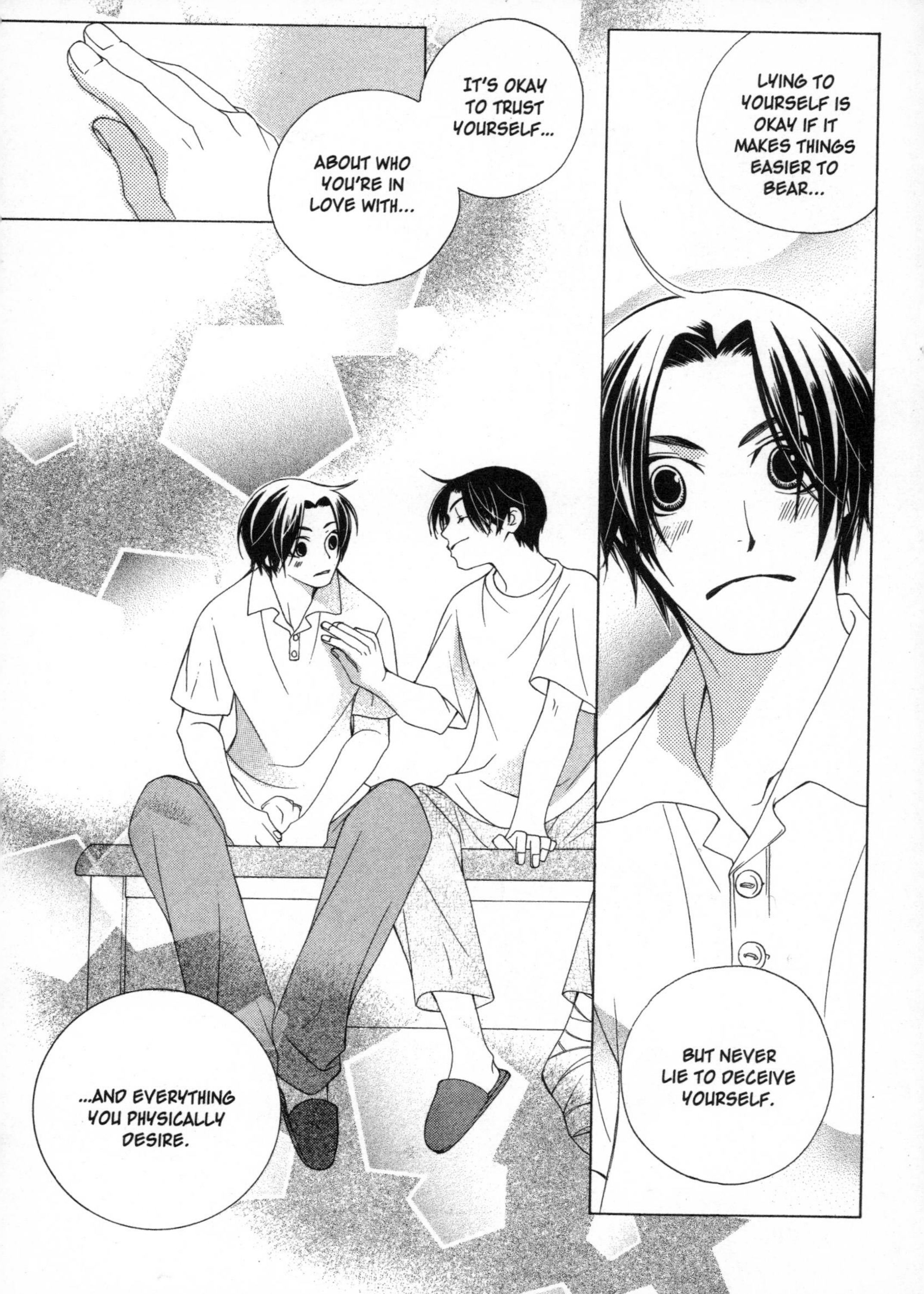
LYING TO YOURSELF IS OKAY IF IT MAKES THINGS EASIER TO BEAR...
BUT NEVER LIE TO DECEIVE YOURSELF.
IT'S OKAY TO TRUST YOURSELF...
ABOUT WHO YOU'RE IN LOVE WITH...
...AND EVERYTHING YOU PHYSICALLY DESIRE.

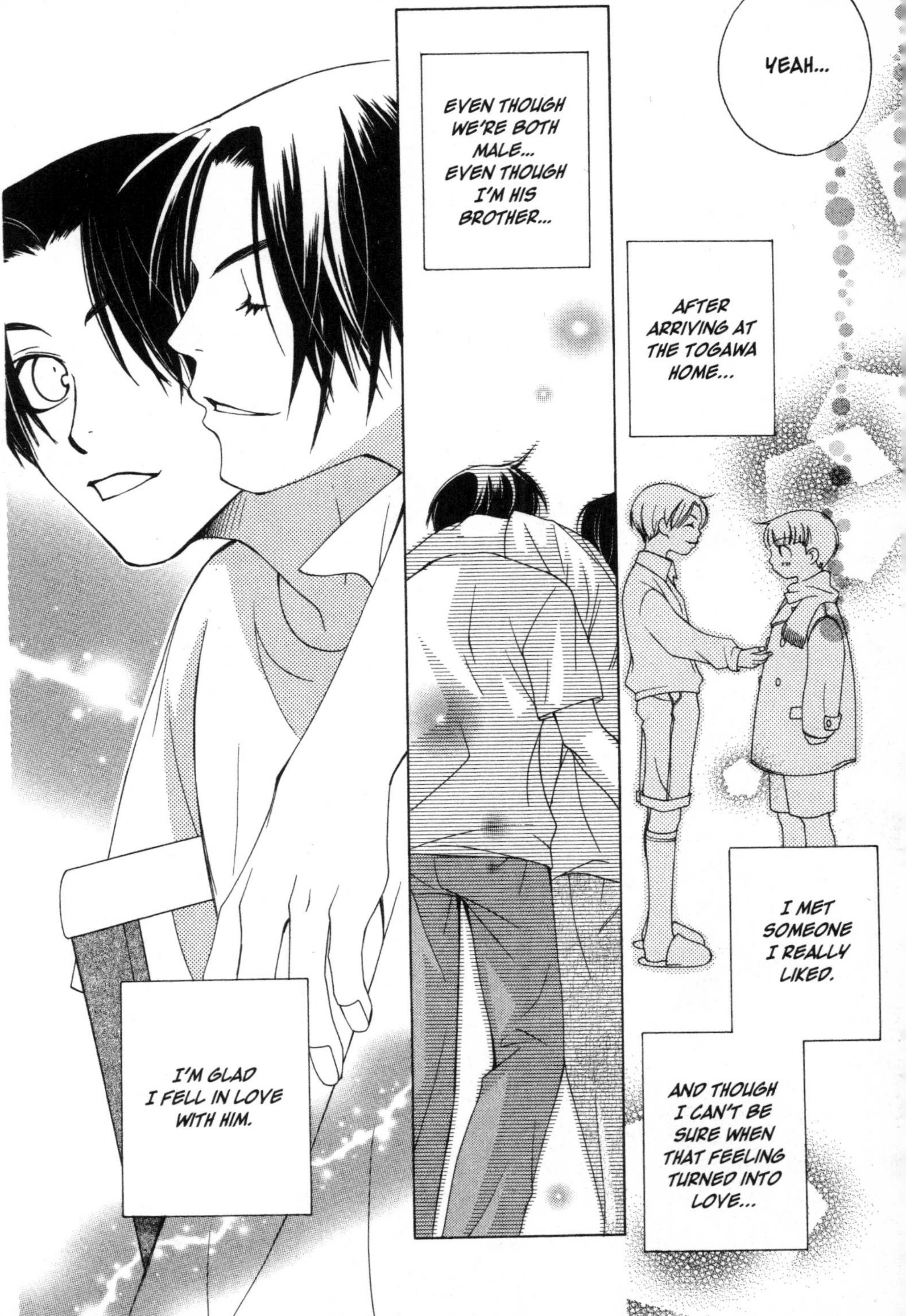
YEAH...
AFTER ARRIVING AT THE TOGAWA HOME...
I MET SOMEONE I REALLY LIKED.
AND THOUGH I CAN'T BE SURE WHEN THAT FEELING TURNED INTO LOVE...
EVEN THOUGH WE'RE BOTH MALE... EVEN THOUGH I'M HIS BROTHER...
I'M GLAD I FELL IN LOVE WITH HIM.

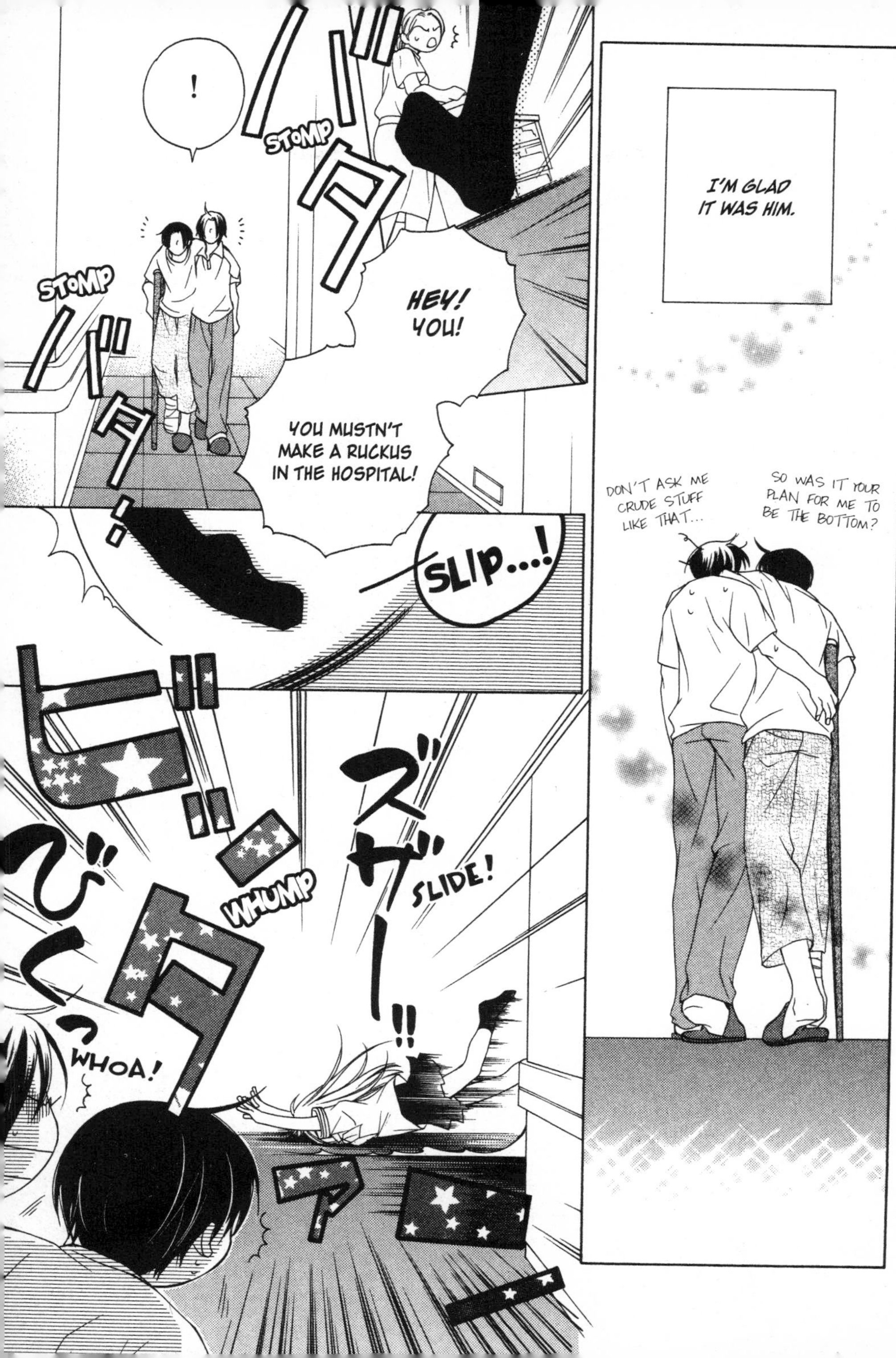
I'M GLAD IT WAS HIM.
SO WAS IT YOUR PLAN FOR ME TO BE THE BOTTOM?
DON'T ASK ME CRUDE STUFF LIKE THAT...
STOMP
!
HEY! YOU!
YOU MUSTN'T MAKE A RUCKUS IN THE HOSPITAL!
STOMP
SLIP...!
SLIDE!
WHUMP
WHOA!

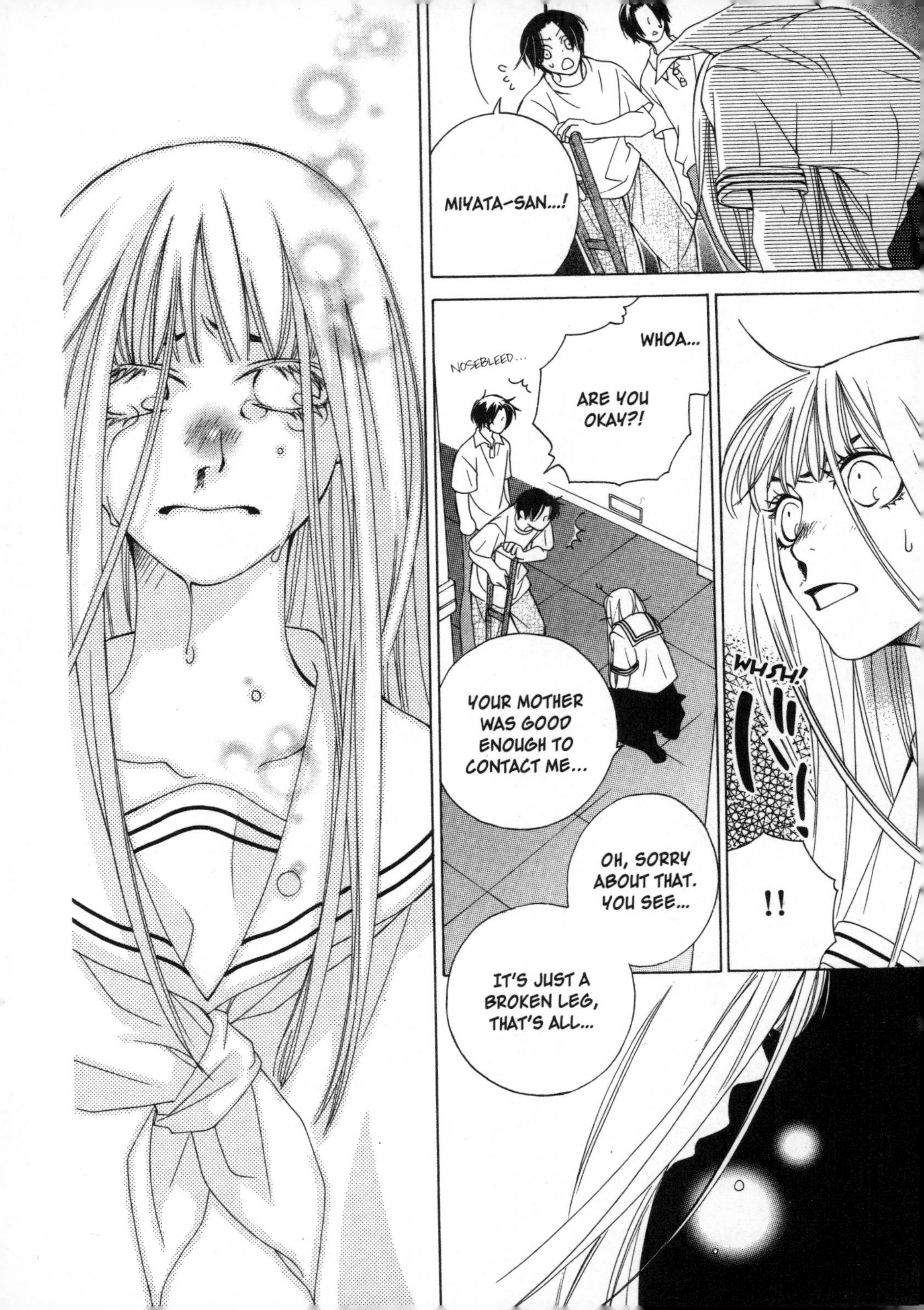
MIYATA-SAN...!
WHSH!
!!
WHOA...
ARE YOU OKAY?!
NOSEBLEED...
YOUR MOTHER WAS GOOD ENOUGH TO CONTACT ME...
OH, SORRY ABOUT THAT. YOU SEE...
IT'S JUST A BROKEN LEG, THAT'S ALL...

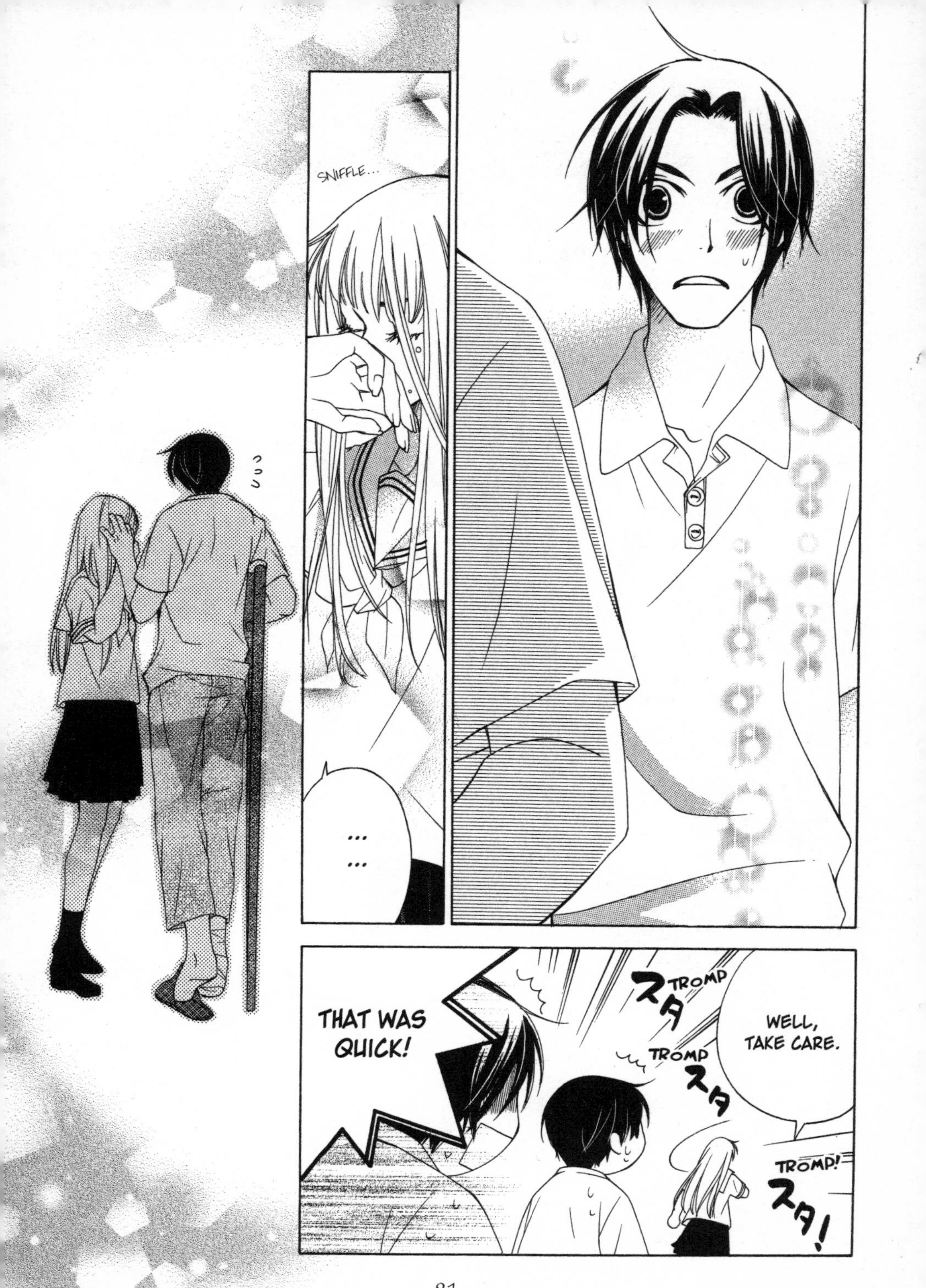
SNIFFLE...
...
...
WELL, TAKE CARE.
TROMP
スタ
TROMP
スタ
TROMP!
スタ!
THAT WAS QUICK!

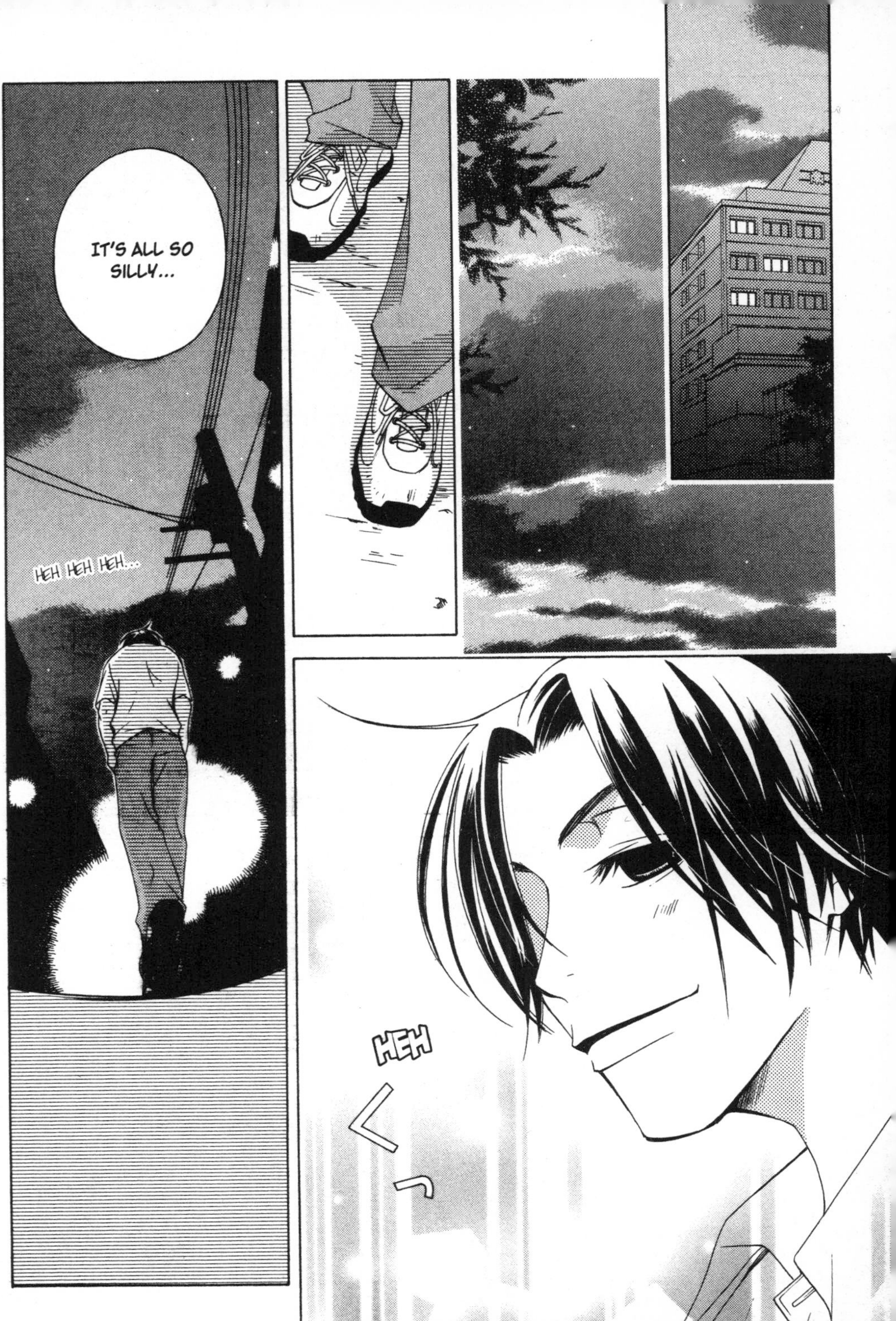
HEH
くっ
IT'S ALL SO SILLY...
HEH HEH HEH...

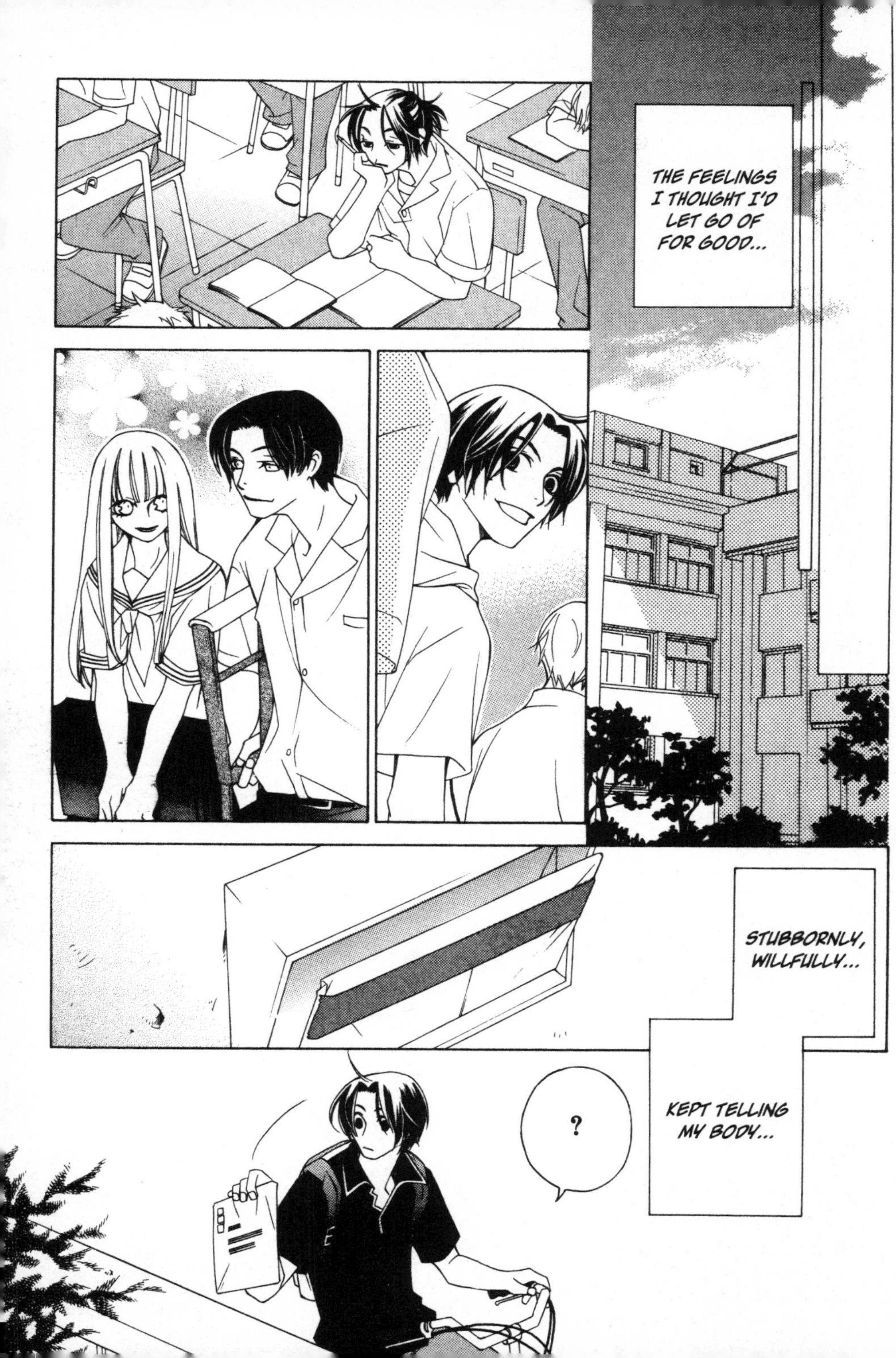
THE FEELINGS I THOUGHT I'D LET GO OF FOR GOOD...
STUBBORNLY, WILLFULLY...
KEPT TELLING MY BODY...
?

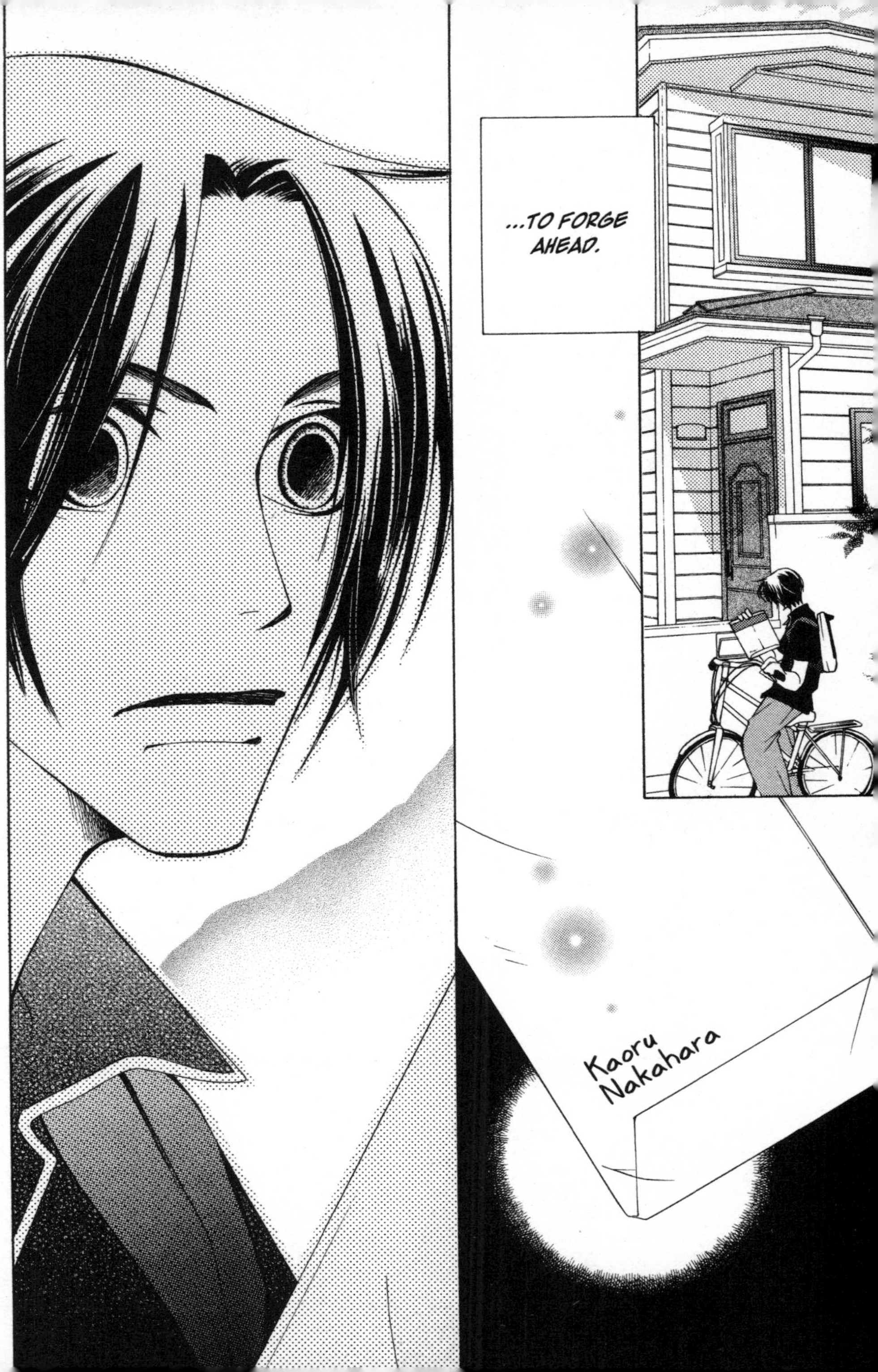
...TO FORGE AHEAD.
Kaoru Nakahara

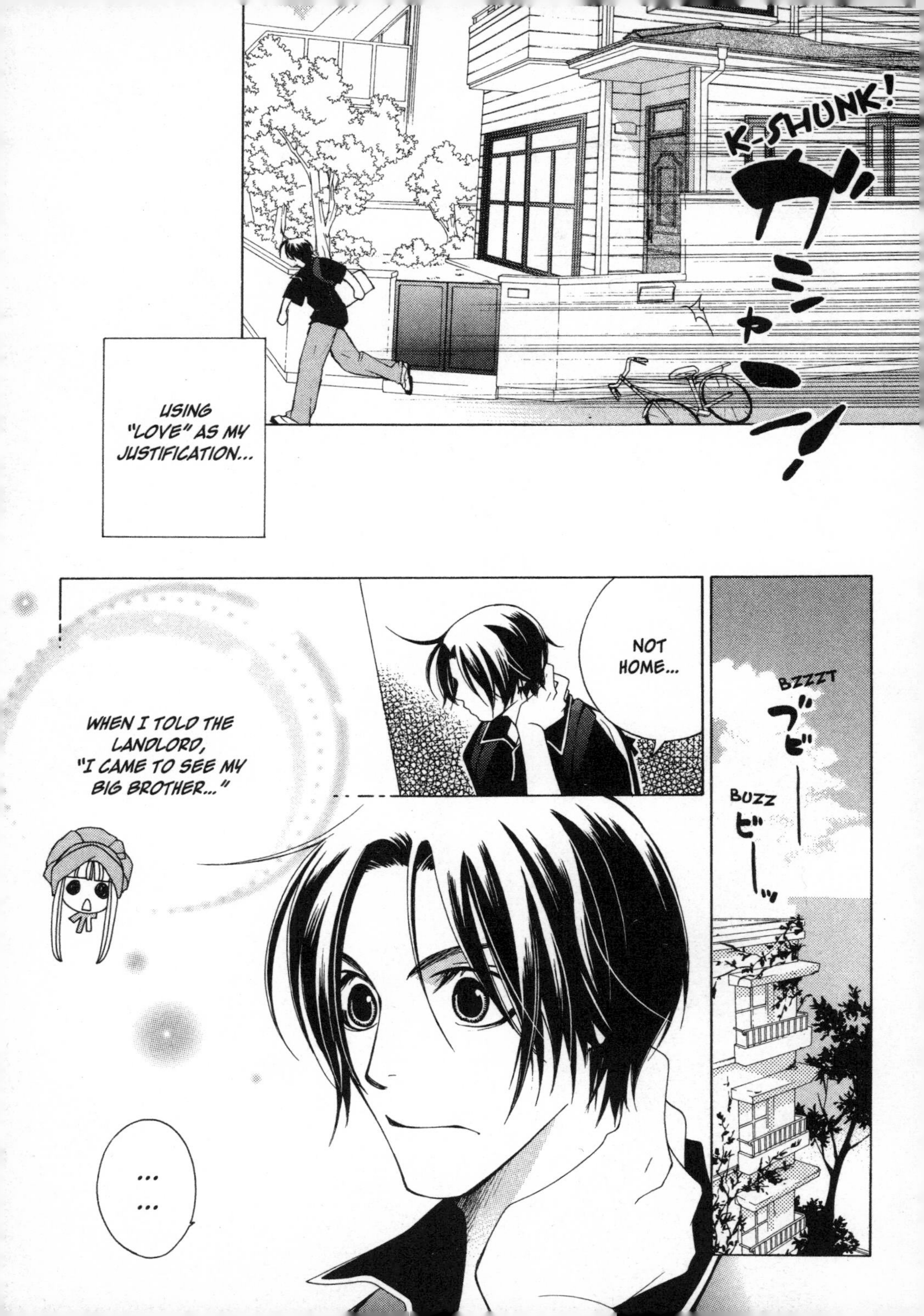
K-SHUNK!
USING "LOVE" AS MY JUSTIFICATION...
BZZZT
BUZZ
NOT HOME...
WHEN I TOLD THE LANDLORD, "I CAME TO SEE MY BIG BROTHER..."
... ...

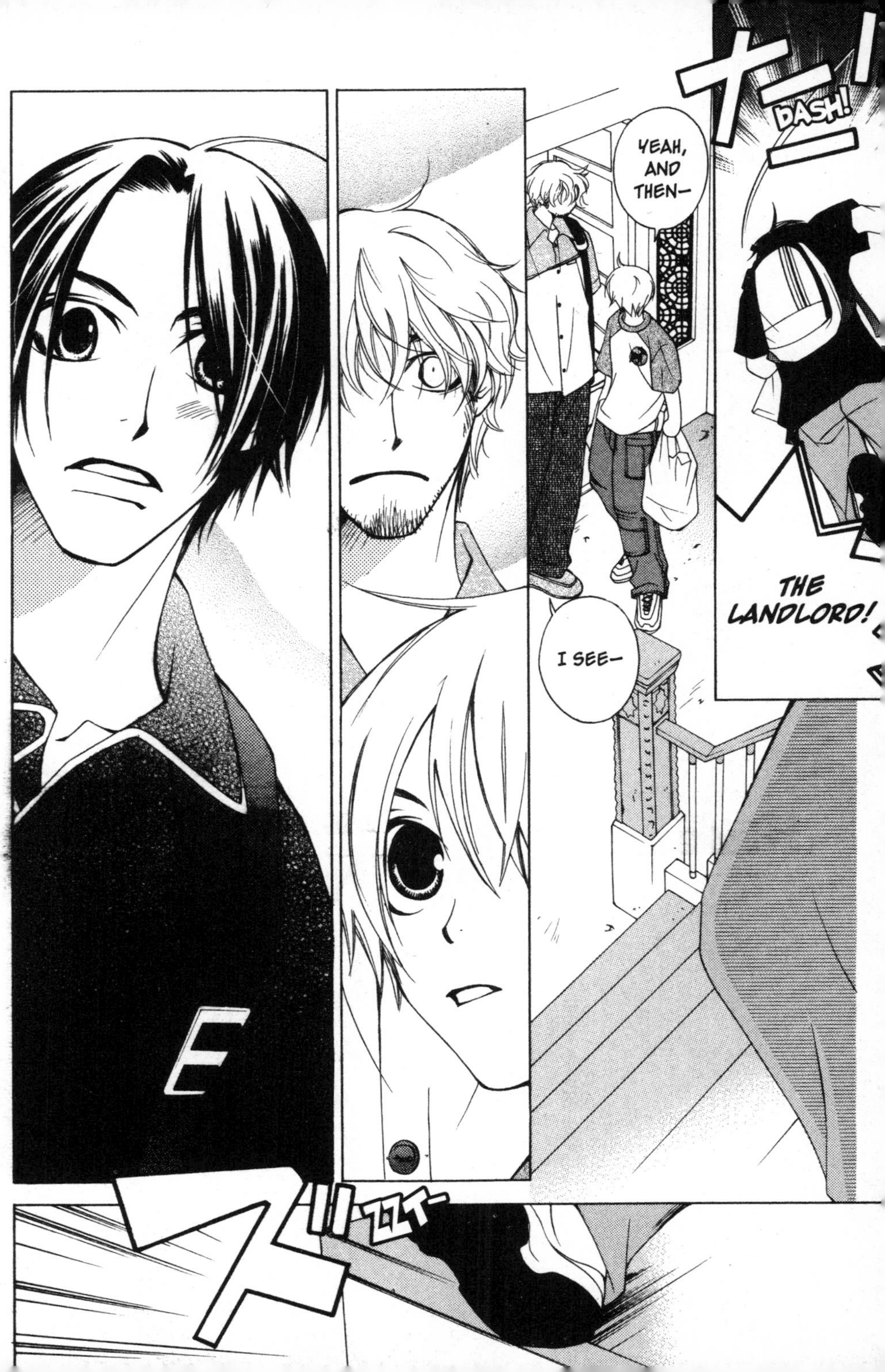
DASH!
THE LANDLORD!
YEAH, AND THEN—
I SEE—
ZZZT-

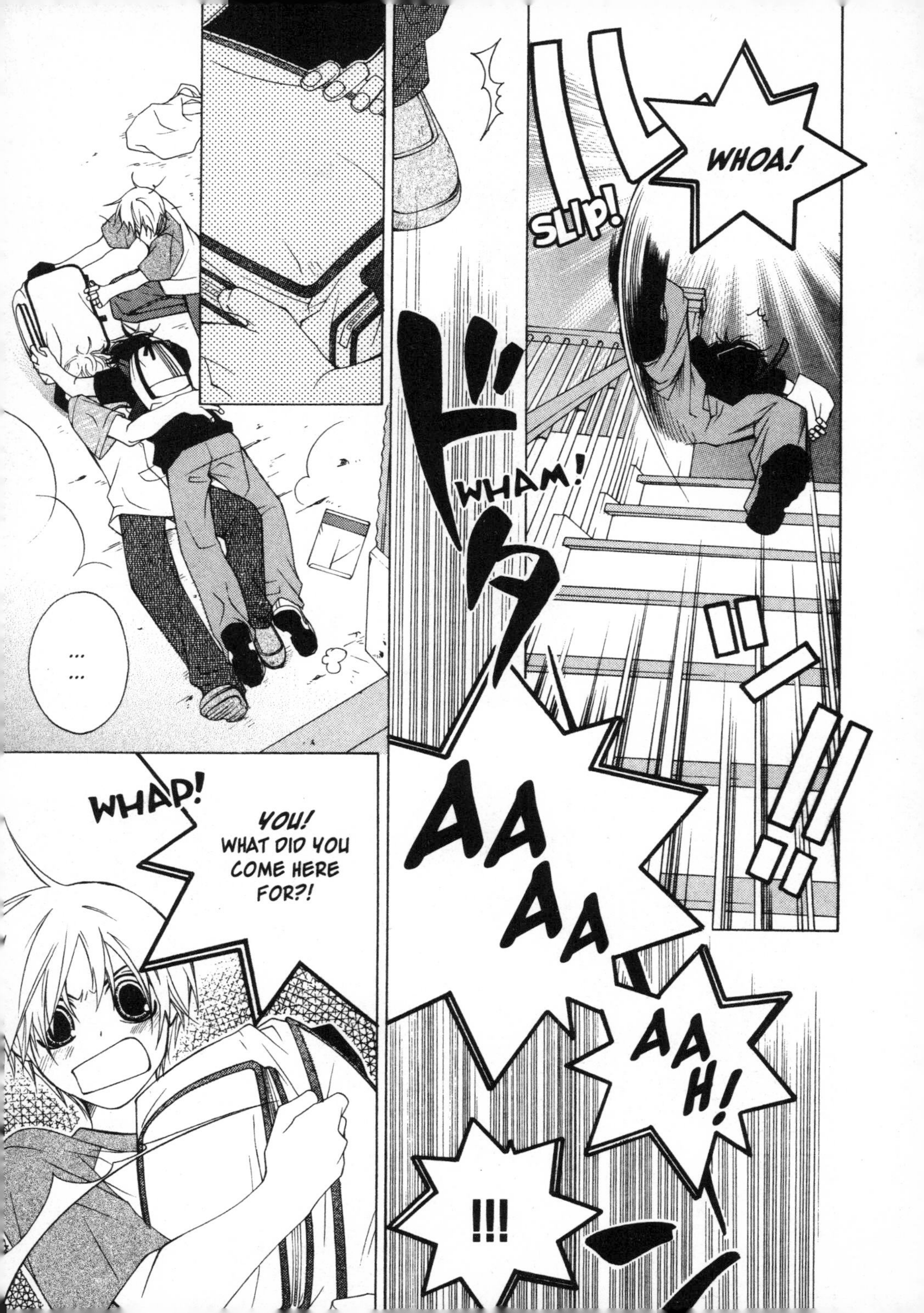

WHOA!
SLIP!
ドタ
WHAM!
AAAAAAH!
!!!
……
WHAP!
YOU! WHAT DID YOU COME HERE FOR?!

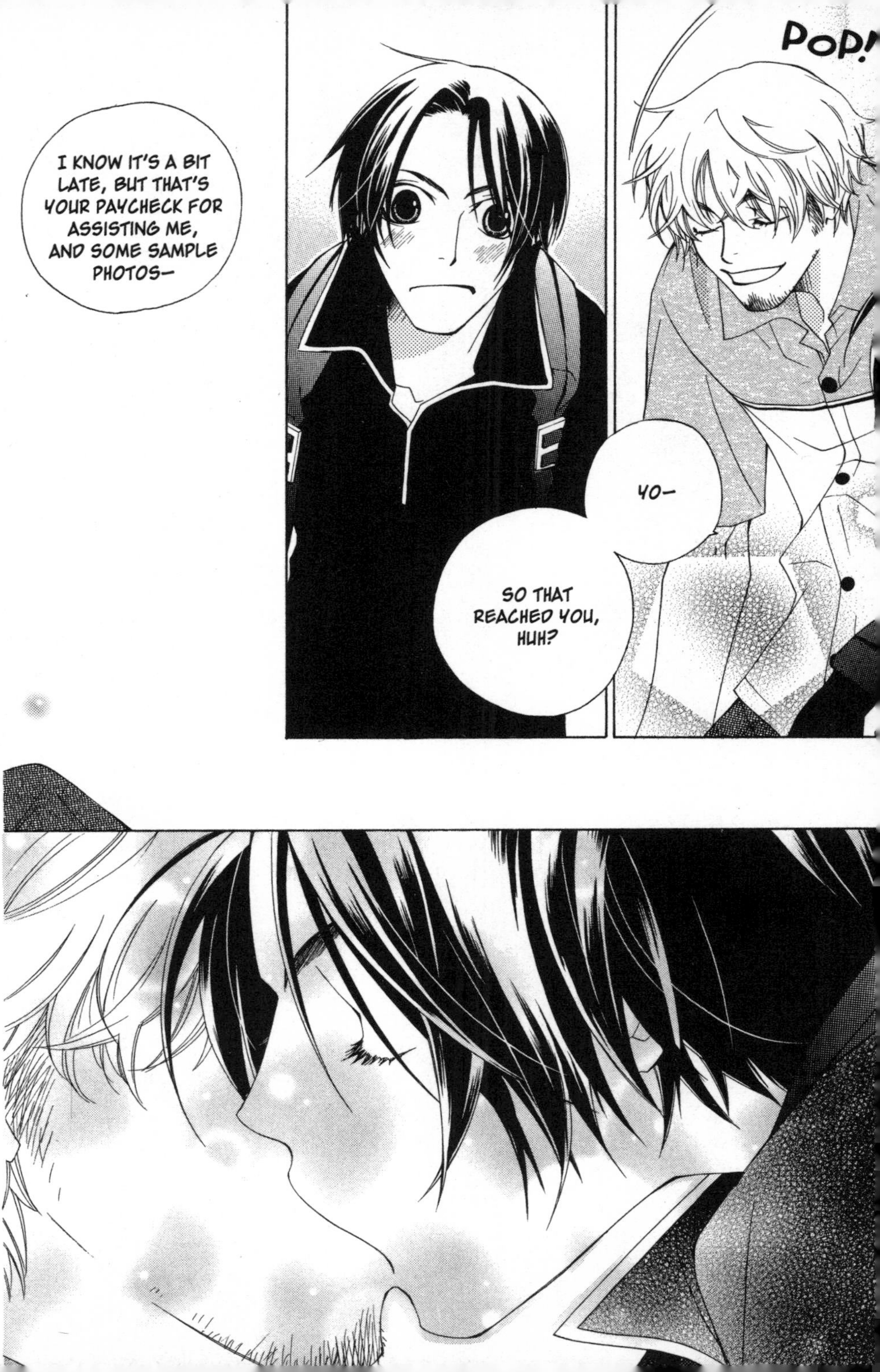
POP!
YO—
SO THAT REACHED YOU, HUH?
I KNOW IT'S A BIT LATE, BUT THAT'S YOUR PAYCHECK FOR ASSISTING ME, AND SOME SAMPLE PHOTOS—

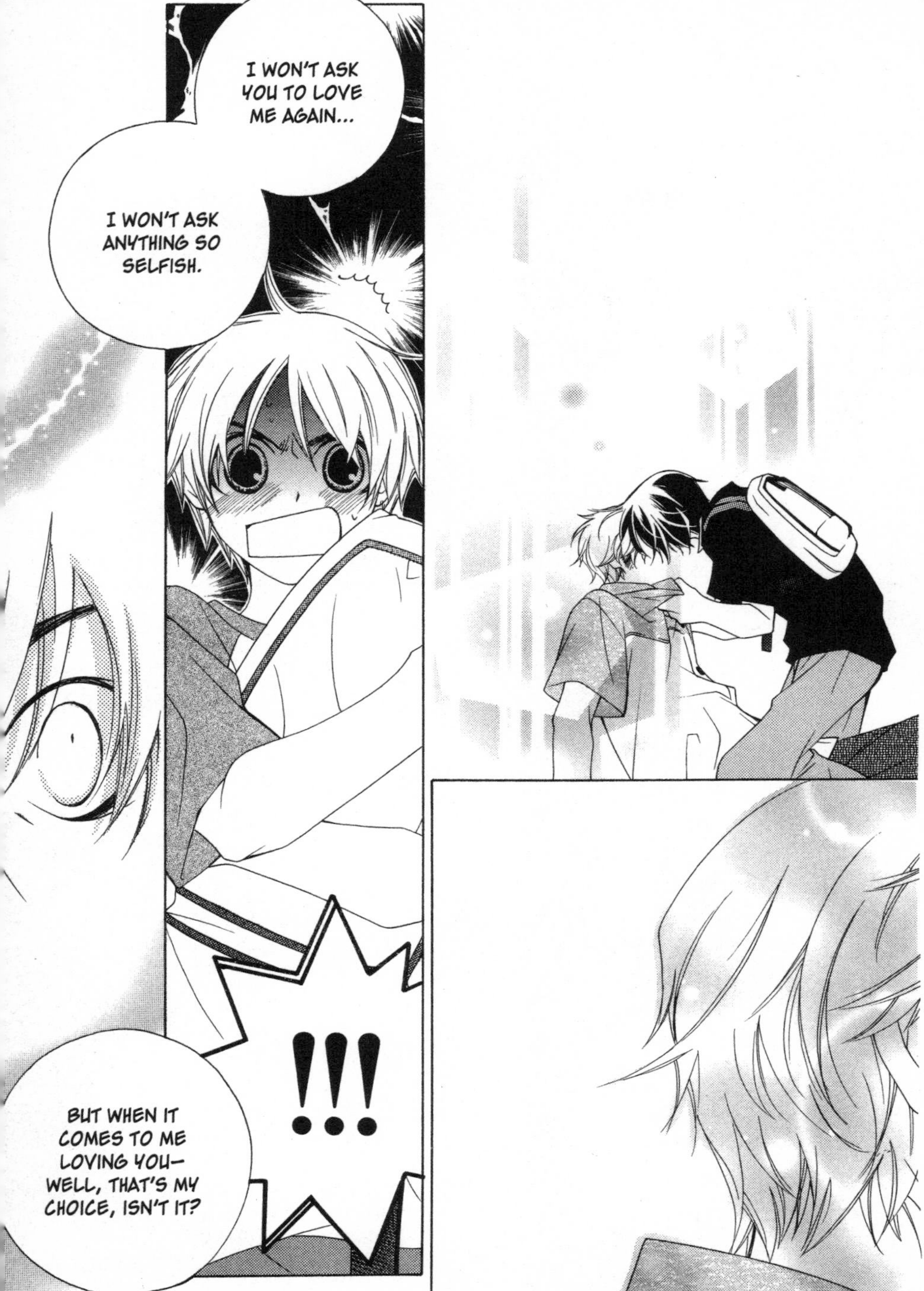
I WON'T ASK YOU TO LOVE ME AGAIN...
I WON'T ASK ANYTHING SO SELFISH.
!!!
BUT WHEN IT COMES TO ME LOVING YOU— WELL, THAT'S MY CHOICE, ISN'T IT?

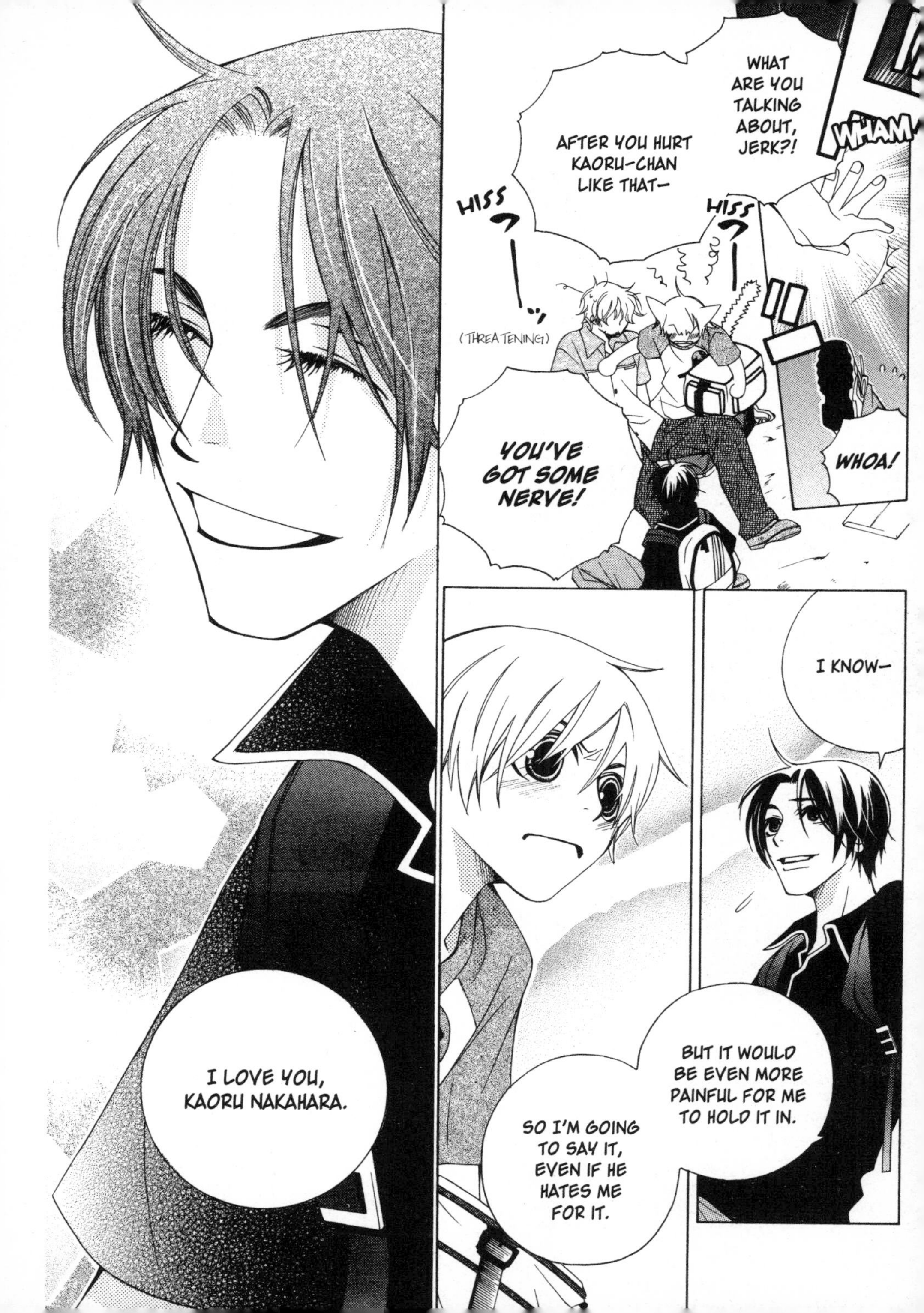
WHAM
WHAT ARE YOU TALKING ABOUT, JERK?!
AFTER YOU HURT KAORU-CHAN LIKE THAT—
HISS
HISS
(THREATENING)
WHOA!
YOU'VE GOT SOME NERVE!
I KNOW—
BUT IT WOULD BE EVEN MORE PAINFUL FOR ME TO HOLD IT IN.
SO I'M GOING TO SAY IT, EVEN IF HE HATES ME FOR IT.
I LOVE YOU, KAORU NAKAHARA.

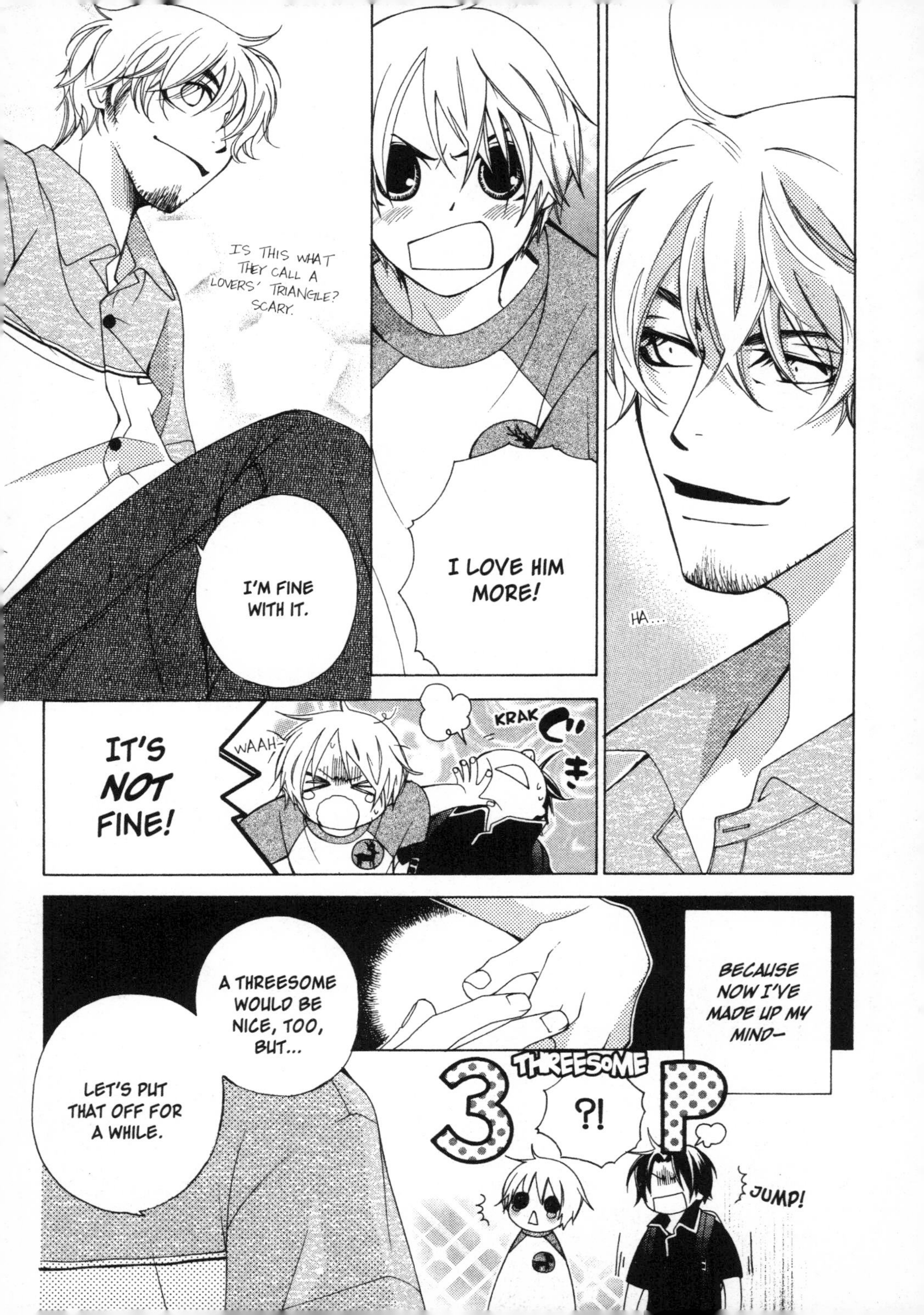

HA...
I LOVE HIM MORE!
IS THIS WHAT THEY CALL A LOVERS' TRIANGLE? SCARY.
I'M FINE WITH IT.
KRAK
WAAH
IT'S NOT FINE!
BECAUSE NOW I'VE MADE UP MY MIND—
A THREESOME WOULD BE NICE, TOO, BUT...
LET'S PUT THAT OFF FOR A WHILE.
3P
THREESOME
?!
JUMP!

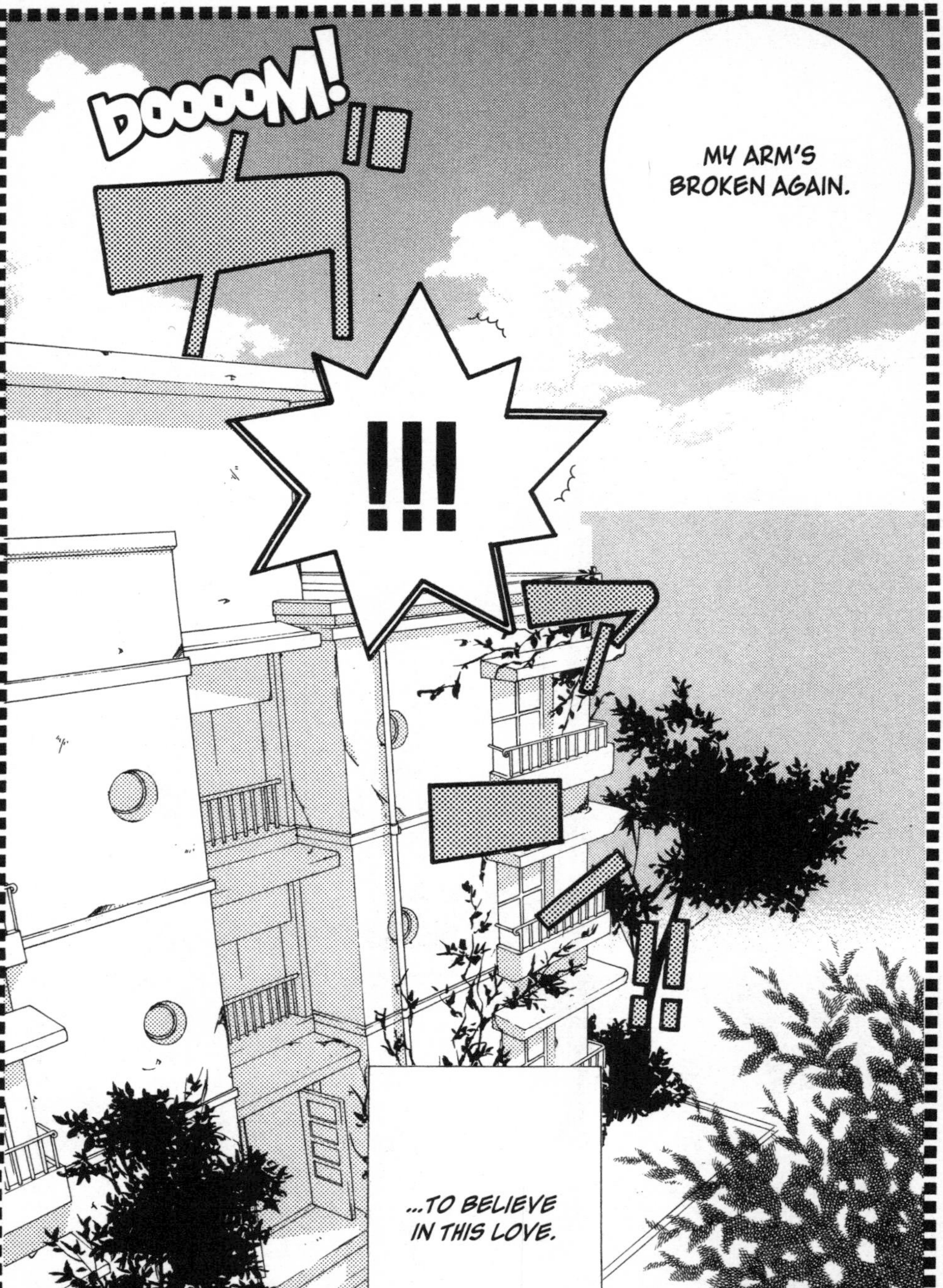
MY ARM'S BROKEN AGAIN.
BOOOOM!!!
!!!
...TO BELIEVE IN THIS LOVE.

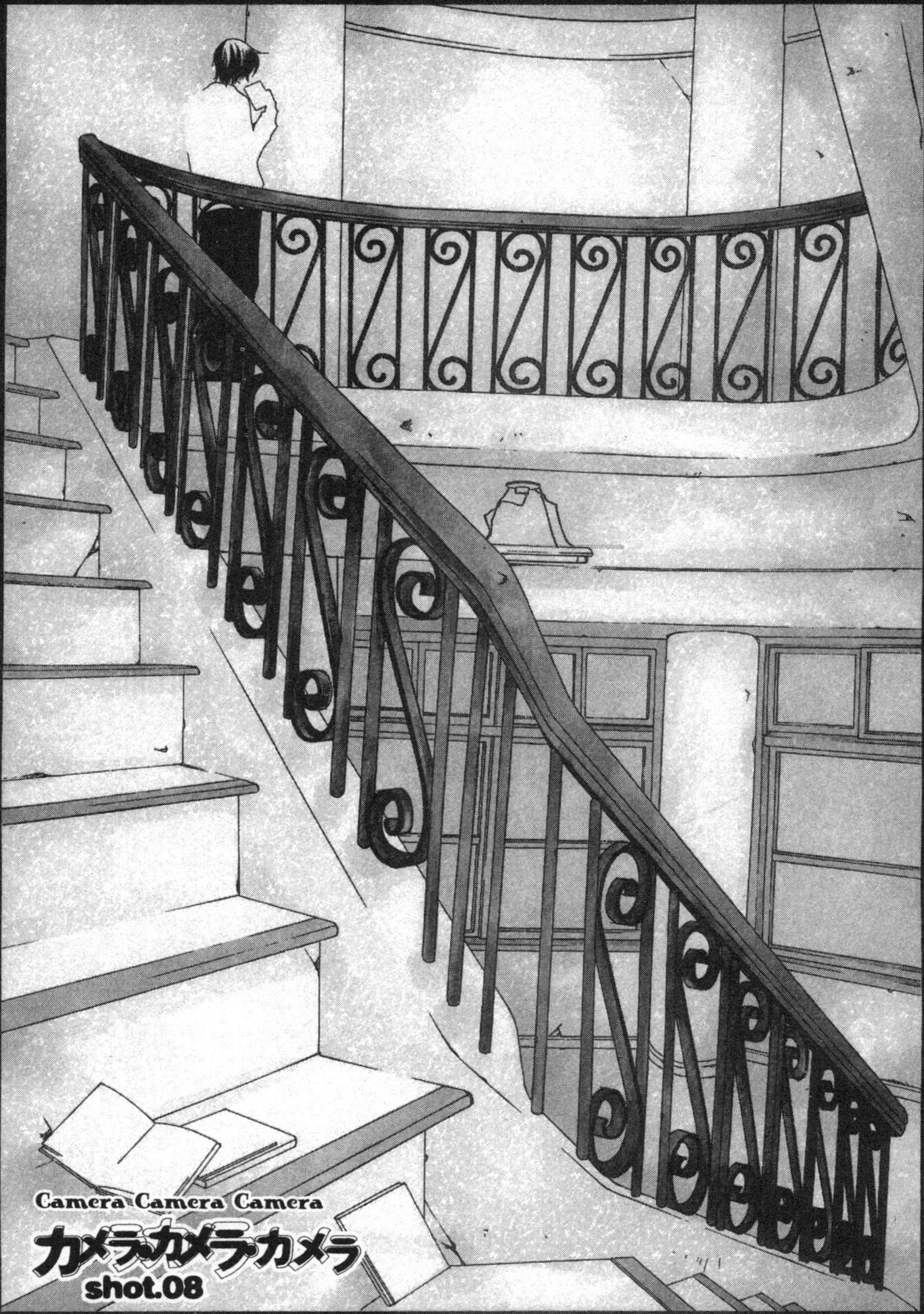
Camera Camera Camera
カメラ・カメラ・カメラ
shot.08

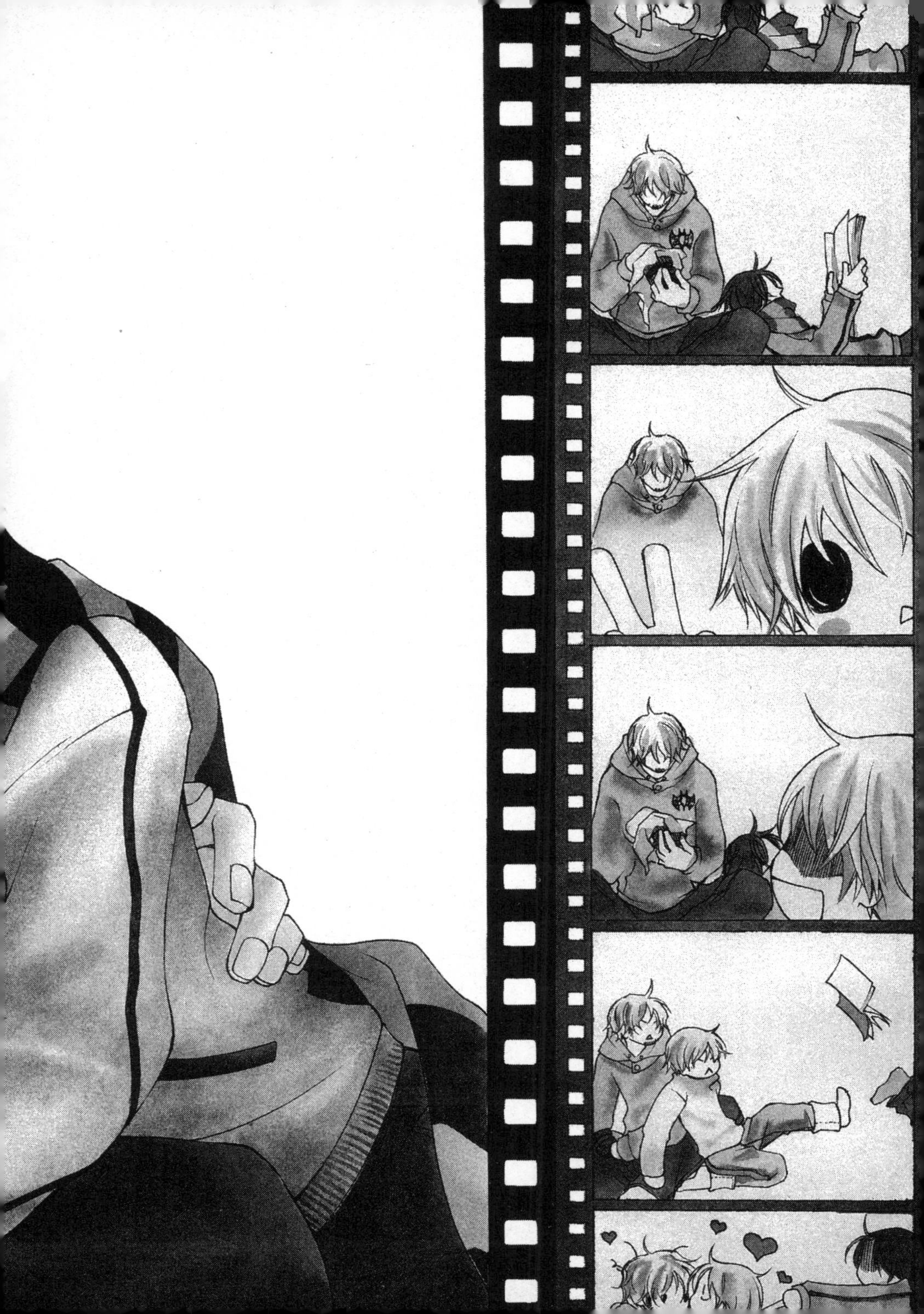

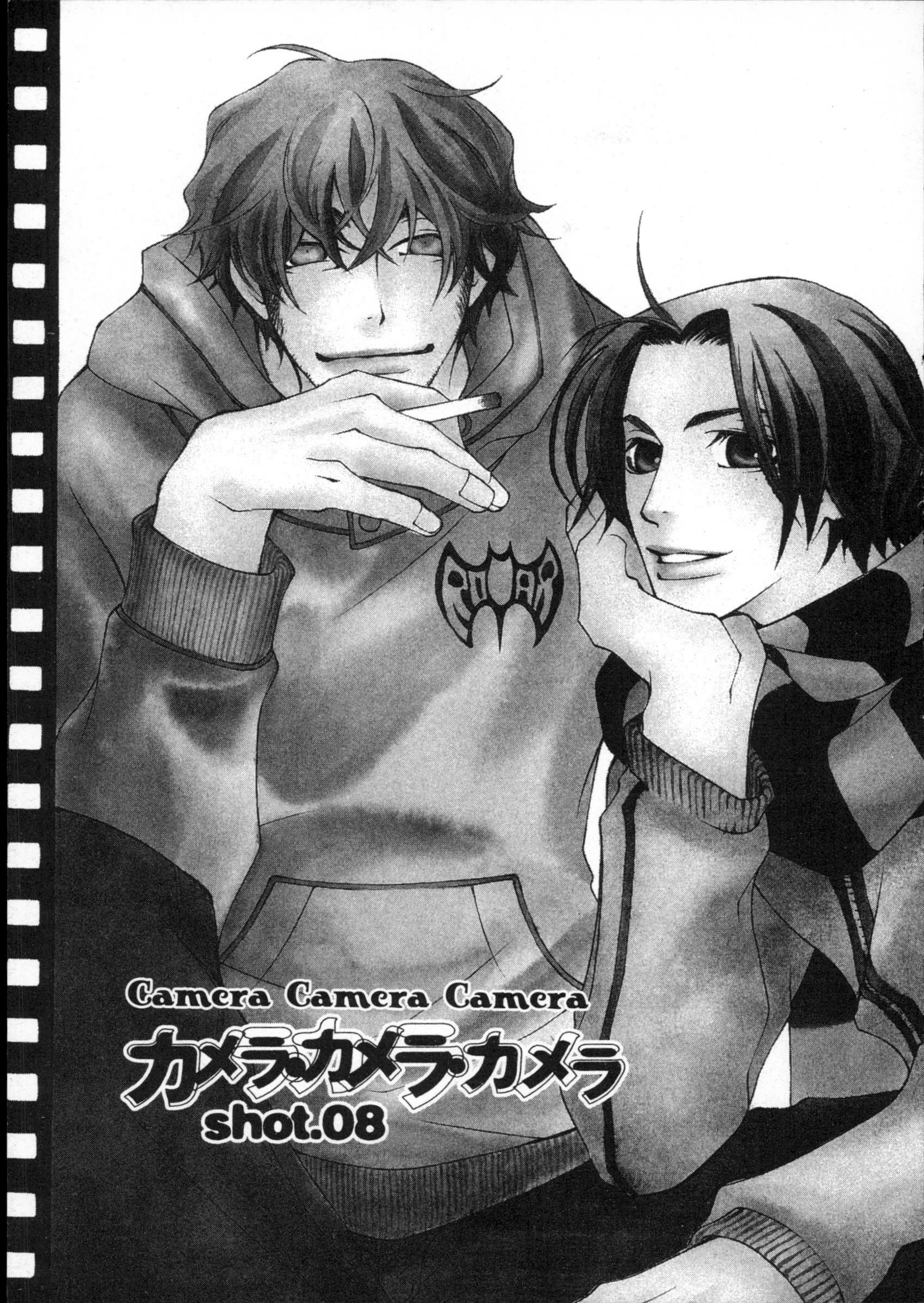
Camera Camera Camera
カメラ・カメラ・カメラ
shot.08

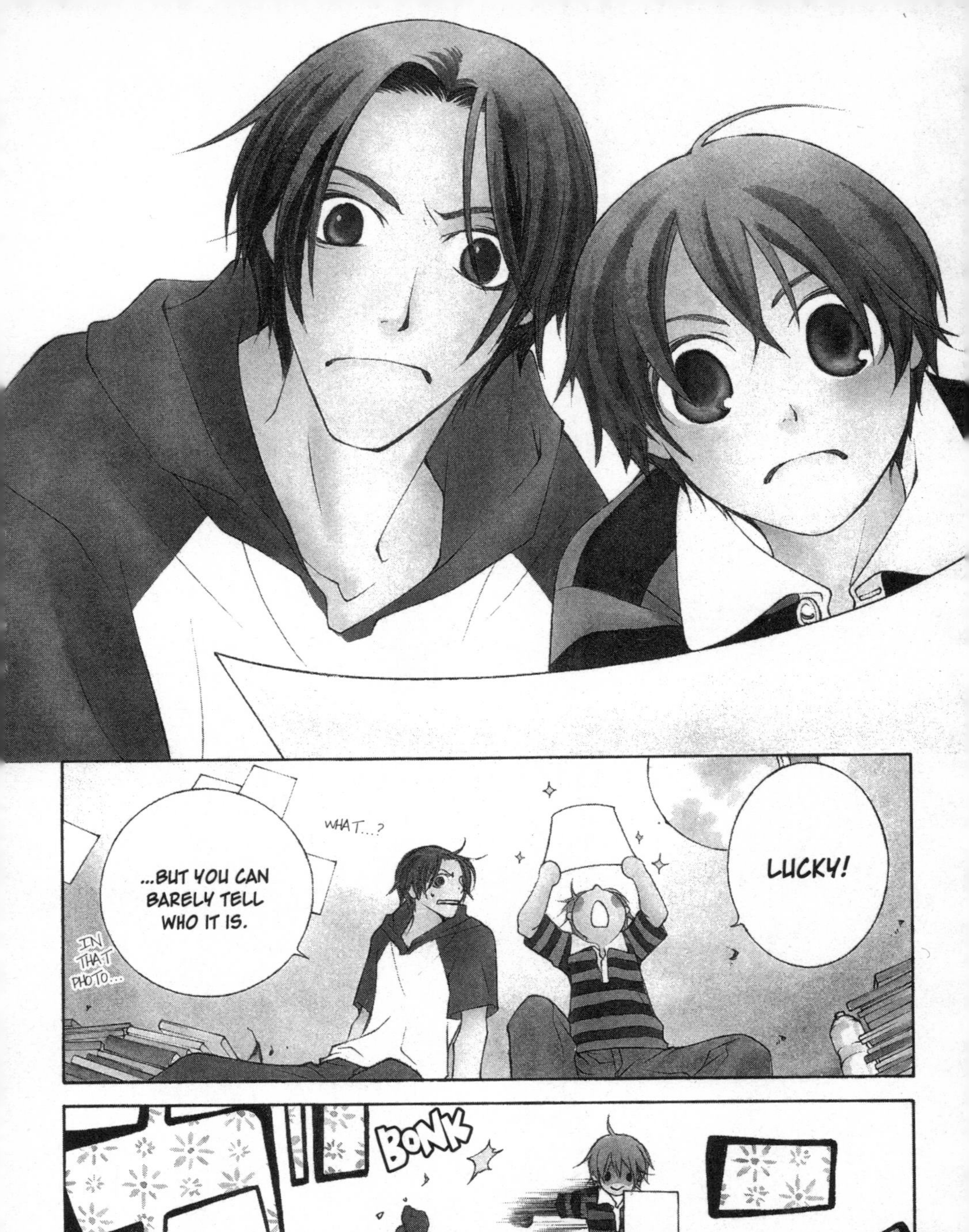
LUCKY!
WHAT...?
...BUT YOU CAN BARELY TELL WHO IT IS.
IN THAT PHOTO...
BONK

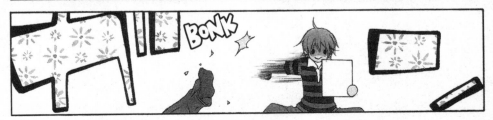

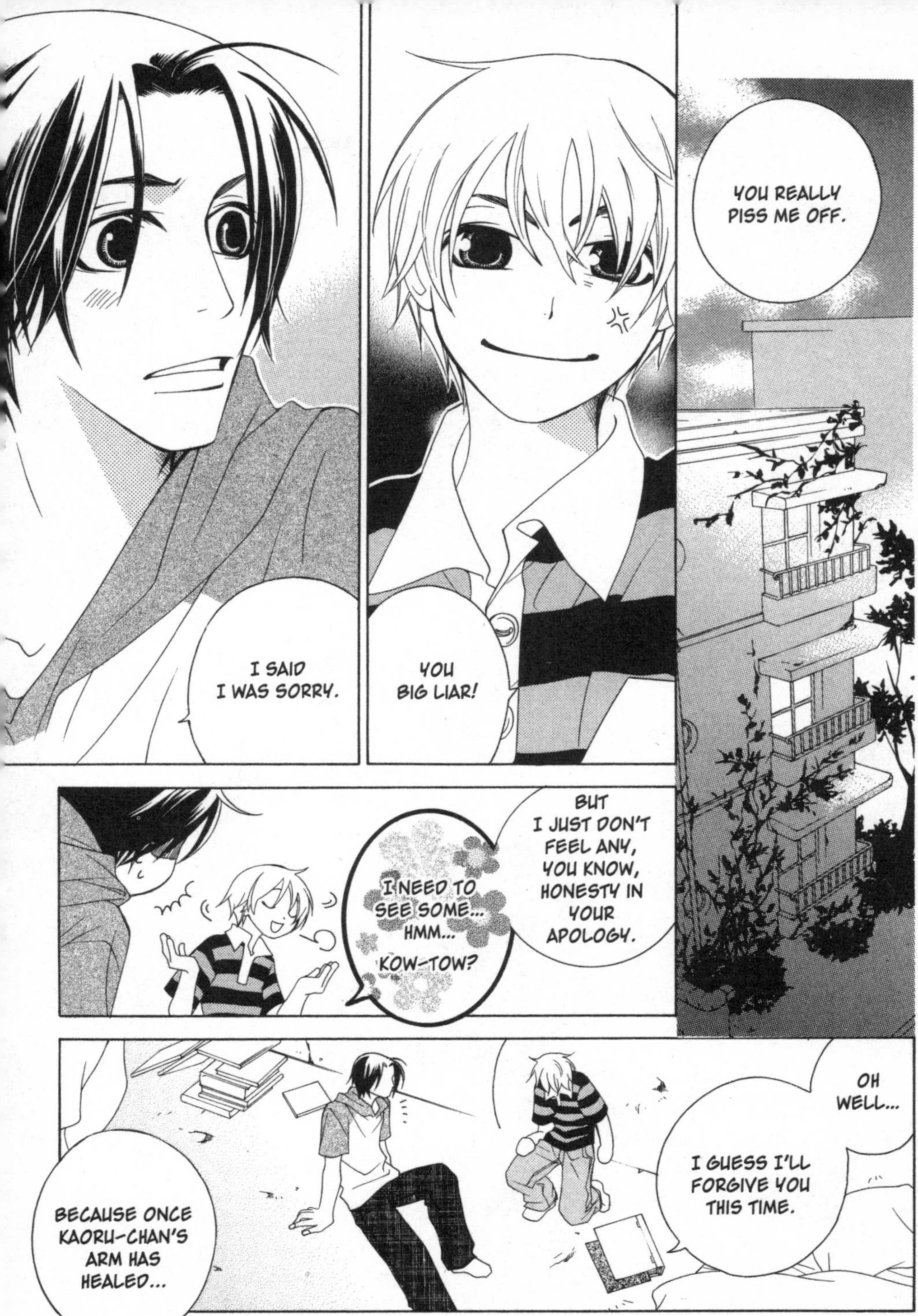
YOU REALLY PISS ME OFF.
YOU BIG LIAR!
I SAID I WAS SORRY.
BUT I JUST DON'T FEEL ANY, YOU KNOW, HONESTY IN YOUR APOLOGY.
I NEED TO SEE SOME... HMM... KOW-TOW?
OH WELL...
I GUESS I'LL FORGIVE YOU THIS TIME.
BECAUSE ONCE KAORU-CHAN'S ARM HAS HEALED...

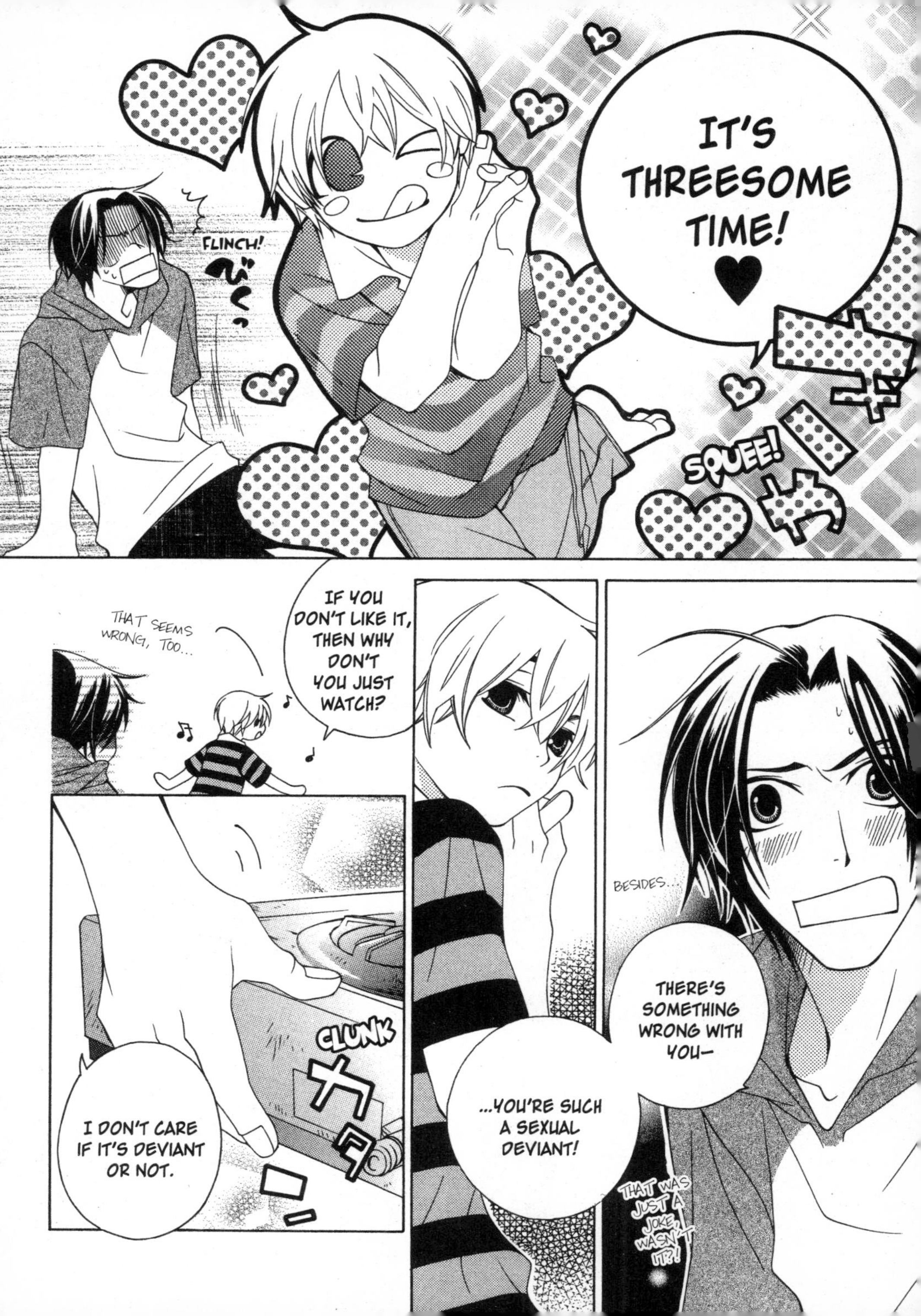
IT'S THREESOME TIME! ♥
SQUEE!
FLINCH!
BESIDES...
THERE'S SOMETHING WRONG WITH YOU—
THAT WAS JUST A JOKE, WASN'T IT!?
...YOU'RE SUCH A SEXUAL DEVIANT!
IF YOU DON'T LIKE IT, THEN WHY DON'T YOU JUST WATCH?
THAT SEEMS WRONG, TOO...
CLUNK
I DON'T CARE IF IT'S DEVIANT OR NOT.

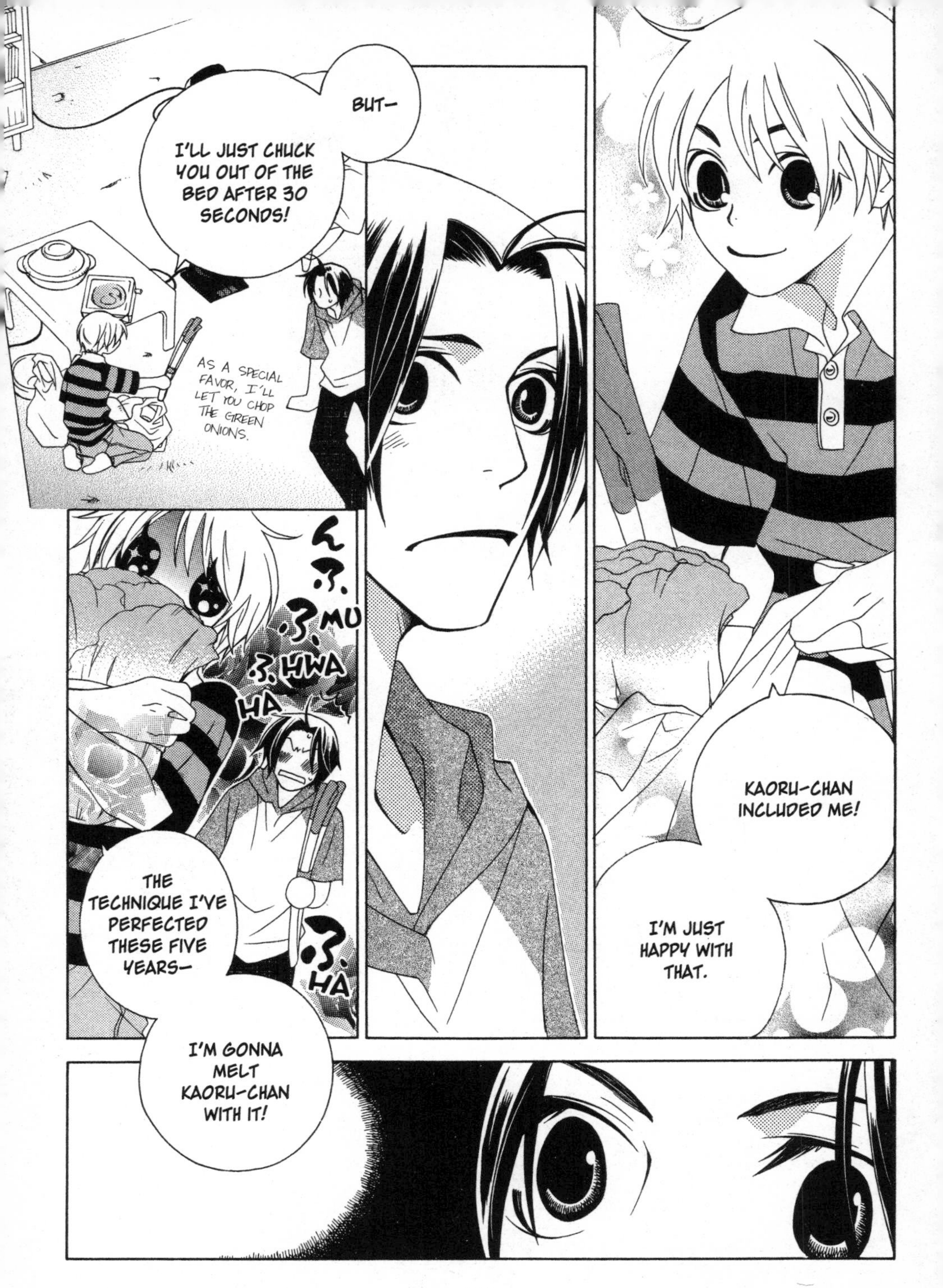
KAORU-CHAN INCLUDED ME!
I'M JUST HAPPY WITH THAT.
BUT—
I'LL JUST CHUCK YOU OUT OF THE BED AFTER 30 SECONDS!
AS A SPECIAL FAVOR, I'LL LET YOU CHOP THE GREEN ONIONS.
んふふ MU
ふふ HWA
HA
THE TECHNIQUE I'VE PERFECTED THESE FIVE YEARS—
ふ HA
I'M GONNA MELT KAORU-CHAN WITH IT!

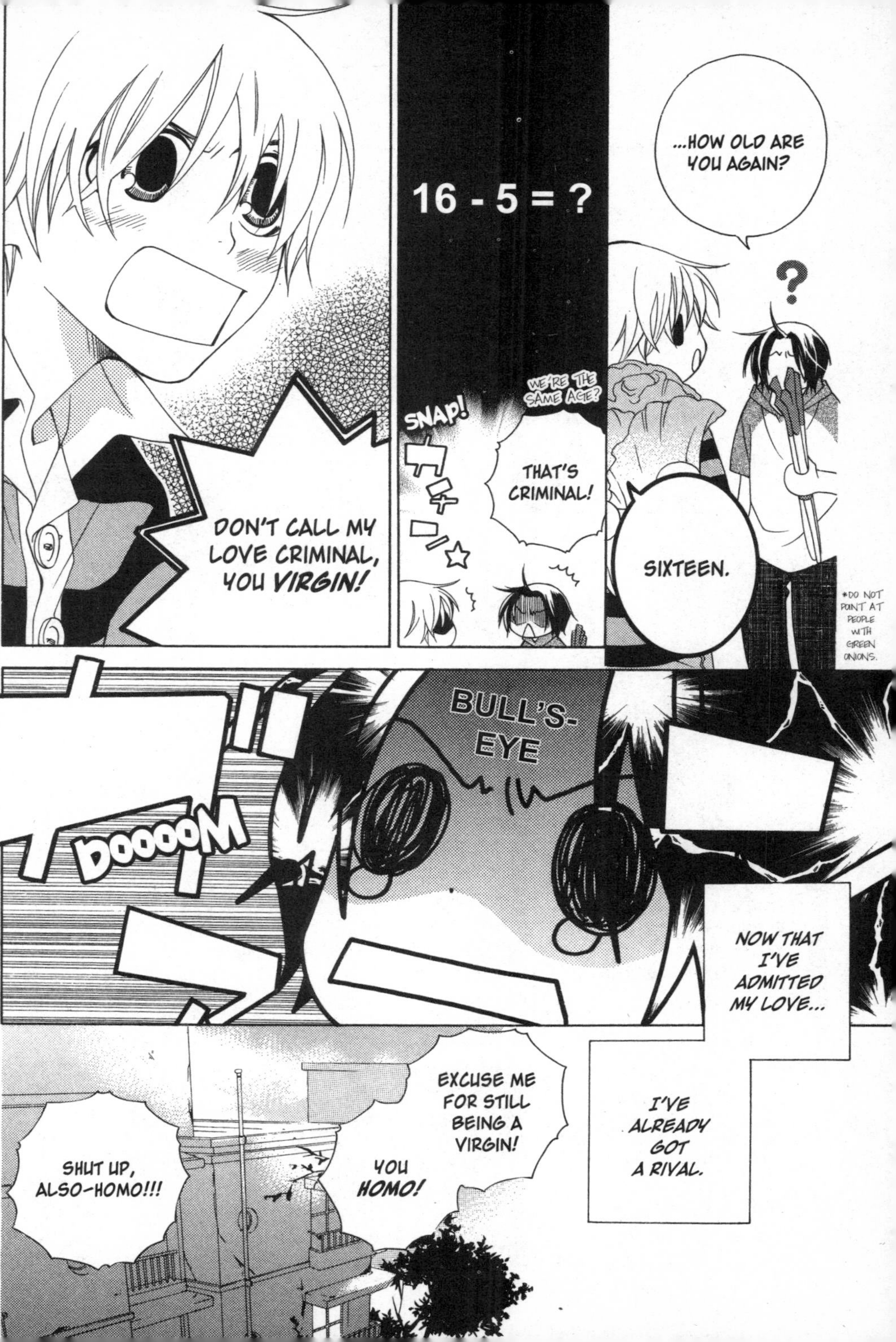
...HOW OLD ARE YOU AGAIN?
?
SIXTEEN.
*DO NOT POINT AT PEOPLE WITH GREEN ONIONS.
16 - 5 = ?
WE'RE THE SAME AGE?
SNAP!
THAT'S CRIMINAL!
DON'T CALL MY LOVE CRIMINAL, YOU VIRGIN!
BULL'S-EYE
DOOOOM
NOW THAT I'VE ADMITTED MY LOVE...
I'VE ALREADY GOT A RIVAL.
EXCUSE ME FOR STILL BEING A VIRGIN!
YOU HOMO!
SHUT UP, ALSO-HOMO!!!

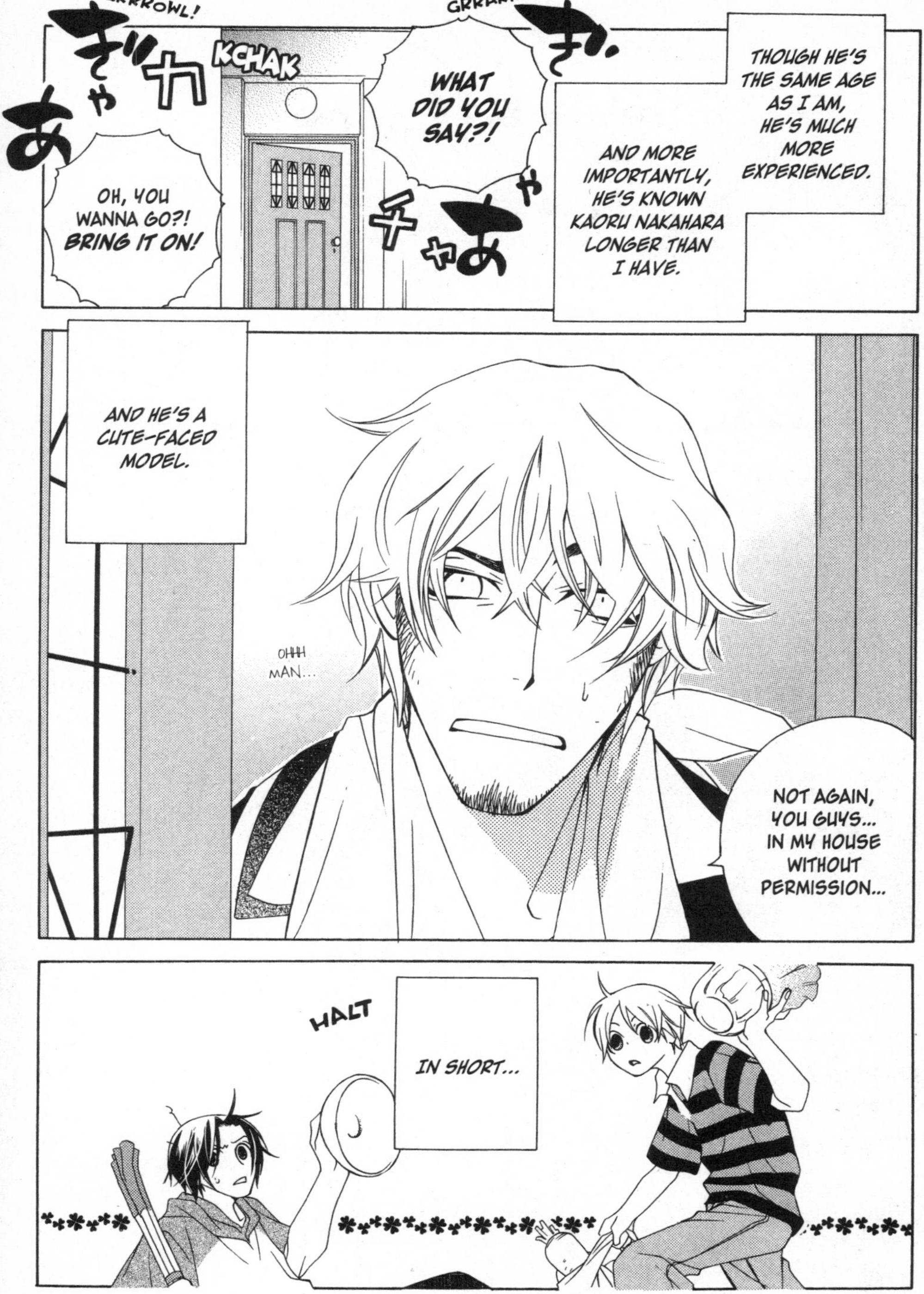
THOUGH HE'S THE SAME AGE AS I AM, HE'S MUCH MORE EXPERIENCED.
AND MORE IMPORTANTLY, HE'S KNOWN KAORU NAKAHARA LONGER THAN I HAVE.
GRRARRGH!
WHAT DID YOU SAY?!
KCHAK
GRRROWL!
OH, YOU WANNA GO?! BRING IT ON!
AND HE'S A CUTE-FACED MODEL.
NOT AGAIN, YOU GUYS... IN MY HOUSE WITHOUT PERMISSION...
OHHH MAN...
IN SHORT...
HALT

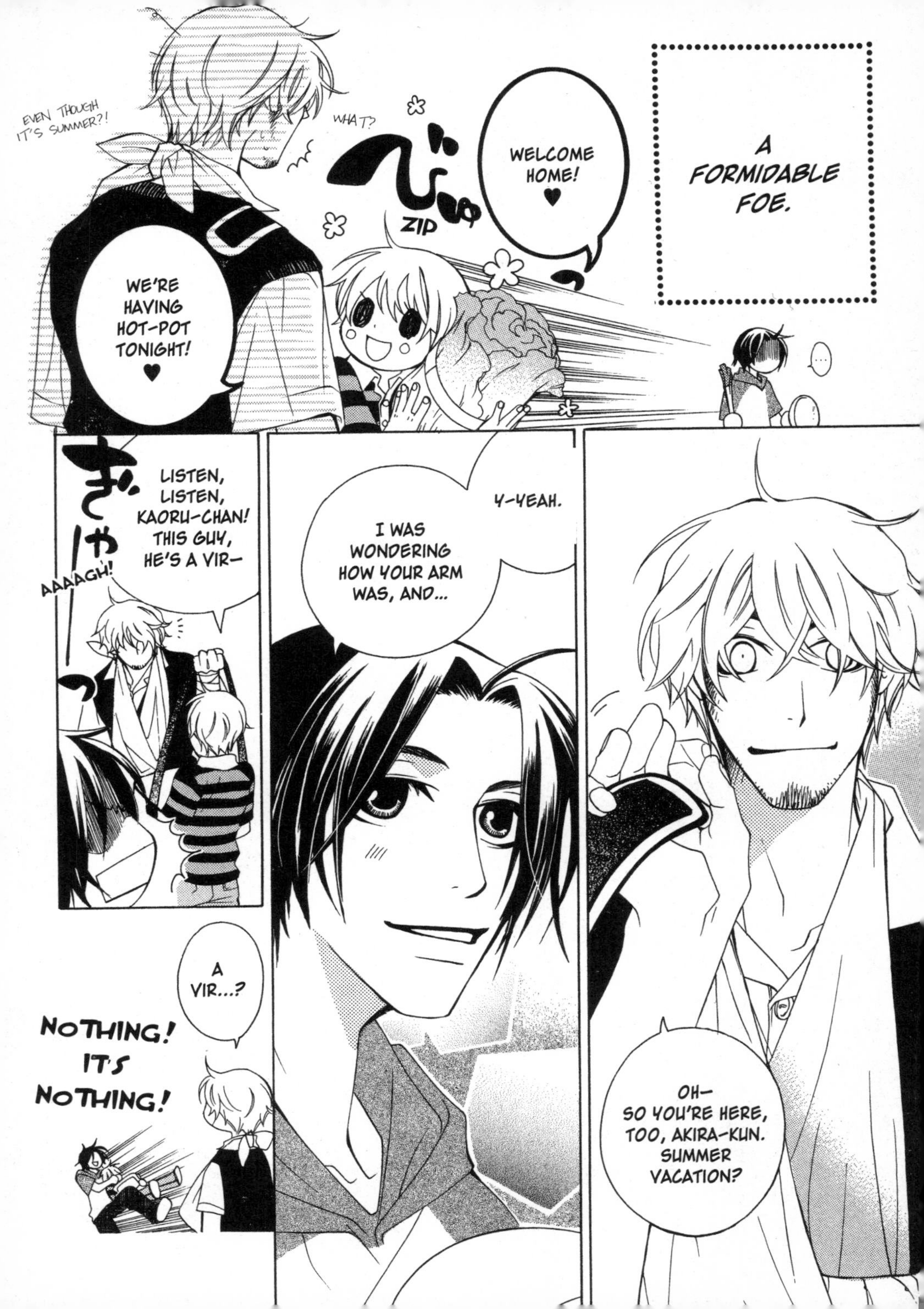
A FORMIDABLE FOE.
WELCOME HOME! ♥
...
ZIP
WHAT?
EVEN THOUGH IT'S SUMMER?!
WE'RE HAVING HOT-POT TONIGHT! ♥
OH— SO YOU'RE HERE, TOO, AKIRA-KUN. SUMMER VACATION?
Y-YEAH.
I WAS WONDERING HOW YOUR ARM WAS, AND...
LISTEN, LISTEN, KAORU-CHAN! THIS GUY, HE'S A VIR—
AAAAGH!
A VIR...?
NOTHING! IT'S NOTHING!

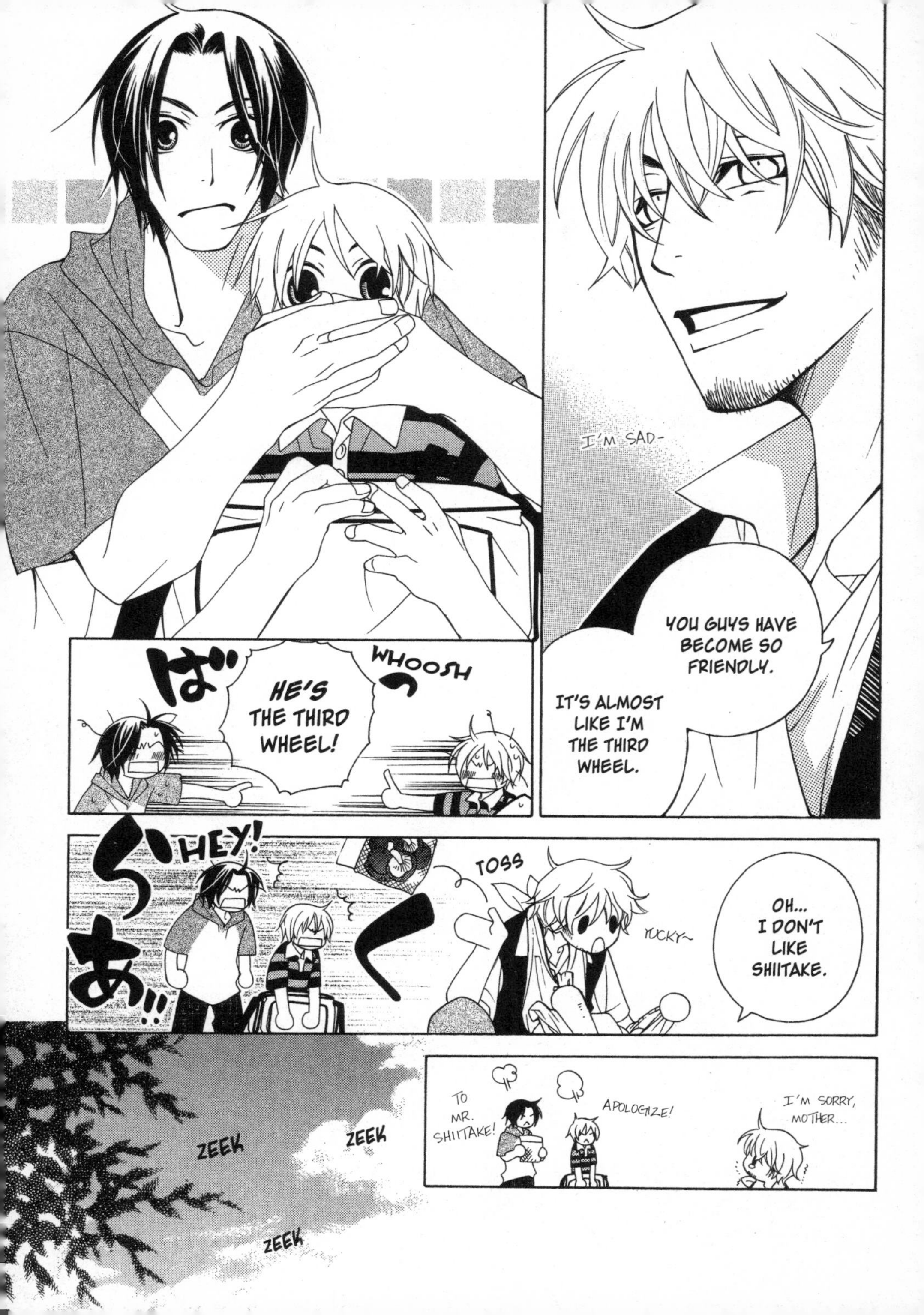
I'M SAD-
YOU GUYS HAVE BECOME SO FRIENDLY.
IT'S ALMOST LIKE I'M THE THIRD WHEEL.
WHOOSH
HE'S THE THIRD WHEEL!
ぱっ
OH... I DON'T LIKE SHIITAKE.
YUCKY~
TOSS
HEY!
らあ!!
I'M SORRY, MOTHER...
APOLOGIZE!
TO MR. SHIITAKE!
ZEEK
ZEEK
ZEEK

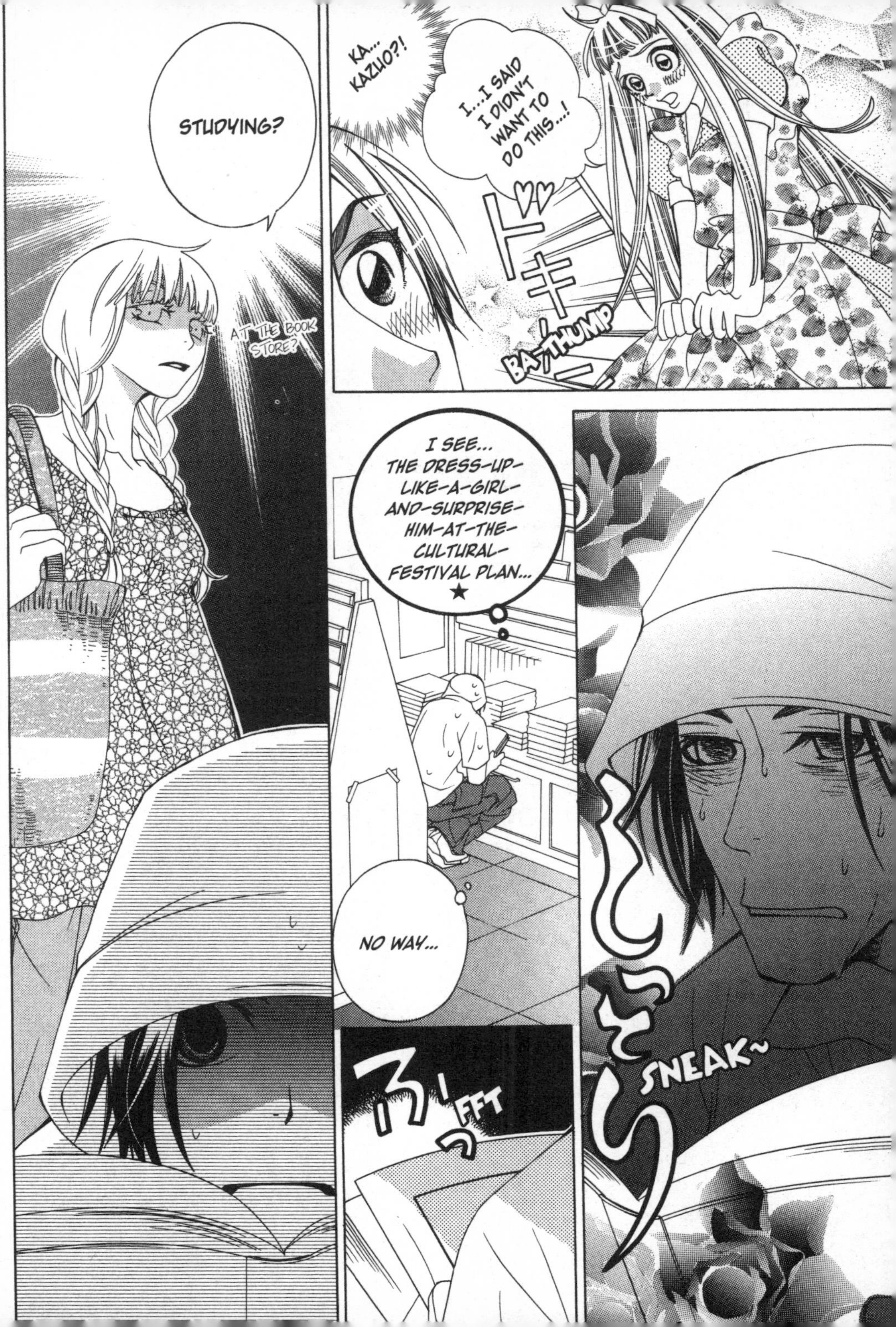
I...I SAID I DIDN'T WANT TO DO THIS...!
KA... KAZUO?!
BA-THUMP
SNEAK~
I SEE... THE DRESS-UP-LIKE-A-GIRL-AND-SURPRISE-HIM-AT-THE-CULTURAL-FESTIVAL PLAN... ★
NO WAY...
FFT
STUDYING?
AT THE BOOK STORE?

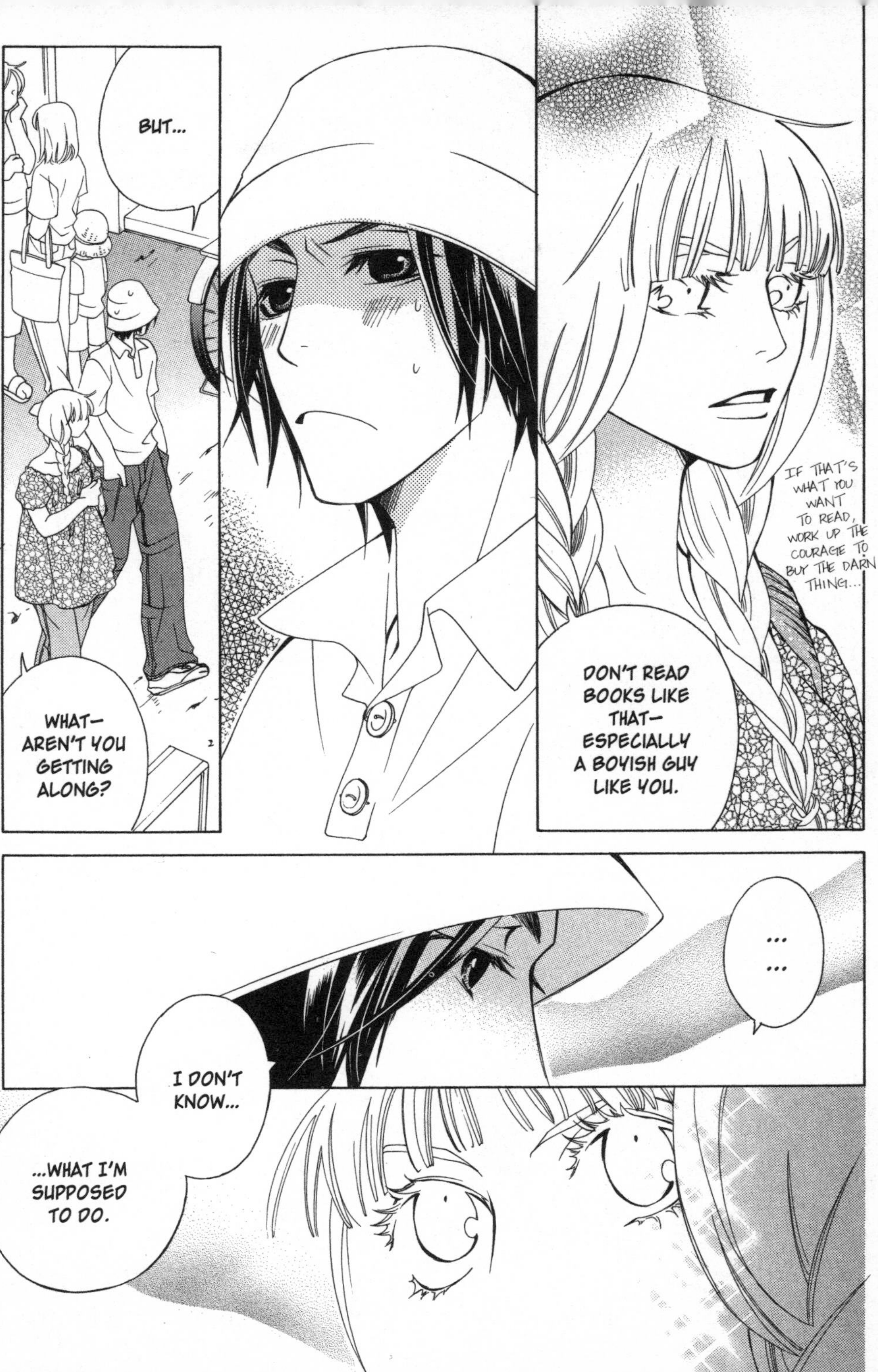
IF THAT'S WHAT YOU WANT TO READ, WORK UP THE COURAGE TO BUY THE DARN THING...
DON'T READ BOOKS LIKE THAT— ESPECIALLY A BOYISH GUY LIKE YOU.
BUT...
WHAT— AREN'T YOU GETTING ALONG?
... ...
I DON'T KNOW...
...WHAT I'M SUPPOSED TO DO.

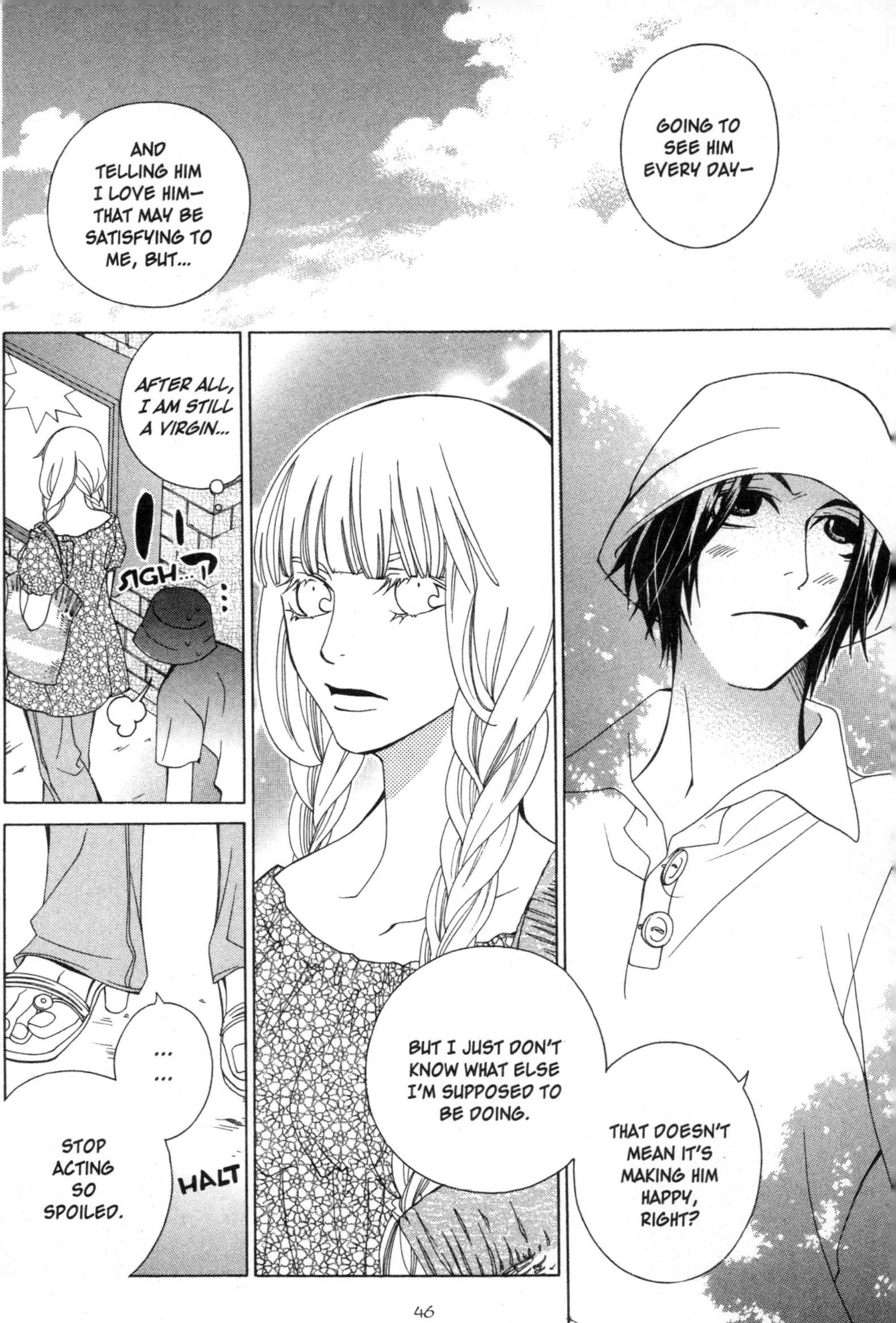
GOING TO SEE HIM EVERY DAY—
AND TELLING HIM I LOVE HIM— THAT MAY BE SATISFYING TO ME, BUT...
THAT DOESN'T MEAN IT'S MAKING HIM HAPPY, RIGHT?
BUT I JUST DON'T KNOW WHAT ELSE I'M SUPPOSED TO BE DOING.
AFTER ALL, I AM STILL A VIRGIN...
SIGH...
... ...
HALT
STOP ACTING SO SPOILED.

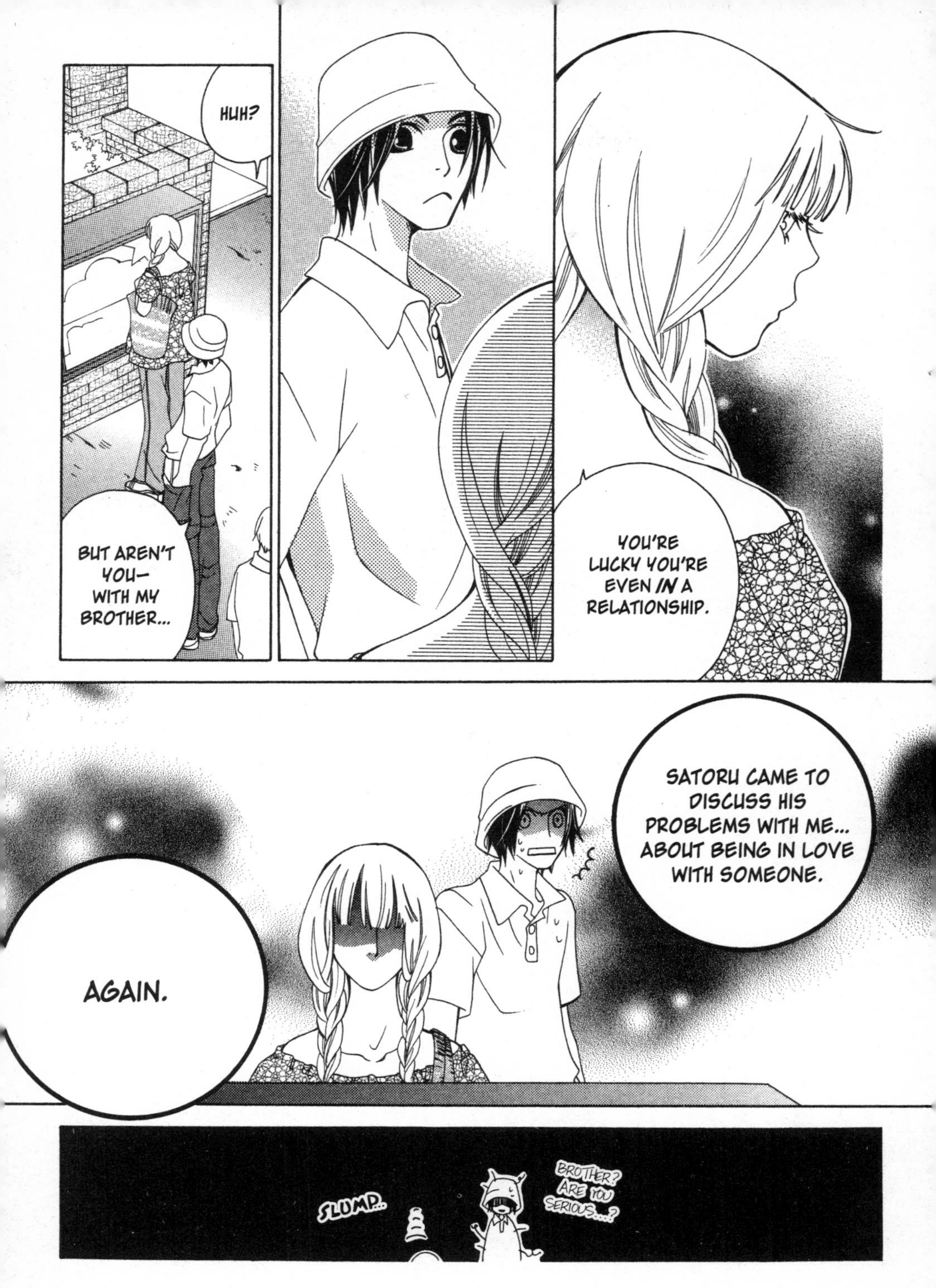
YOU'RE LUCKY YOU'RE EVEN *IN* A RELATIONSHIP.
HUH?
BUT AREN'T YOU— WITH MY BROTHER...
SATORU CAME TO DISCUSS HIS PROBLEMS WITH ME... ABOUT BEING IN LOVE WITH SOMEONE.
AGAIN.
BROTHER? ARE YOU SERIOUS...?
SLUMP...

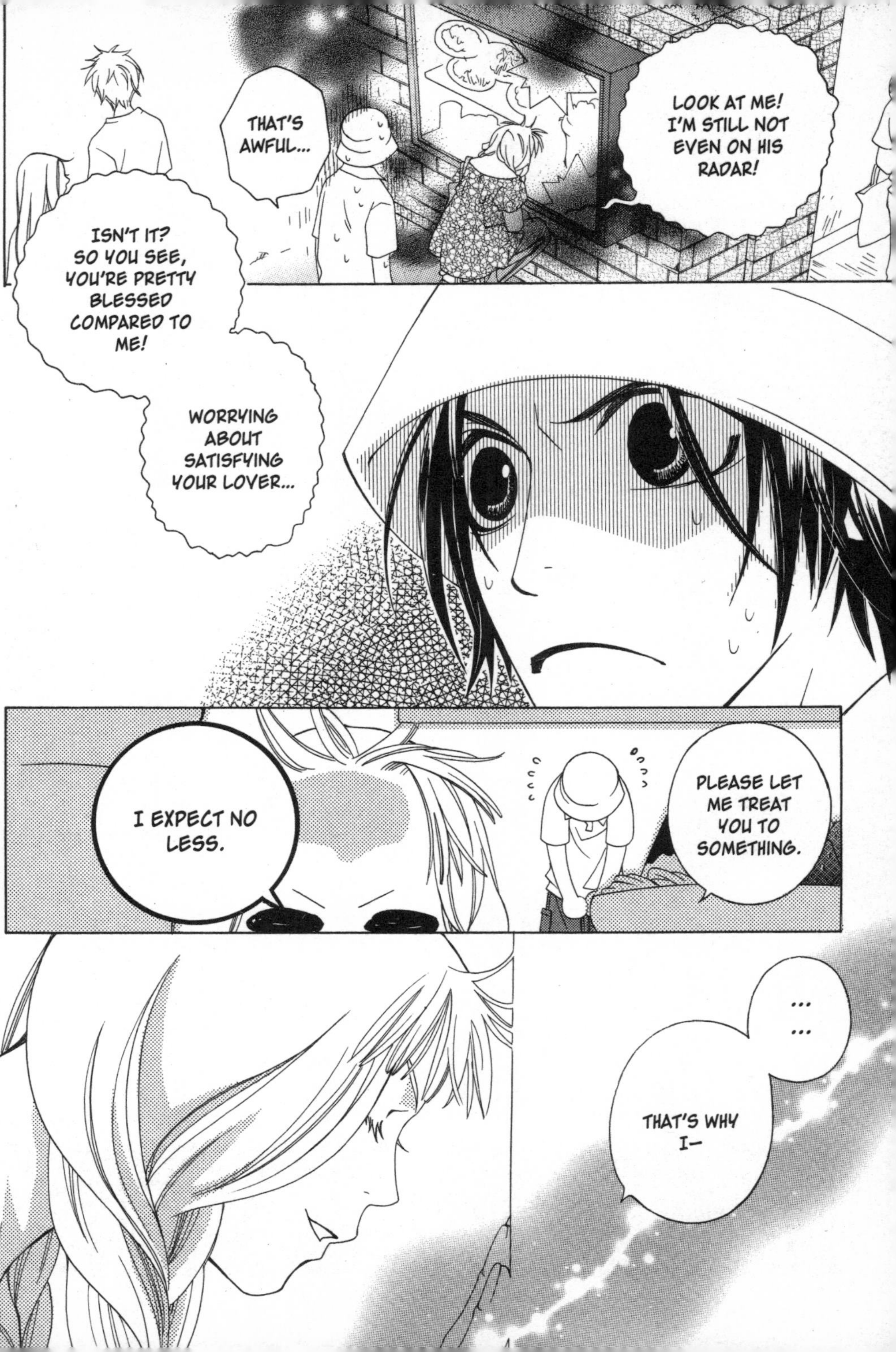

LOOK AT ME! I'M STILL NOT EVEN ON HIS RADAR!
THAT'S AWFUL...
ISN'T IT? SO YOU SEE, YOU'RE PRETTY BLESSED COMPARED TO ME!
WORRYING ABOUT SATISFYING YOUR LOVER...
PLEASE LET ME TREAT YOU TO SOMETHING.
I EXPECT NO LESS.
……
THAT'S WHY I—

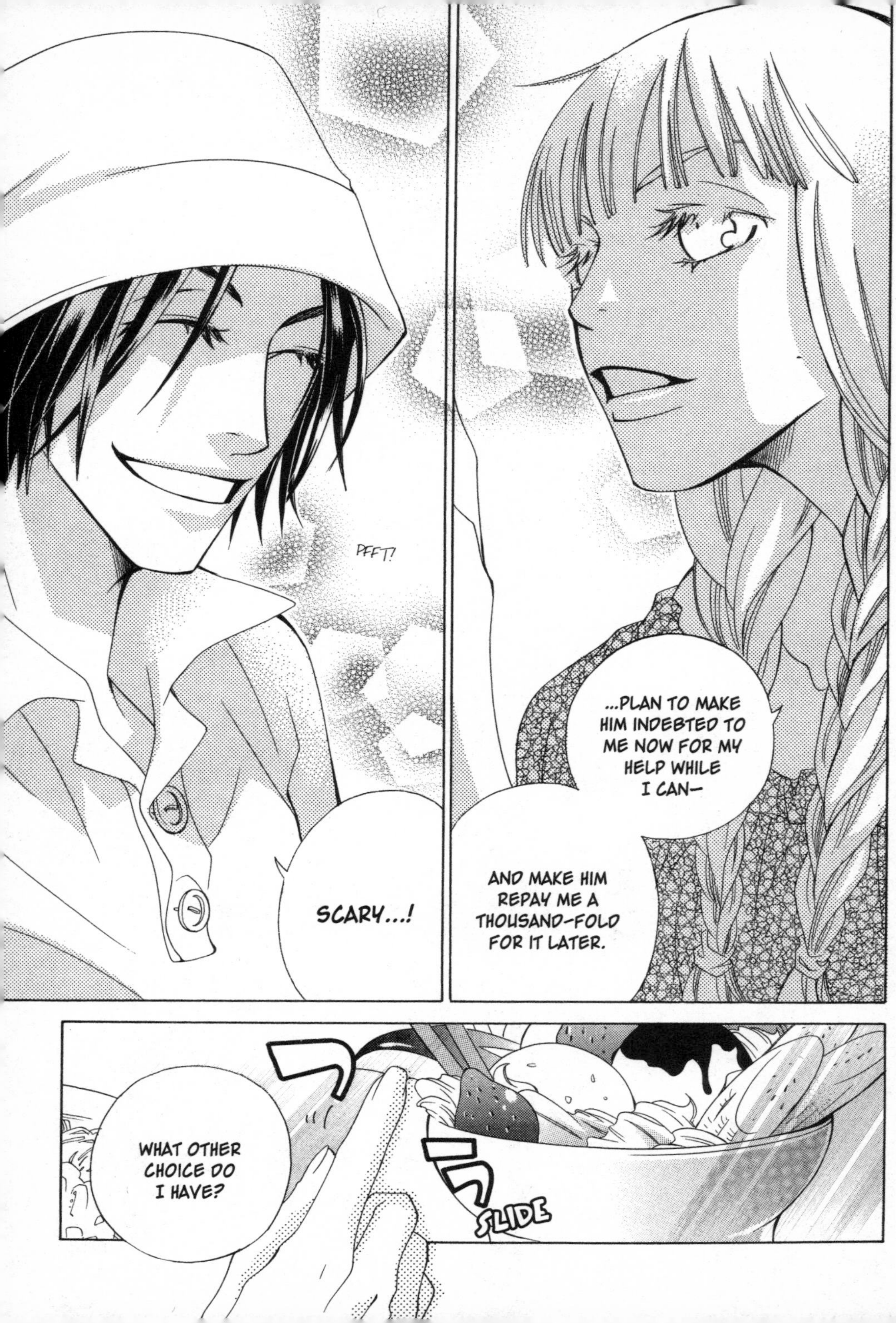
...PLAN TO MAKE HIM INDEBTED TO ME NOW FOR MY HELP WHILE I CAN—
AND MAKE HIM REPAY ME A THOUSAND-FOLD FOR IT LATER.
PFFT!
SCARY...!
WHAT OTHER CHOICE DO I HAVE?
SLIDE

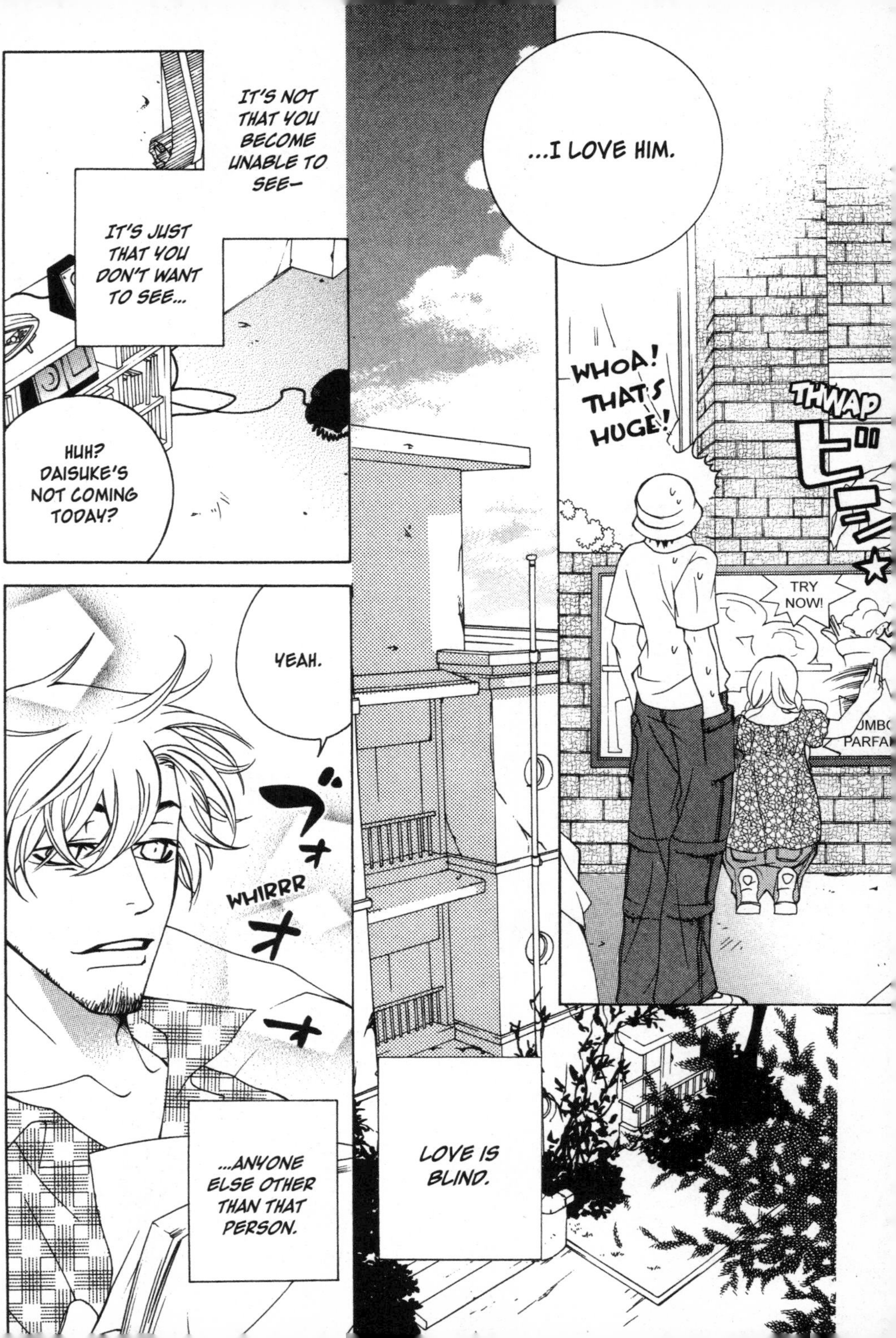
...I LOVE HIM.
WHOA! THAT'S HUGE!
THWAP
TRY NOW!
LOVE IS BLIND.
IT'S NOT THAT YOU BECOME UNABLE TO SEE—
IT'S JUST THAT YOU DON'T WANT TO SEE...
HUH? DAISUKE'S NOT COMING TODAY?
YEAH.
WHIRRR
...ANYONE ELSE OTHER THAN THAT PERSON.

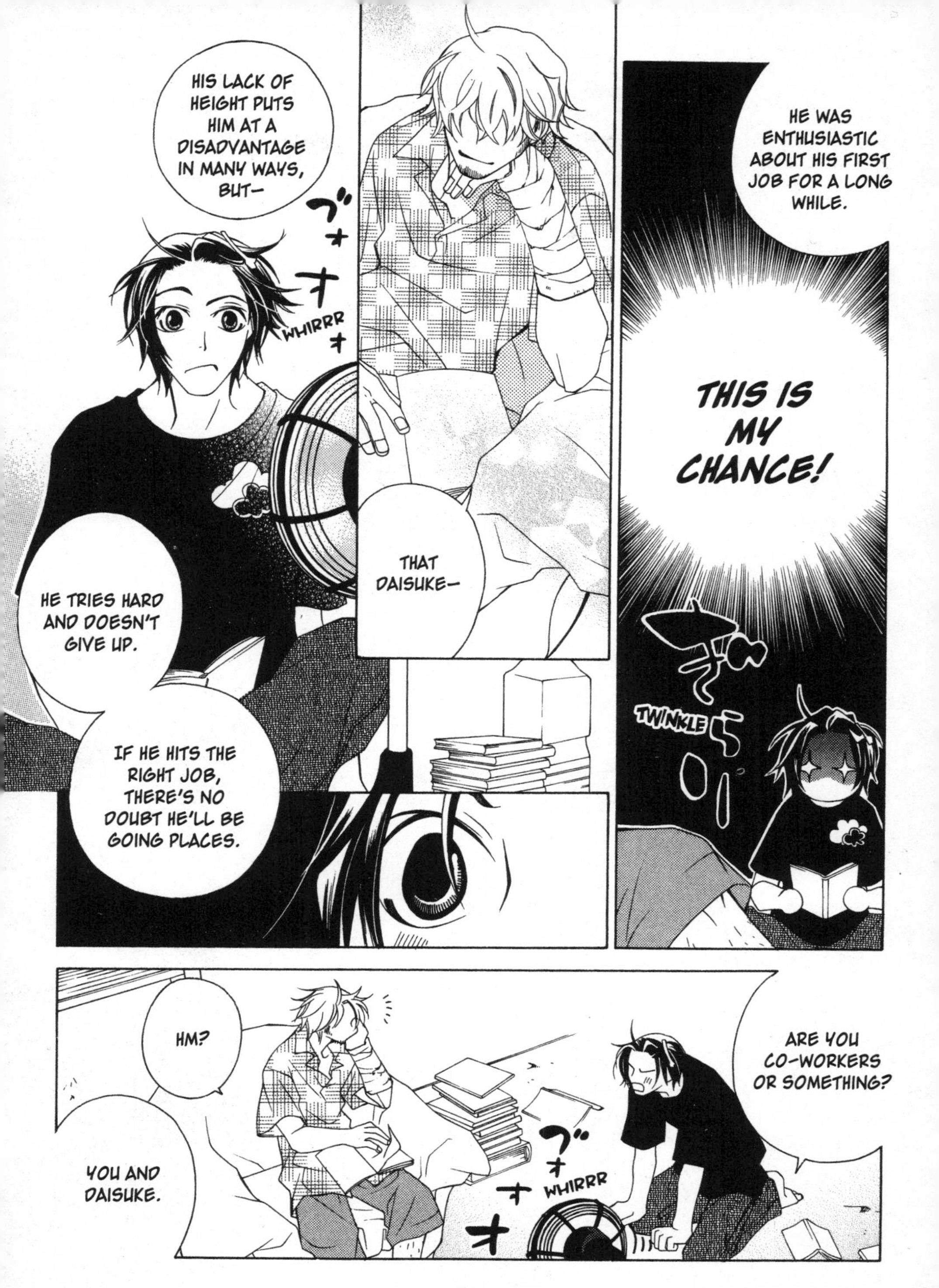
HE WAS ENTHUSIASTIC ABOUT HIS FIRST JOB FOR A LONG WHILE.
THIS IS MY CHANCE!
TWINKLE
THAT DAISUKE—
HIS LACK OF HEIGHT PUTS HIM AT A DISADVANTAGE IN MANY WAYS, BUT—
WHIRRR
HE TRIES HARD AND DOESN'T GIVE UP.
IF HE HITS THE RIGHT JOB, THERE'S NO DOUBT HE'LL BE GOING PLACES.
ARE YOU CO-WORKERS OR SOMETHING?
WHIRRR
HM?
YOU AND DAISUKE.

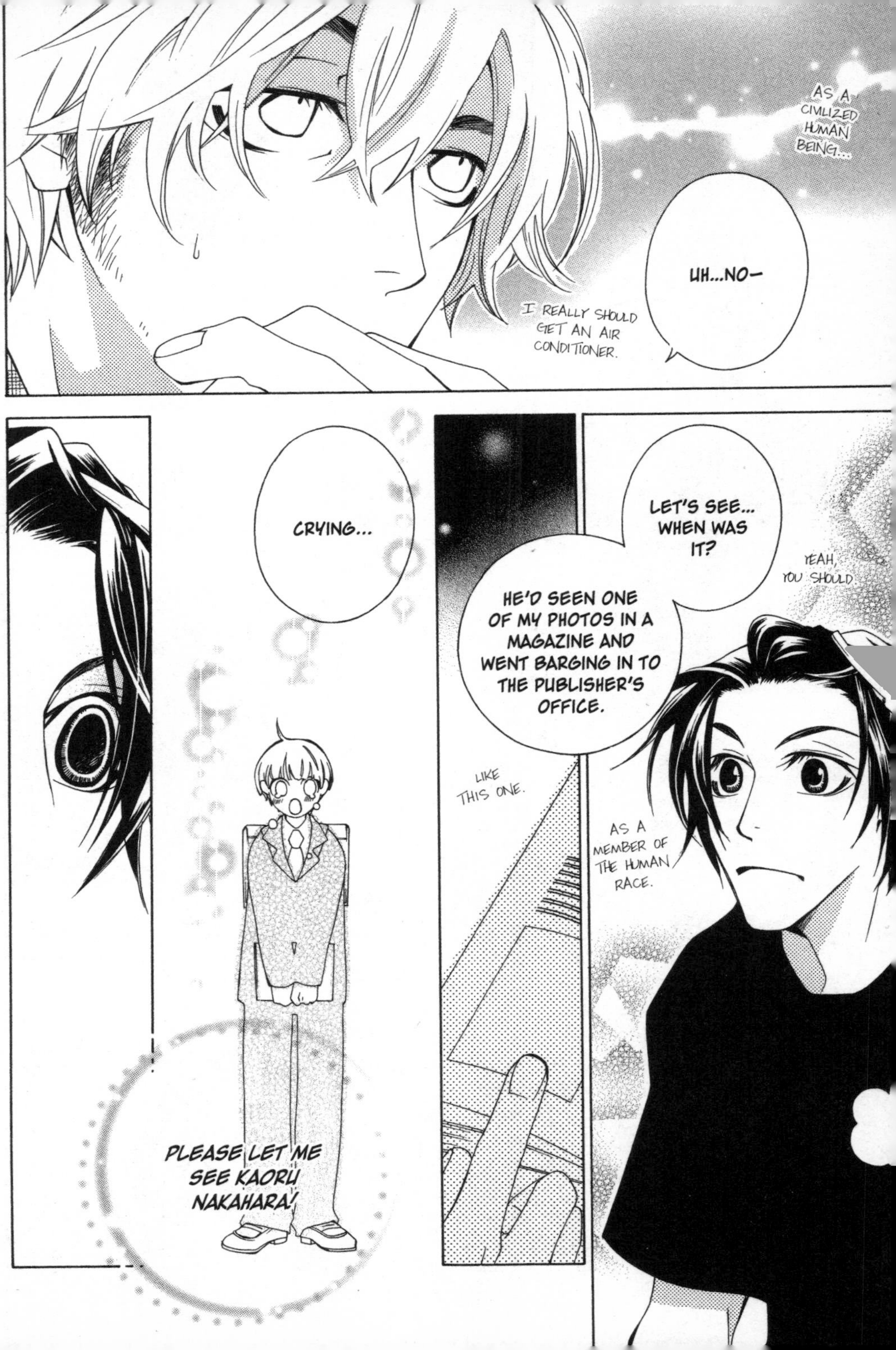
AS A CIVILIZED HUMAN BEING...
UH...NO—
I REALLY SHOULD GET AN AIR CONDITIONER.
LET'S SEE... WHEN WAS IT?
YEAH, YOU SHOULD.
HE'D SEEN ONE OF MY PHOTOS IN A MAGAZINE AND WENT BARGING IN TO THE PUBLISHER'S OFFICE.
AS A MEMBER OF THE HUMAN RACE.
LIKE THIS ONE.
CRYING...
PLEASE LET ME SEE KAORU NAKAHARA!

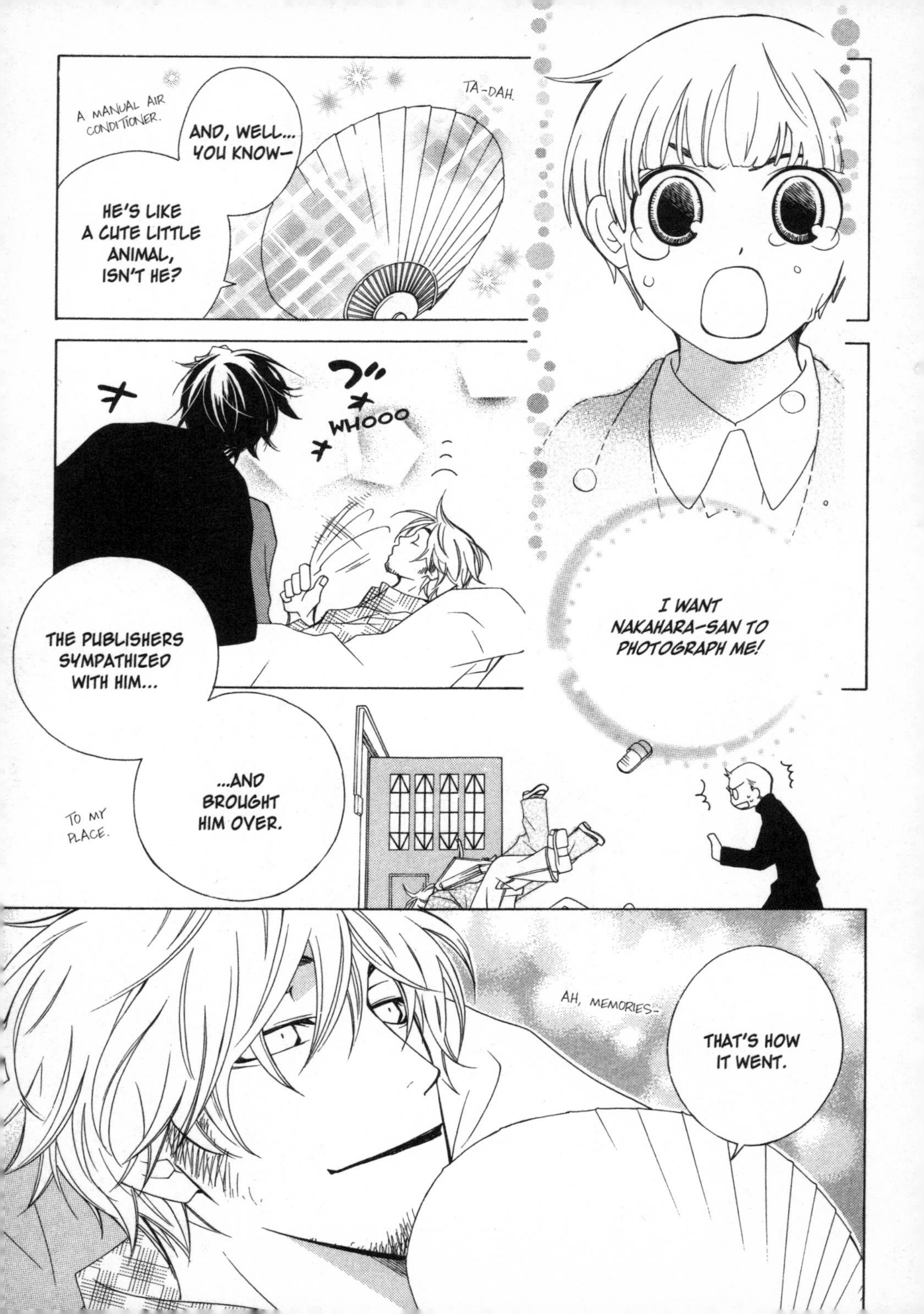
I WANT NAKAHARA-SAN TO PHOTOGRAPH ME!
TA-DAH.
AND, WELL... YOU KNOW—
A MANUAL AIR CONDITIONER.
HE'S LIKE A CUTE LITTLE ANIMAL, ISN'T HE?
WHOOO
THE PUBLISHERS SYMPATHIZED WITH HIM...
...AND BROUGHT HIM OVER.
TO MY PLACE.
AH, MEMORIES—
THAT'S HOW IT WENT.

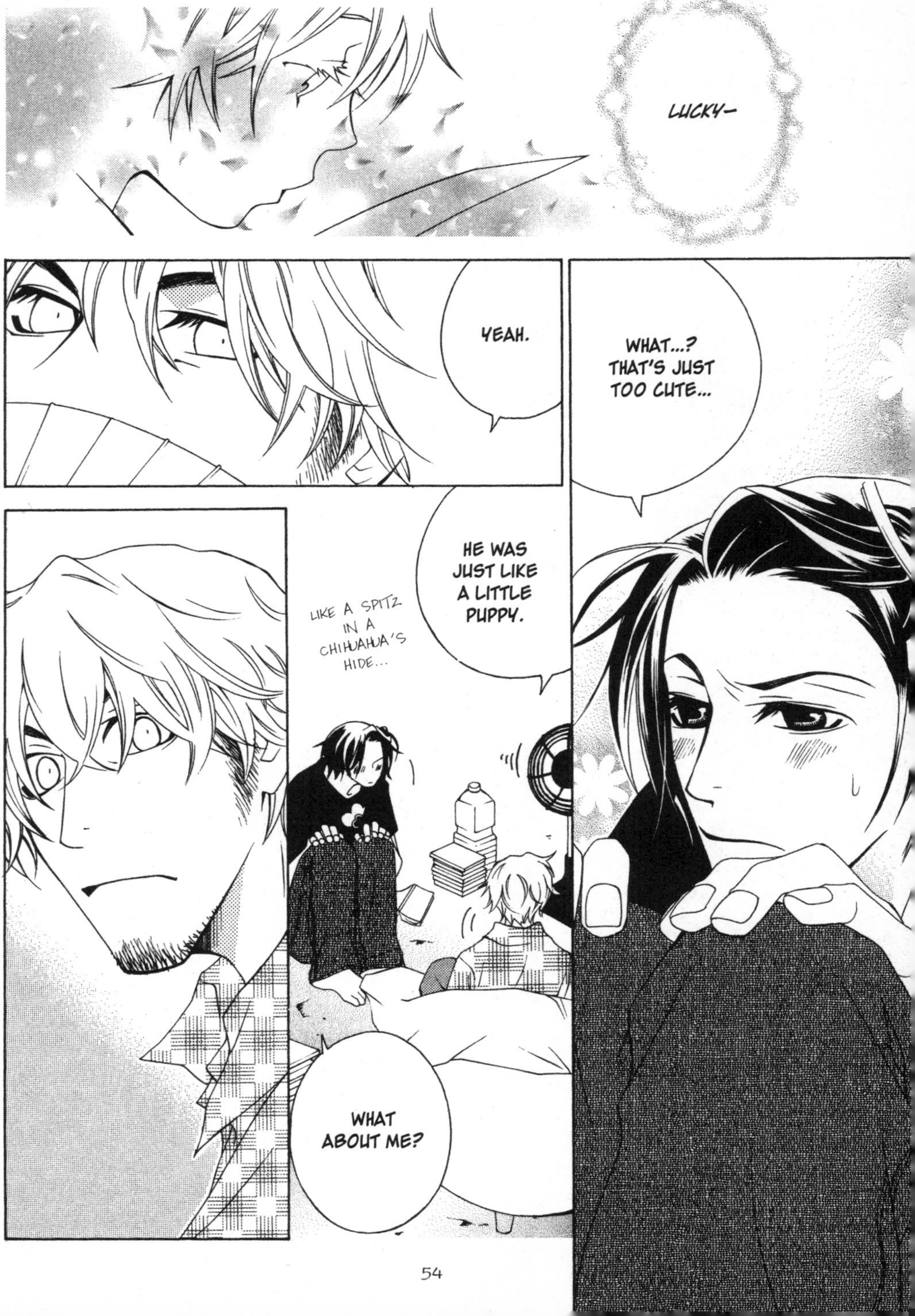
LUCKY—
WHAT...? THAT'S JUST TOO CUTE...
YEAH.
HE WAS JUST LIKE A LITTLE PUPPY.
LIKE A SPITZ IN A CHIHUAHUA'S HIDE...
WHAT ABOUT ME?

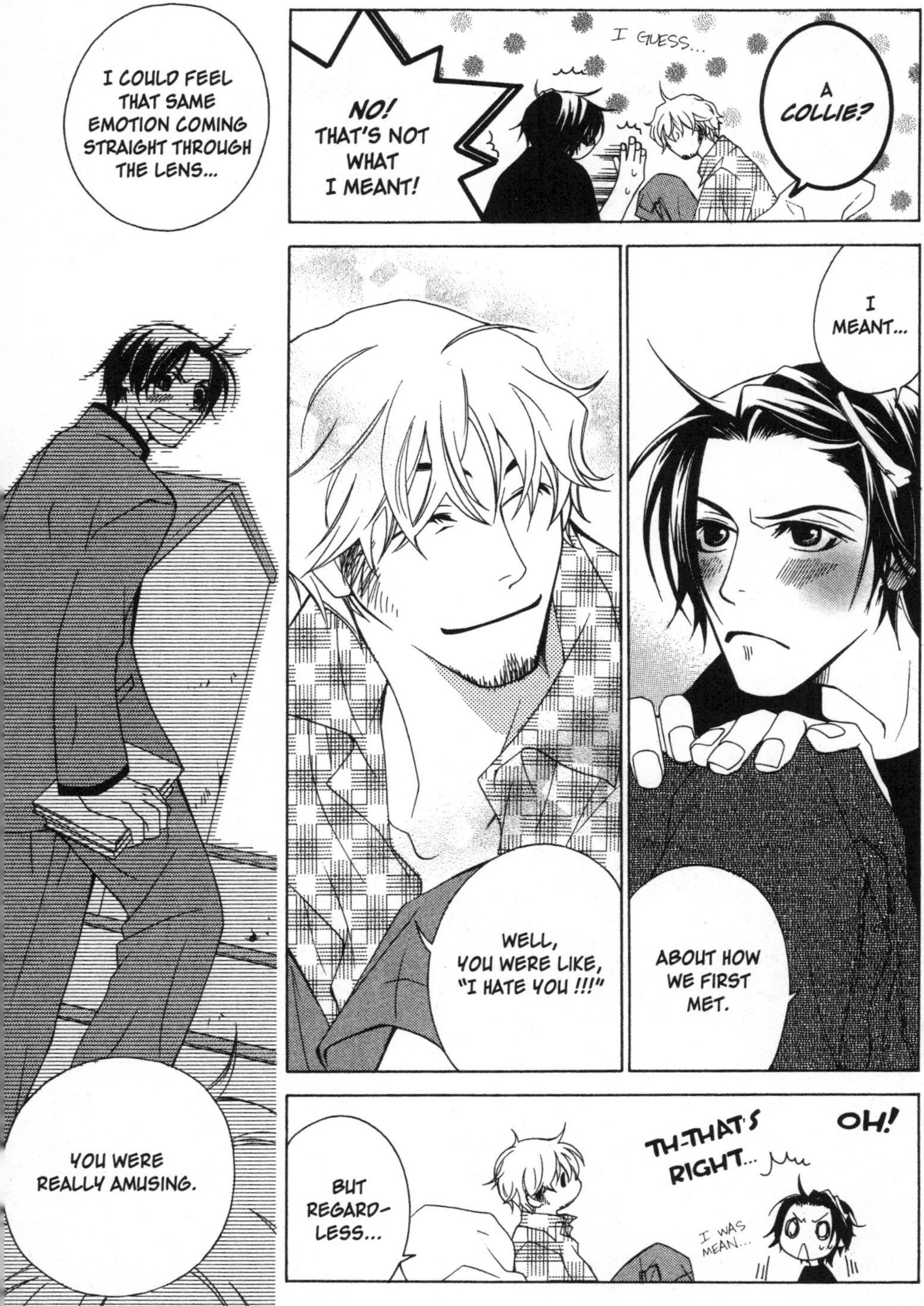
A COLLIE?
I GUESS...
NO! THAT'S NOT WHAT I MEANT!
I MEANT...
ABOUT HOW WE FIRST MET.
WELL, YOU WERE LIKE, "I HATE YOU !!!"
OH!
TH-THAT'S RIGHT...
I WAS MEAN...
BUT REGARD-LESS...
I COULD FEEL THAT SAME EMOTION COMING STRAIGHT THROUGH THE LENS...
YOU WERE REALLY AMUSING.

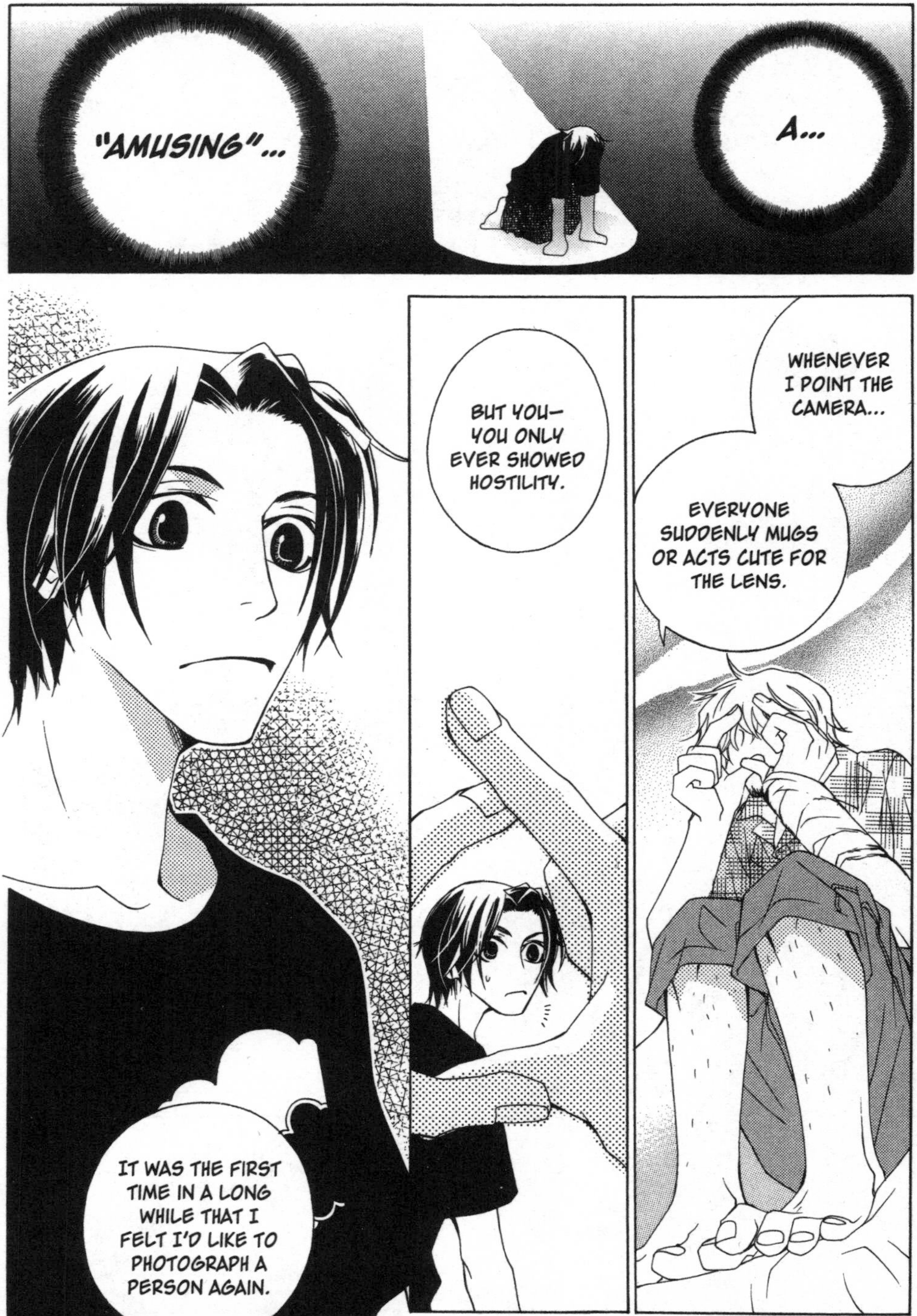
A...
"AMUSING"...
WHENEVER I POINT THE CAMERA...
EVERYONE SUDDENLY MUGS OR ACTS CUTE FOR THE LENS.
BUT YOU— YOU ONLY EVER SHOWED HOSTILITY.
IT WAS THE FIRST TIME IN A LONG WHILE THAT I FELT I'D LIKE TO PHOTOGRAPH A PERSON AGAIN.

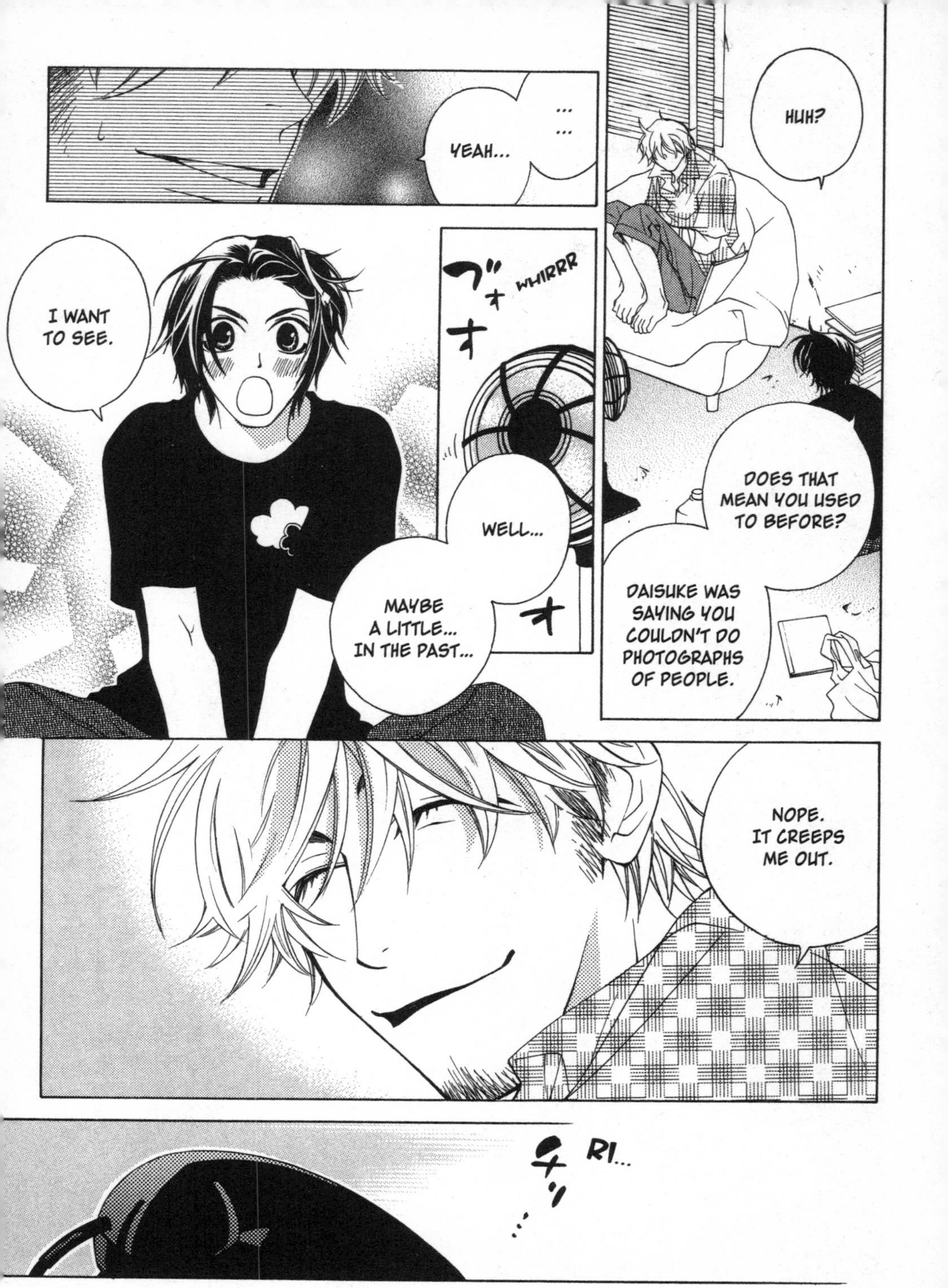
HUH?
DOES THAT MEAN YOU USED TO BEFORE?
DAISUKE WAS SAYING YOU COULDN'T DO PHOTOGRAPHS OF PEOPLE.
......
YEAH...
WHIRRR
WELL...
MAYBE A LITTLE... IN THE PAST...
I WANT TO SEE.
NOPE. IT CREEPS ME OUT.
RI...

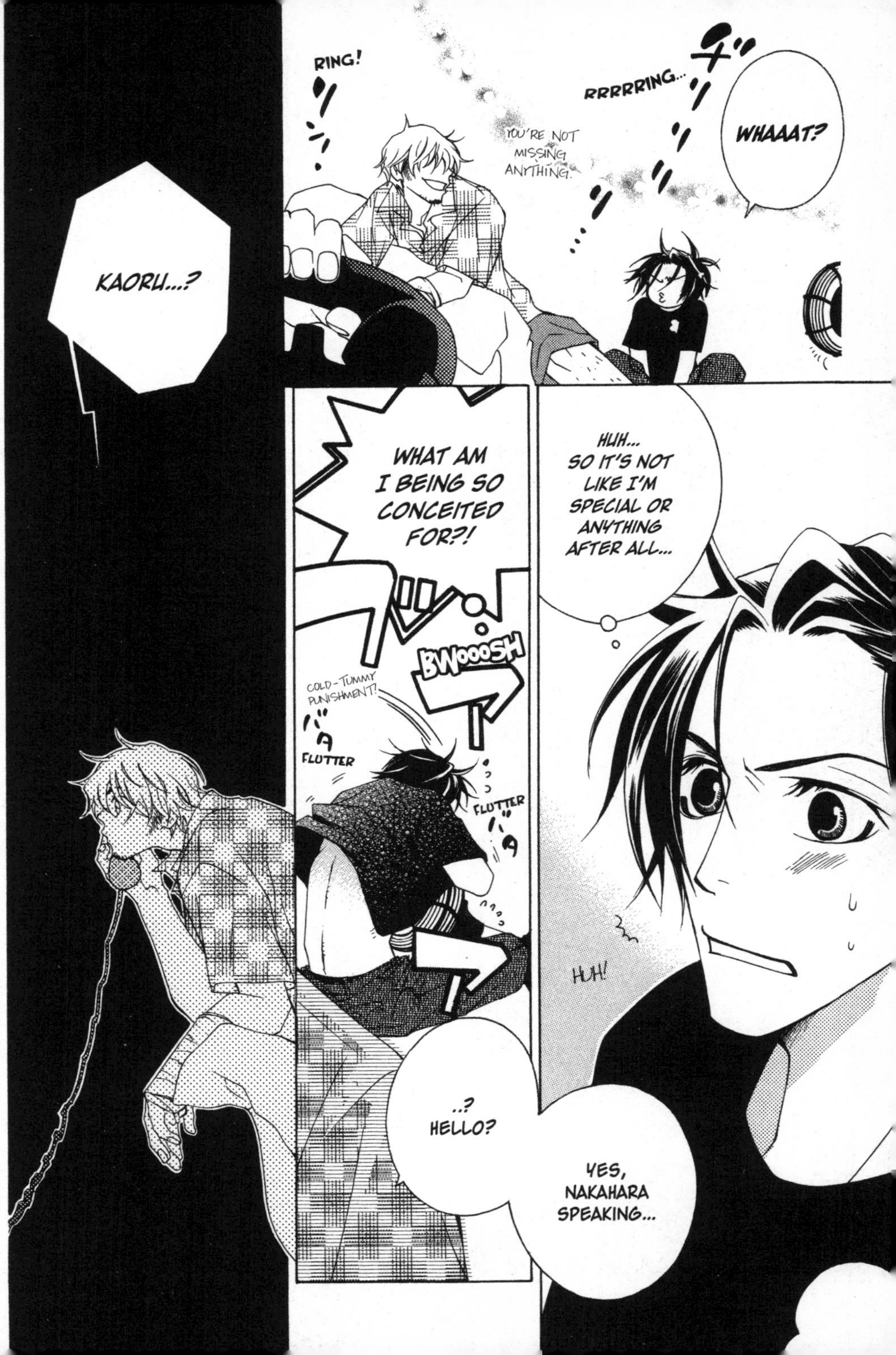
WHAAAT?
RRRRRING...
YOU'RE NOT MISSING ANYTHING.
RING!
HUH... SO IT'S NOT LIKE I'M SPECIAL OR ANYTHING AFTER ALL...
HUH!
YES, NAKAHARA SPEAKING...
WHAT AM I BEING SO CONCEITED FOR?!
BWOOOSH
COLD-TUMMY PUNISHMENT!
FLUTTER
FLUTTER
..? HELLO?
KAORU...?

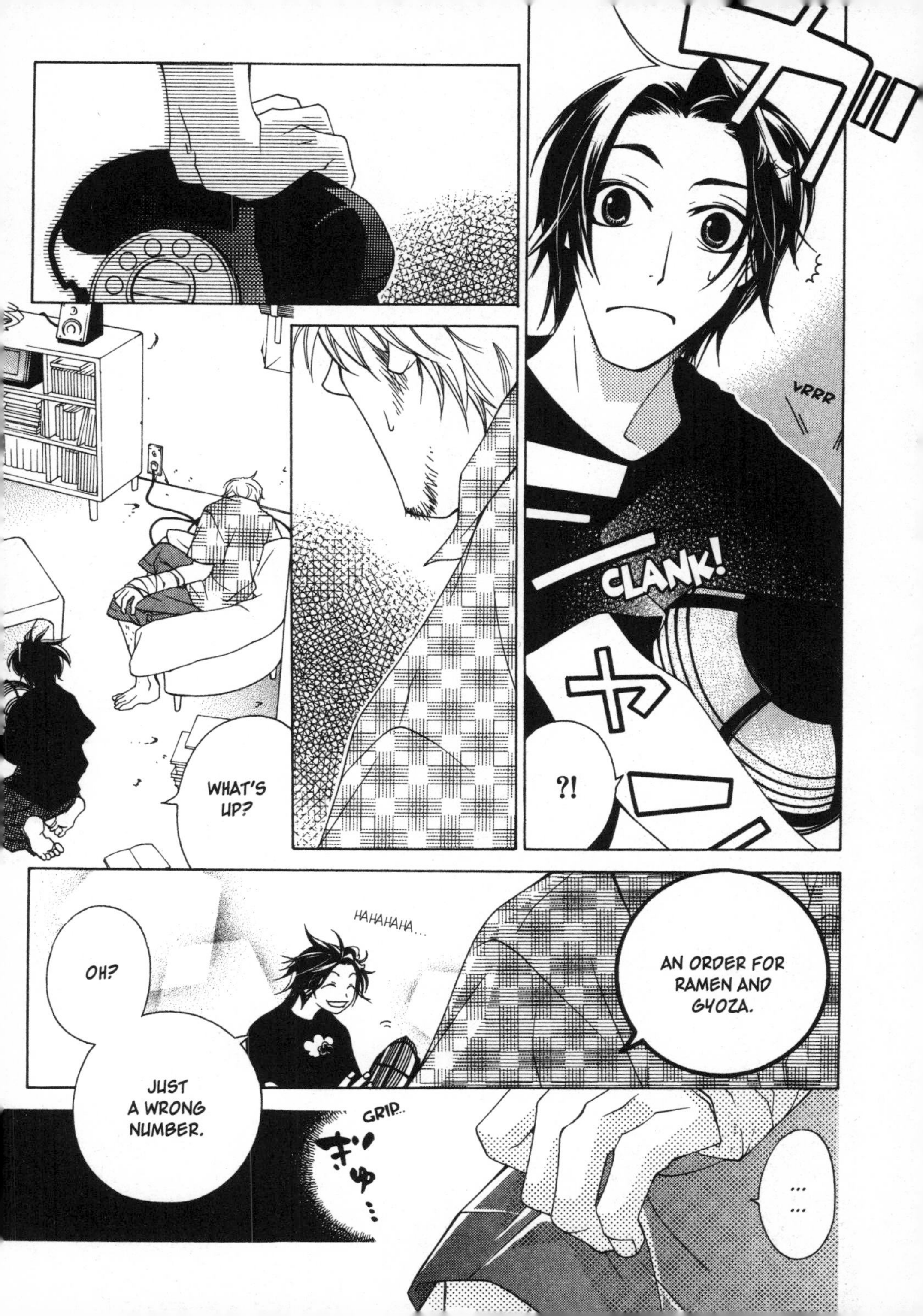
VRRR
CLANK!
?!
WHAT'S UP?
AN ORDER FOR RAMEN AND GYOZA.
HAHAHAHA...
OH?
JUST A WRONG NUMBER.
...
...
GRIP..
ぎゅ...

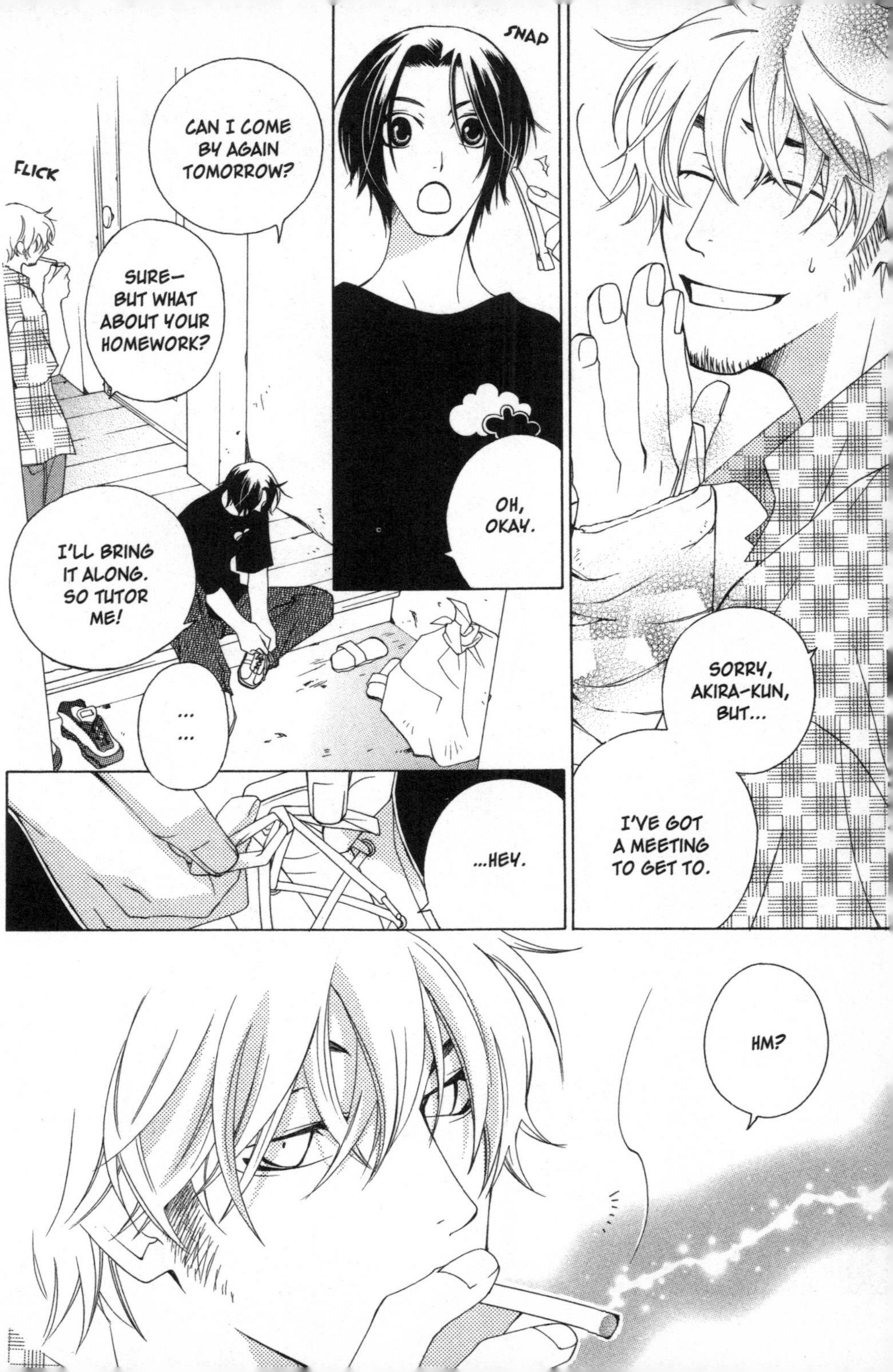
SORRY, AKIRA-KUN, BUT...
I'VE GOT A MEETING TO GET TO.
SNAP
OH, OKAY.
FLICK
CAN I COME BY AGAIN TOMORROW?
SURE— BUT WHAT ABOUT YOUR HOMEWORK?
I'LL BRING IT ALONG. SO TUTOR ME!
... ...
...HEY.
HM?

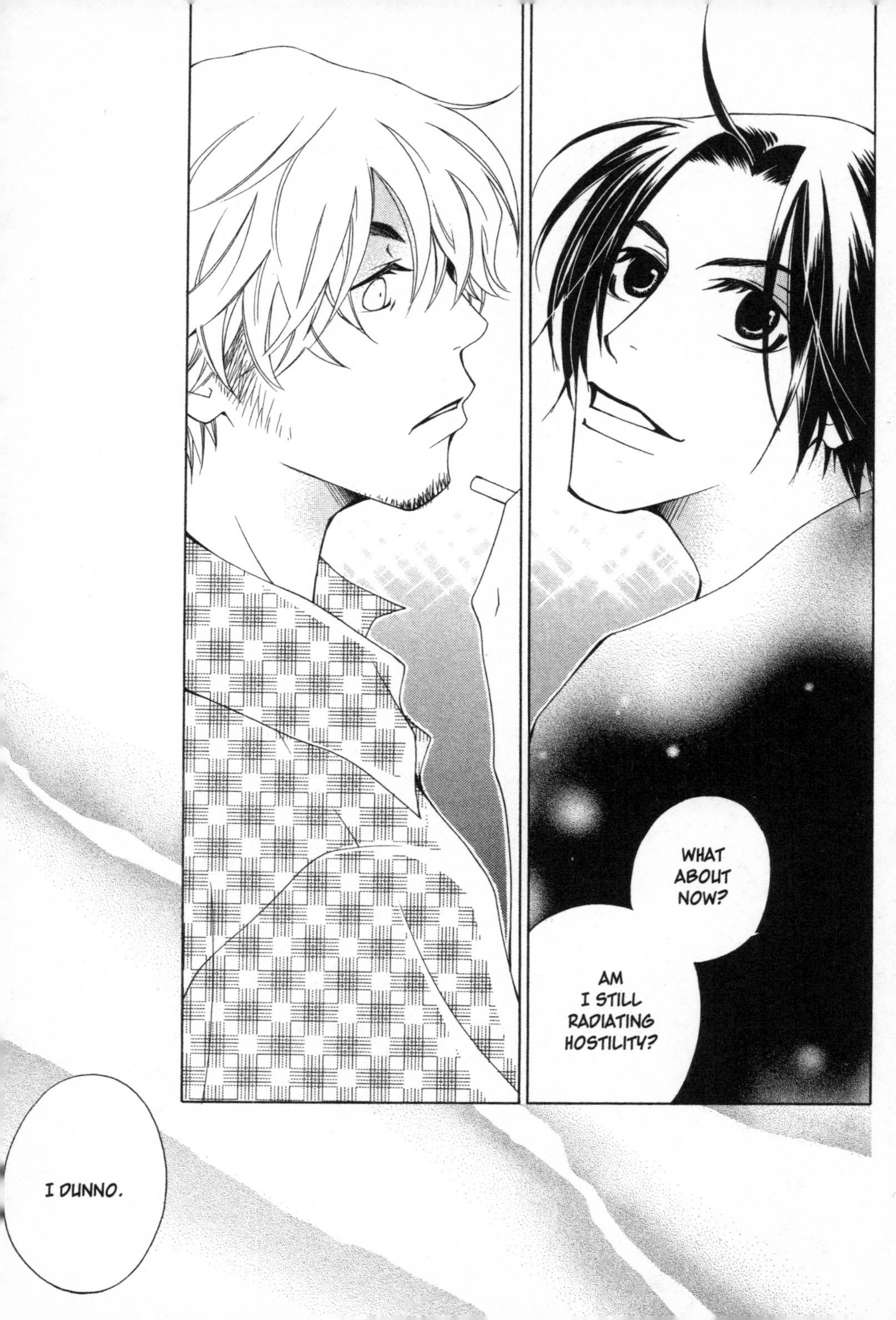
WHAT ABOUT NOW?
AM I STILL RADIATING HOSTILITY?
I DUNNO.

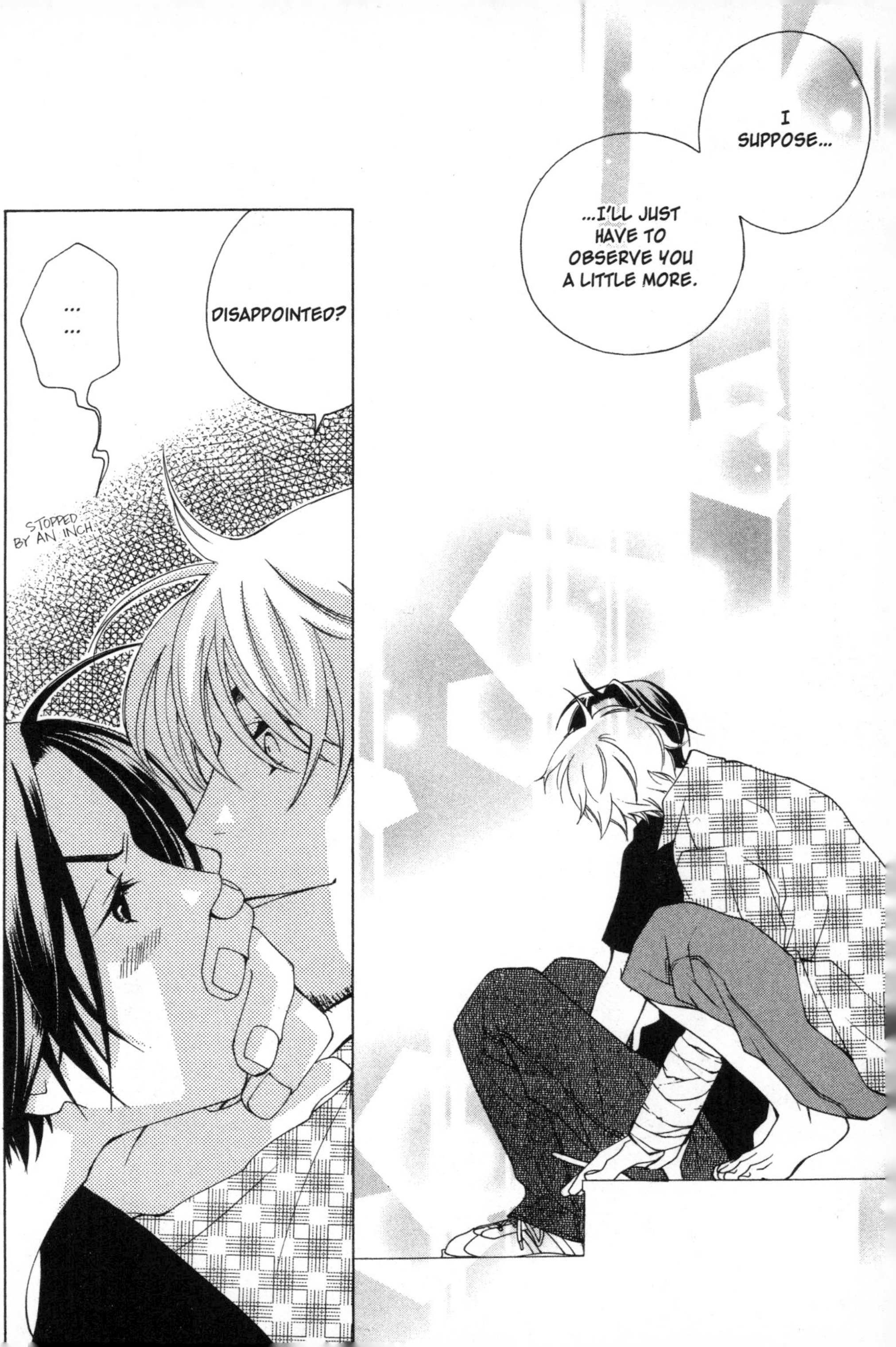
I SUPPOSE...
...I'LL JUST HAVE TO OBSERVE YOU A LITTLE MORE.
DISAPPOINTED?
... ...
STOPPED BY AN INCH.

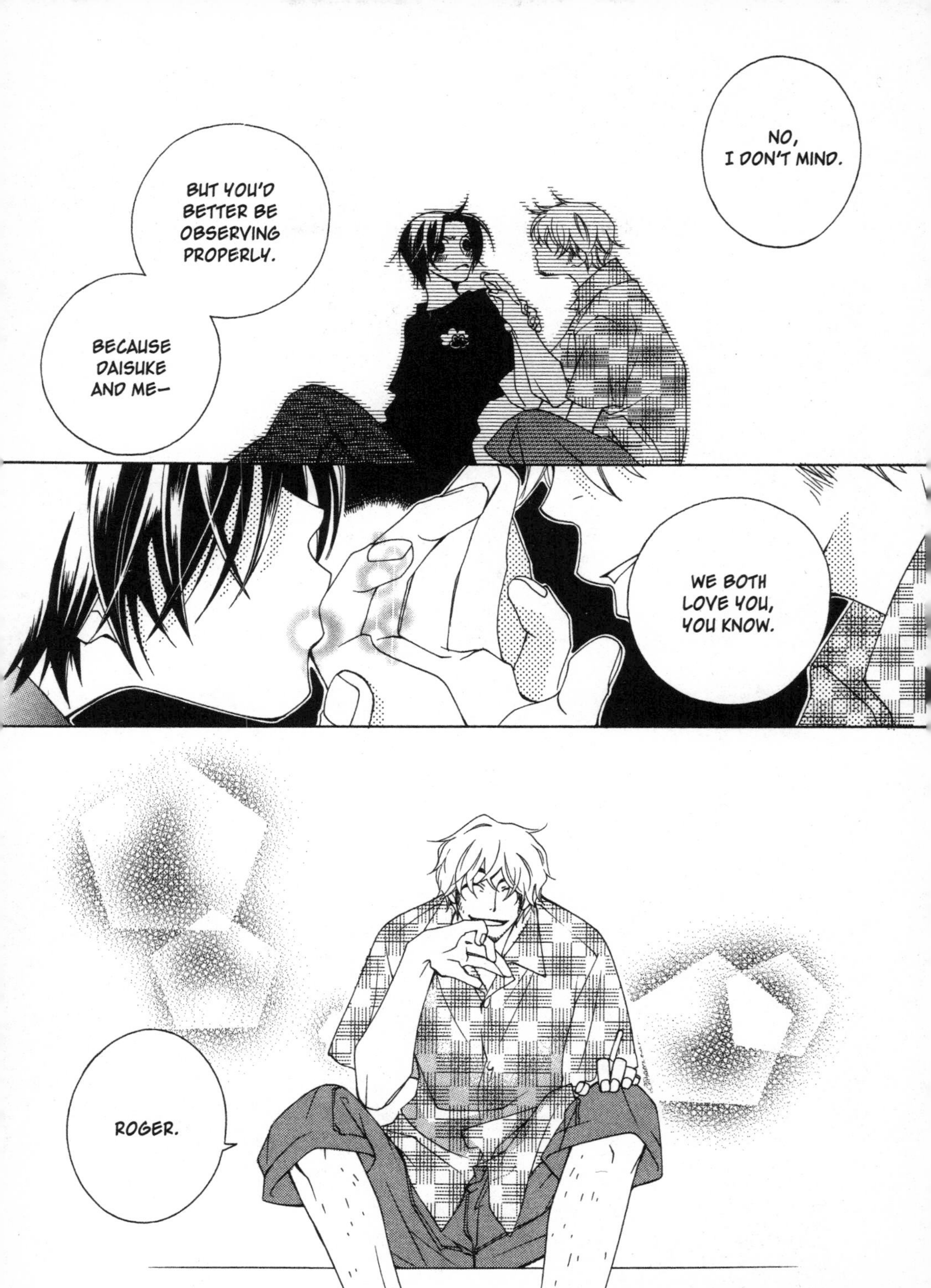
NO, I DON'T MIND.
BUT YOU'D BETTER BE OBSERVING PROPERLY.
BECAUSE DAISUKE AND ME—
WE BOTH LOVE YOU, YOU KNOW.
ROGER.

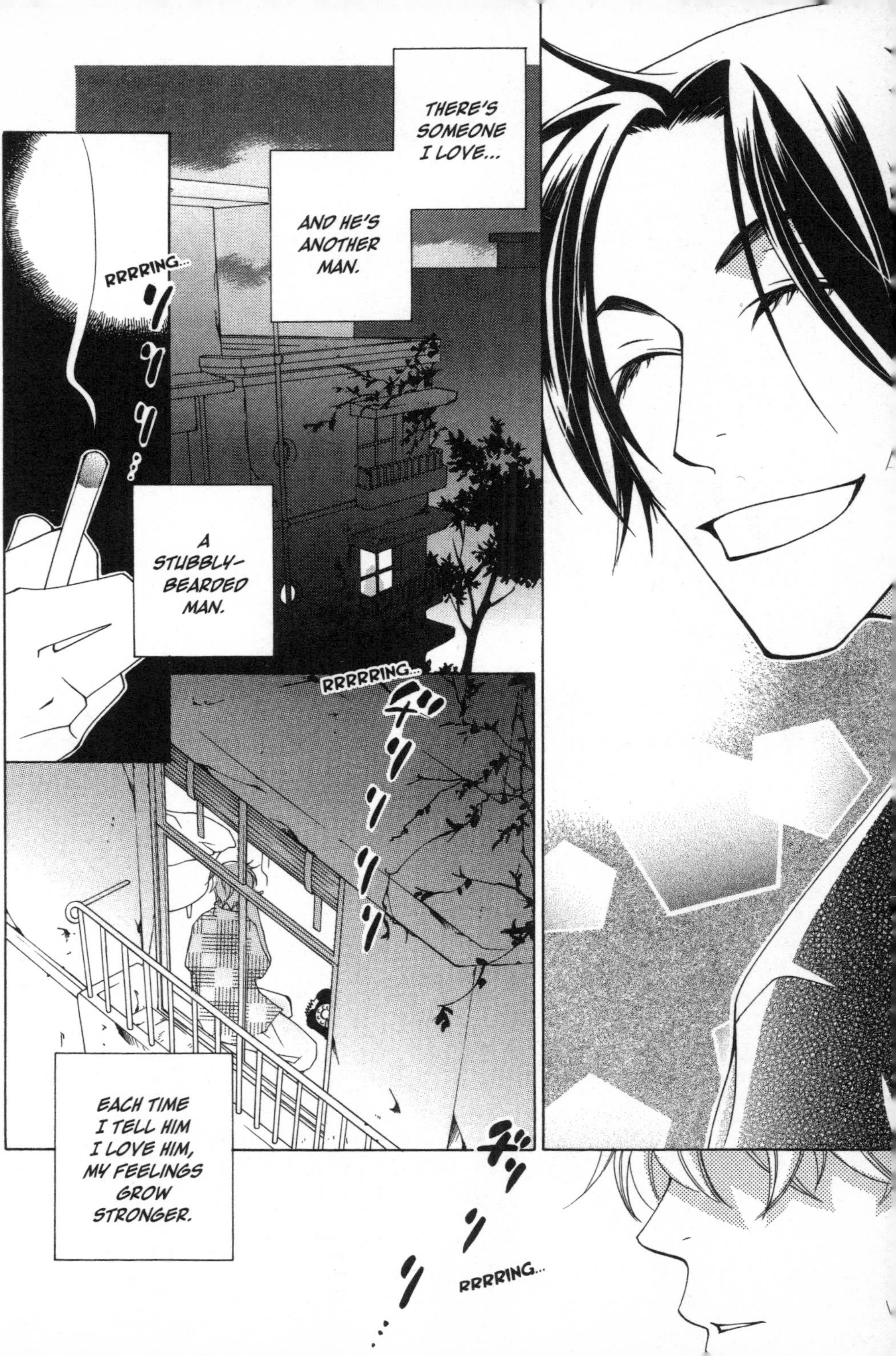
THERE'S SOMEONE I LOVE...
AND HE'S ANOTHER MAN.
RRRRING...
A STUBBLY-BEARDED MAN.
RRRRRING...
EACH TIME I TELL HIM I LOVE HIM, MY FEELINGS GROW STRONGER.
RRRRING...

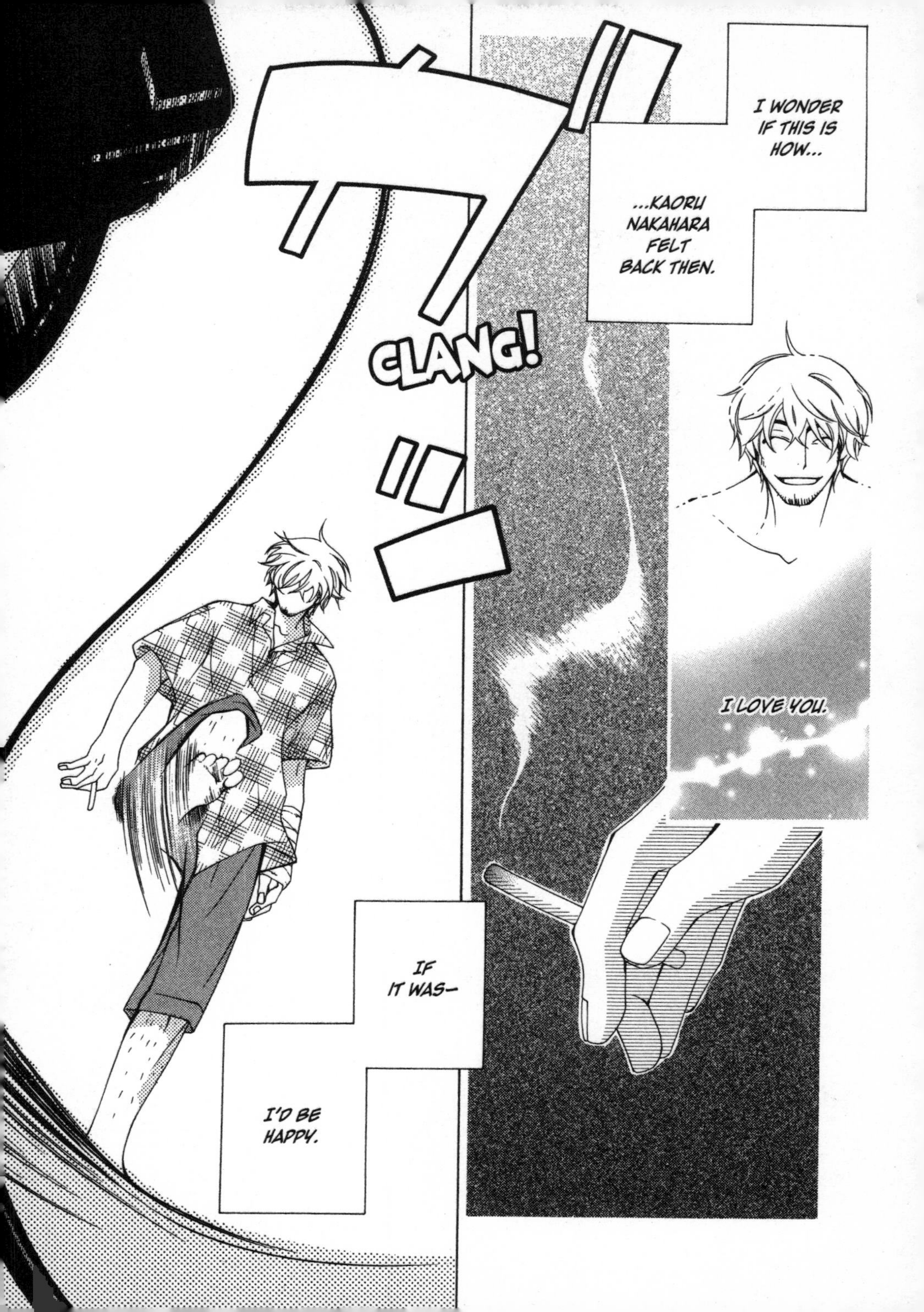
I WONDER IF THIS IS HOW...
...KAORU NAKAHARA FELT BACK THEN.
I LOVE YOU.
CLANG!
IF IT WAS—
I'D BE HAPPY.

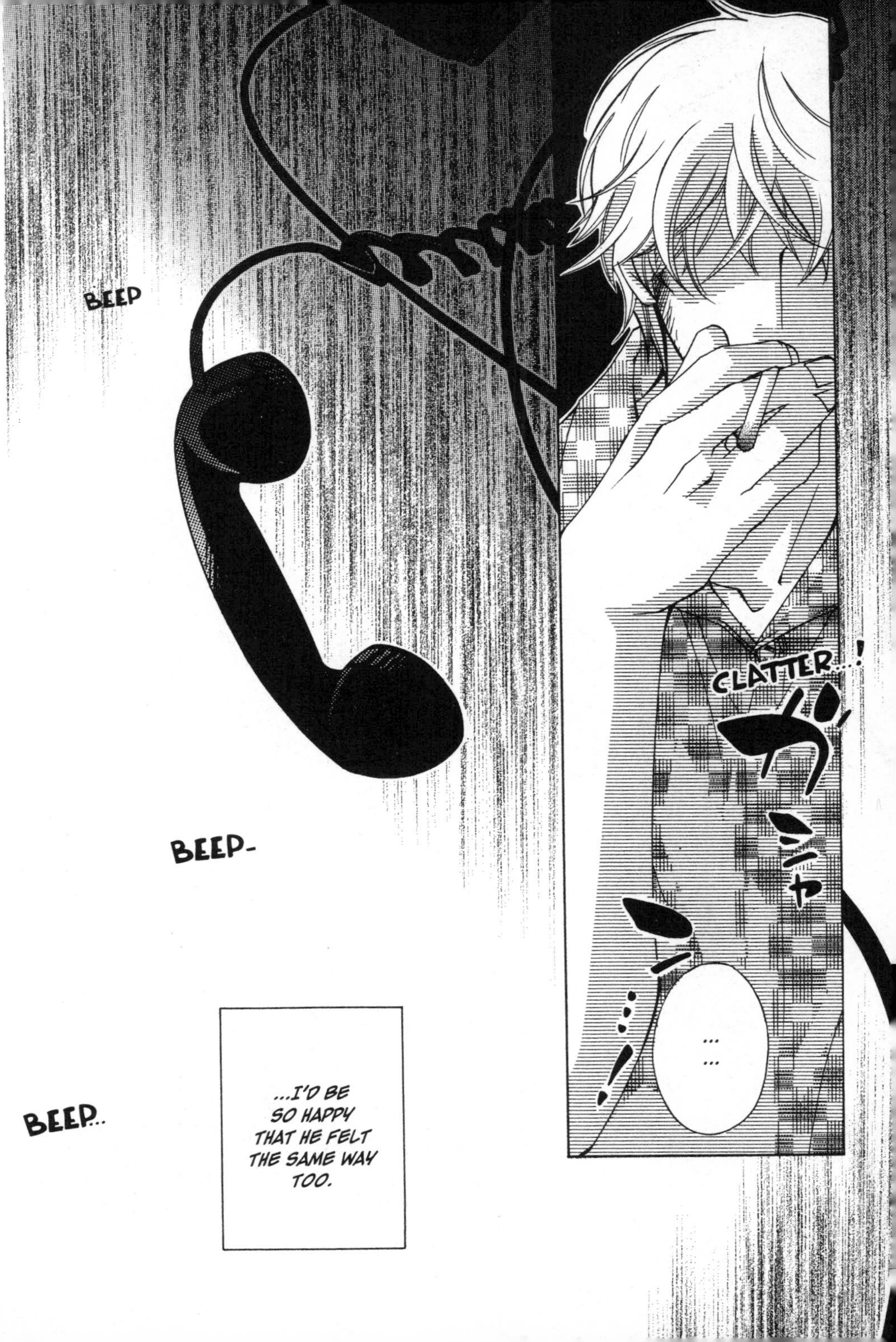
CLATTER...!
... ...
BEEP
BEEP-
BEEP...
...I'D BE SO HAPPY THAT HE FELT THE SAME WAY TOO.

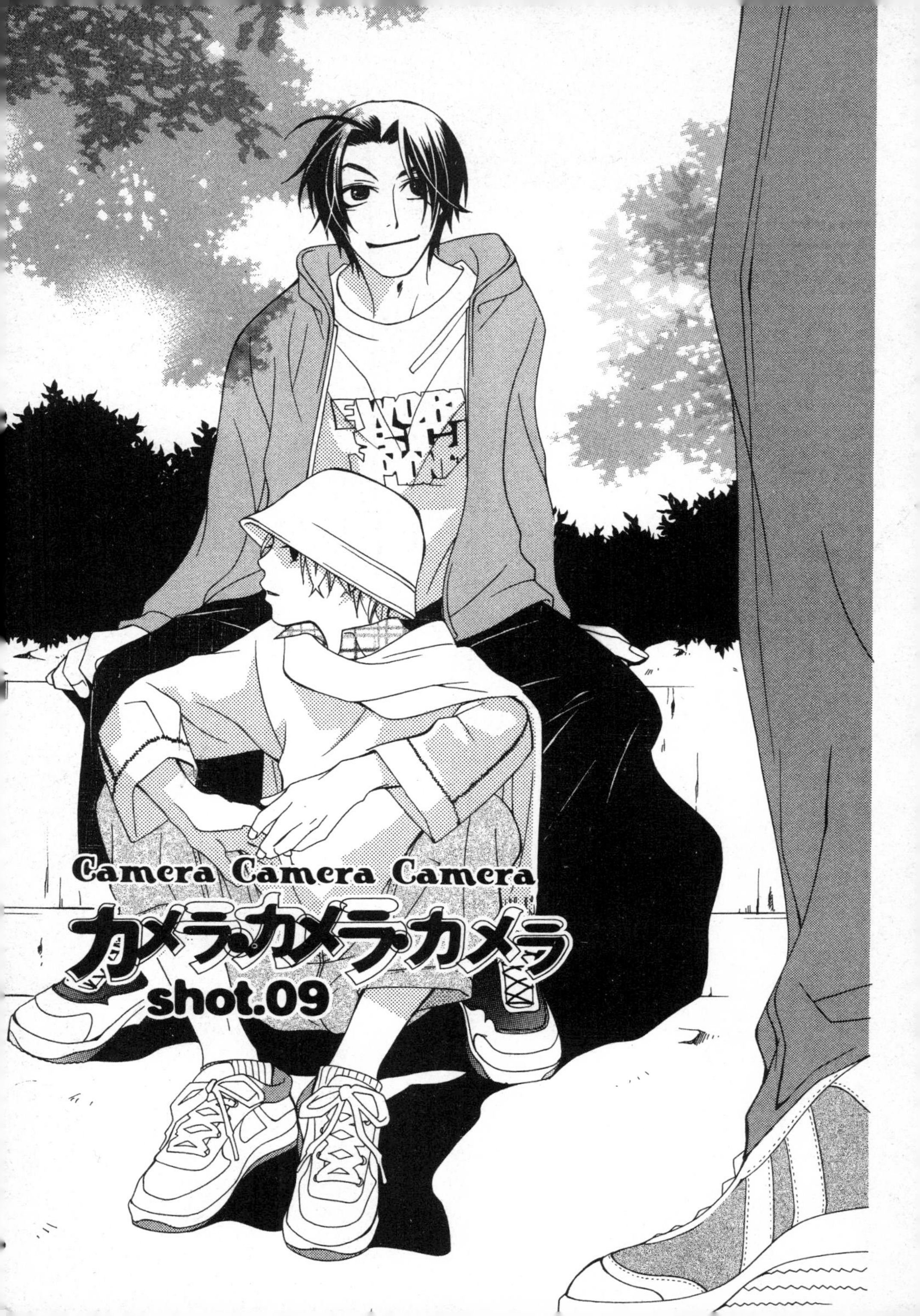
Camera Camera Camera
カメラ・カメラ・カメラ
shot.09

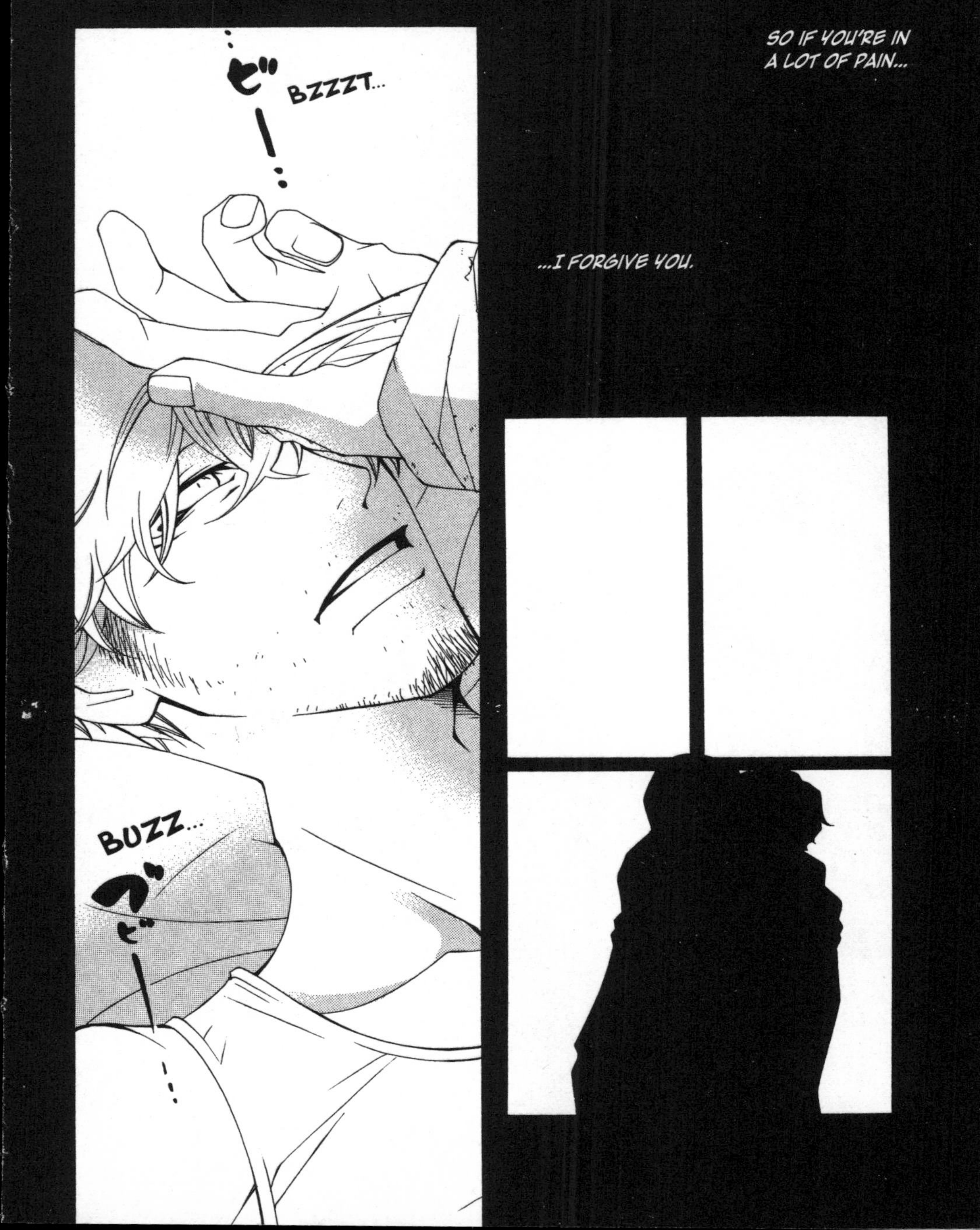
SO IF YOU'RE IN A LOT OF PAIN...
...I FORGIVE YOU.
BZZZT...
BUZZ...

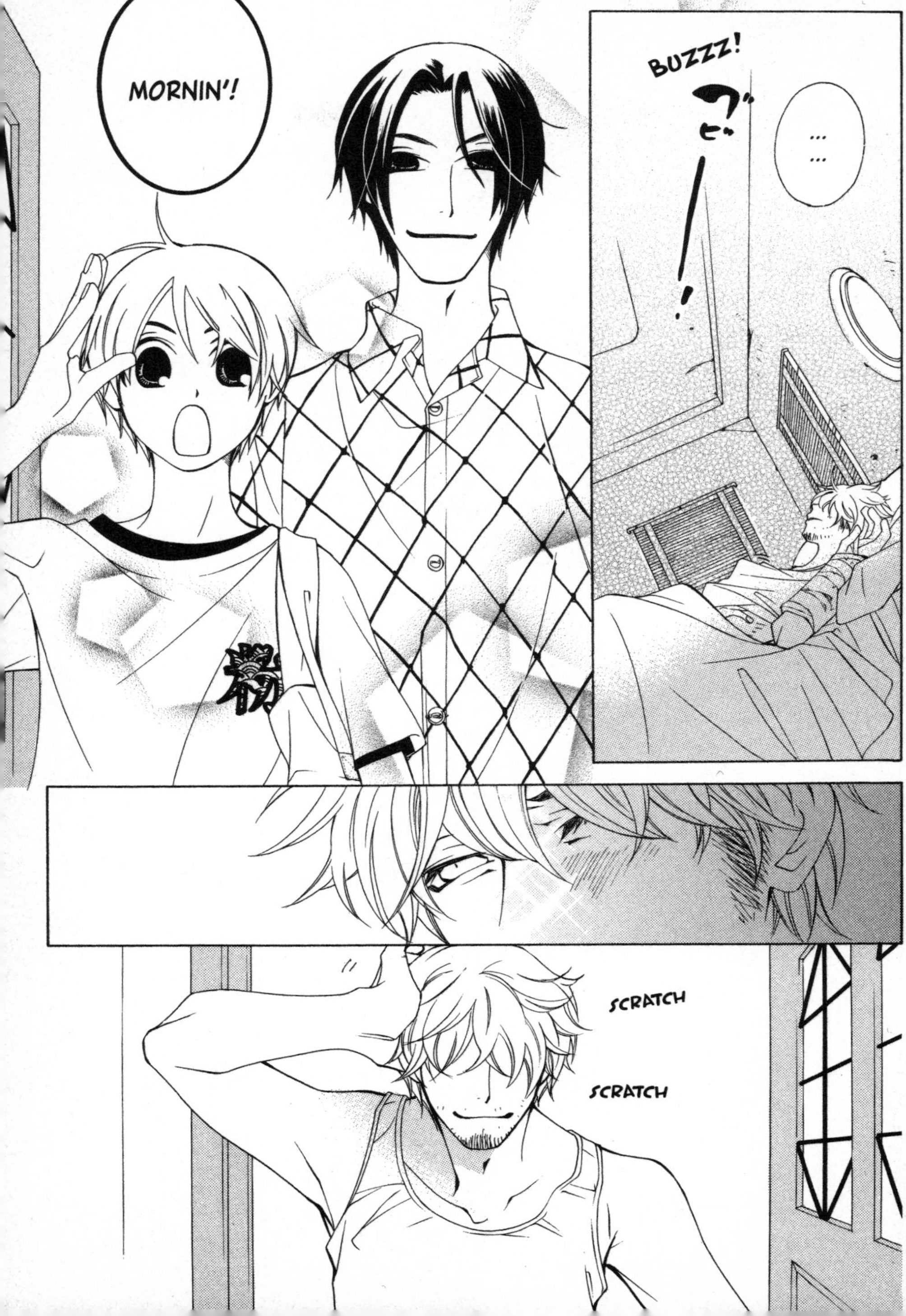
BUZZZ!
ブビー!!
...
...
MORNIN'!
SCRATCH
SCRATCH

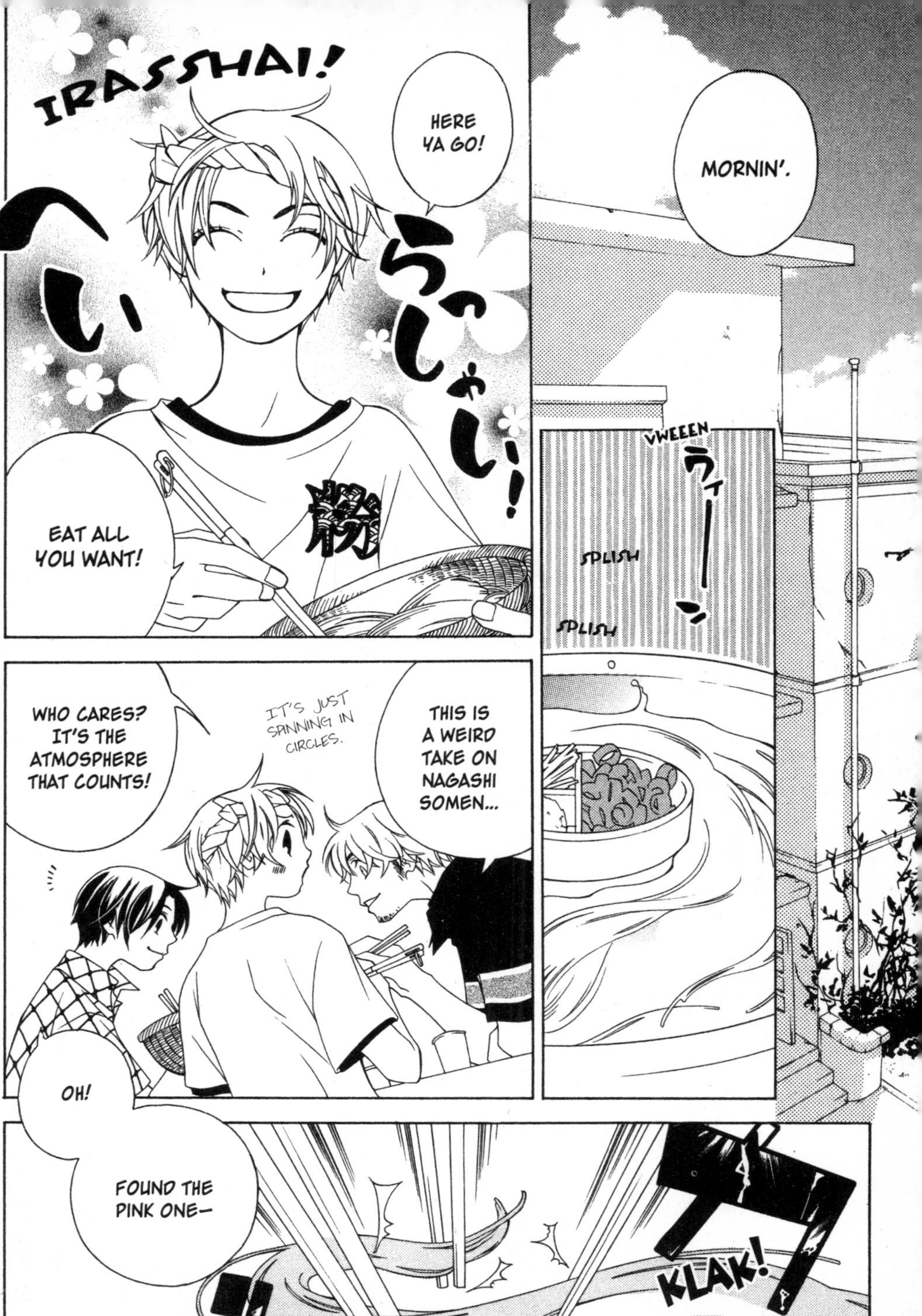
MORNIN'.
VWEEEN
ウィーーッ
SPLISH
SPLISH
IRASSHAI!
へいらっしゃい!
HERE YA GO!
EAT ALL YOU WANT!
THIS IS A WEIRD TAKE ON NAGASHI SOMEN...
IT'S JUST SPINNING IN CIRCLES.
WHO CARES? IT'S THE ATMOSPHERE THAT COUNTS!
OH!
FOUND THE PINK ONE—
KLAK!

*NAGASHI SOMEN: FLOWING BUCKWHEAT NOODLES THAT ARE VERY THIN AND WHITE IN COLOR. THEY ARE PLACED IN WATER AND FLOW DOWN A BAMBOO TRACK, WHERE ONE CATCHES THEM WITH CHOPSTICKS AND EATS THEM IN A BROTH TO EAT.

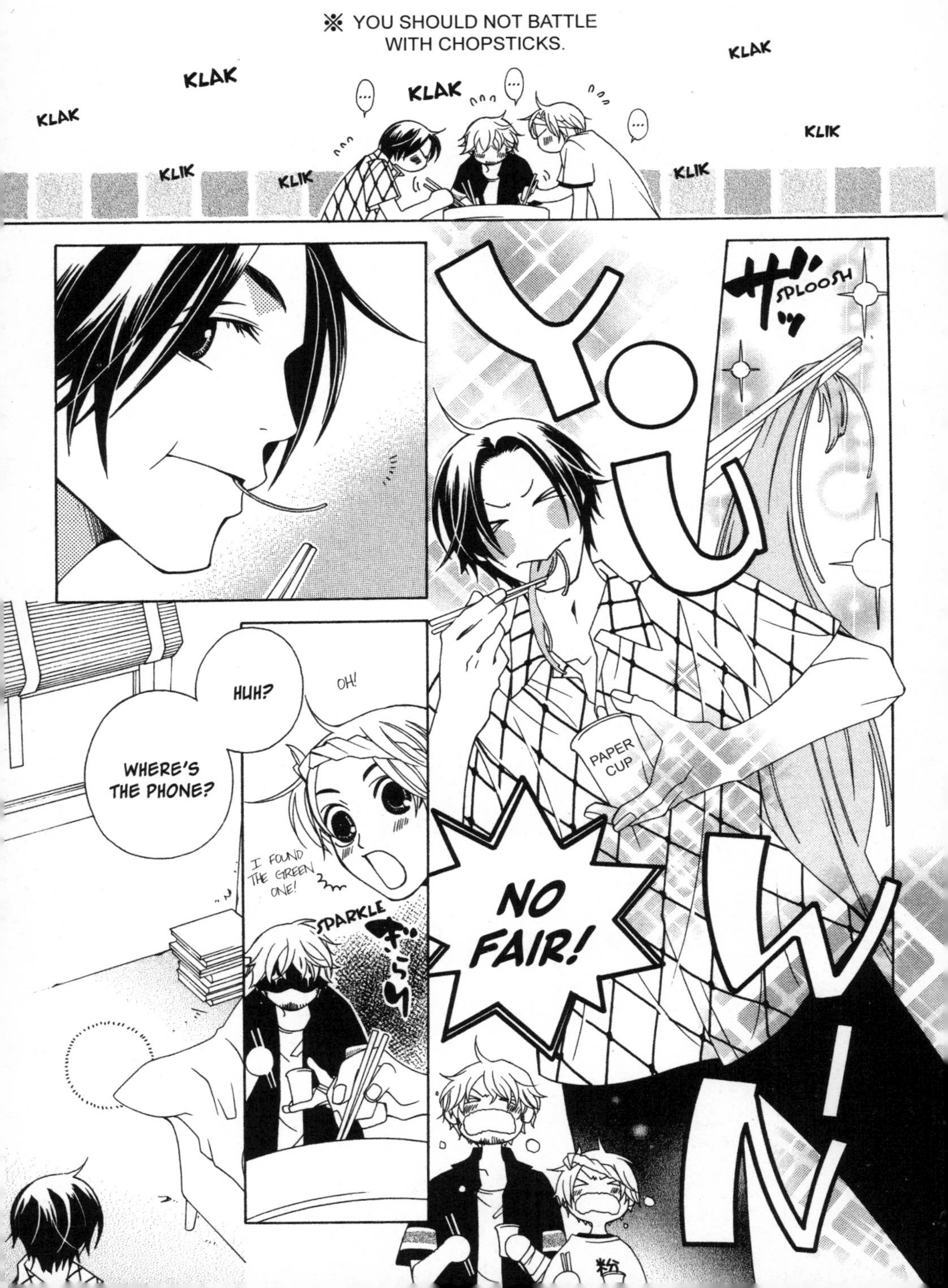
※ YOU SHOULD NOT BATTLE WITH CHOPSTICKS.
KLAK
KLIK
KLAK
KLIK
KLAK
KLIK
KLAK
KLIK
...
...
...
SPLOOSH
YOU WIN
PAPER CUP
OH!
HUH?
WHERE'S THE PHONE?
I FOUND THE GREEN ONE!
SPARKLE
NO FAIR!

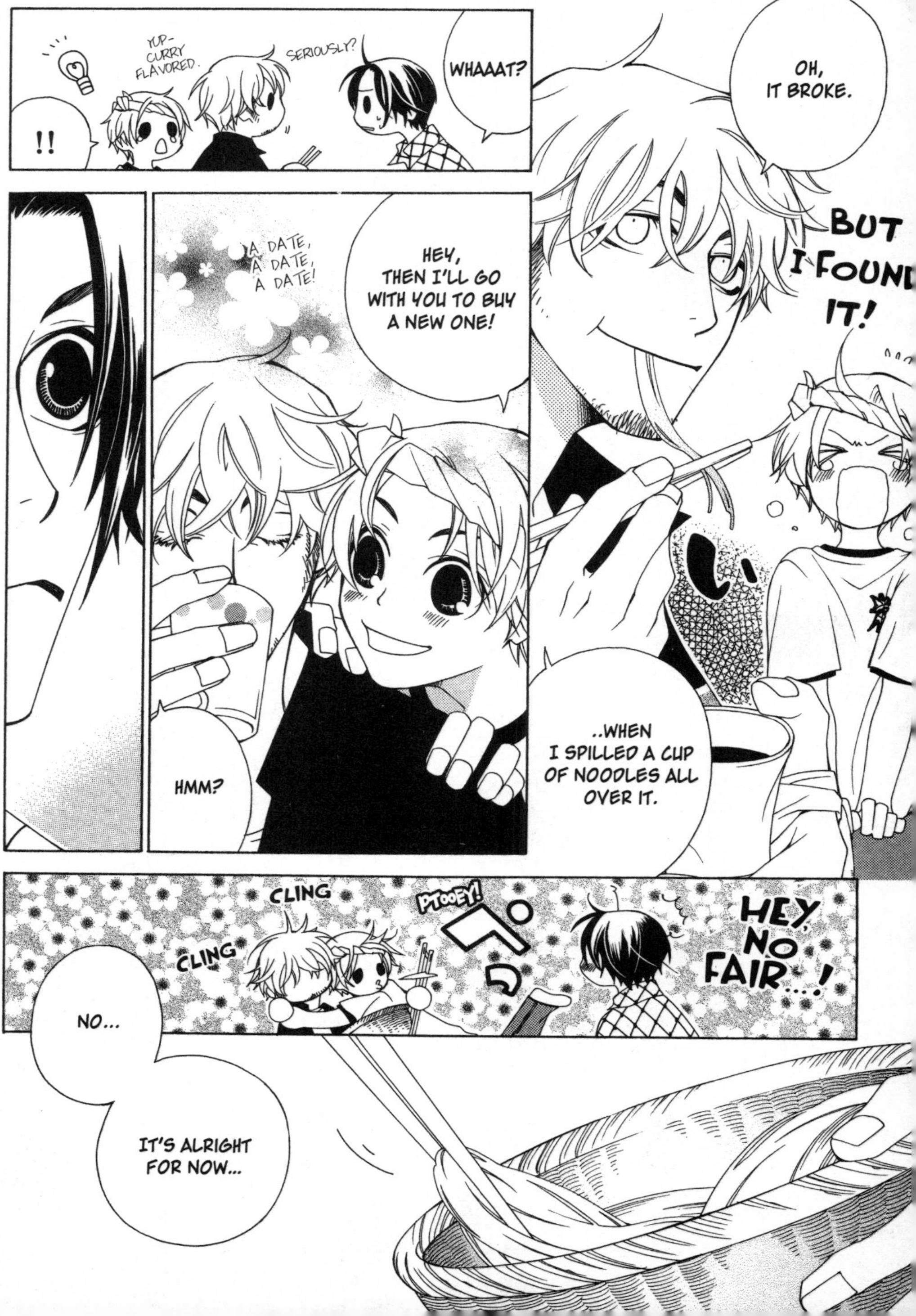
OH, IT BROKE.
BUT I FOUND IT!
..WHEN I SPILLED A CUP OF NOODLES ALL OVER IT.
WHAAAT?
SERIOUSLY?
YUP- CURRY FLAVORED.
!!
HEY, THEN I'LL GO WITH YOU TO BUY A NEW ONE!
A DATE, A DATE, A DATE!
HMM?
HEY, NO FAIR...!
PTOOEY!
CLING
CLING
NO...
IT'S ALRIGHT FOR NOW...

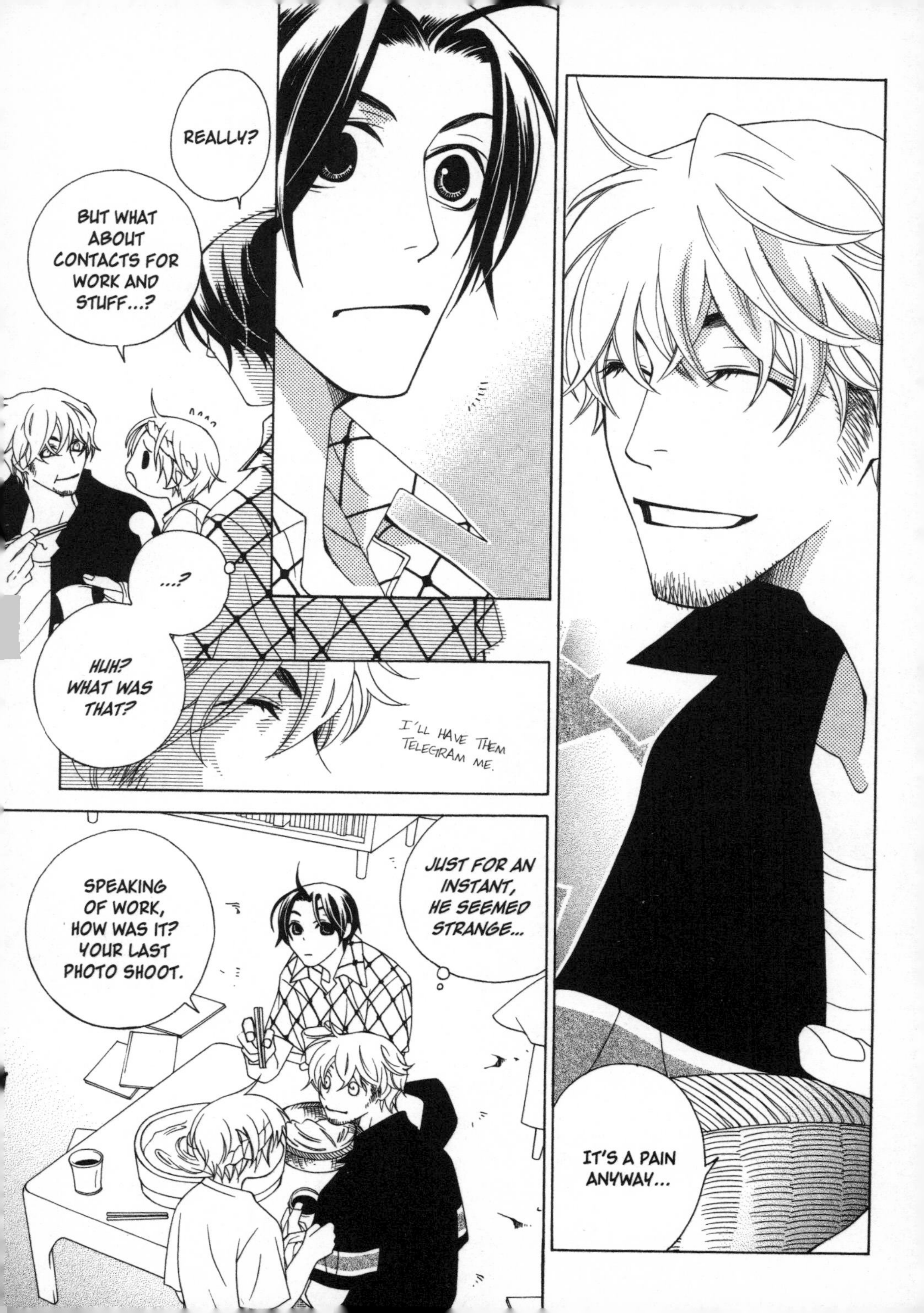
IT'S A PAIN ANYWAY...
REALLY?
BUT WHAT ABOUT CONTACTS FOR WORK AND STUFF...?
I'LL HAVE THEM TELEGRAM ME.
...?
HUH? WHAT WAS THAT?
JUST FOR AN INSTANT, HE SEEMED STRANGE...
SPEAKING OF WORK, HOW WAS IT? YOUR LAST PHOTO SHOOT.

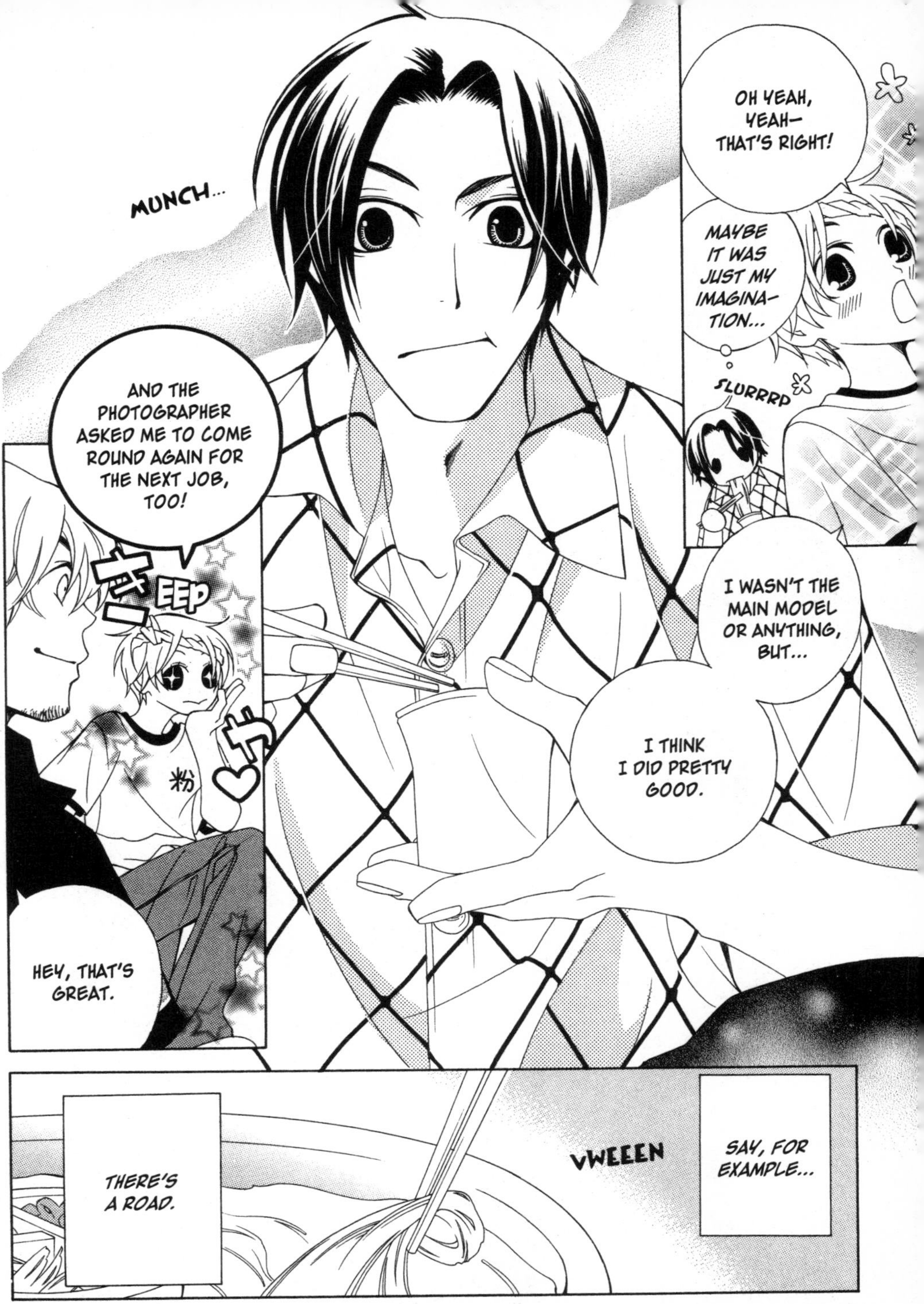
OH YEAH, YEAH—THAT'S RIGHT!
MAYBE IT WAS JUST MY IMAGINATION...
SLURRRP
MUNCH...
I WASN'T THE MAIN MODEL OR ANYTHING, BUT...
I THINK I DID PRETTY GOOD.
AND THE PHOTOGRAPHER ASKED ME TO COME ROUND AGAIN FOR THE NEXT JOB, TOO!
EEP
HEY, THAT'S GREAT.
SAY, FOR EXAMPLE...
VWEEEN
THERE'S A ROAD.

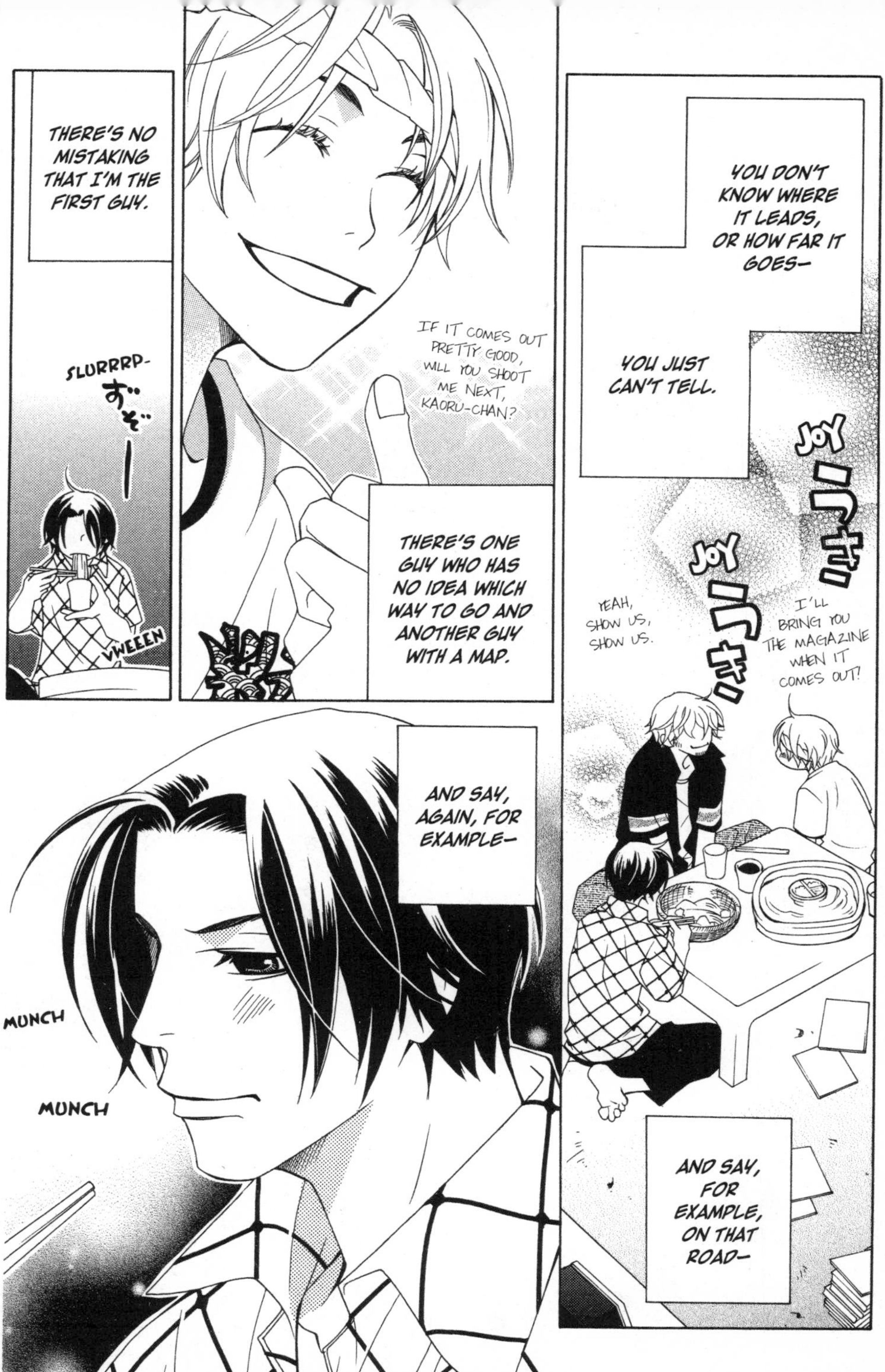
YOU DON'T KNOW WHERE IT LEADS, OR HOW FAR IT GOES—
YOU JUST CAN'T TELL.
JOY
うきっ
JOY
うきっ
I'LL BRING YOU THE MAGAZINE WHEN IT COMES OUT!
YEAH, SHOW US, SHOW US.
AND SAY, FOR EXAMPLE, ON THAT ROAD—
IF IT COMES OUT PRETTY GOOD, WILL YOU SHOOT ME NEXT, KAORU-CHAN?
THERE'S ONE GUY WHO HAS NO IDEA WHICH WAY TO GO AND ANOTHER GUY WITH A MAP.
THERE'S NO MISTAKING THAT I'M THE FIRST GUY.
SLURRRP-
ずぞー
VWEEEN
AND SAY, AGAIN, FOR EXAMPLE—
MUNCH
MUNCH

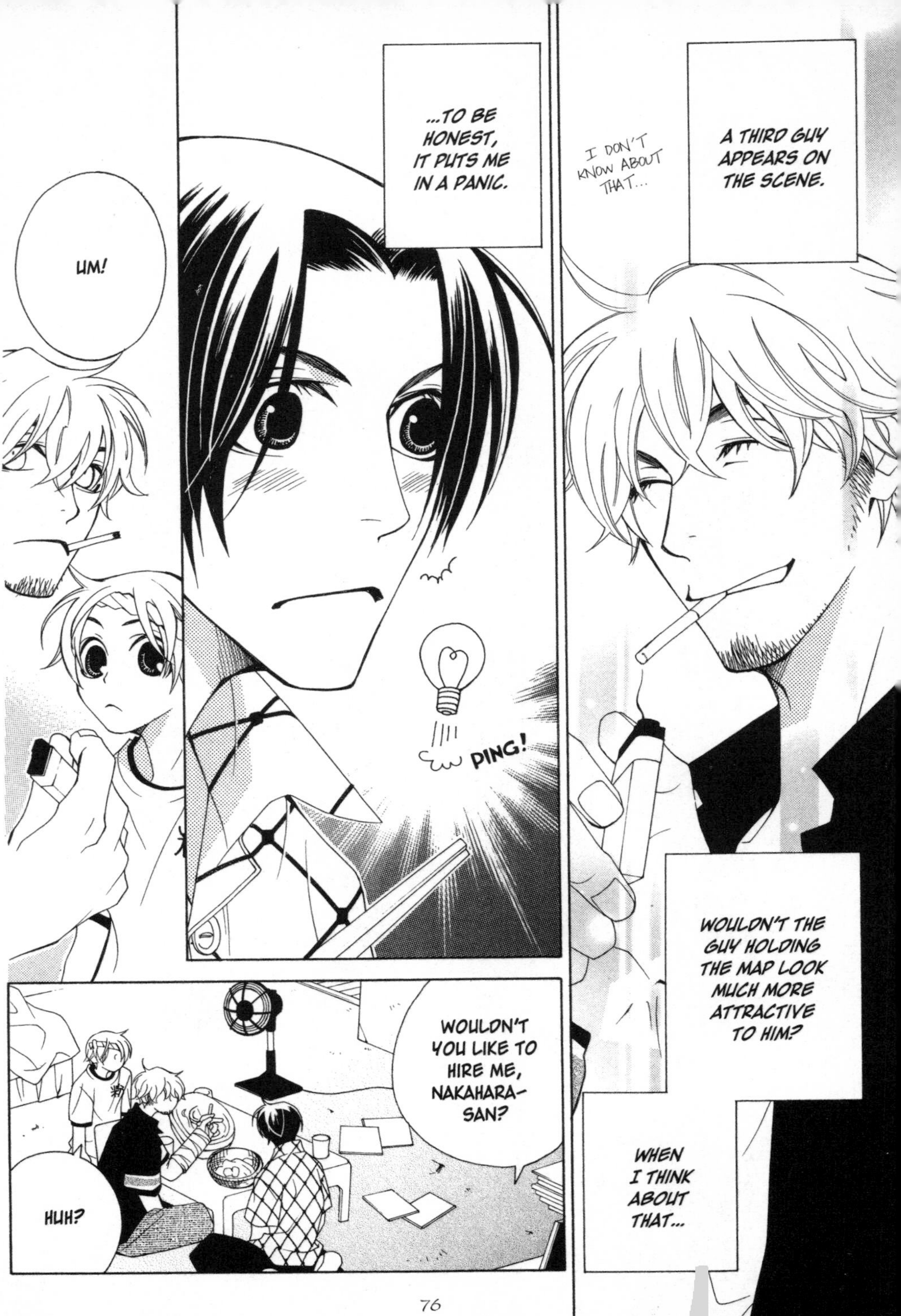
A THIRD GUY APPEARS ON THE SCENE.
I DON'T KNOW ABOUT THAT...
WOULDN'T THE GUY HOLDING THE MAP LOOK MUCH MORE ATTRACTIVE TO HIM?
WHEN I THINK ABOUT THAT...
...TO BE HONEST, IT PUTS ME IN A PANIC.
PING!
UM!
WOULDN'T YOU LIKE TO HIRE ME, NAKAHARA-SAN?
HUH?

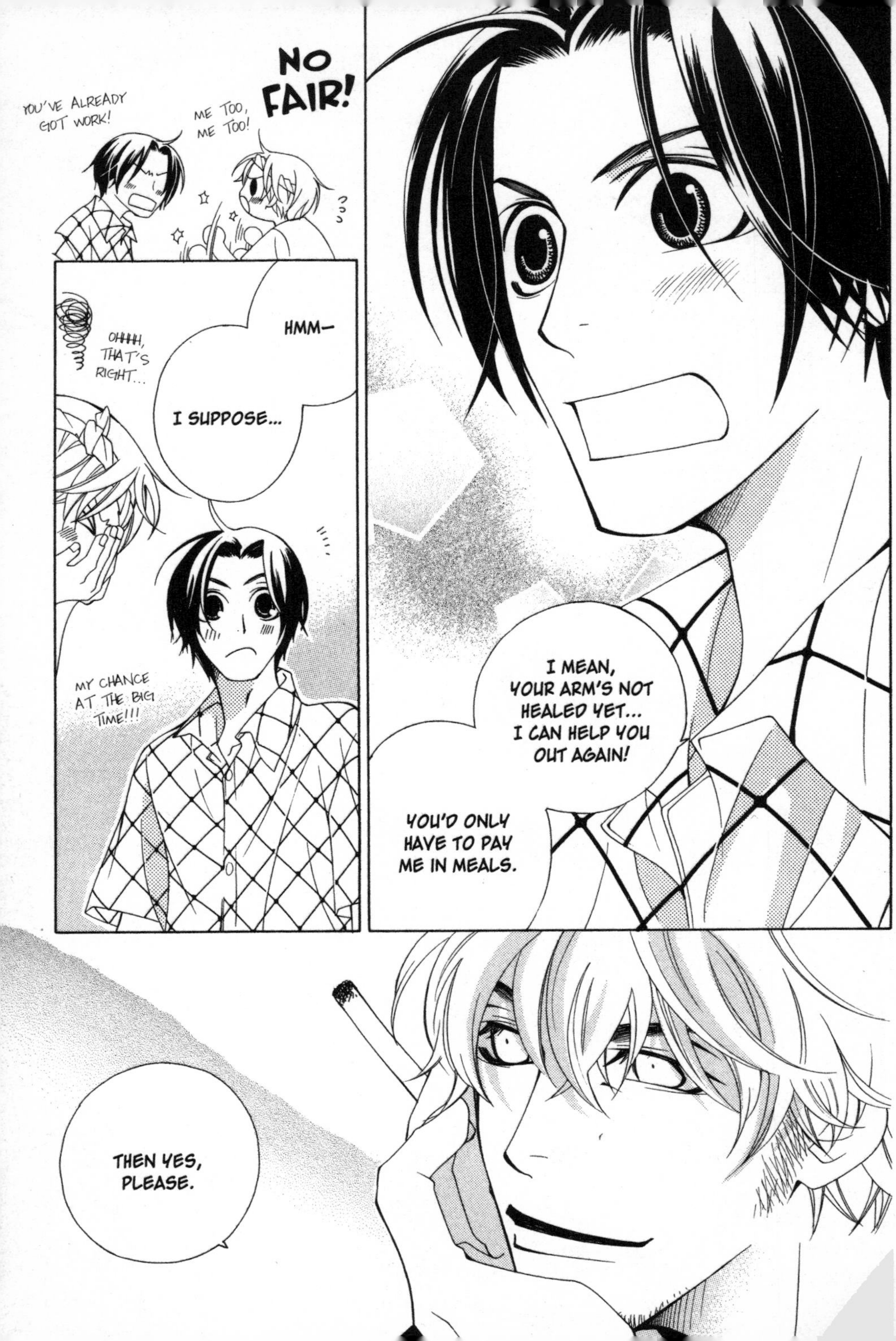
I MEAN, YOUR ARM'S NOT HEALED YET... I CAN HELP YOU OUT AGAIN!
YOU'D ONLY HAVE TO PAY ME IN MEALS.
NO FAIR!
ME TOO, ME TOO!
YOU'VE ALREADY GOT WORK!
HMM—
I SUPPOSE...
OHHHH, THAT'S RIGHT...
MY CHANCE AT THE BIG TIME!!!
THEN YES, PLEASE.

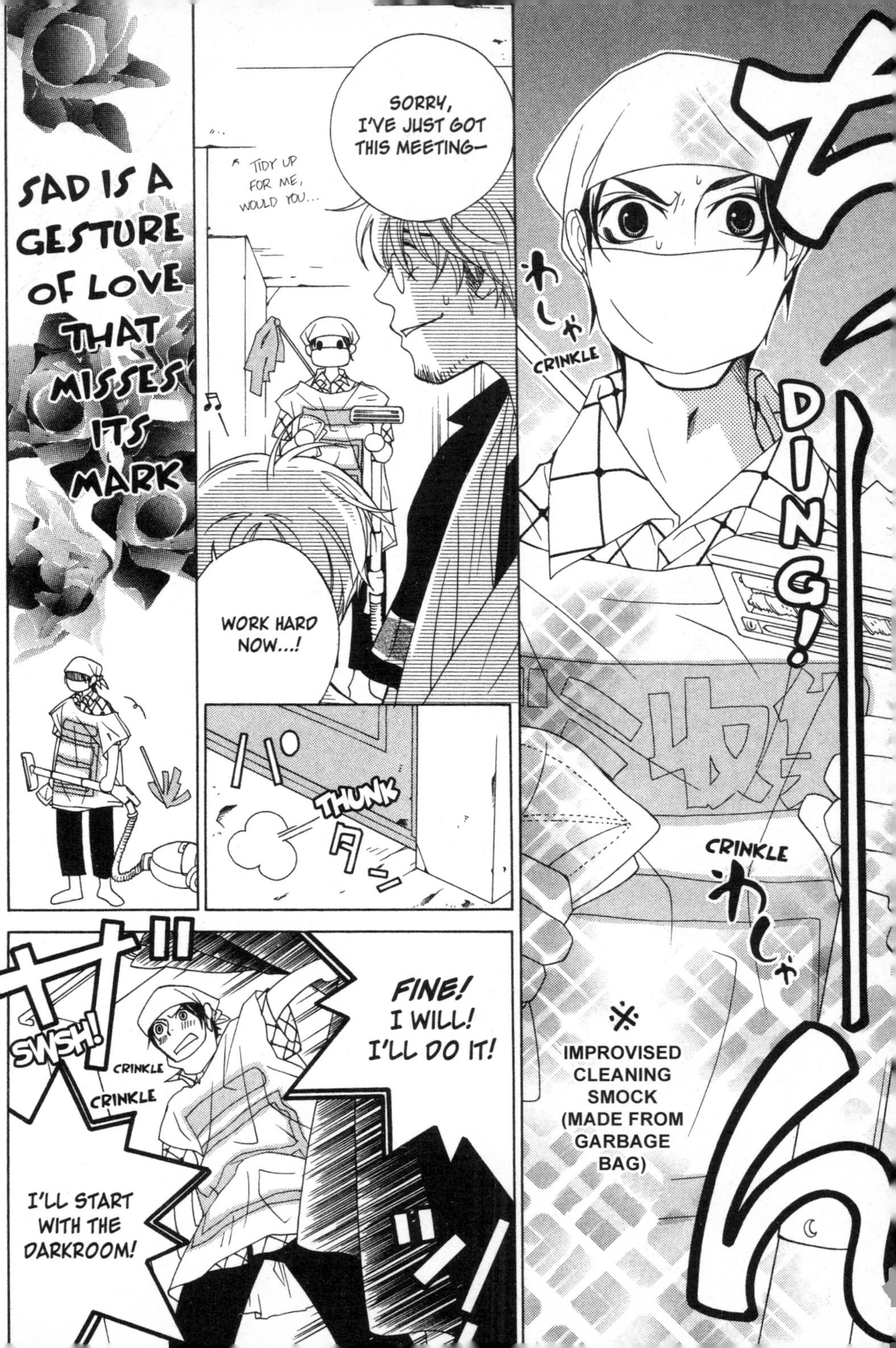
わしゃ
CRINKLE
DING!
CRINKLE
わしゃ
※ IMPROVISED CLEANING SMOCK (MADE FROM GARBAGE BAG)
SORRY, I'VE JUST GOT THIS MEETING—
TIDY UP FOR ME, WOULD YOU...
WORK HARD NOW...!
THUNK
SAD IS A GESTURE OF LOVE THAT MISSES ITS MARK
FINE! I WILL! I'LL DO IT!
SWSH!
CRINKLE
CRINKLE
I'LL START WITH THE DARKROOM!

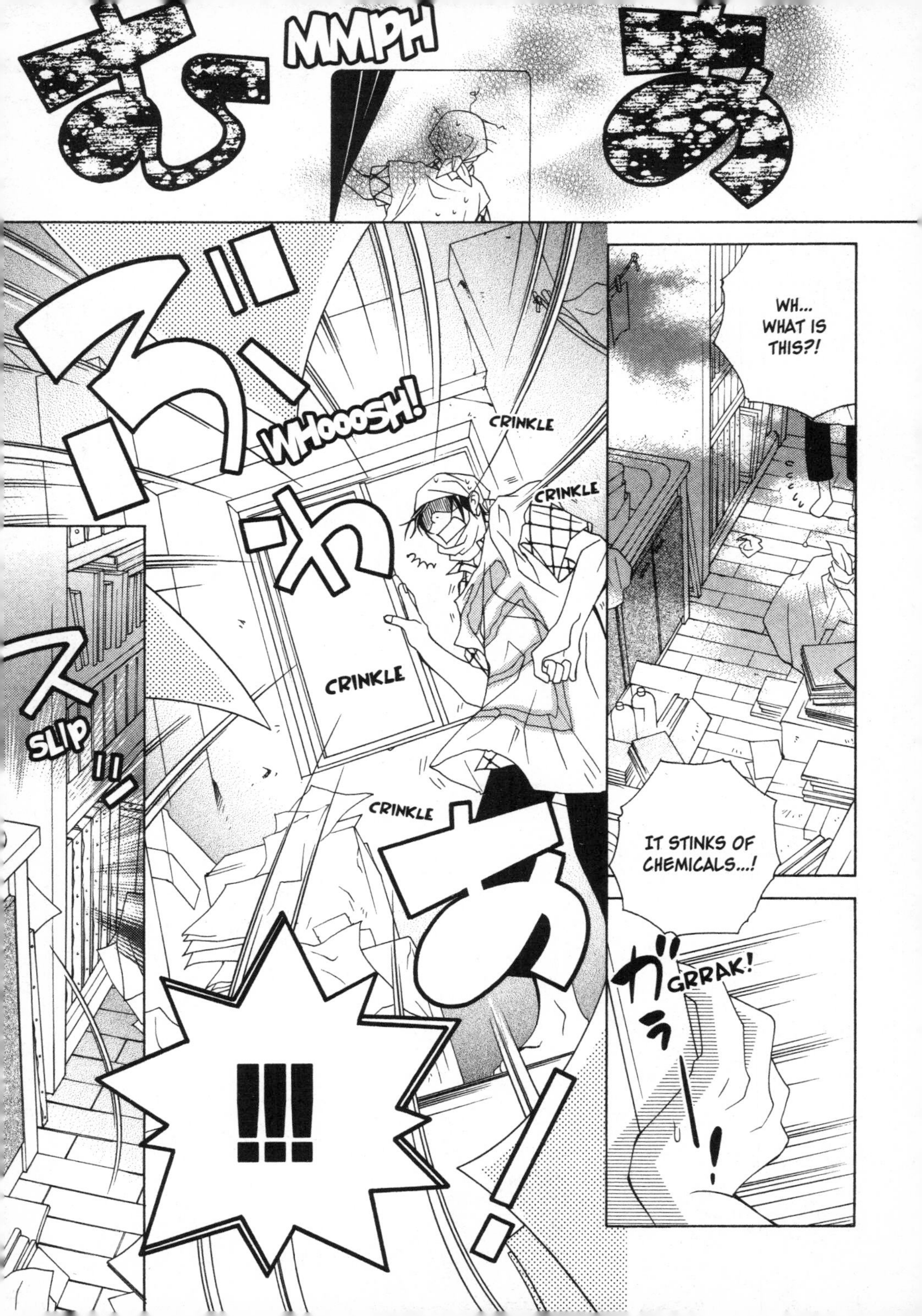
MMPH
WH... WHAT IS THIS?!
IT STINKS OF CHEMICALS...!
GRRAK!
WHOOOSH!
CRINKLE
CRINKLE
CRINKLE
CRINKLE
SLIP
!!!

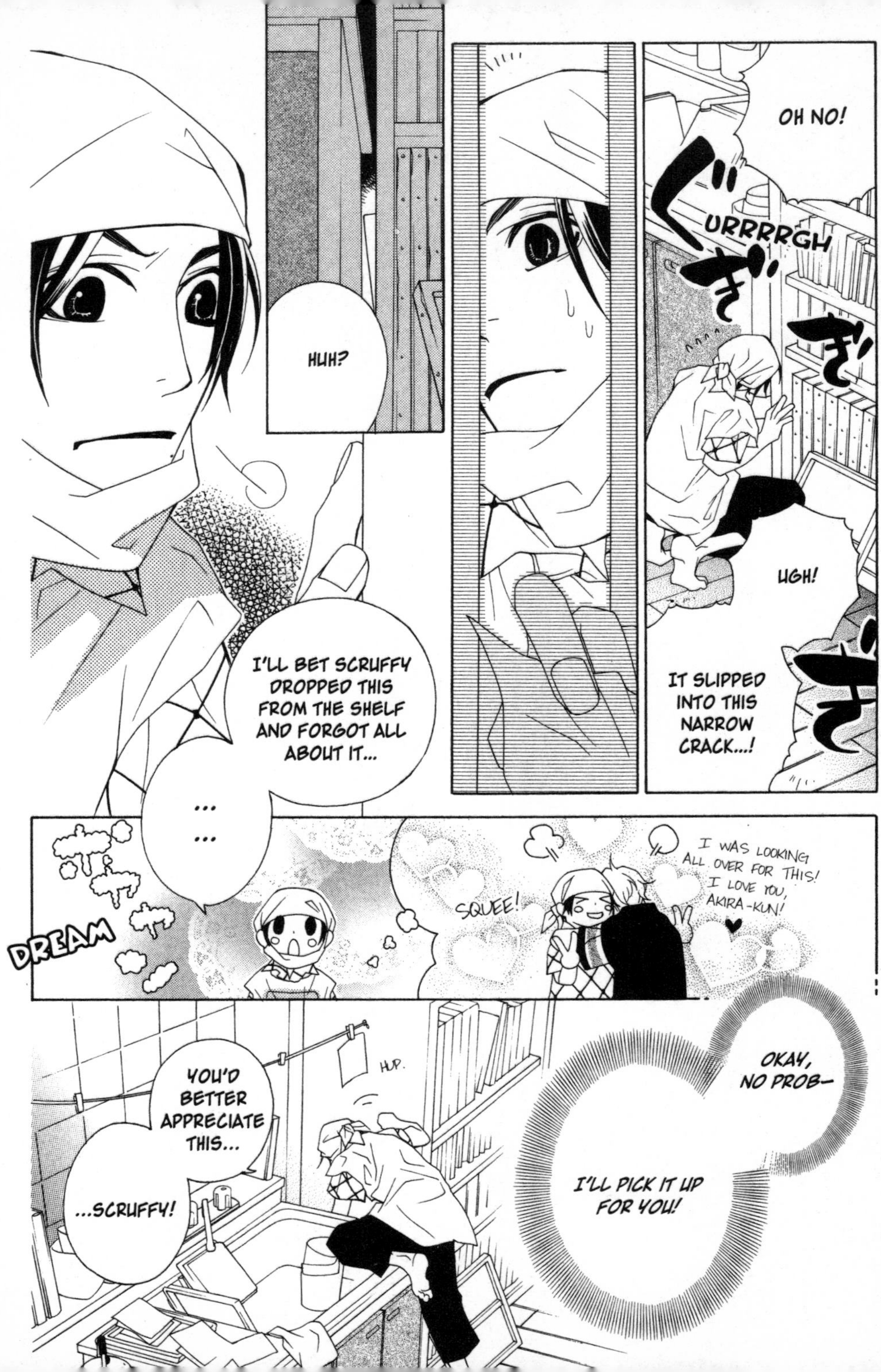
OH NO!
URRRRGH
UGH!
IT SLIPPED INTO THIS NARROW CRACK...!
HUH?
I'LL BET SCRUFFY DROPPED THIS FROM THE SHELF AND FORGOT ALL ABOUT IT...
... ...
I WAS LOOKING ALL OVER FOR THIS! I LOVE YOU, AKIRA-KUN!
SQUEE!
DREAM
OKAY, NO PROB—
I'LL PICK IT UP FOR YOU!
HUP.
YOU'D BETTER APPRECIATE THIS...
...SCRUFFY!

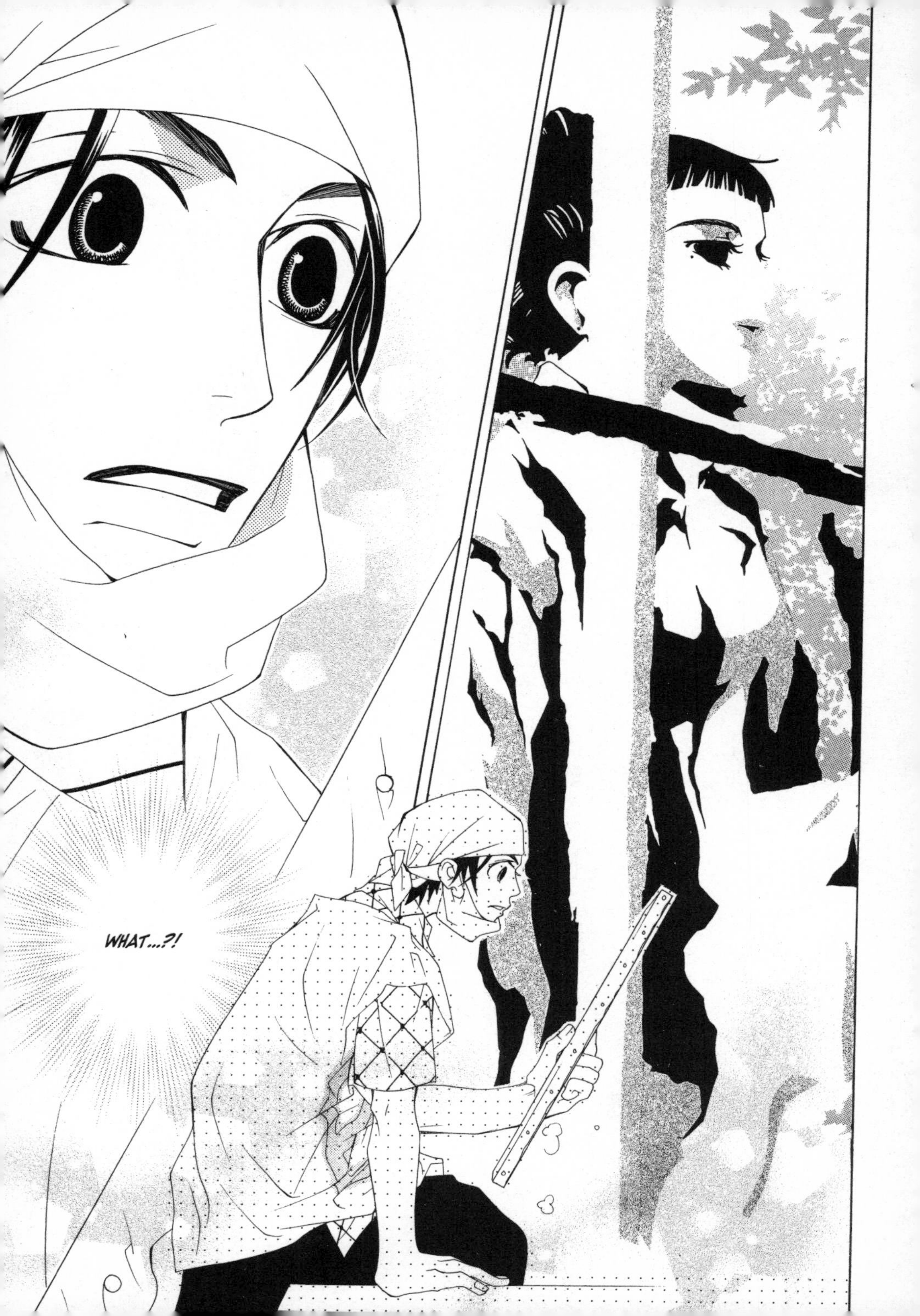
WHAT...?!

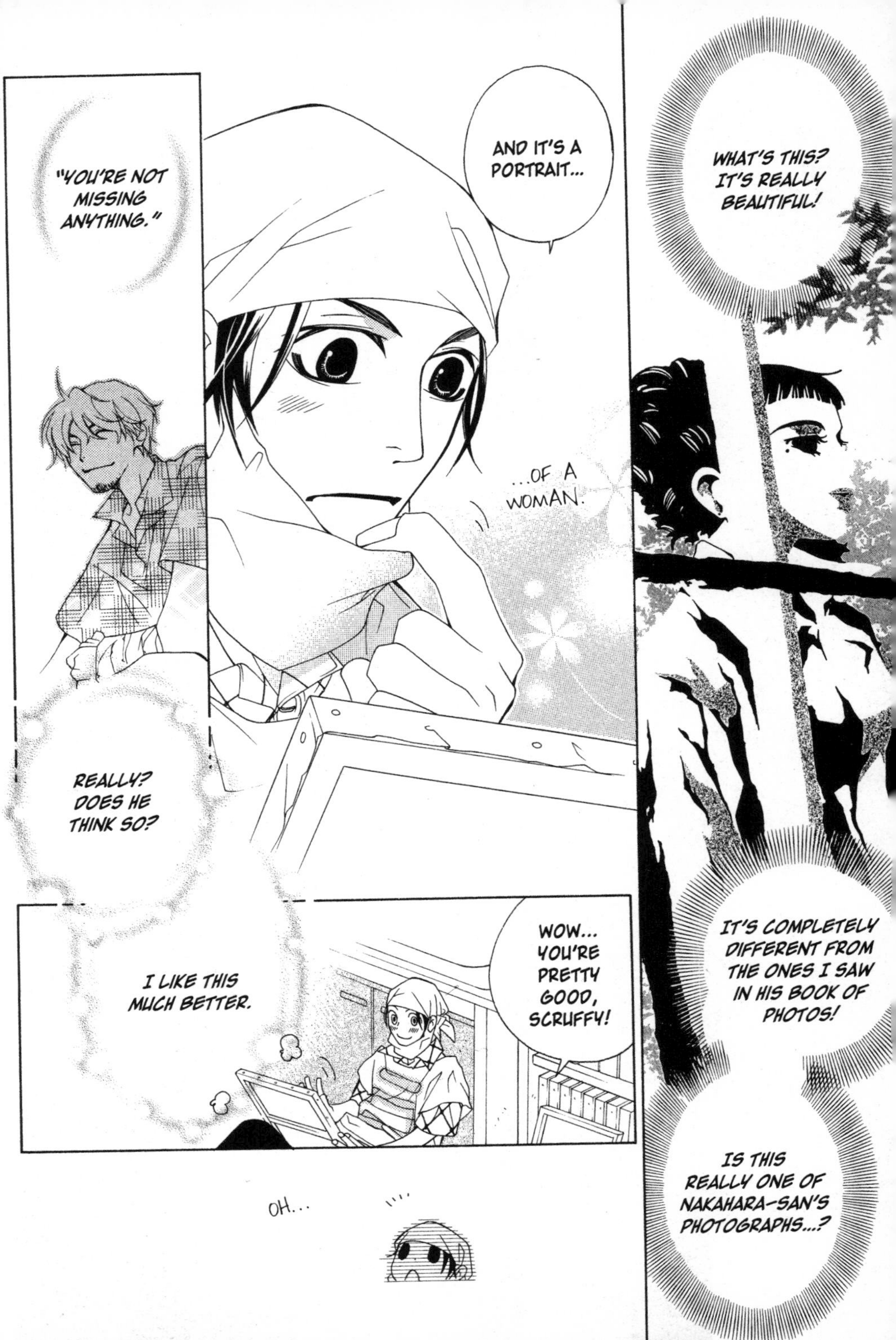
WHAT'S THIS? IT'S REALLY BEAUTIFUL!
IT'S COMPLETELY DIFFERENT FROM THE ONES I SAW IN HIS BOOK OF PHOTOS!
IS THIS REALLY ONE OF NAKAHARA-SAN'S PHOTOGRAPHS...?
AND IT'S A PORTRAIT...
...OF A WOMAN.
"YOU'RE NOT MISSING ANYTHING."
REALLY? DOES HE THINK SO?
WOW... YOU'RE PRETTY GOOD, SCRUFFY!
I LIKE THIS MUCH BETTER.
OH...

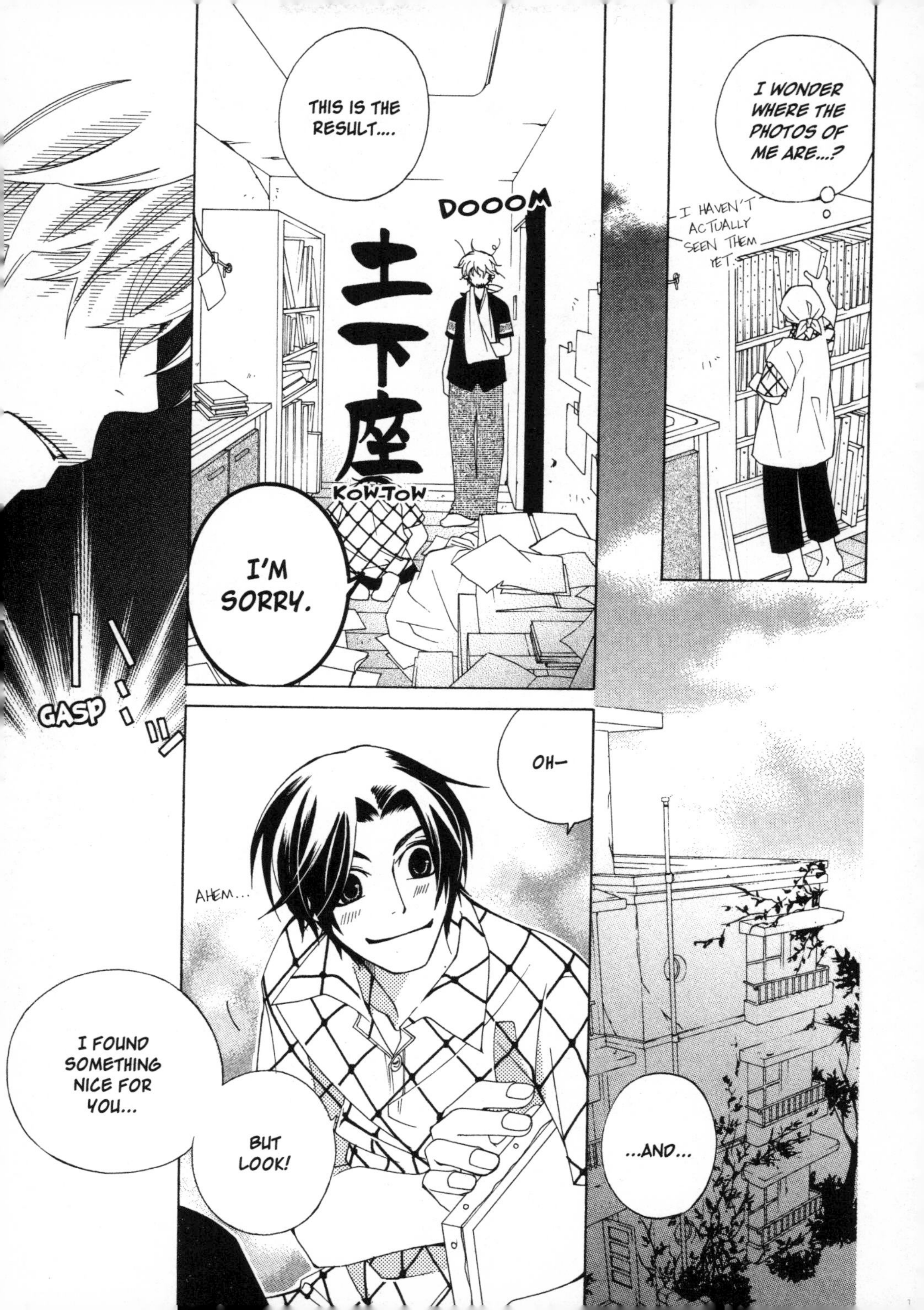

I WONDER WHERE THE PHOTOS OF ME ARE...?
I HAVEN'T ACTUALLY SEEN THEM YET.
THIS IS THE RESULT....
DOOOM
土下座
KOW-TOW
I'M SORRY.
GASP
...AND...
OH—
AHEM...
I FOUND SOMETHING NICE FOR YOU...
BUT LOOK!

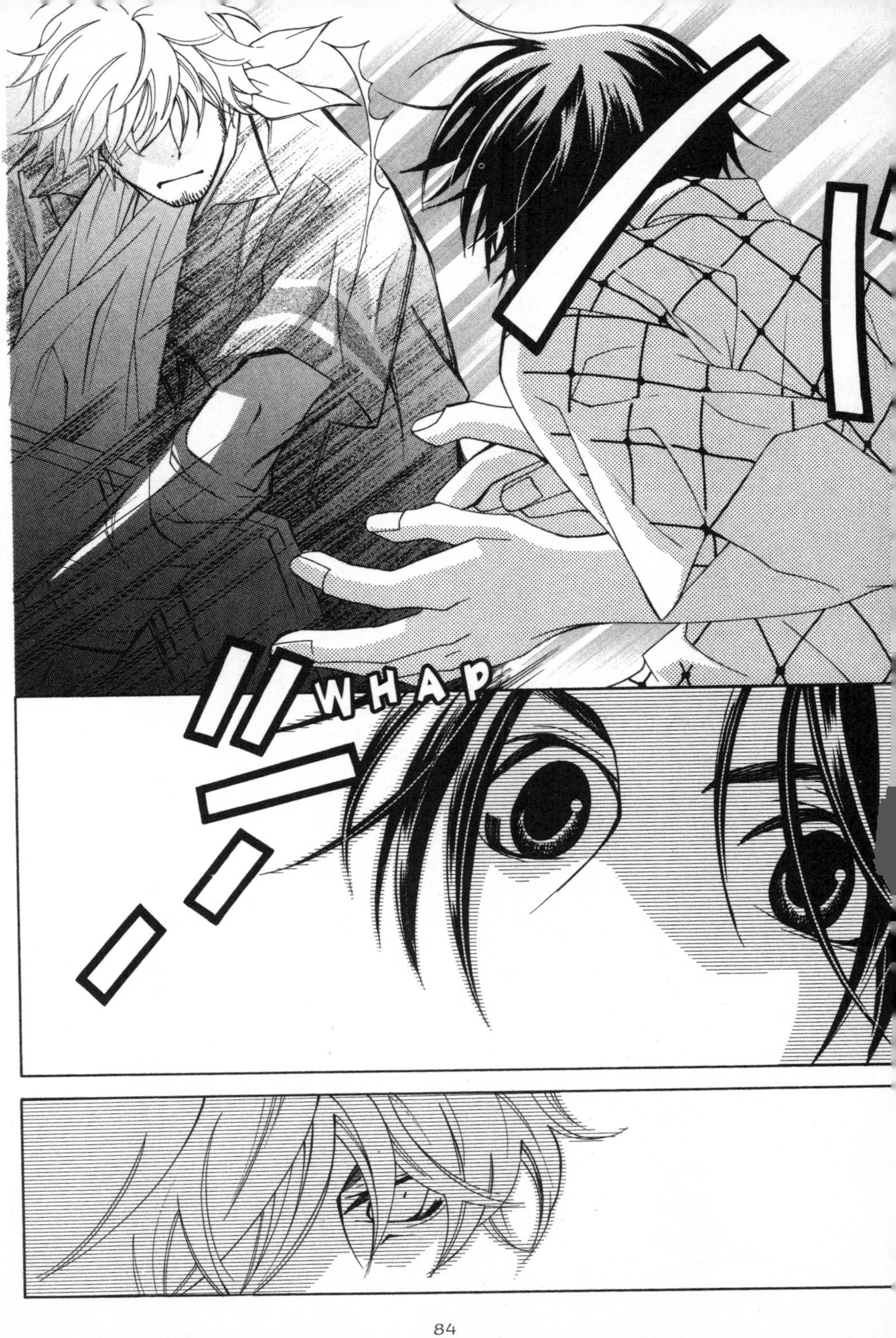
WHAP

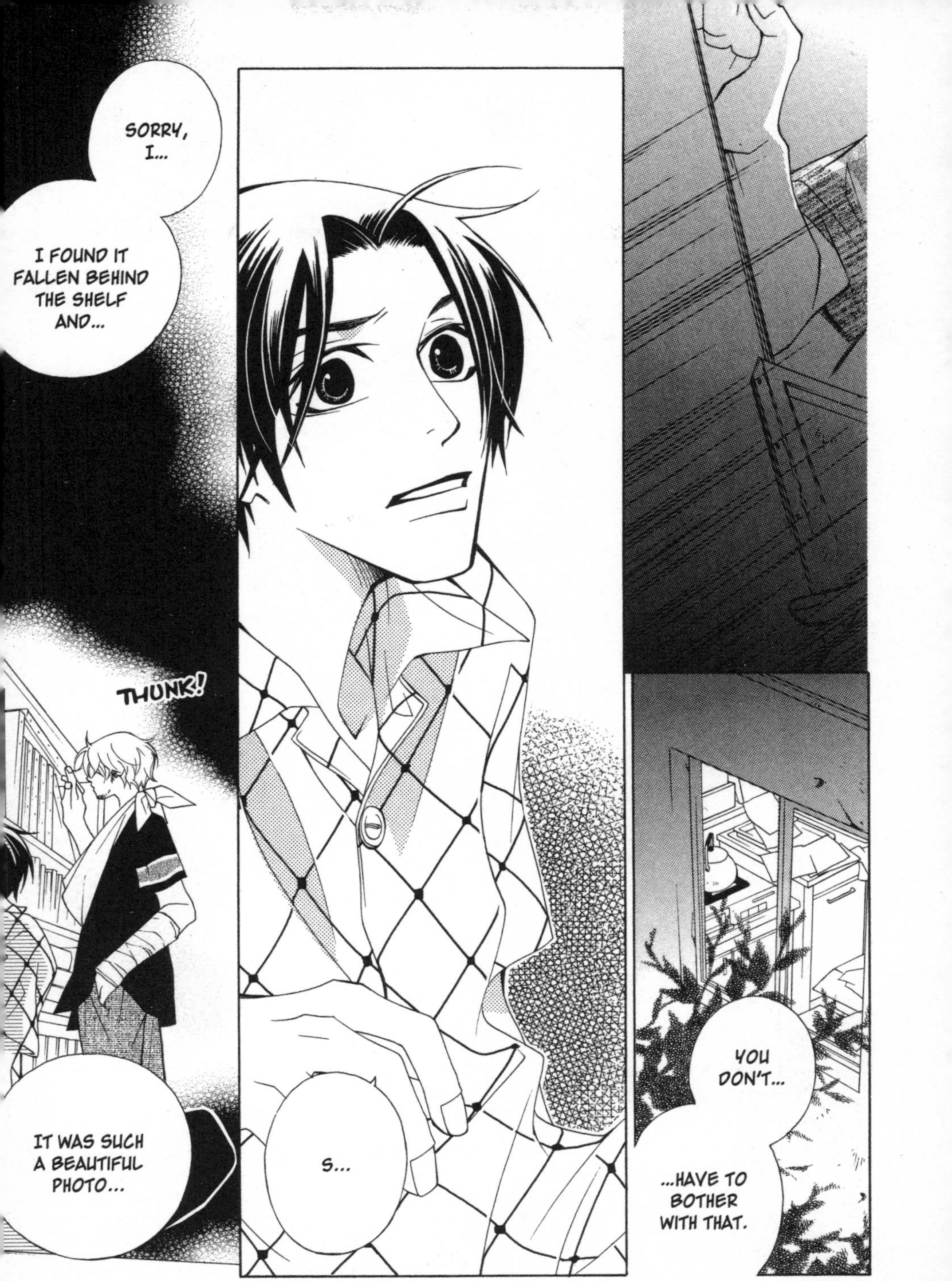
YOU DON'T...
...HAVE TO BOTHER WITH THAT.
S...
SORRY, I...
I FOUND IT FALLEN BEHIND THE SHELF AND...
THUNK!
IT WAS SUCH A BEAUTIFUL PHOTO...

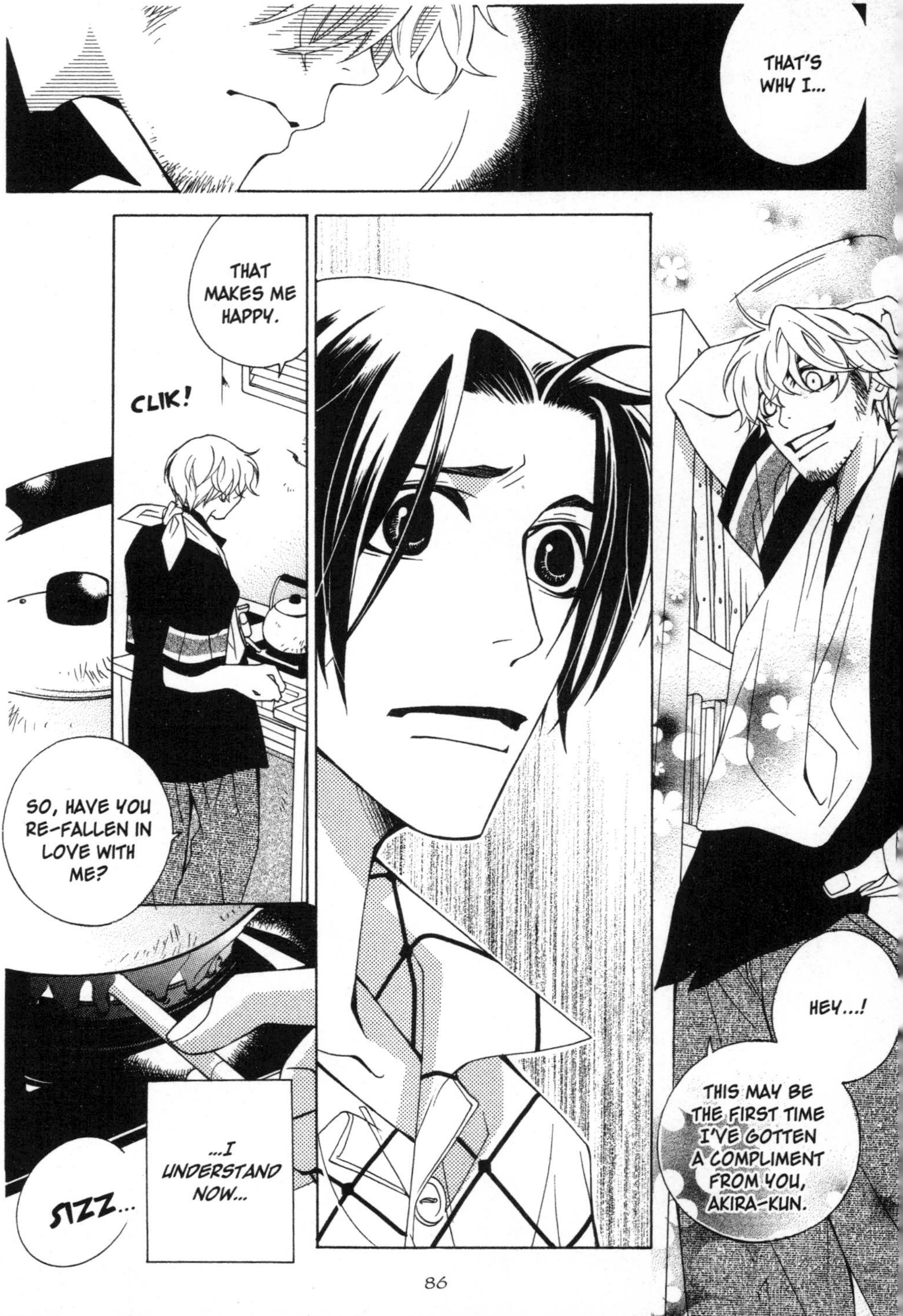
THAT'S WHY I...
HEY...!
THIS MAY BE THE FIRST TIME I'VE GOTTEN A COMPLIMENT FROM YOU, AKIRA-KUN.
THAT MAKES ME HAPPY.
CLIK!
SO, HAVE YOU RE-FALLEN IN LOVE WITH ME?
...I UNDERSTAND NOW...
SIZZ...

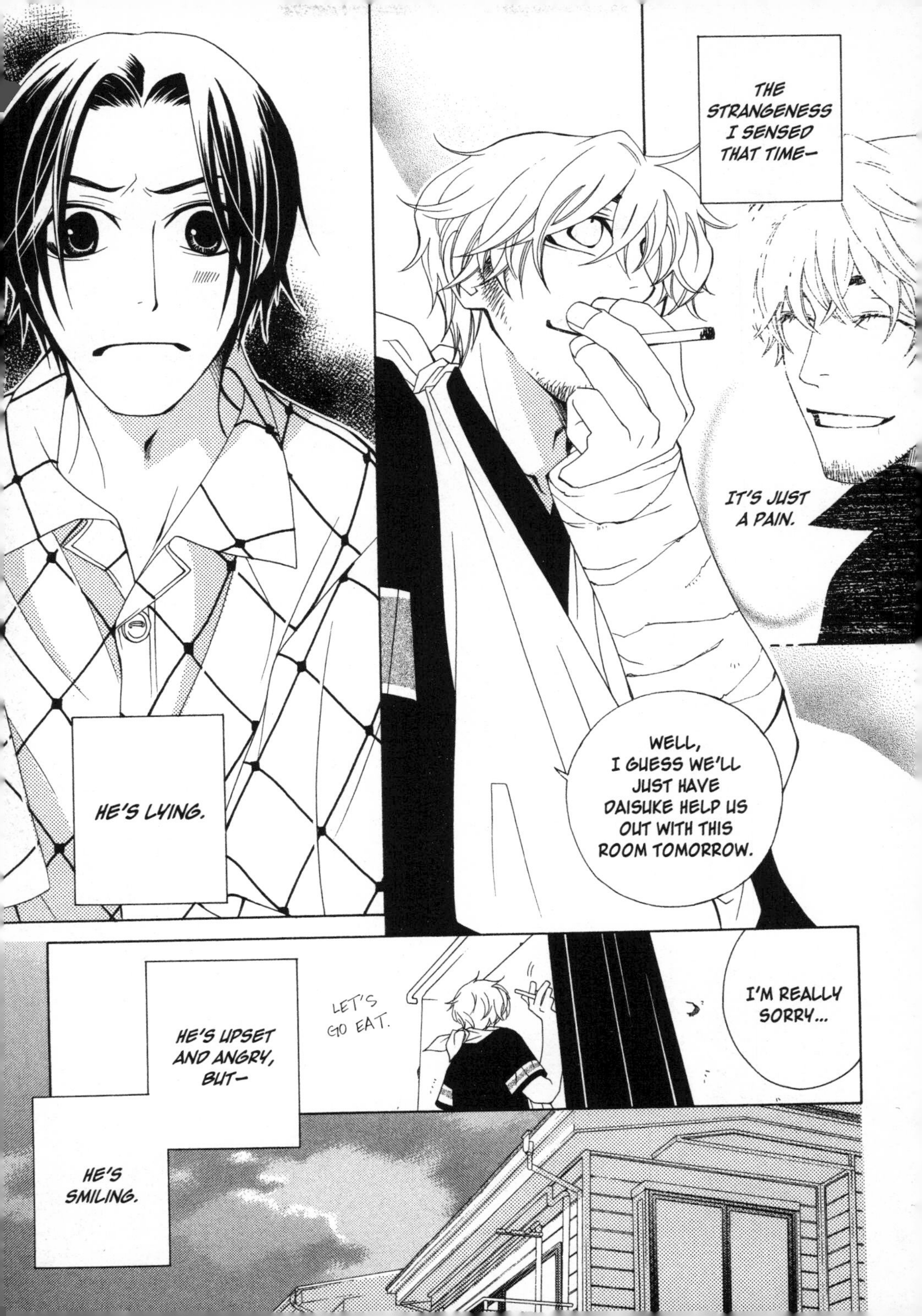
THE STRANGENESS I SENSED THAT TIME—
IT'S JUST A PAIN.
WELL, I GUESS WE'LL JUST HAVE DAISUKE HELP US OUT WITH THIS ROOM TOMORROW.
HE'S LYING.
I'M REALLY SORRY...
LET'S GO EAT.
HE'S UPSET AND ANGRY, BUT—
HE'S SMILING.

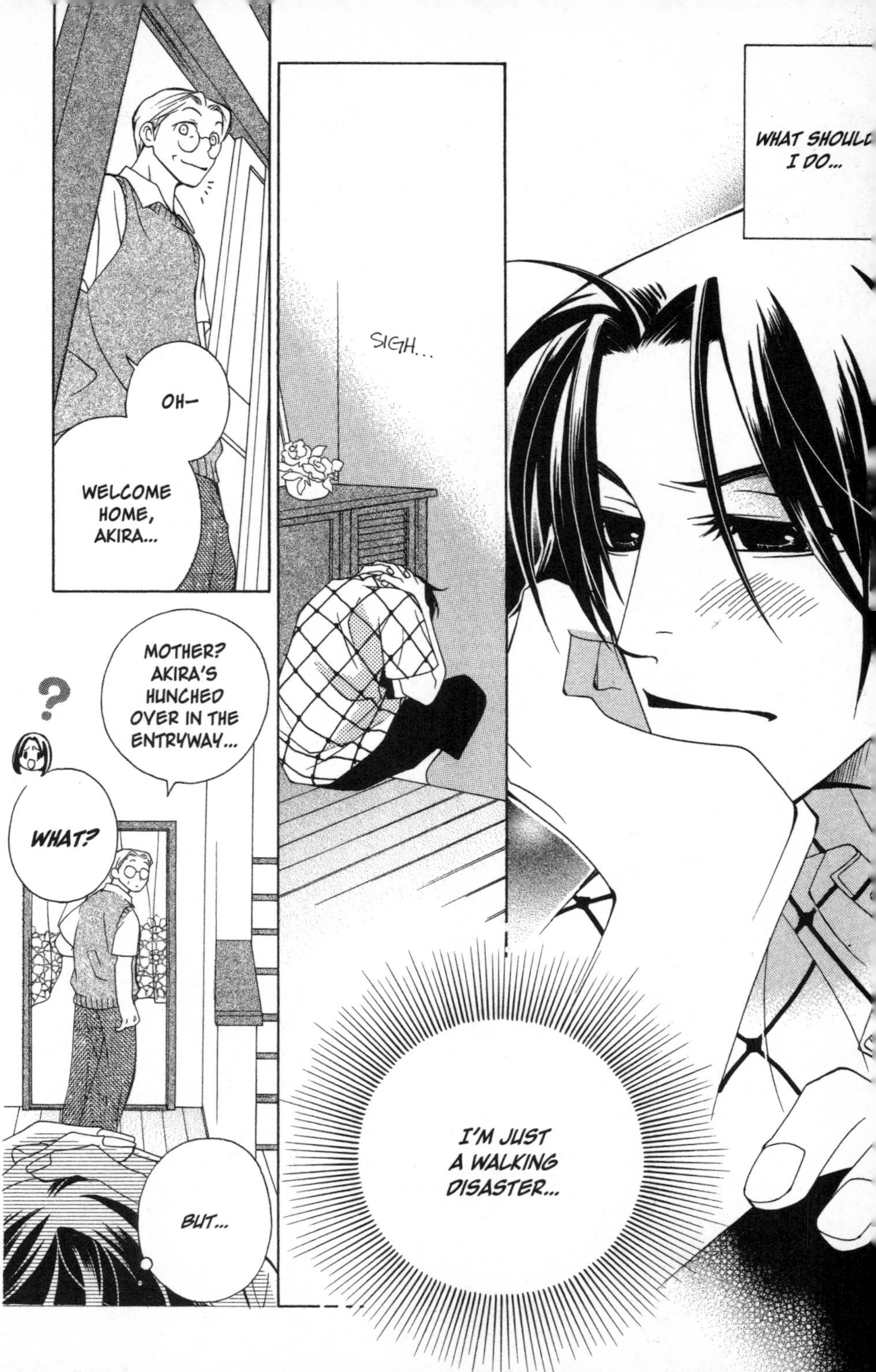
WHAT SHOULD I DO...
I'M JUST A WALKING DISASTER...
SIGH...
OH—
WELCOME HOME, AKIRA...
MOTHER? AKIRA'S HUNCHED OVER IN THE ENTRYWAY...
?
WHAT?
BUT...

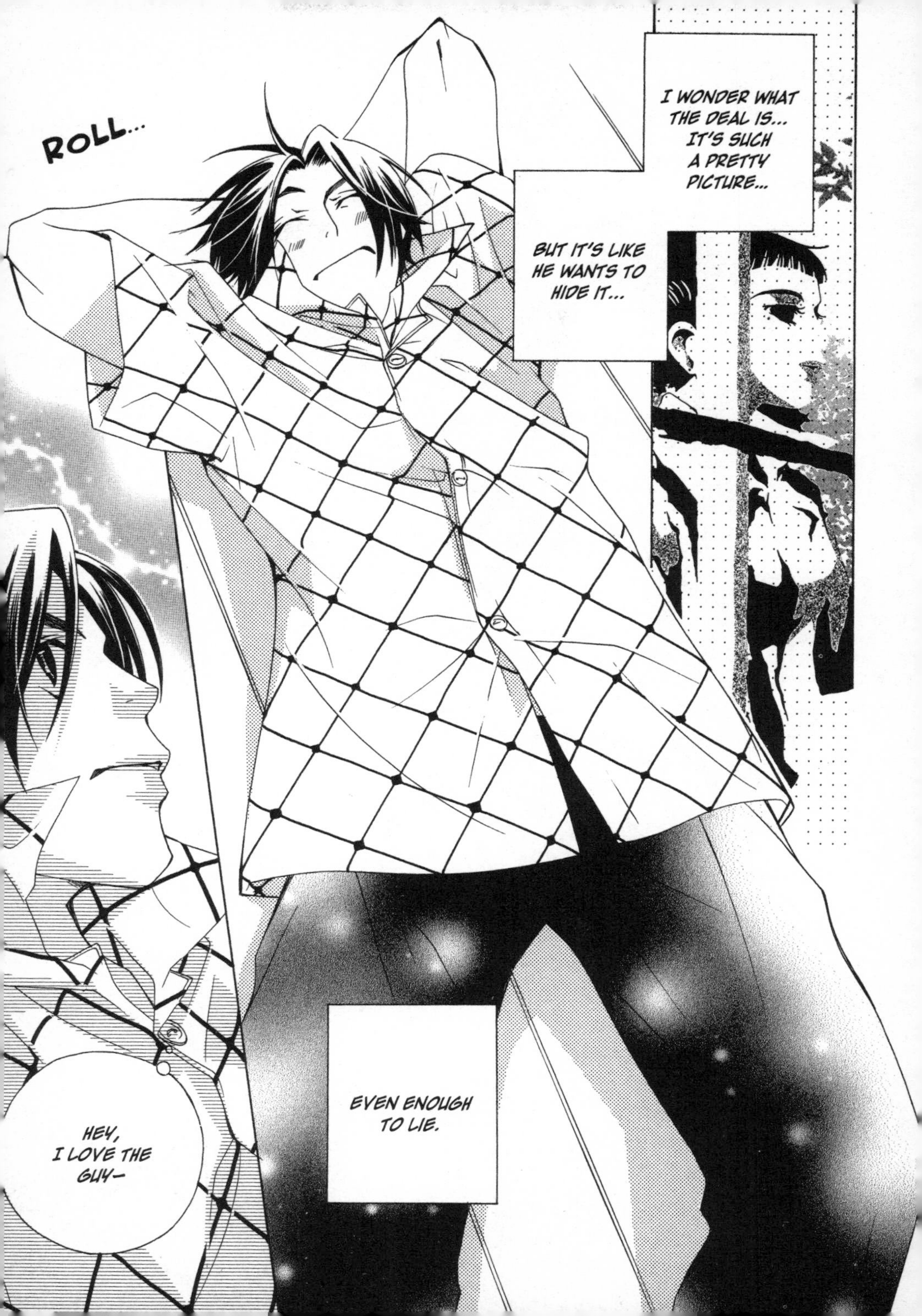
I WONDER WHAT THE DEAL IS... IT'S SUCH A PRETTY PICTURE...
BUT IT'S LIKE HE WANTS TO HIDE IT...
ROLL...
EVEN ENOUGH TO LIE.
HEY, I LOVE THE GUY–

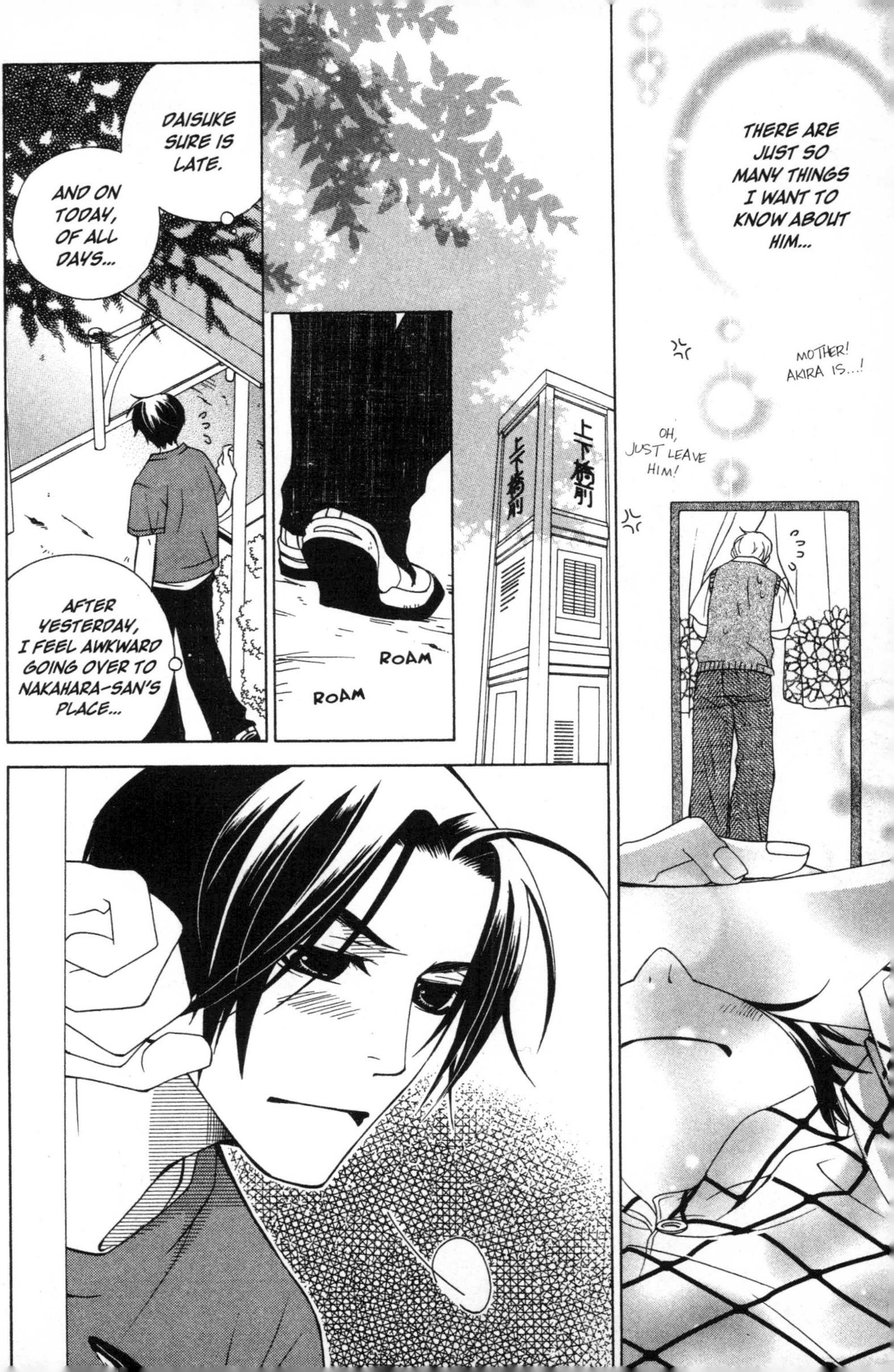
THERE ARE JUST SO MANY THINGS I WANT TO KNOW ABOUT HIM...
MOTHER! AKIRA IS...!
OH, JUST LEAVE HIM!
ROAM
ROAM
DAISUKE SURE IS LATE.
AND ON TODAY, OF ALL DAYS...
AFTER YESTERDAY, I FEEL AWKWARD GOING OVER TO NAKAHARA-SAN'S PLACE...

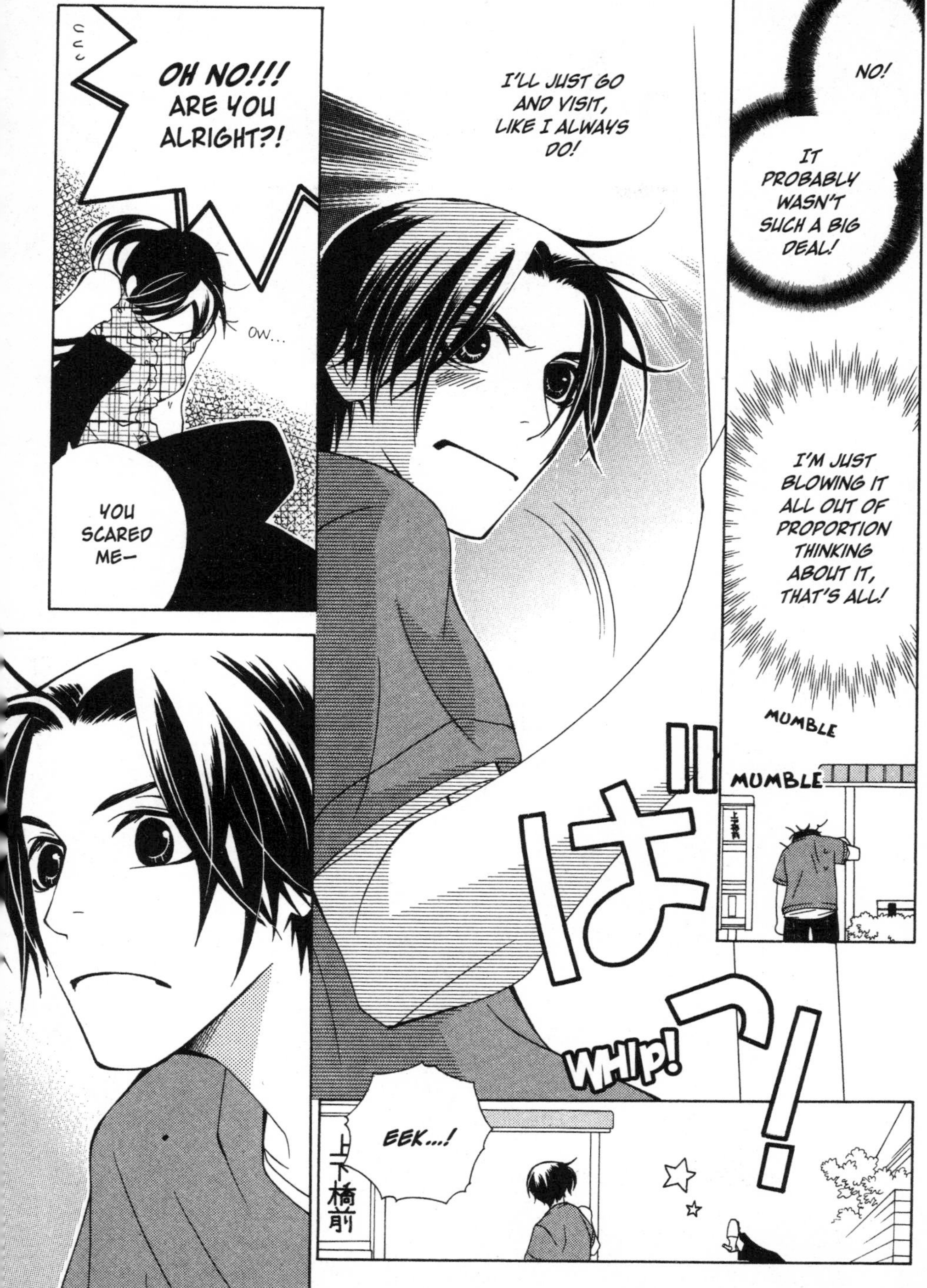
NO!
IT PROBABLY WASN'T SUCH A BIG DEAL!
I'M JUST BLOWING IT ALL OUT OF PROPORTION THINKING ABOUT IT, THAT'S ALL!
MUMBLE
MUMBLE
I'LL JUST GO AND VISIT, LIKE I ALWAYS DO!
はっ!
WHIP!
EEK...!
OH NO!!! ARE YOU ALRIGHT?!
OW...
YOU SCARED ME—

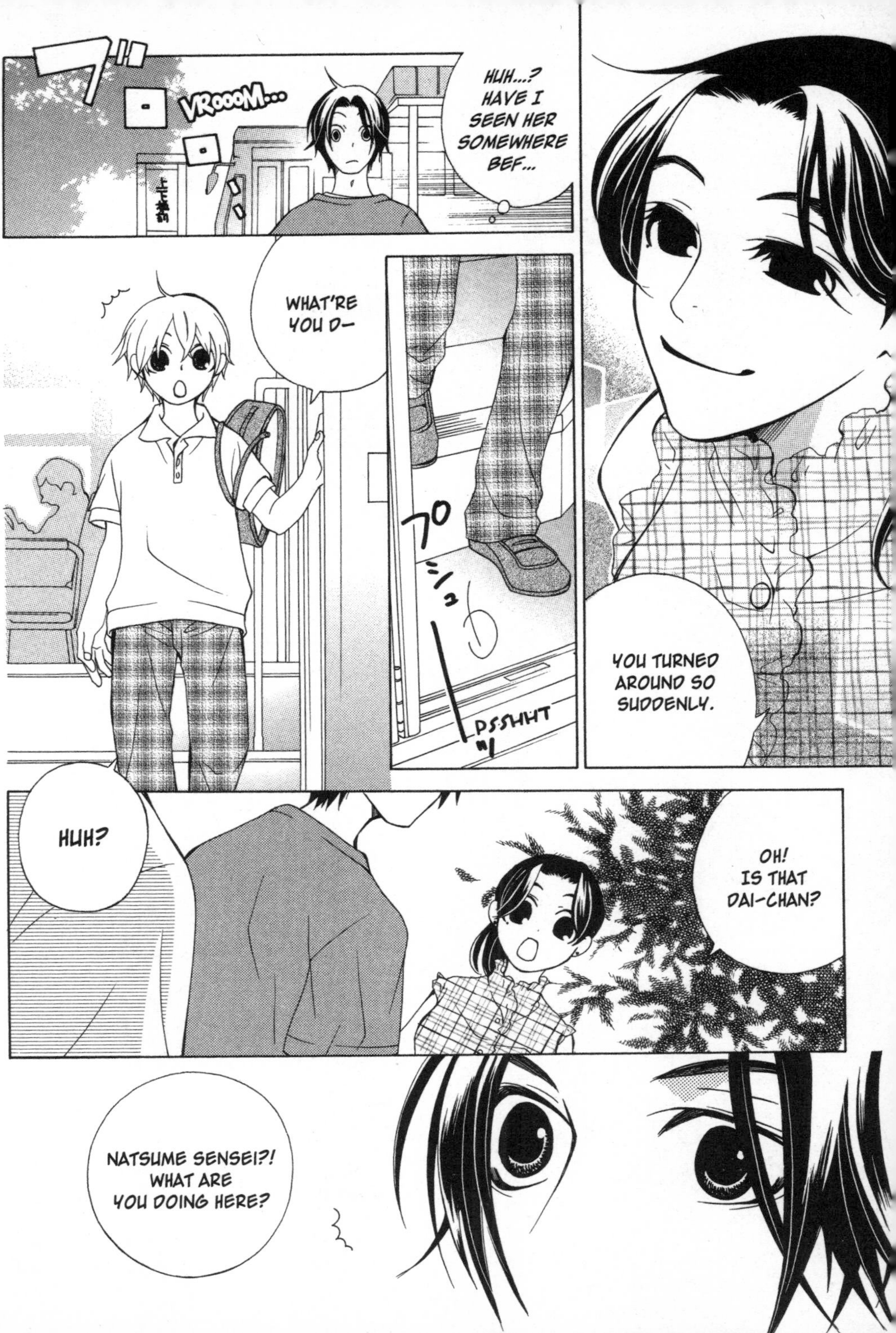
YOU TURNED AROUND SO SUDDENLY.
VROOOM...
HUH...? HAVE I SEEN HER SOMEWHERE BEF...
PSSHHT
WHAT'RE YOU D-
OH! IS THAT DAI-CHAN?
HUH?
NATSUME SENSEI?! WHAT ARE YOU DOING HERE?

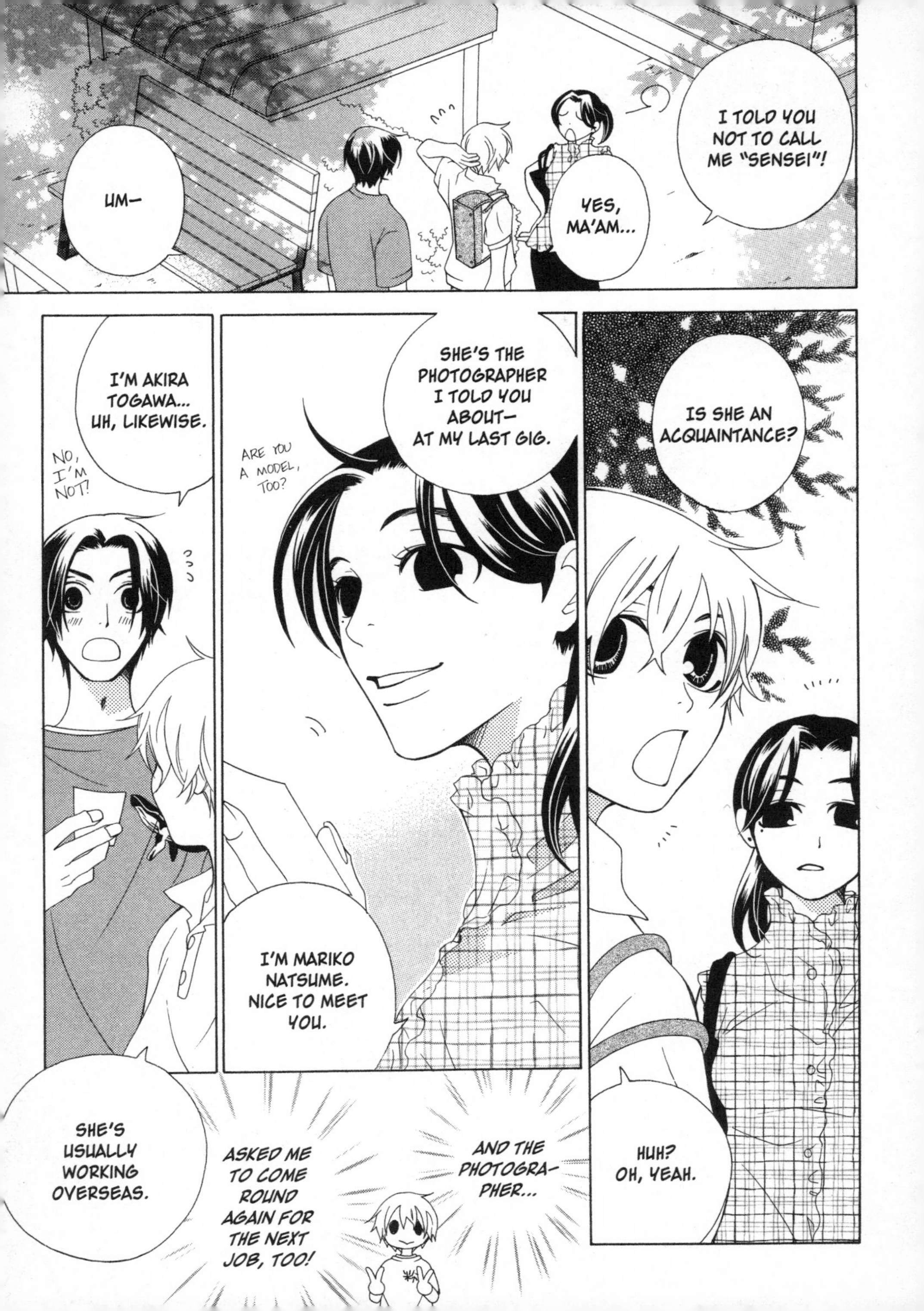
I TOLD YOU NOT TO CALL ME "SENSEI"!
YES, MA'AM...
UM—
IS SHE AN ACQUAINTANCE?
HUH? OH, YEAH.
SHE'S THE PHOTOGRAPHER I TOLD YOU ABOUT— AT MY LAST GIG.
ARE YOU A MODEL, TOO?
I'M MARIKO NATSUME. NICE TO MEET YOU.
I'M AKIRA TOGAWA... UH, LIKEWISE.
NO, I'M NOT!
AND THE PHOTOGRA-PHER...
ASKED ME TO COME ROUND AGAIN FOR THE NEXT JOB, TOO!
SHE'S USUALLY WORKING OVERSEAS.

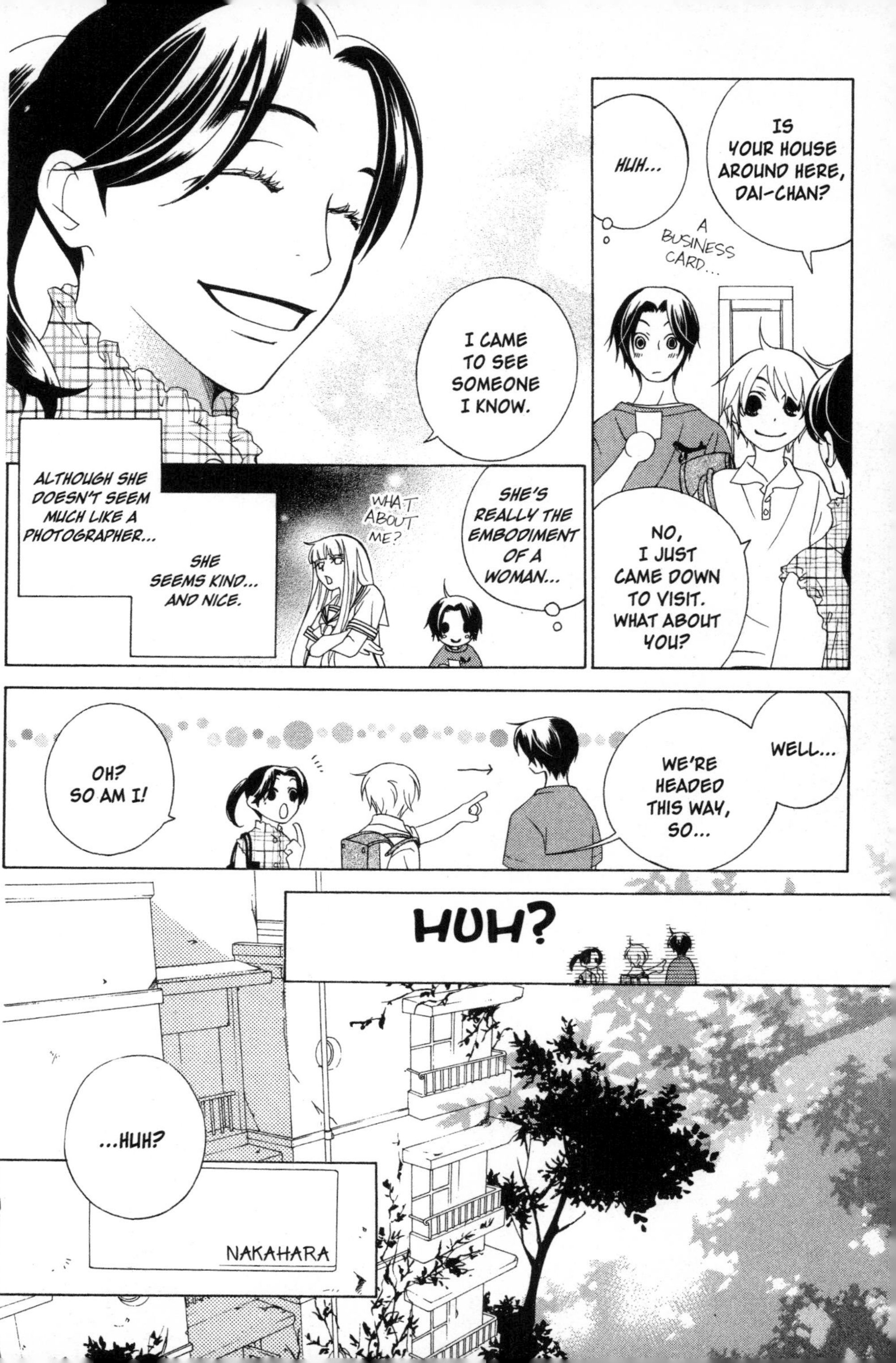
IS YOUR HOUSE AROUND HERE, DAI-CHAN?
HUH...
A BUSINESS CARD...
NO, I JUST CAME DOWN TO VISIT. WHAT ABOUT YOU?
I CAME TO SEE SOMEONE I KNOW.
SHE'S REALLY THE EMBODIMENT OF A WOMAN...
WHAT ABOUT ME?
ALTHOUGH SHE DOESN'T SEEM MUCH LIKE A PHOTOGRAPHER...
SHE SEEMS KIND... AND NICE.
WELL...
WE'RE HEADED THIS WAY, SO...
OH? SO AM I!
HUH?
...HUH?
NAKAHARA

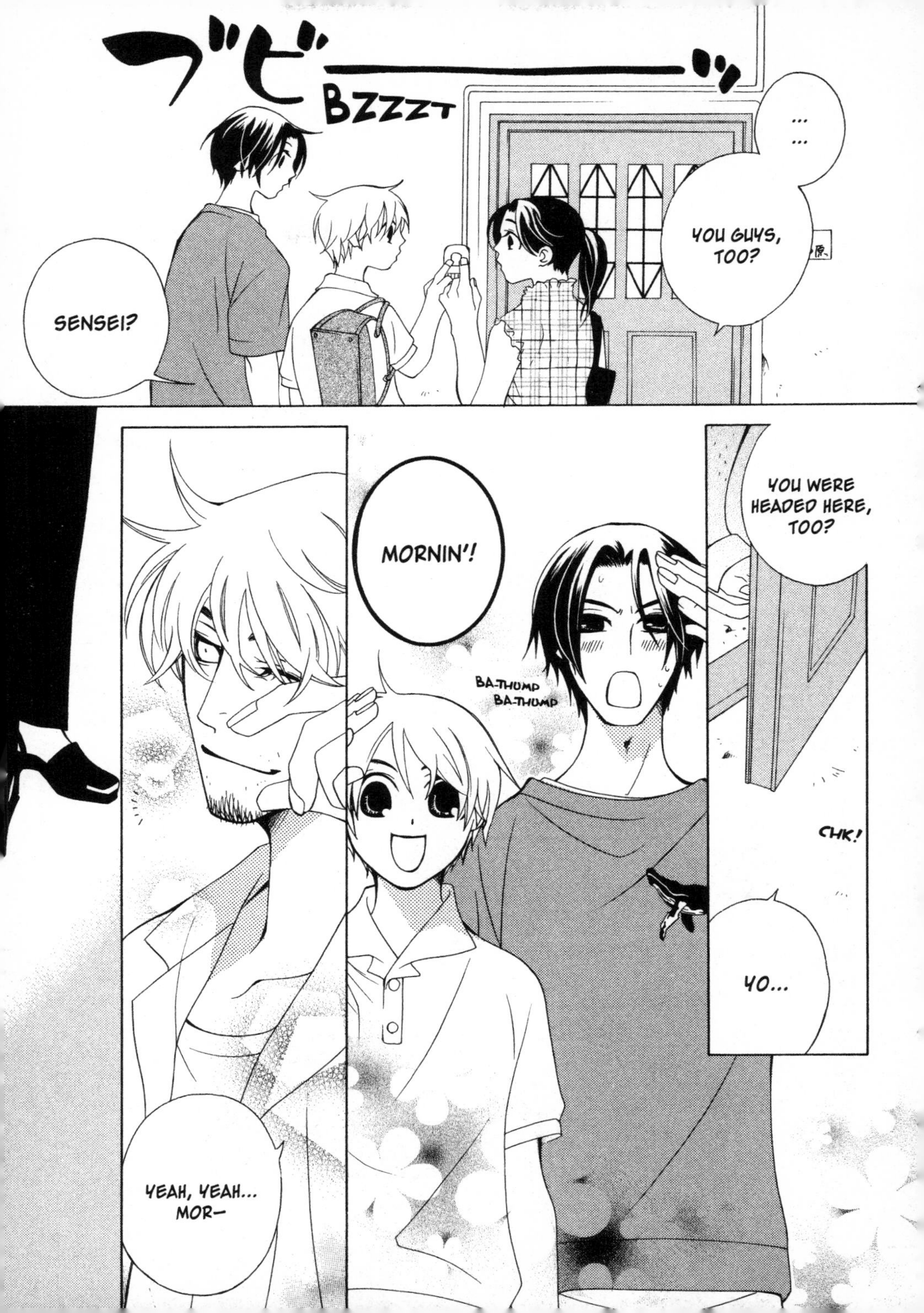
ブビーーーッ
BZZZT
...
...
YOU GUYS, TOO?
SENSEI?
YOU WERE HEADED HERE, TOO?
CHK!
YO...
MORNIN'!
BA-THUMP BA-THUMP
YEAH, YEAH... MOR—

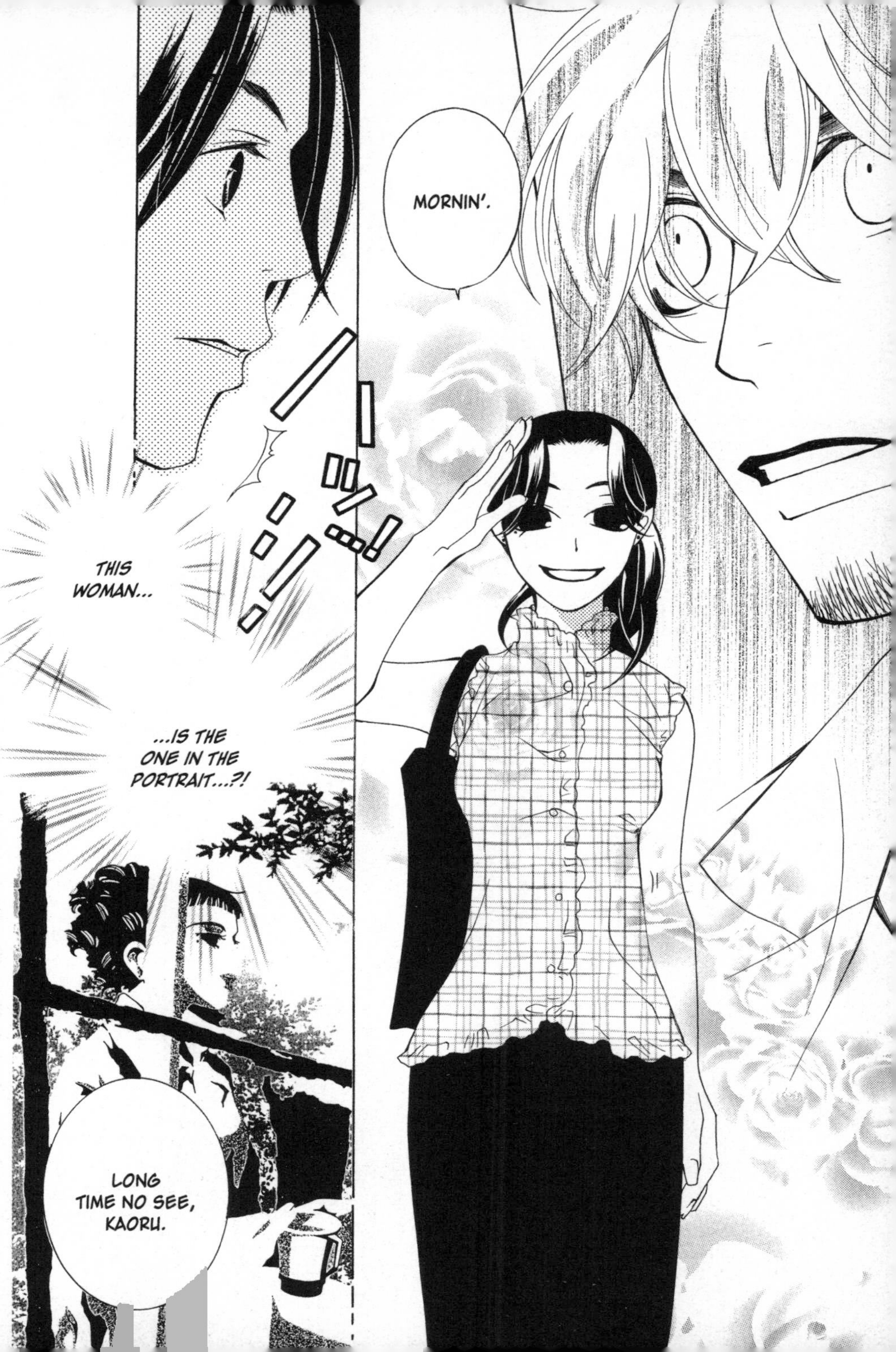
MORNIN'.
THIS WOMAN...
...IS THE ONE IN THE PORTRAIT...?!
LONG TIME NO SEE, KAORU.

Camera Camera Camera

カメラ・カメラ・カメラ
shot.10

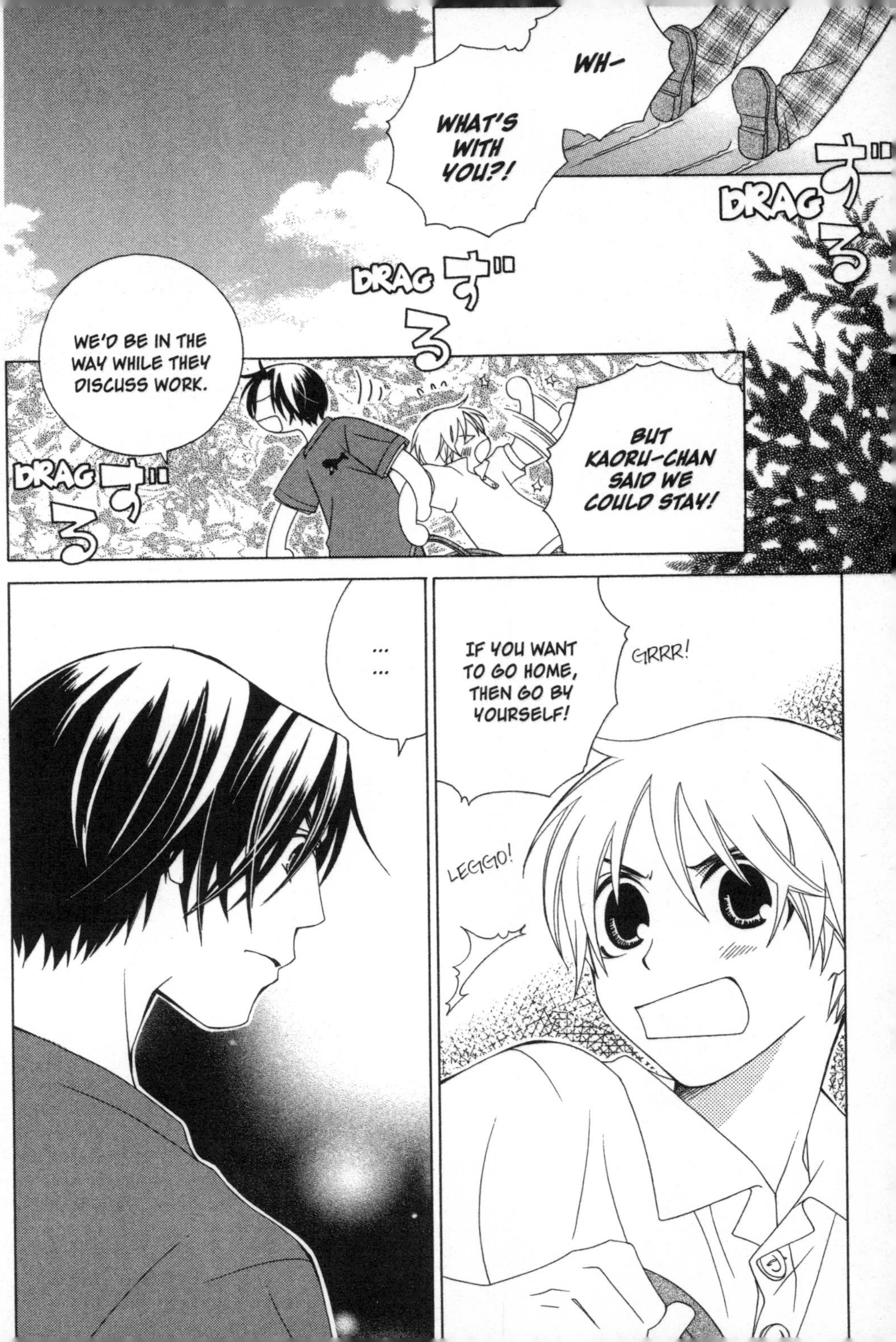
WH-
WHAT'S WITH YOU?!
DRAG
DRAG
BUT KAORU-CHAN SAID WE COULD STAY!
WE'D BE IN THE WAY WHILE THEY DISCUSS WORK.
DRAG
GRRR!
IF YOU WANT TO GO HOME, THEN GO BY YOURSELF!
LEGGO!
...
...

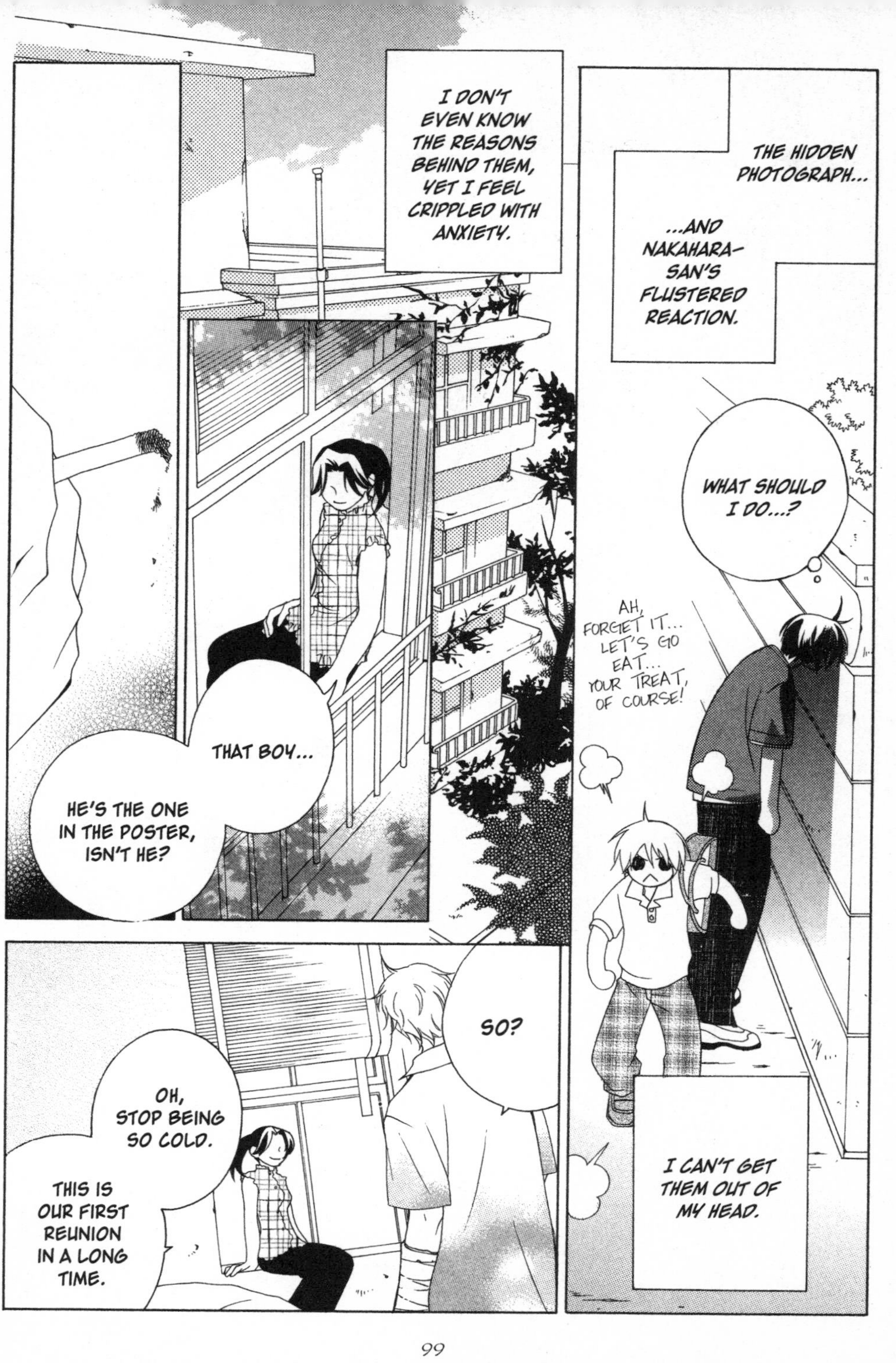
THE HIDDEN PHOTOGRAPH...
...AND NAKAHARA-SAN'S FLUSTERED REACTION.
WHAT SHOULD I DO...?
AH, FORGET IT... LET'S GO EAT... YOUR TREAT, OF COURSE!
I CAN'T GET THEM OUT OF MY HEAD.
I DON'T EVEN KNOW THE REASONS BEHIND THEM, YET I FEEL CRIPPLED WITH ANXIETY.
THAT BOY...
HE'S THE ONE IN THE POSTER, ISN'T HE?
SO?
OH, STOP BEING SO COLD.
THIS IS OUR FIRST REUNION IN A LONG TIME.

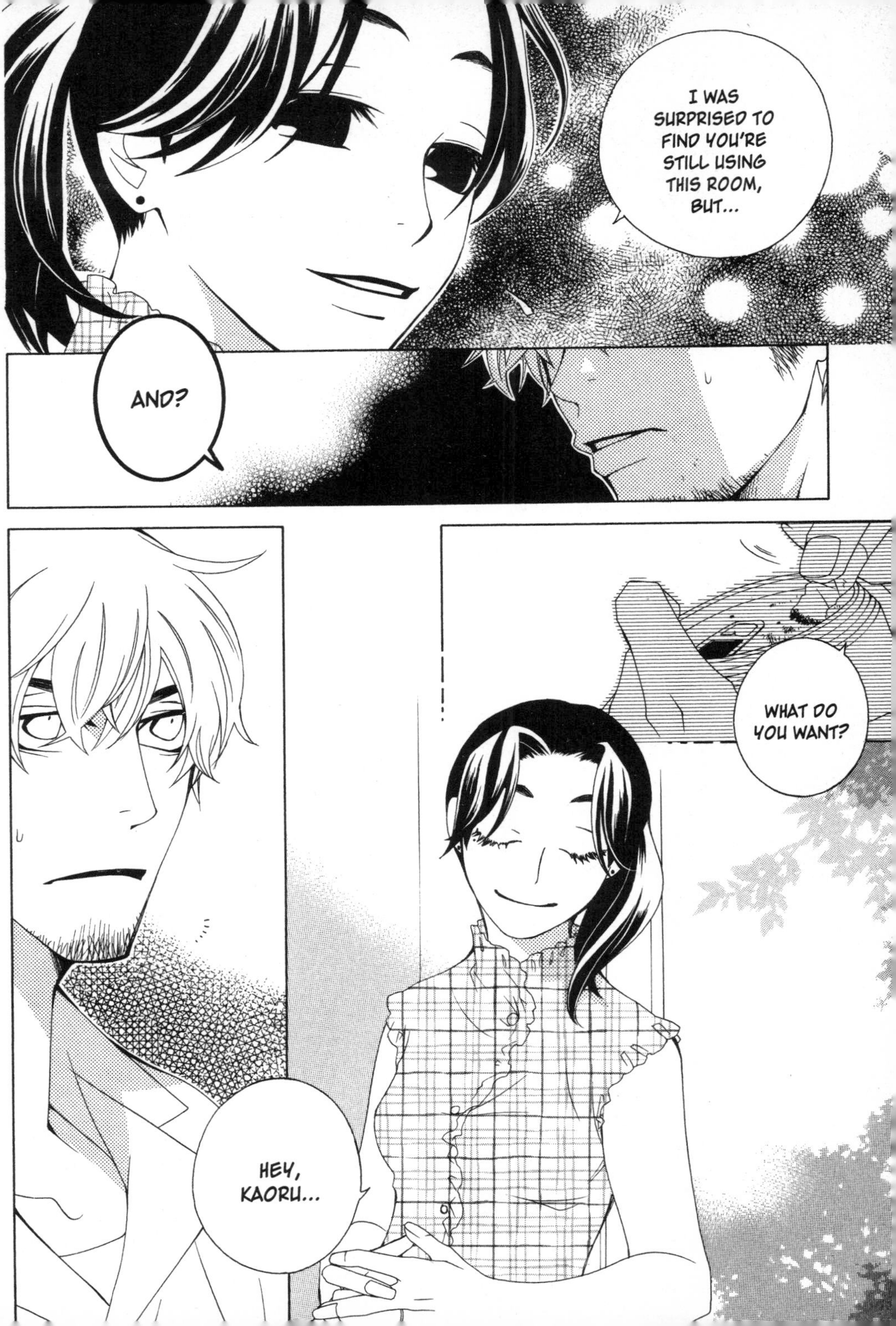
I WAS SURPRISED TO FIND YOU'RE STILL USING THIS ROOM, BUT...
AND?
WHAT DO YOU WANT?
HEY, KAORU...

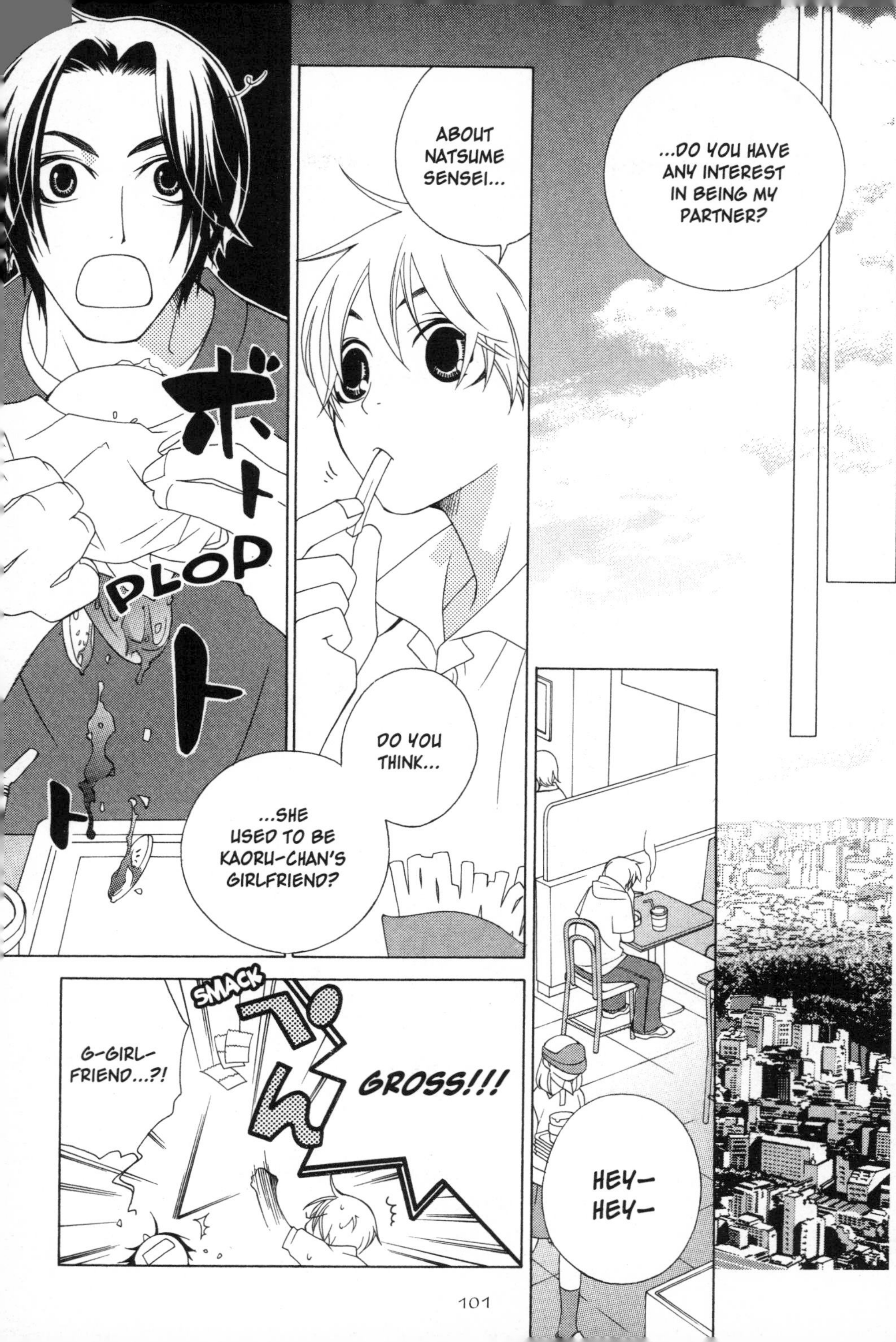
...DO YOU HAVE ANY INTEREST IN BEING MY PARTNER?
HEY- HEY-
ABOUT NATSUME SENSEI...
DO YOU THINK...
...SHE USED TO BE KAORU-CHAN'S GIRLFRIEND?
ボト
PLOP
トト
GROSS!!!
SMACK
G-GIRL-FRIEND...?!

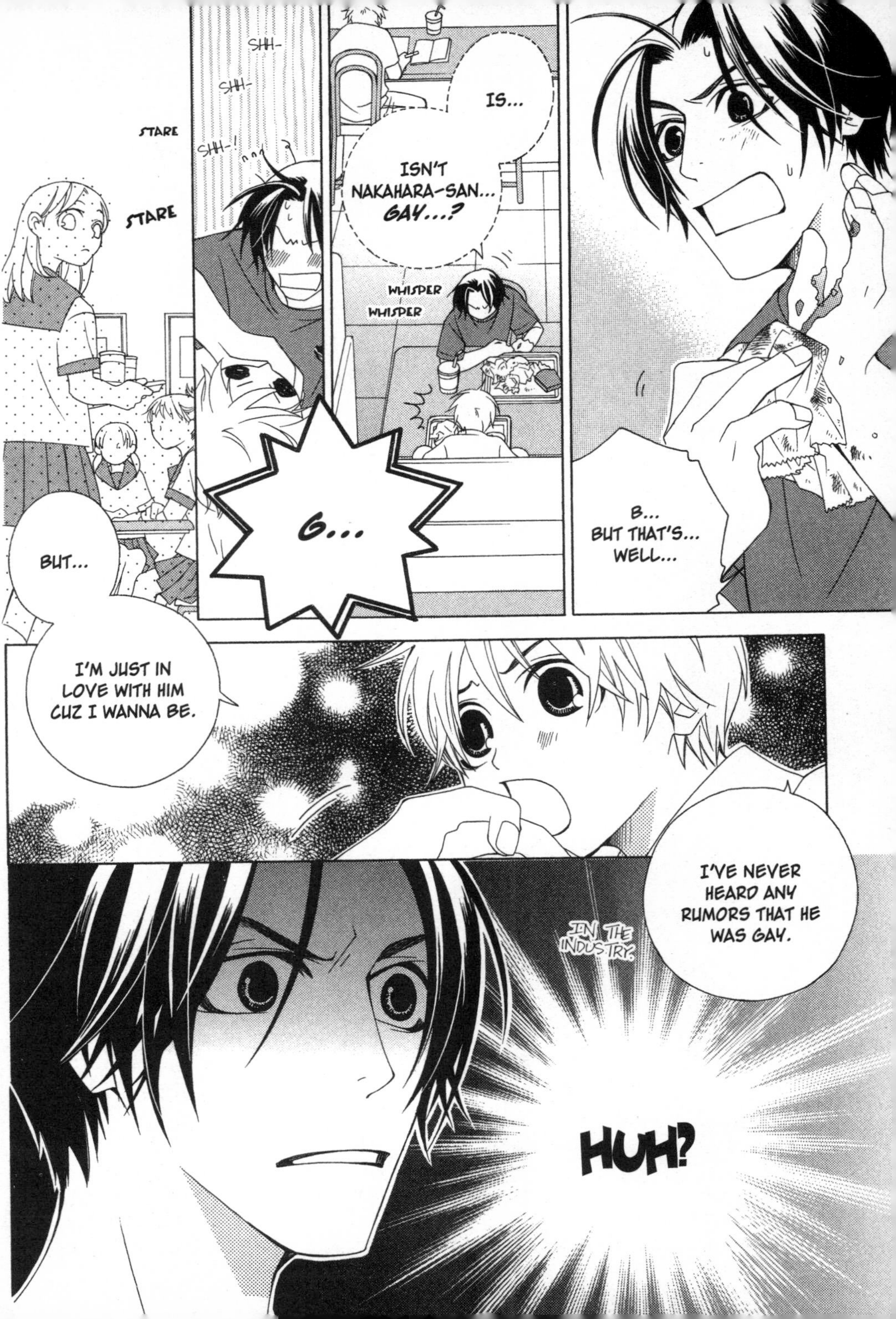
B... BUT THAT'S... WELL...
SHH-
SHH-
SHH-!
IS...
ISN'T NAKAHARA-SAN... GAY...?
WHISPER
WHISPER
G...
STARE
STARE
BUT...
I'M JUST IN LOVE WITH HIM CUZ I WANNA BE.
I'VE NEVER HEARD ANY RUMORS THAT HE WAS GAY.
IN THE INDUSTRY.
HUH?

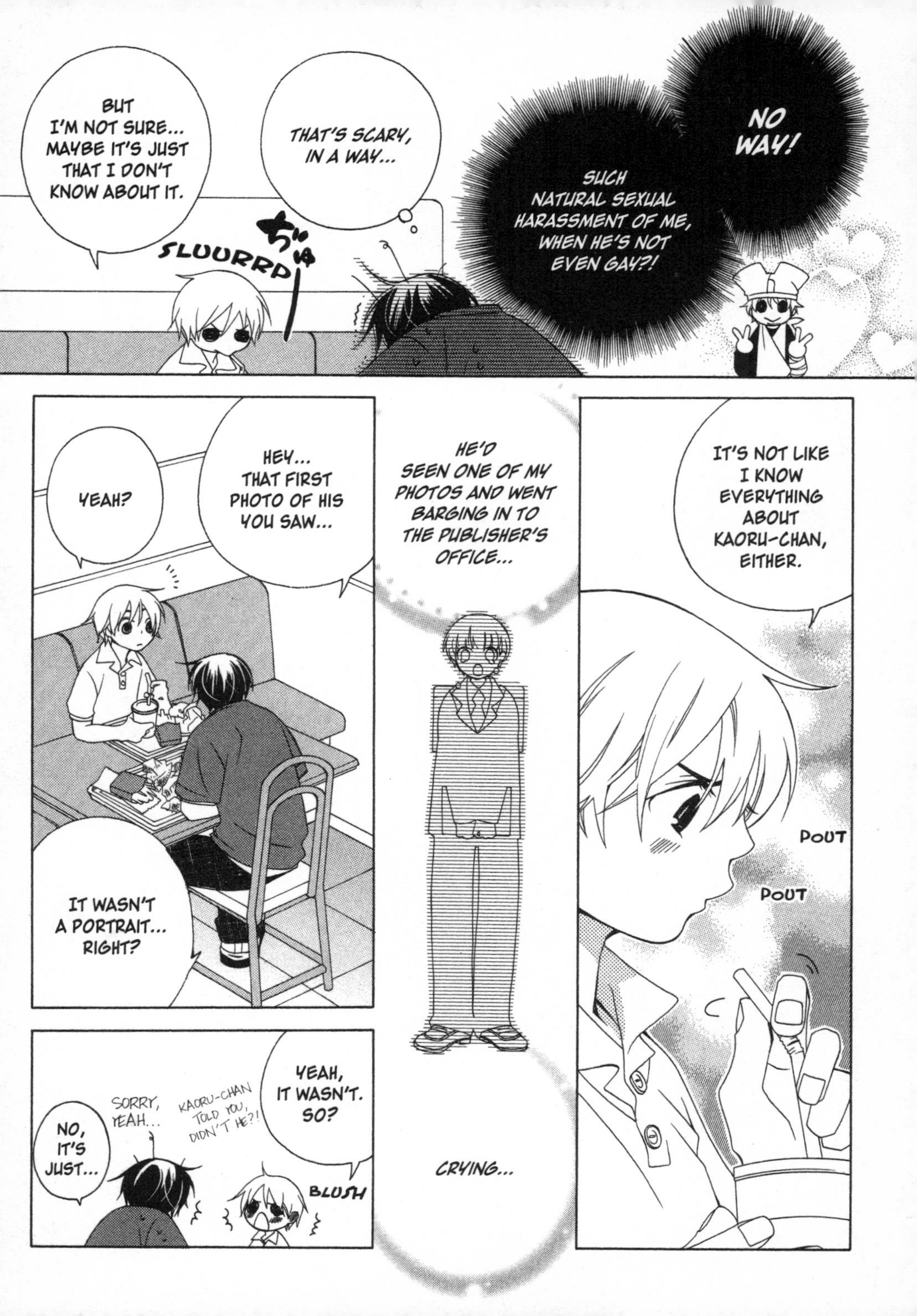
NO WAY!
SUCH NATURAL SEXUAL HARASSMENT OF ME, WHEN HE'S NOT EVEN GAY?!
THAT'S SCARY, IN A WAY...
BUT I'M NOT SURE... MAYBE IT'S JUST THAT I DON'T KNOW ABOUT IT.
SLUURRP
IT'S NOT LIKE I KNOW EVERYTHING ABOUT KAORU-CHAN, EITHER.
POUT
POUT
HE'D SEEN ONE OF MY PHOTOS AND WENT BARGING IN TO THE PUBLISHER'S OFFICE...
CRYING...
HEY... THAT FIRST PHOTO OF HIS YOU SAW...
YEAH?
IT WASN'T A PORTRAIT... RIGHT?
YEAH, IT WASN'T. SO?
KAORU-CHAN TOLD YOU, DIDN'T HE?!
SORRY, YEAH...
NO, IT'S JUST...
BLUSH

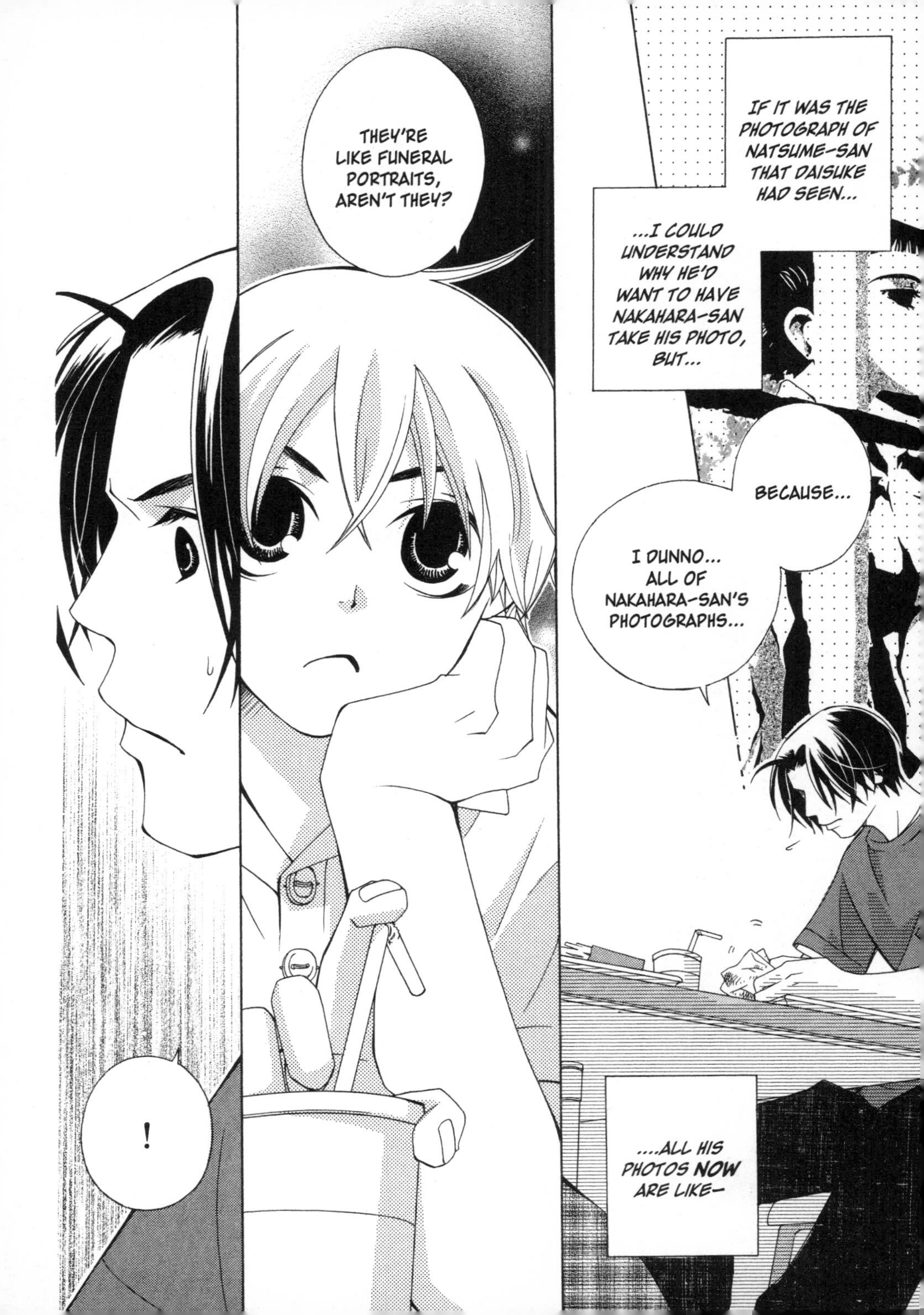
IF IT WAS THE PHOTOGRAPH OF NATSUME-SAN THAT DAISUKE HAD SEEN...
...I COULD UNDERSTAND WHY HE'D WANT TO HAVE NAKAHARA-SAN TAKE HIS PHOTO, BUT...
BECAUSE...
I DUNNO... ALL OF NAKAHARA-SAN'S PHOTOGRAPHS...
....ALL HIS PHOTOS **NOW** ARE LIKE—
THEY'RE LIKE FUNERAL PORTRAITS, AREN'T THEY?
!

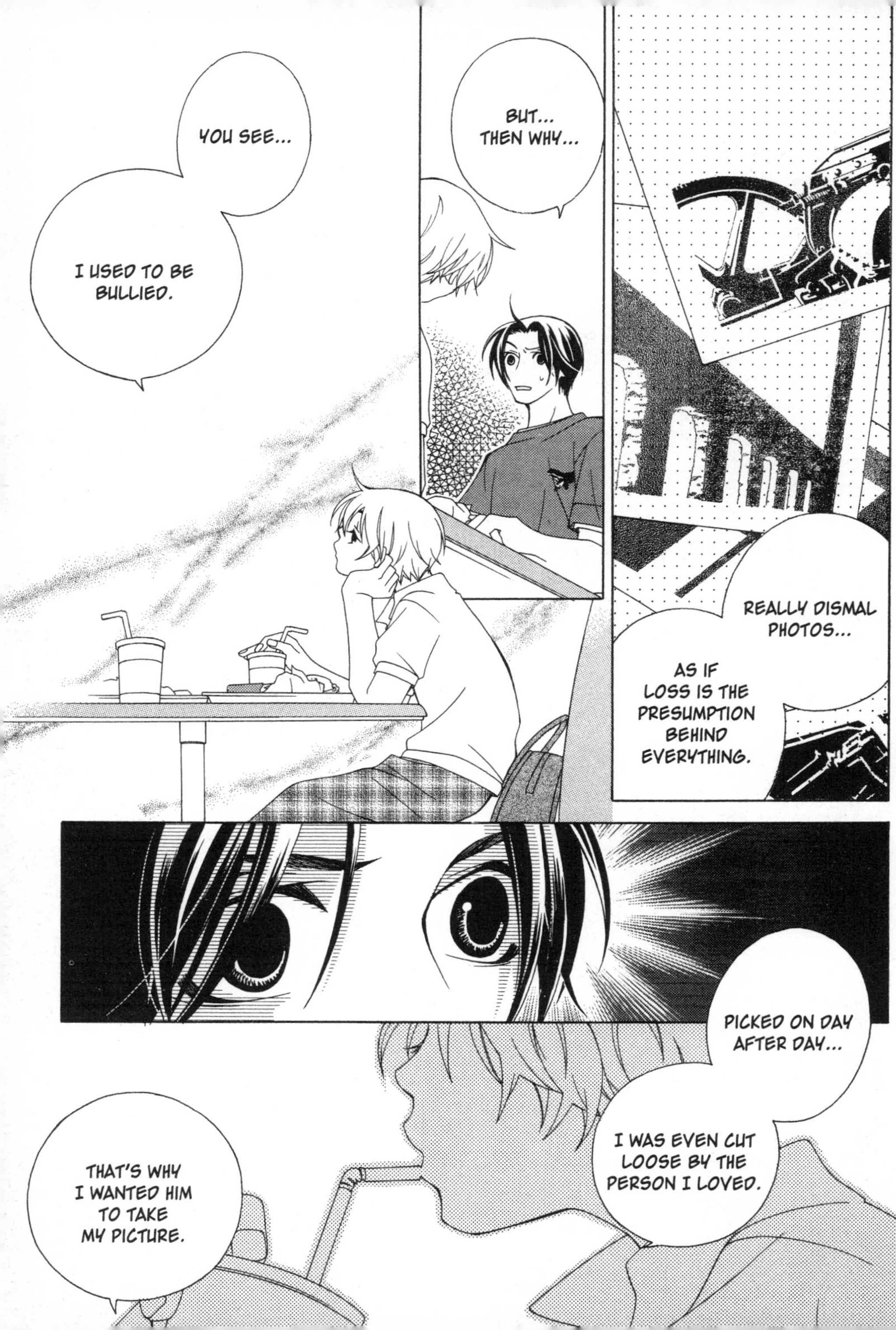
REALLY DISMAL PHOTOS...
AS IF LOSS IS THE PRESUMPTION BEHIND EVERYTHING.
BUT... THEN WHY...
YOU SEE...
I USED TO BE BULLIED.
PICKED ON DAY AFTER DAY...
I WAS EVEN CUT LOOSE BY THE PERSON I LOVED.
THAT'S WHY I WANTED HIM TO TAKE MY PICTURE.

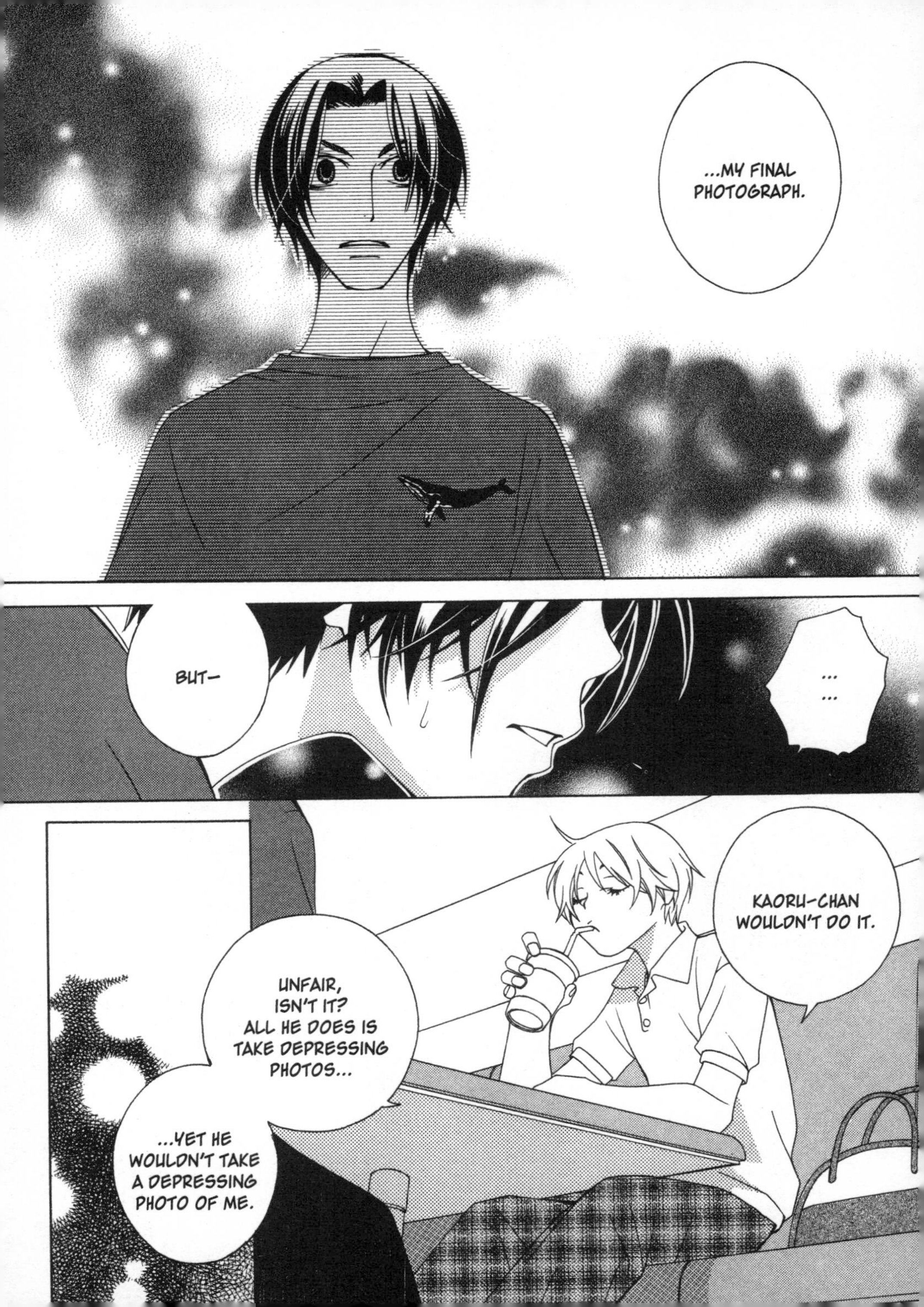
...MY FINAL PHOTOGRAPH.
...
...
BUT—
KAORU-CHAN WOULDN'T DO IT.
UNFAIR, ISN'T IT? ALL HE DOES IS TAKE DEPRESSING PHOTOS...
...YET HE WOULDN'T TAKE A DEPRESSING PHOTO OF ME.

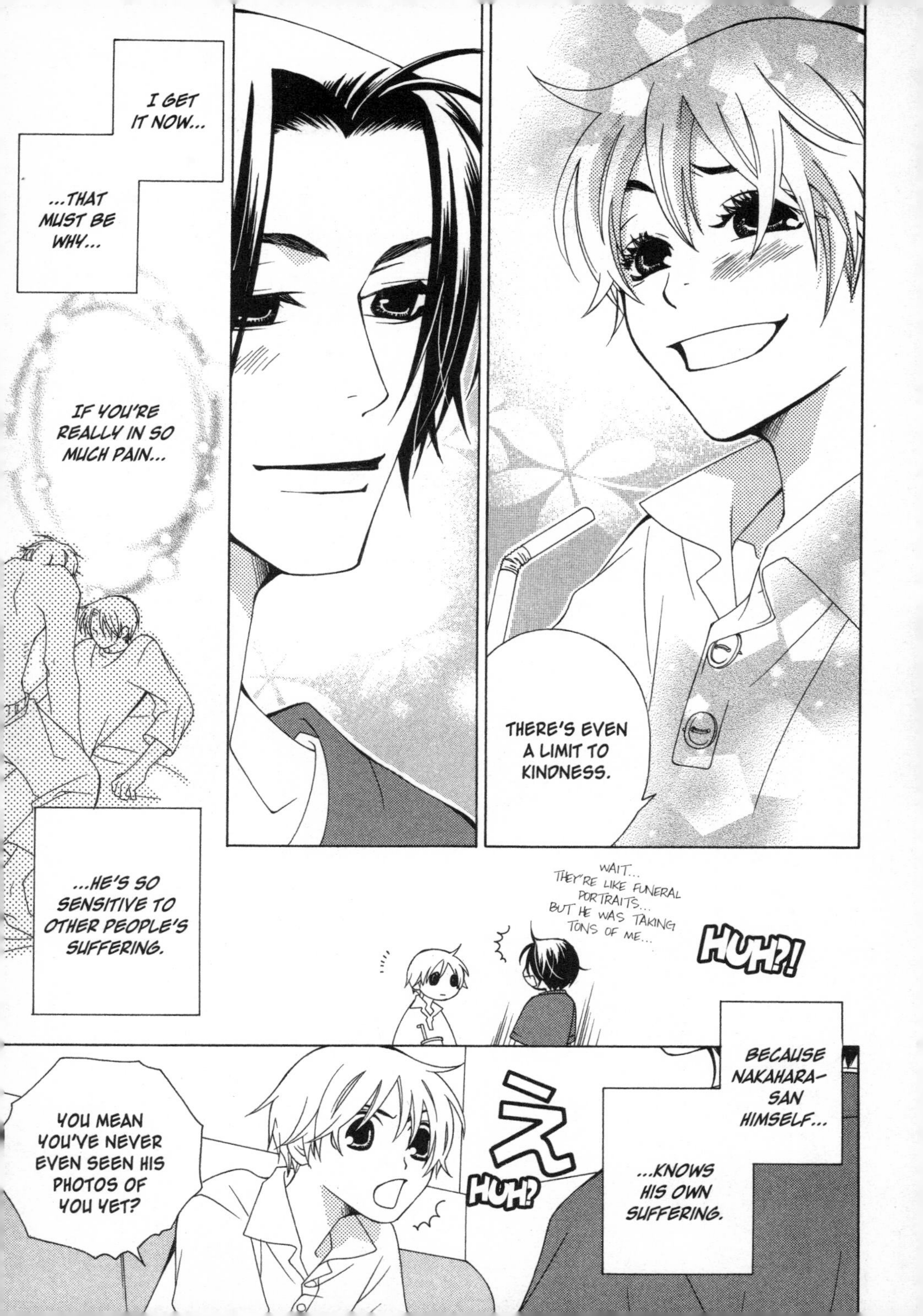
THERE'S EVEN A LIMIT TO KINDNESS.
I GET IT NOW...
...THAT MUST BE WHY...
IF YOU'RE REALLY IN SO MUCH PAIN...
...HE'S SO SENSITIVE TO OTHER PEOPLE'S SUFFERING.
HUH?!
WAIT... THEY'RE LIKE FUNERAL PORTRAITS... BUT HE WAS TAKING TONS OF ME...
BECAUSE NAKAHARA-SAN HIMSELF...
...KNOWS HIS OWN SUFFERING.
え
HUH?
YOU MEAN YOU'VE NEVER EVEN SEEN HIS PHOTOS OF YOU YET?

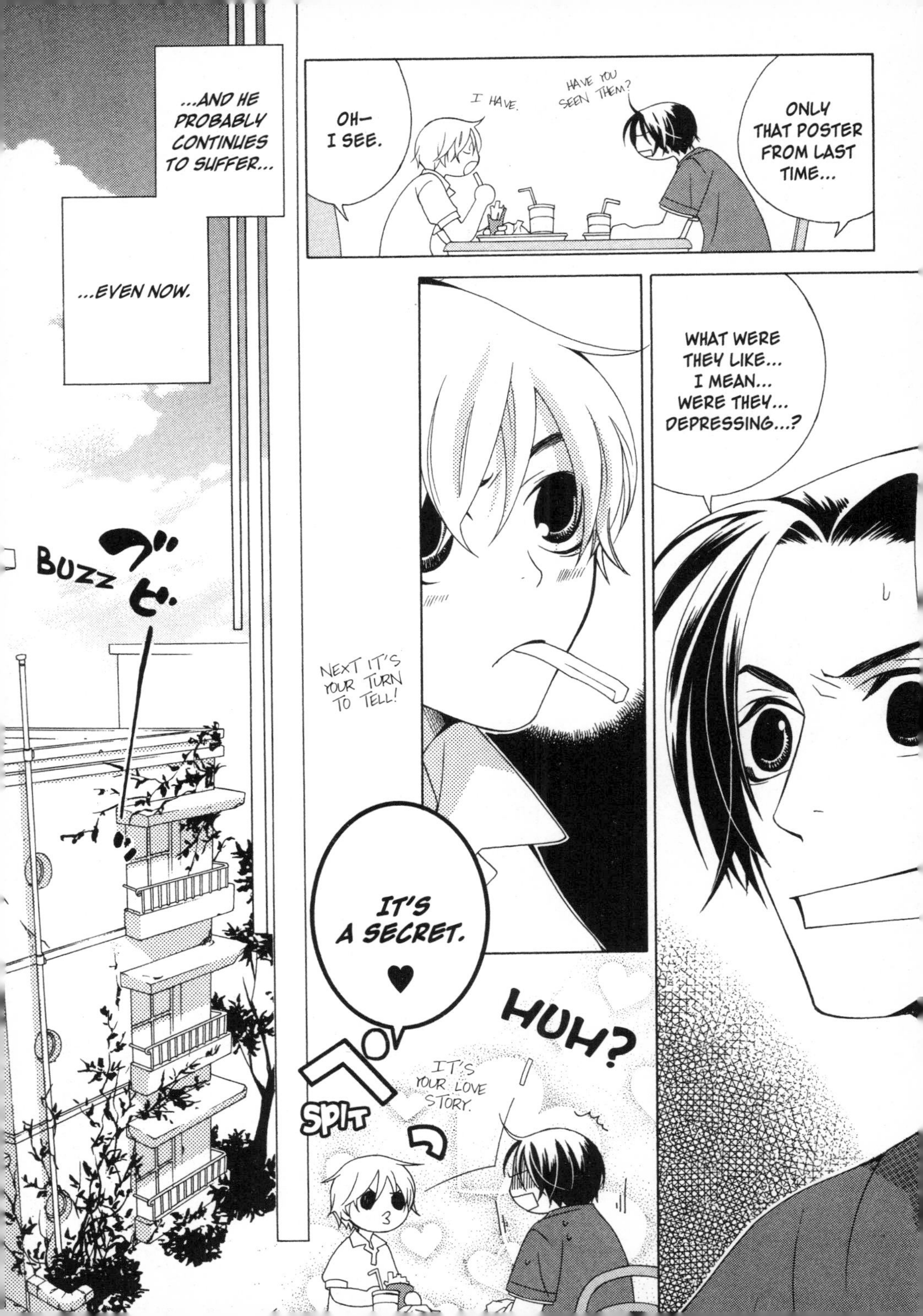
ONLY THAT POSTER FROM LAST TIME...
HAVE YOU SEEN THEM?
I HAVE.
OH— I SEE.
WHAT WERE THEY LIKE... I MEAN... WERE THEY... DEPRESSING...?
NEXT IT'S YOUR TURN TO TELL!
IT'S A SECRET. ♥
HUH?
IT'S YOUR LOVE STORY.
SPIT
...AND HE PROBABLY CONTINUES TO SUFFER...
...EVEN NOW.
BUZZ

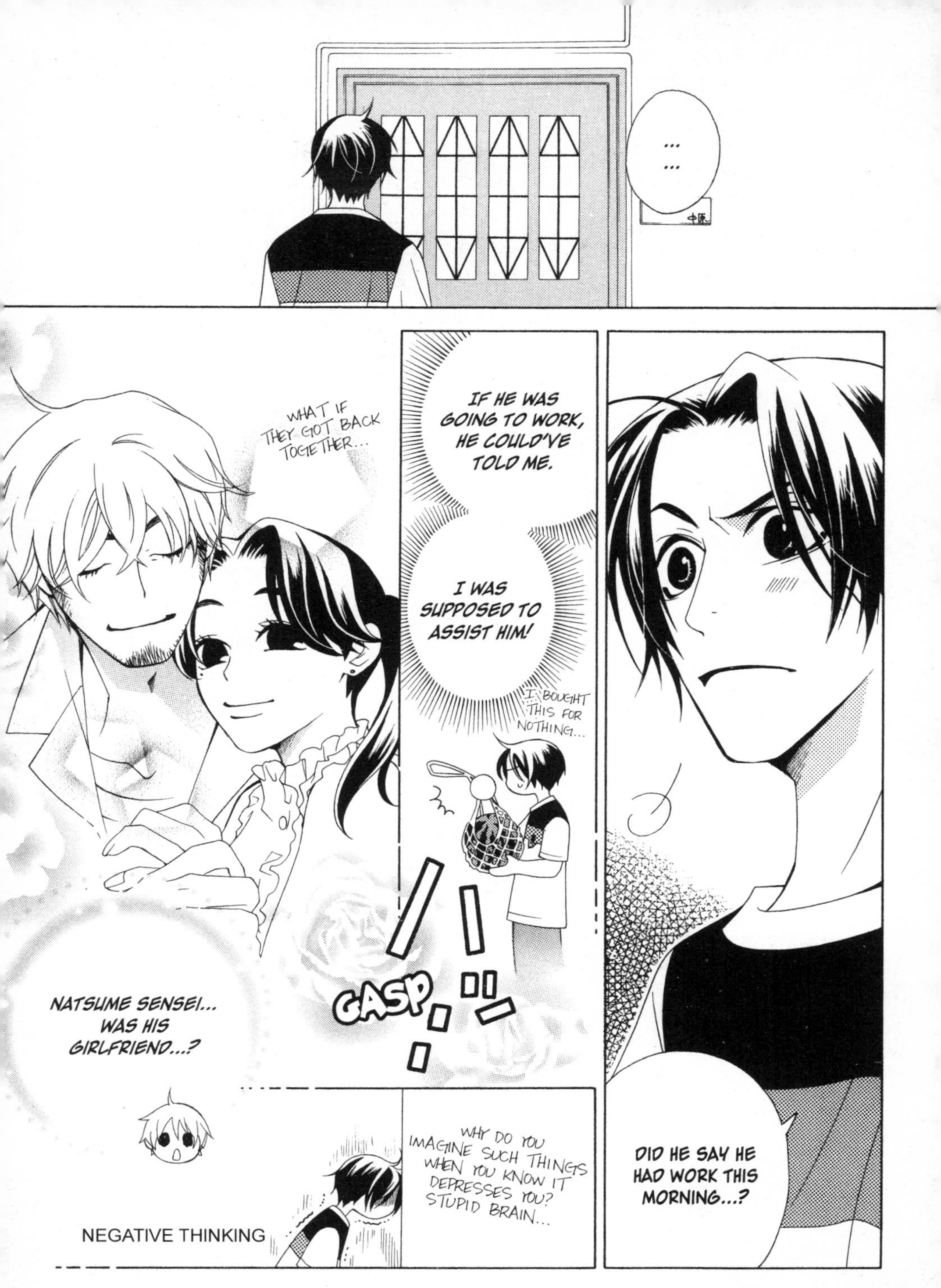
...
...
DID HE SAY HE HAD WORK THIS MORNING...?
IF HE WAS GOING TO WORK, HE COULD'VE TOLD ME.
I WAS SUPPOSED TO ASSIST HIM!
...I BOUGHT THIS FOR NOTHING...
WHAT IF THEY GOT BACK TOGETHER...
GASP
NATSUME SENSEI... WAS HIS GIRLFRIEND...?
WHY DO YOU IMAGINE SUCH THINGS WHEN YOU KNOW IT DEPRESSES YOU? STUPID BRAIN...
NEGATIVE THINKING

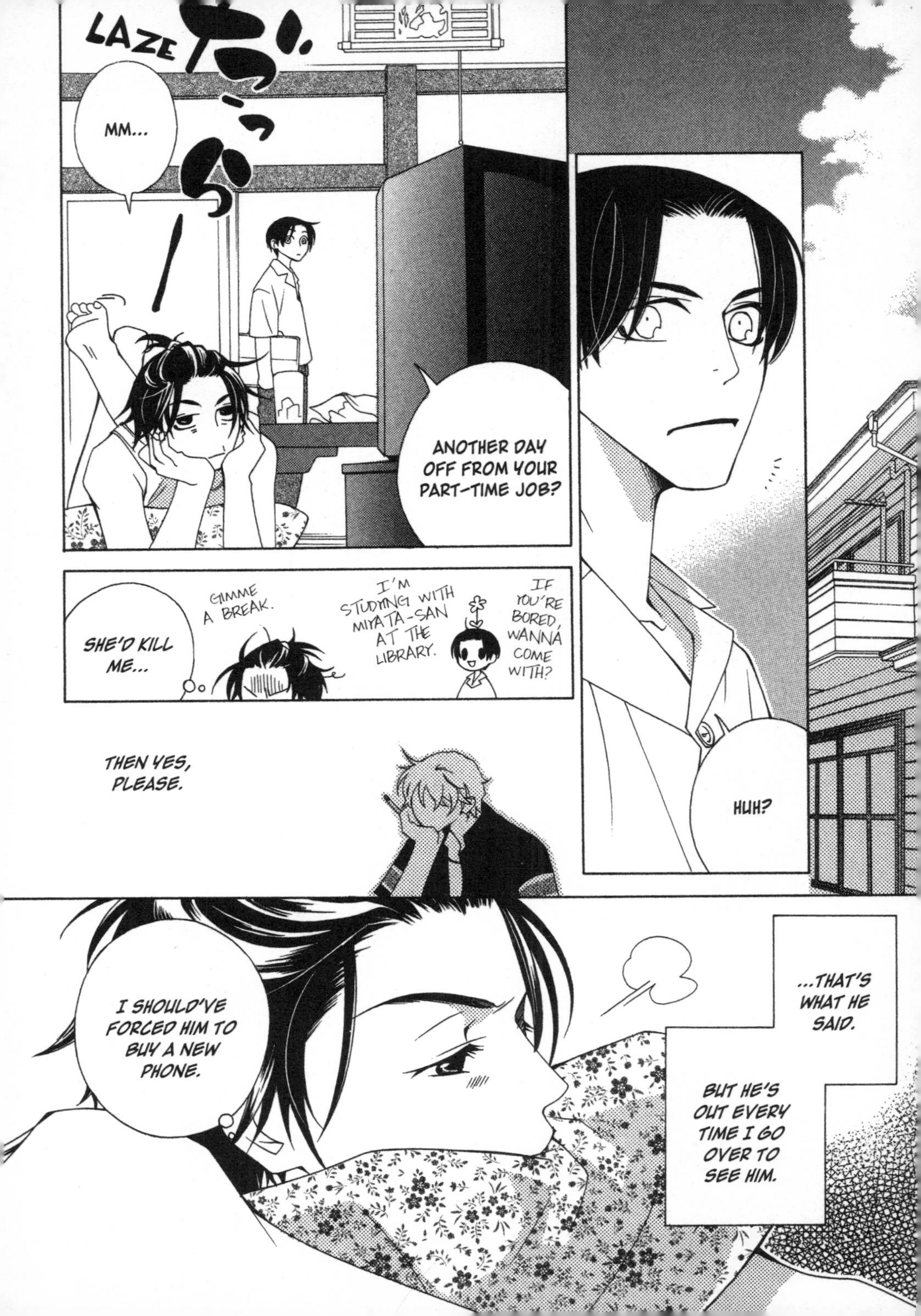
LAZE
MM...
ANOTHER DAY OFF FROM YOUR PART-TIME JOB?
I'M STUDYING WITH MIYATA-SAN AT THE LIBRARY.
IF YOU'RE BORED, WANNA COME WITH?
GIMME A BREAK.
SHE'D KILL ME...
THEN YES, PLEASE.
HUH?
...THAT'S WHAT HE SAID.
BUT HE'S OUT EVERY TIME I GO OVER TO SEE HIM.
I SHOULD'VE FORCED HIM TO BUY A NEW PHONE.

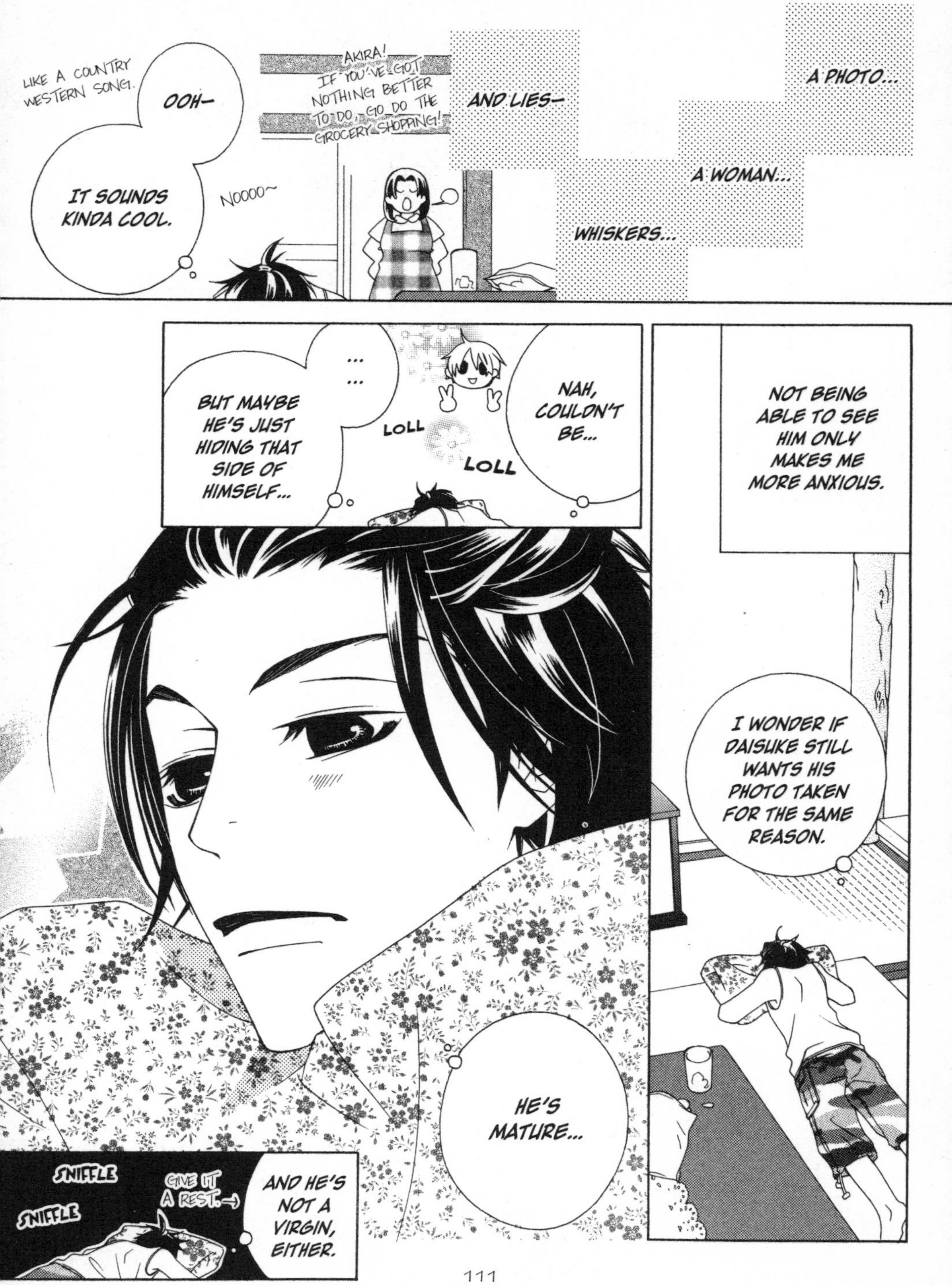
A PHOTO...
A WOMAN...
WHISKERS...
AND LIES—
AKIRA! IF YOU'VE GOT NOTHING BETTER TO DO, GO DO THE GROCERY SHOPPING!
NOOOO~
OOH—
LIKE A COUNTRY WESTERN SONG.
IT SOUNDS KINDA COOL.
NOT BEING ABLE TO SEE HIM ONLY MAKES ME MORE ANXIOUS.
I WONDER IF DAISUKE STILL WANTS HIS PHOTO TAKEN FOR THE SAME REASON.
NAH, COULDN'T BE...
LOLL
LOLL
... ...
BUT MAYBE HE'S JUST HIDING THAT SIDE OF HIMSELF...
HE'S MATURE...
AND HE'S NOT A VIRGIN, EITHER.
GIVE IT A REST.
SNIFFLE
SNIFFLE

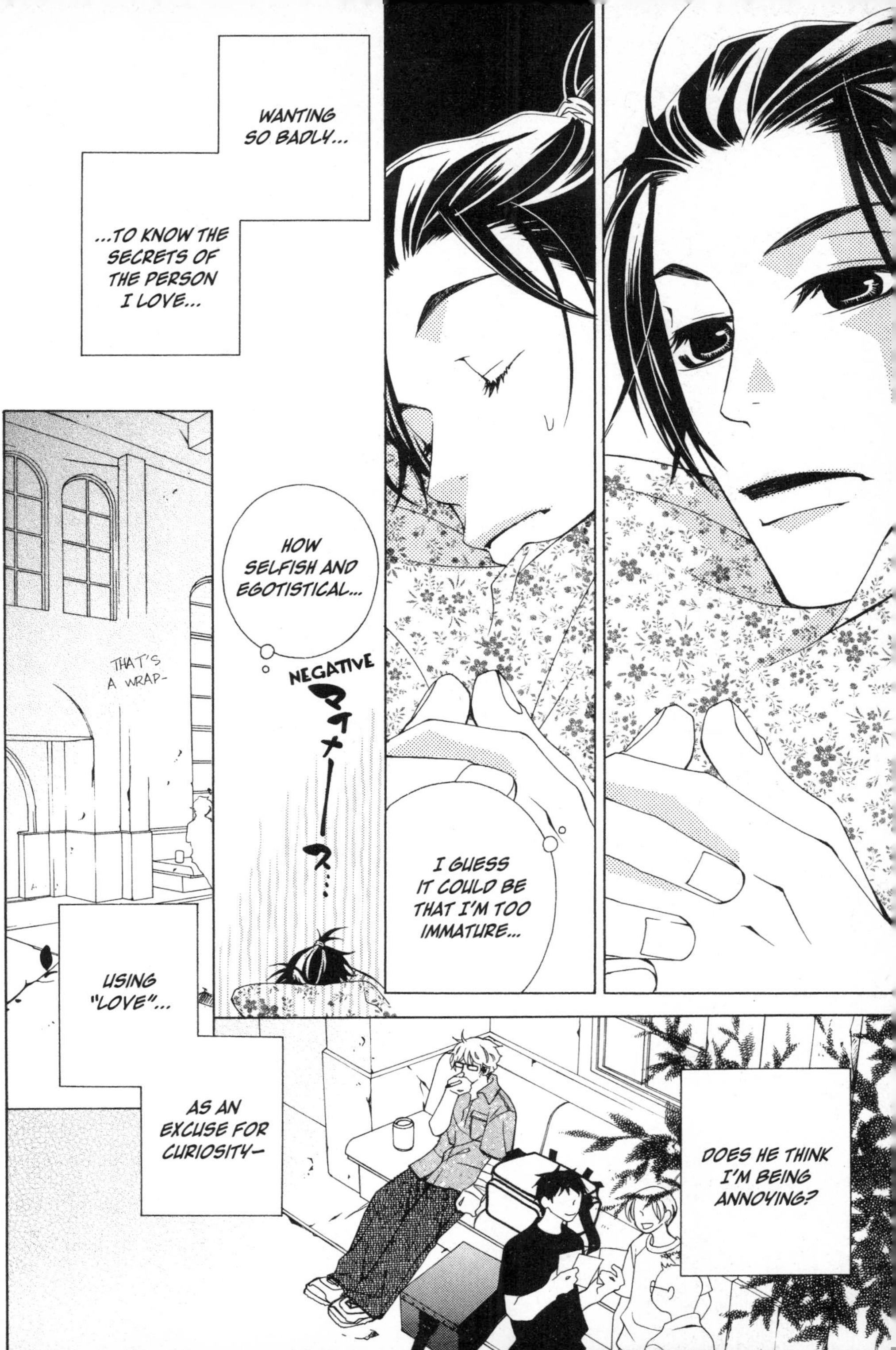
I GUESS IT COULD BE THAT I'M TOO IMMATURE...
WANTING SO BADLY...
...TO KNOW THE SECRETS OF THE PERSON I LOVE...
HOW SELFISH AND EGOTISTICAL...
NEGATIVE
マイナーース...
THAT'S A WRAP-
DOES HE THINK I'M BEING ANNOYING?
USING "LOVE"...
AS AN EXCUSE FOR CURIOSITY-

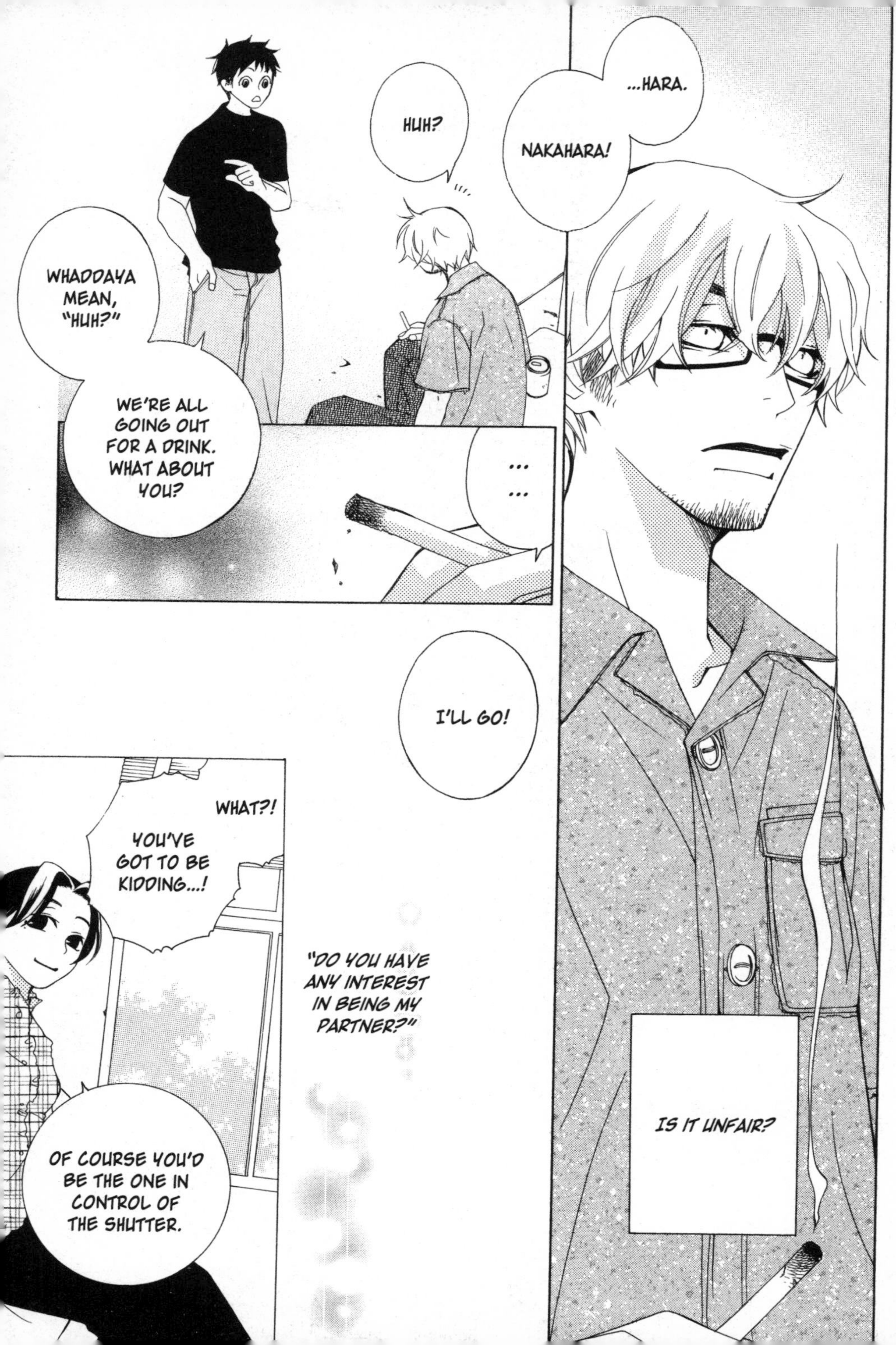
...HARA.
NAKAHARA!
IS IT UNFAIR?
HUH?
WHADDAYA MEAN, "HUH?"
WE'RE ALL GOING OUT FOR A DRINK. WHAT ABOUT YOU?
... ...
I'LL GO!
WHAT?!
YOU'VE GOT TO BE KIDDING...!
"DO YOU HAVE ANY INTEREST IN BEING MY PARTNER?"
OF COURSE YOU'D BE THE ONE IN CONTROL OF THE SHUTTER.

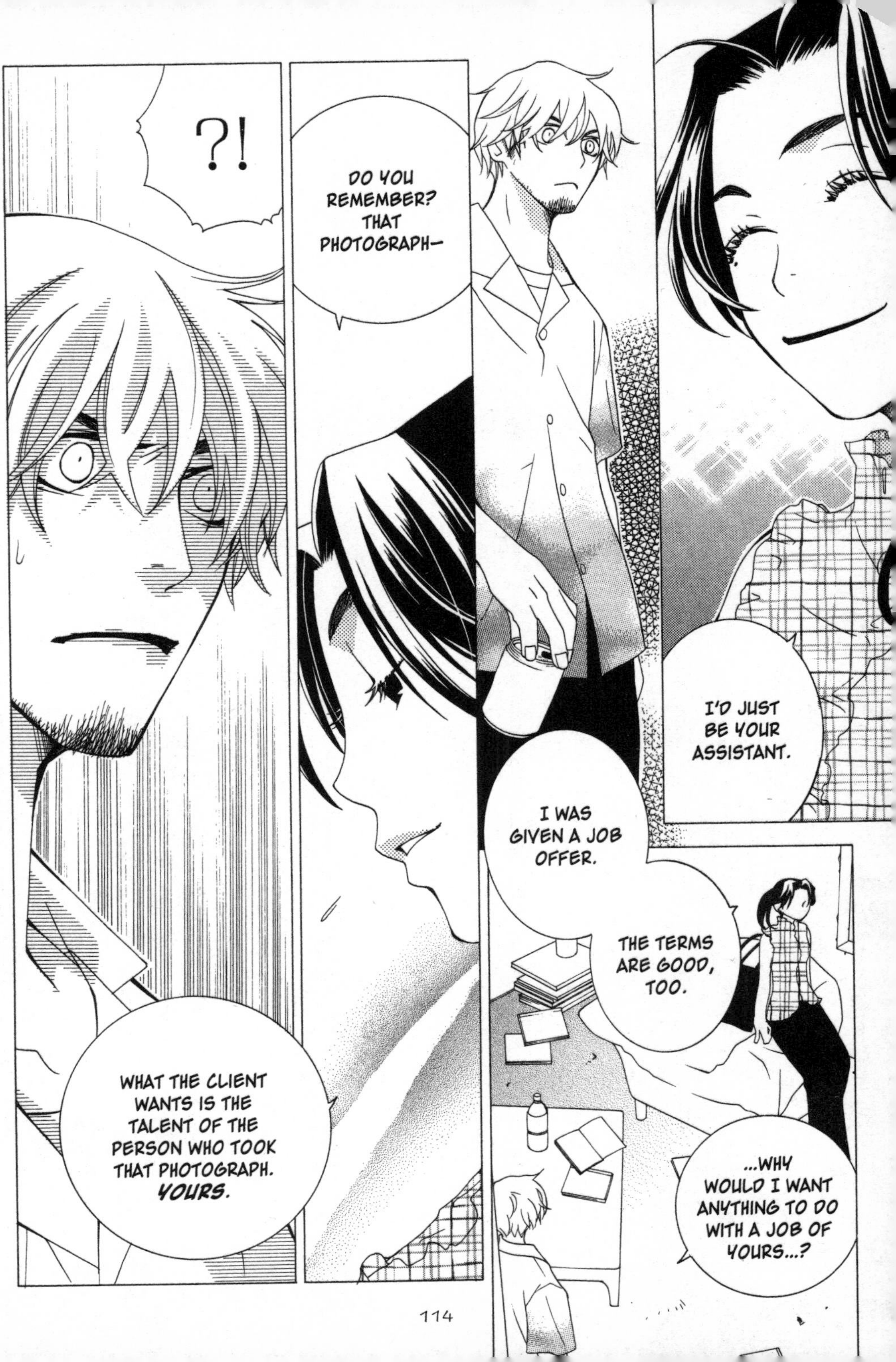
I WAS GIVEN A JOB OFFER.
THE TERMS ARE GOOD, TOO.
...WHY WOULD I WANT ANYTHING TO DO WITH A JOB OF YOURS...?
I'D JUST BE YOUR ASSISTANT.
DO YOU REMEMBER? THAT PHOTOGRAPH—
WHAT THE CLIENT WANTS IS THE TALENT OF THE PERSON WHO TOOK THAT PHOTOGRAPH. *YOURS*.
?!

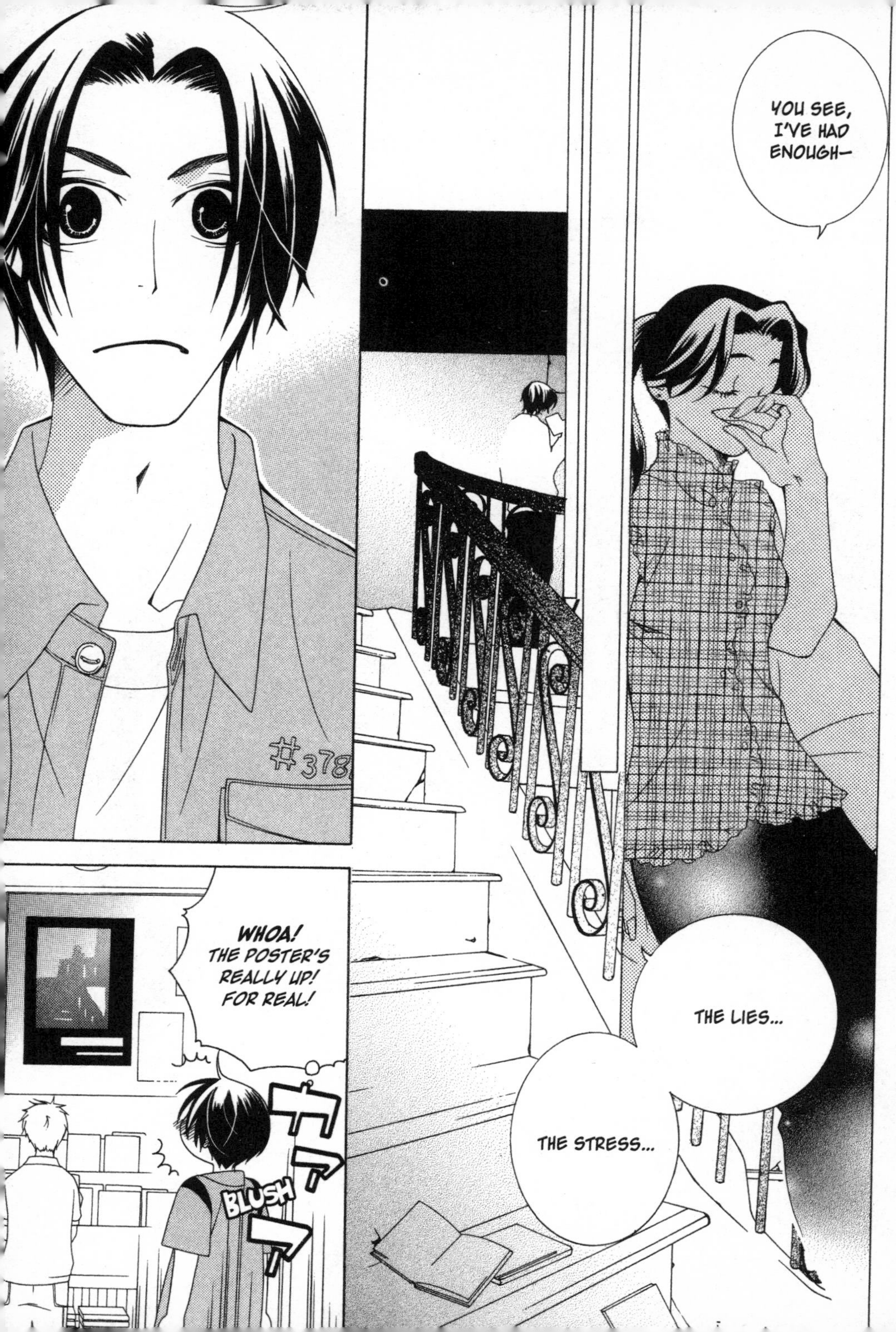
YOU SEE, I'VE HAD ENOUGH—
THE LIES...
THE STRESS...
WHOA! THE POSTER'S REALLY UP! FOR REAL!
BLUSH

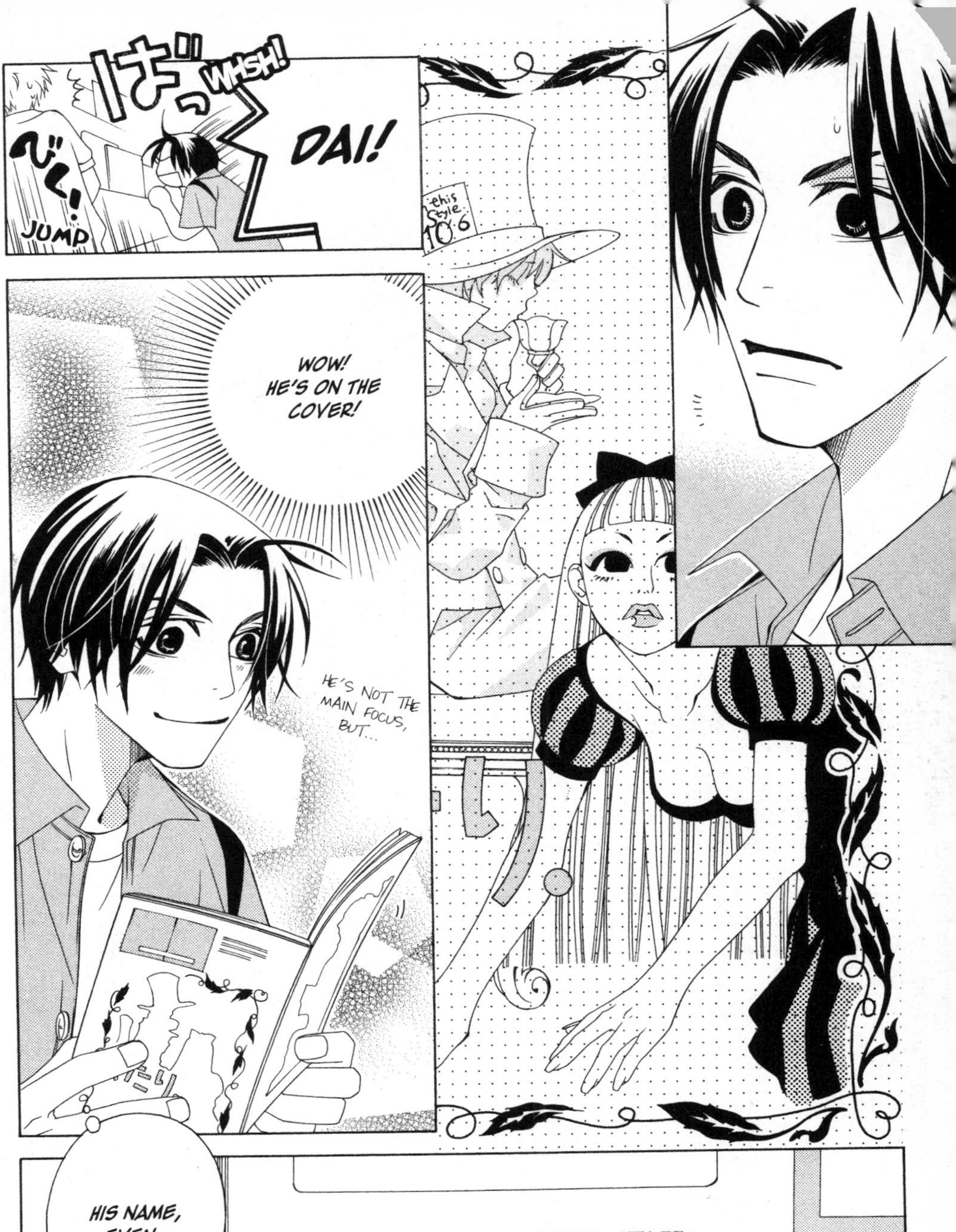
はっ WHSH!
DAI!
びくっ! JUMP
WOW! HE'S ON THE COVER!
HE'S NOT THE MAIN FOCUS, BUT...
HIS NAME, EVEN...
COVER STAFF
PHOTOGRAPHER/ MARIKO NATSUME
MODEL/ KOTOKO, DAISUKE

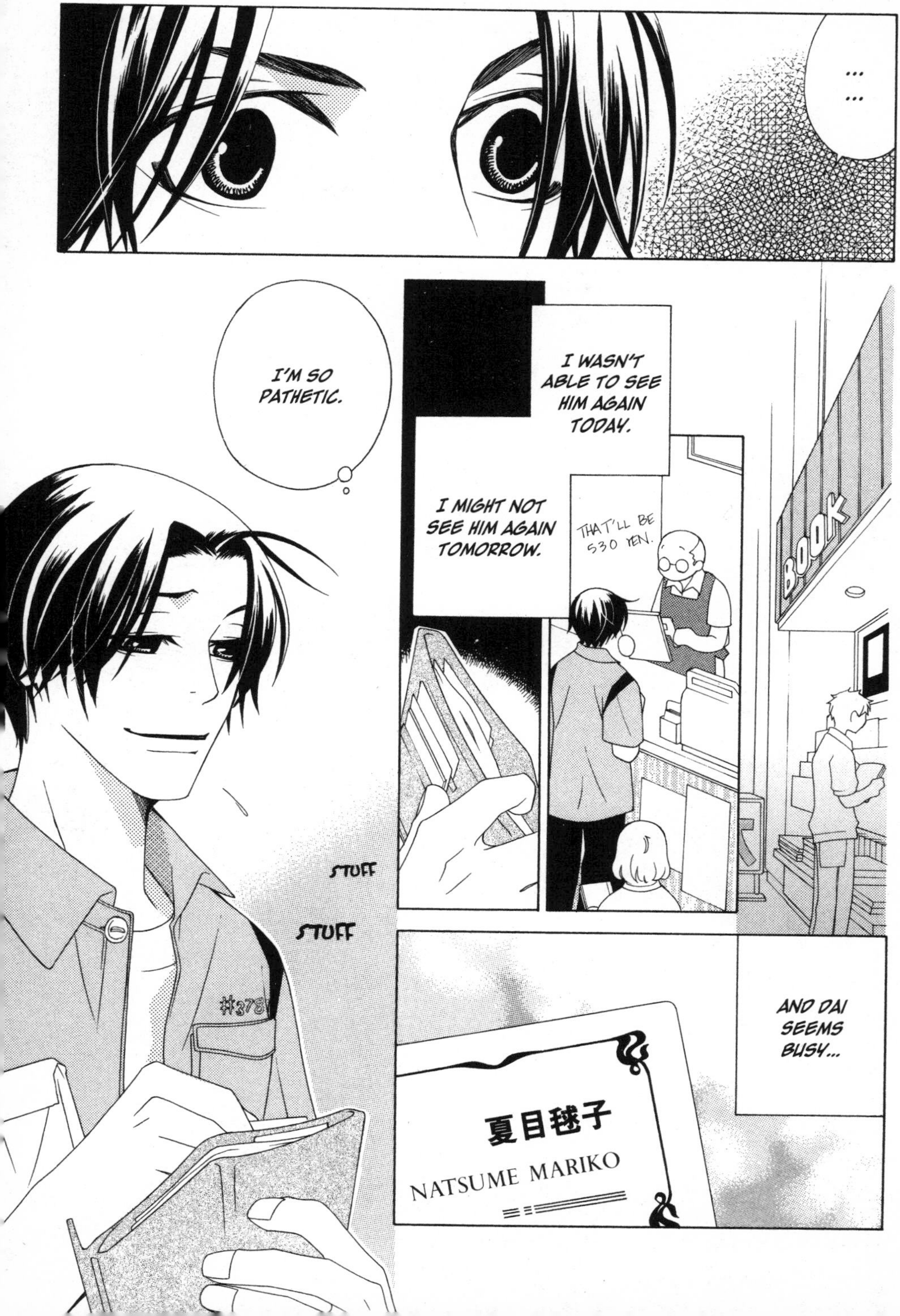

……
I WASN'T ABLE TO SEE HIM AGAIN TODAY.
I MIGHT NOT SEE HIM AGAIN TOMORROW.
THAT'LL BE 530 YEN.
AND DAI SEEMS BUSY...
夏目毬子
NATSUME MARIKO
I'M SO PATHETIC.
STUFF
STUFF

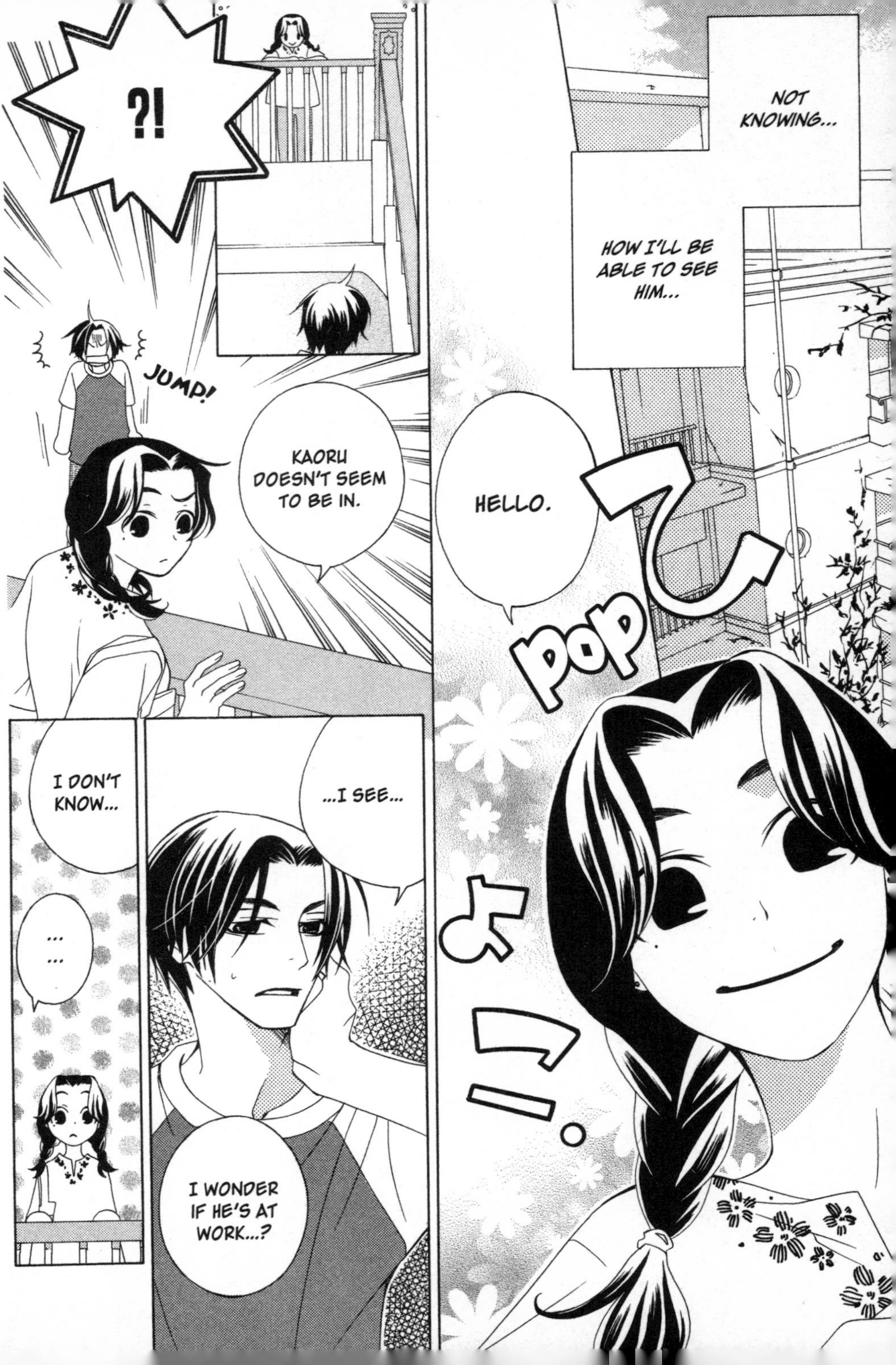
NOT KNOWING...
HOW I'LL BE ABLE TO SEE HIM...
HELLO.
POP
ひょこーっ
?!
JUMP!
KAORU DOESN'T SEEM TO BE IN.
...I SEE...
I WONDER IF HE'S AT WORK...?
I DON'T KNOW...
...
...

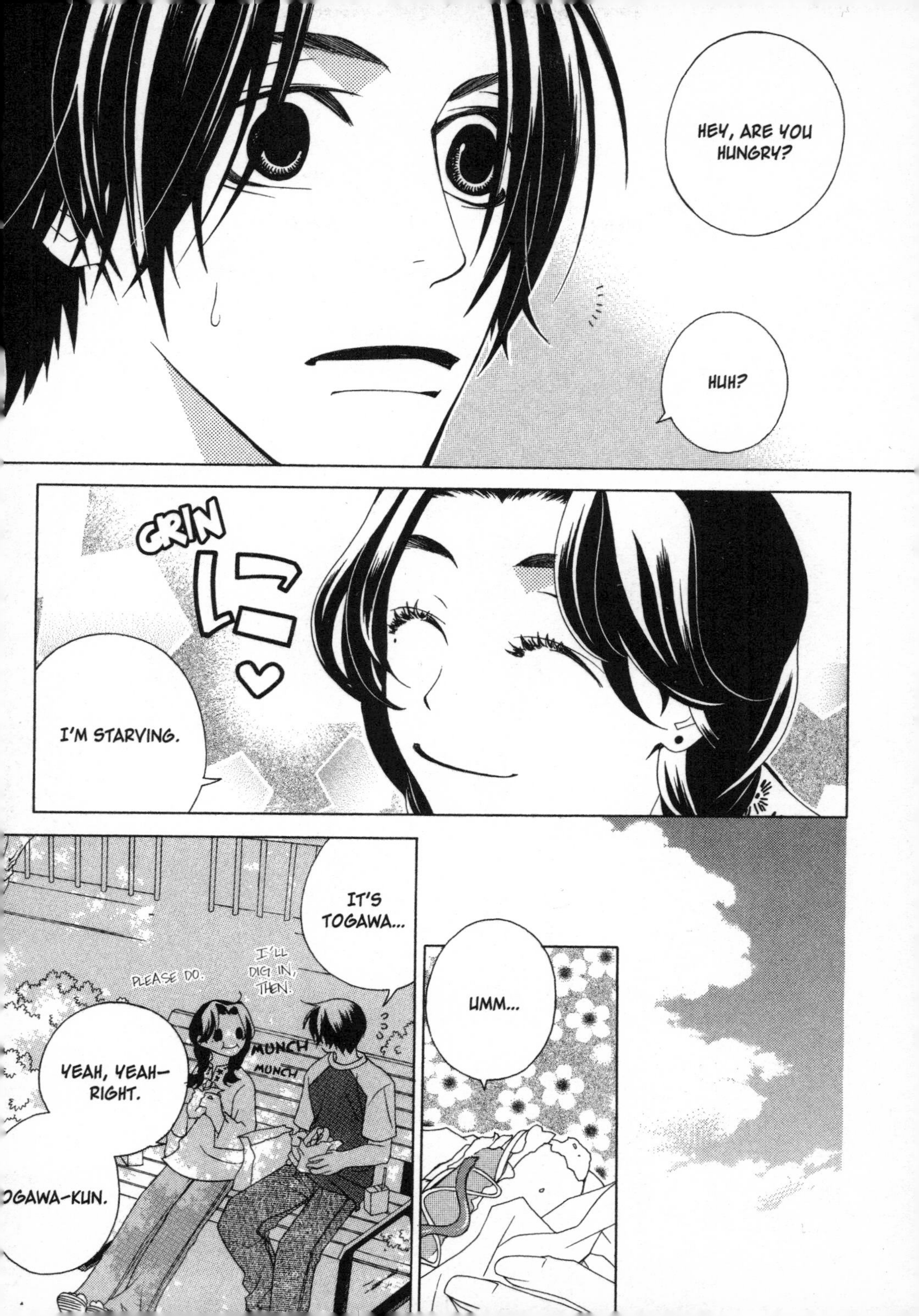
HEY, ARE YOU HUNGRY?
HUH?
GRIN
I'M STARVING.
UMM...
IT'S TOGAWA...
I'LL DIG IN, THEN.
PLEASE DO.
MUNCH
MUNCH
YEAH, YEAH- RIGHT.
OGAWA-KUN.

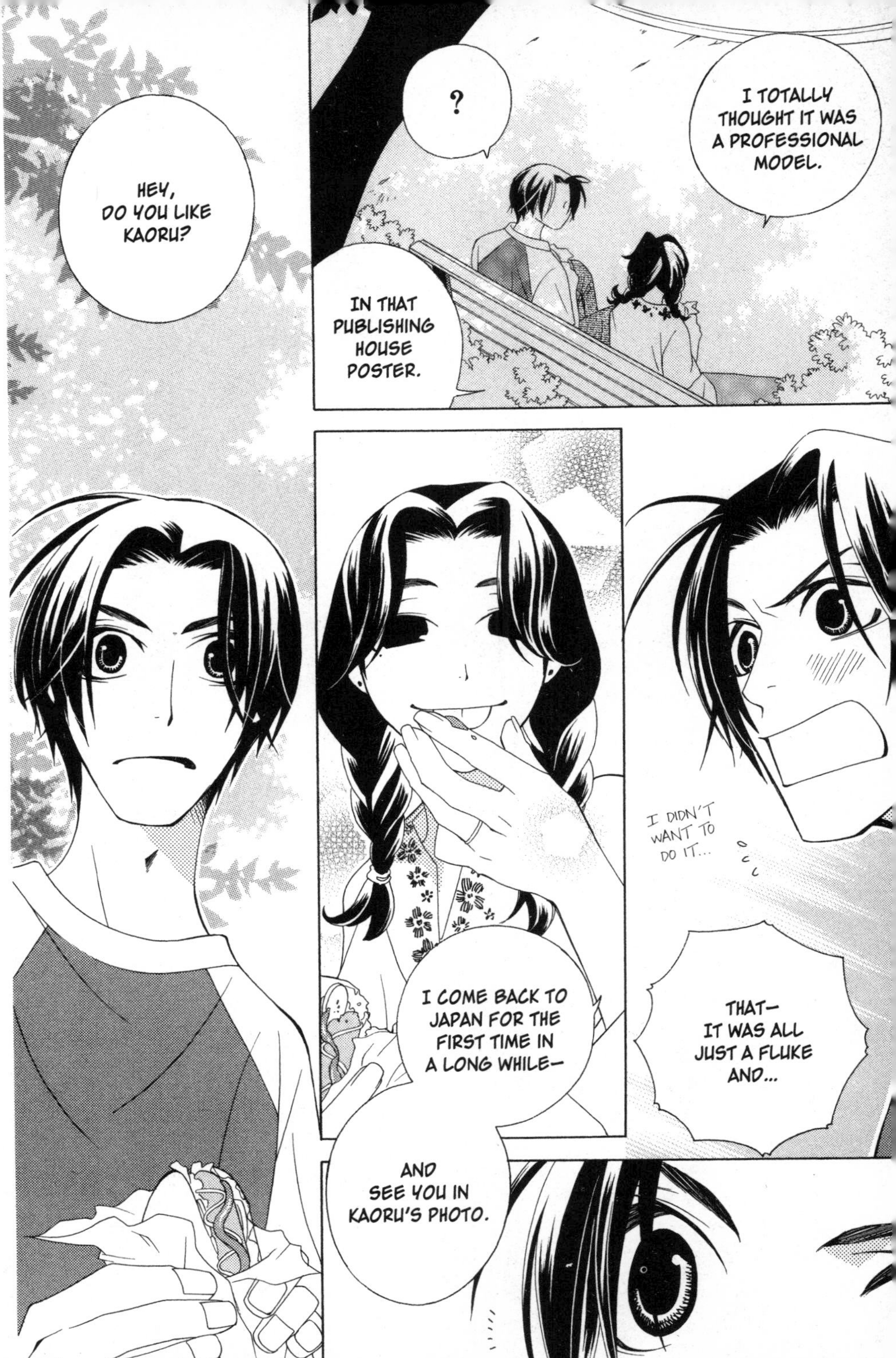
I TOTALLY THOUGHT IT WAS A PROFESSIONAL MODEL.
?
IN THAT PUBLISHING HOUSE POSTER.
THAT— IT WAS ALL JUST A FLUKE AND...
I DIDN'T WANT TO DO IT...
I COME BACK TO JAPAN FOR THE FIRST TIME IN A LONG WHILE—
AND SEE YOU IN KAORU'S PHOTO.
HEY, DO YOU LIKE KAORU?

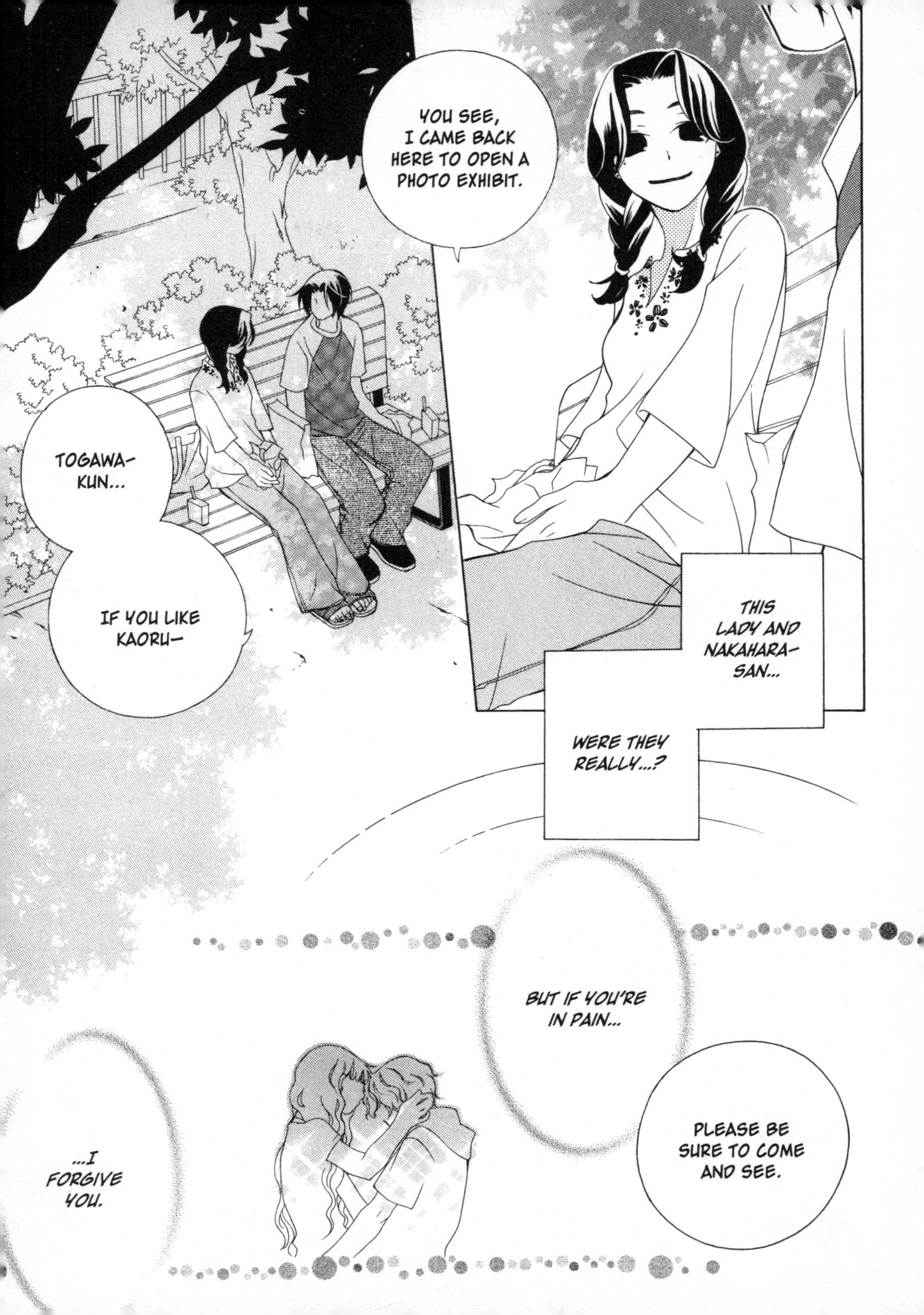
YOU SEE, I CAME BACK HERE TO OPEN A PHOTO EXHIBIT.
TOGAWA-KUN...
IF YOU LIKE KAORU-
THIS LADY AND NAKAHARA-SAN...
WERE THEY REALLY...?
BUT IF YOU'RE IN PAIN...
PLEASE BE SURE TO COME AND SEE.
...I FORGIVE YOU.

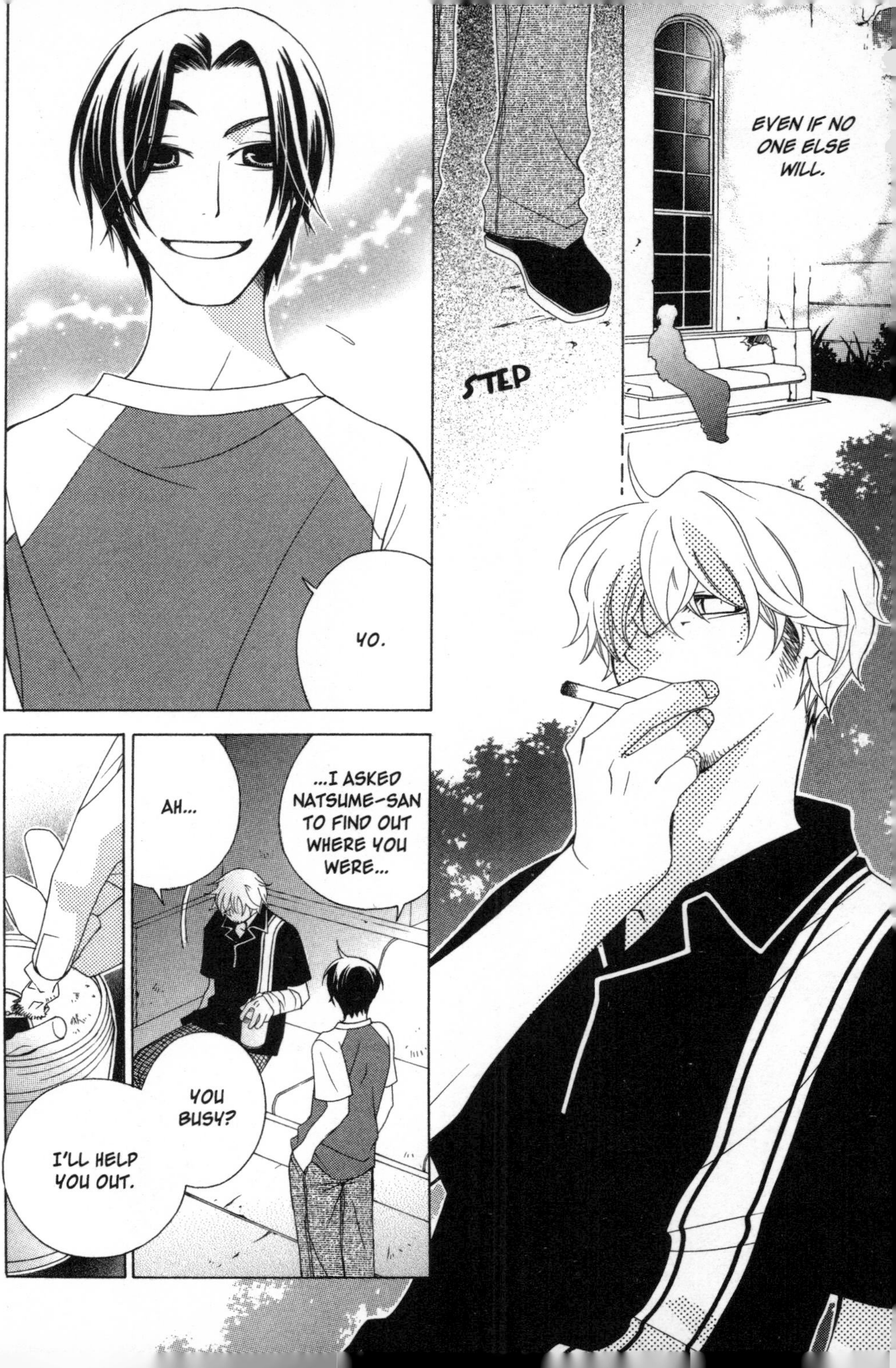
EVEN IF NO ONE ELSE WILL.
STEP
YO.
...I ASKED NATSUME-SAN TO FIND OUT WHERE YOU WERE...
AH...
YOU BUSY?
I'LL HELP YOU OUT.

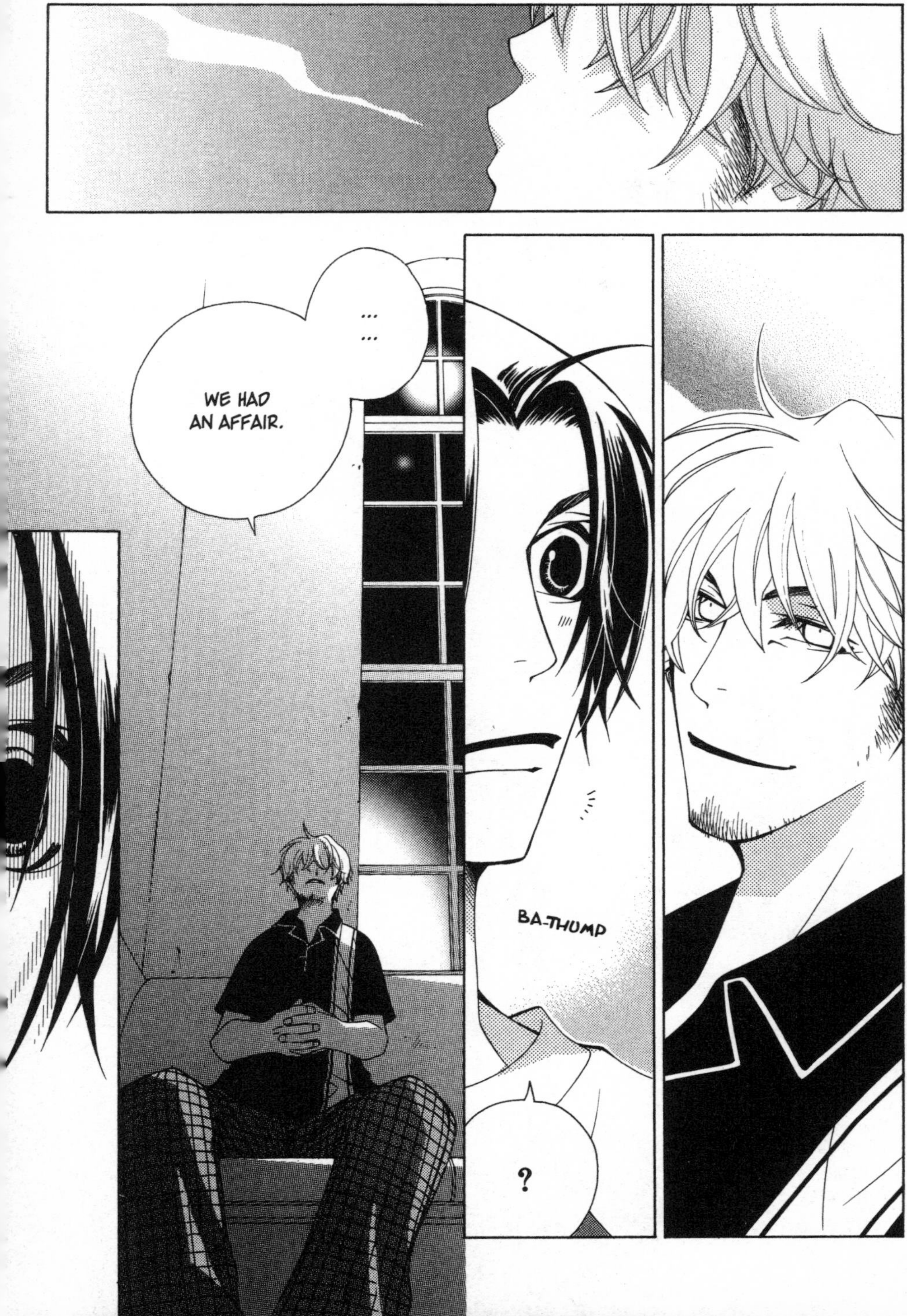
BA-THUMP
?
...
...
WE HAD AN AFFAIR.

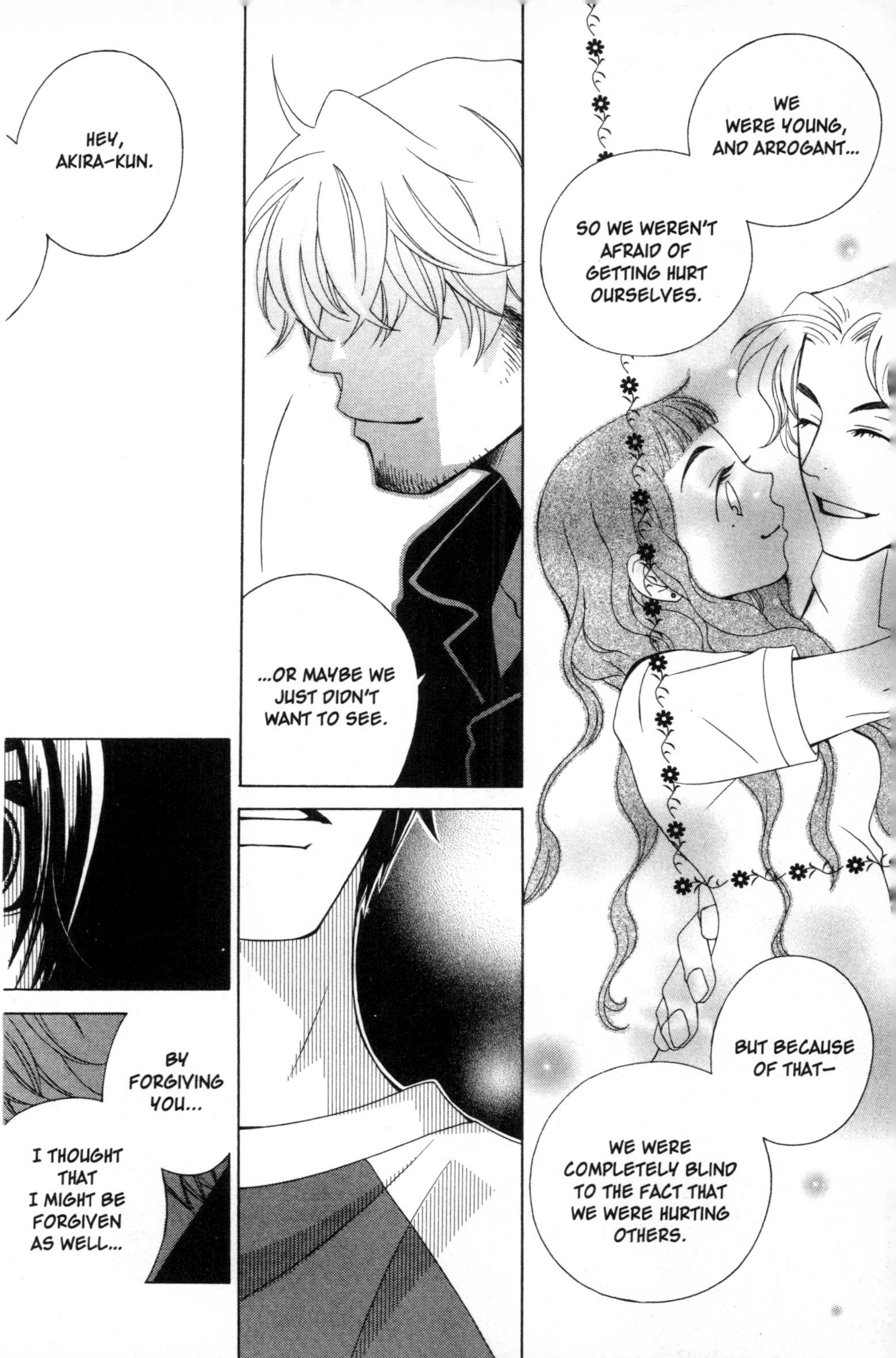
WE WERE YOUNG, AND ARROGANT...
SO WE WEREN'T AFRAID OF GETTING HURT OURSELVES.
BUT BECAUSE OF THAT—
WE WERE COMPLETELY BLIND TO THE FACT THAT WE WERE HURTING OTHERS.
...OR MAYBE WE JUST DIDN'T WANT TO SEE.
HEY, AKIRA-KUN.
BY FORGIVING YOU...
I THOUGHT THAT I MIGHT BE FORGIVEN AS WELL...

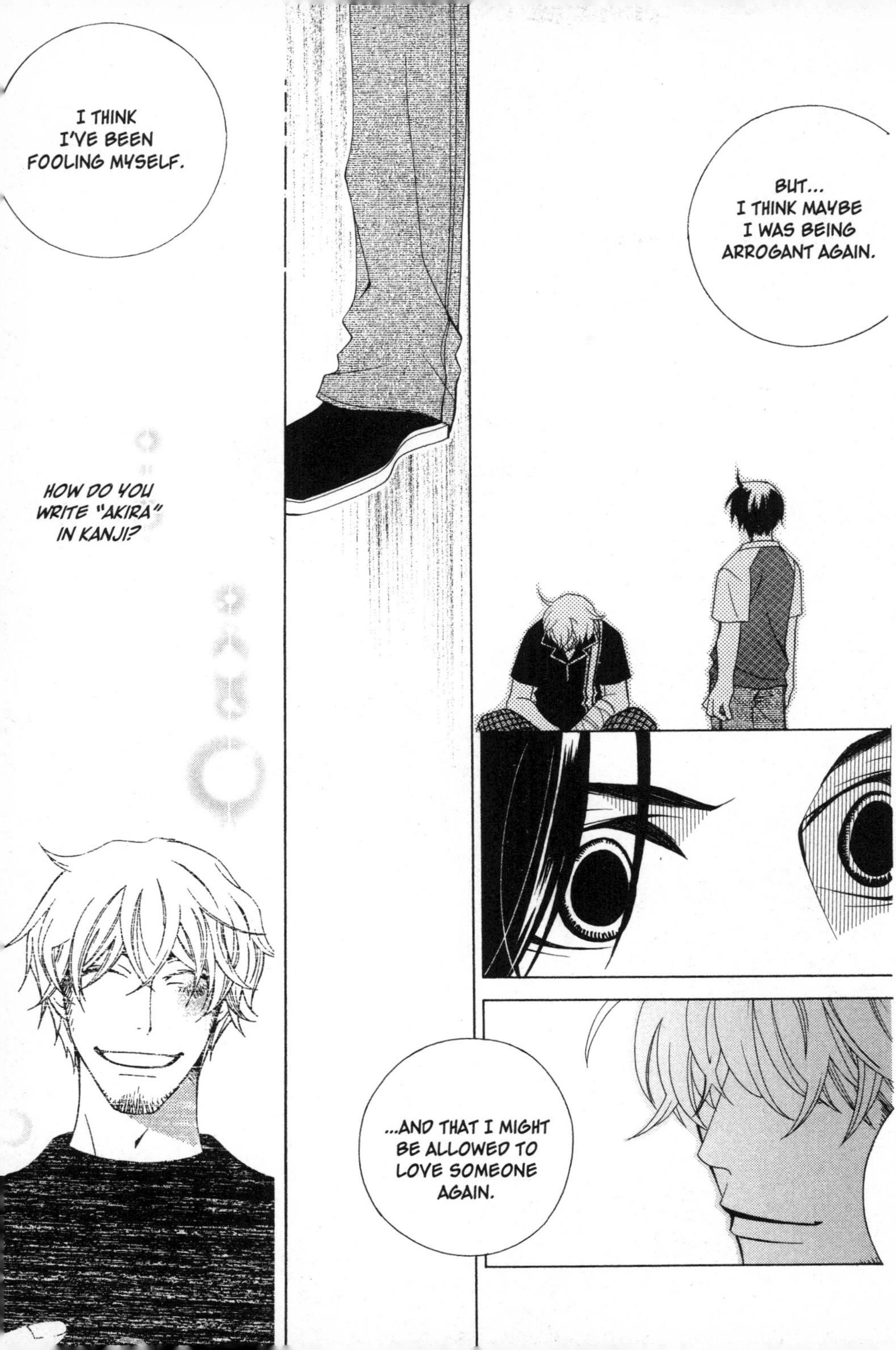
BUT... I THINK MAYBE I WAS BEING ARROGANT AGAIN.
...AND THAT I MIGHT BE ALLOWED TO LOVE SOMEONE AGAIN.
I THINK I'VE BEEN FOOLING MYSELF.
HOW DO YOU WRITE "AKIRA" IN KANJI?

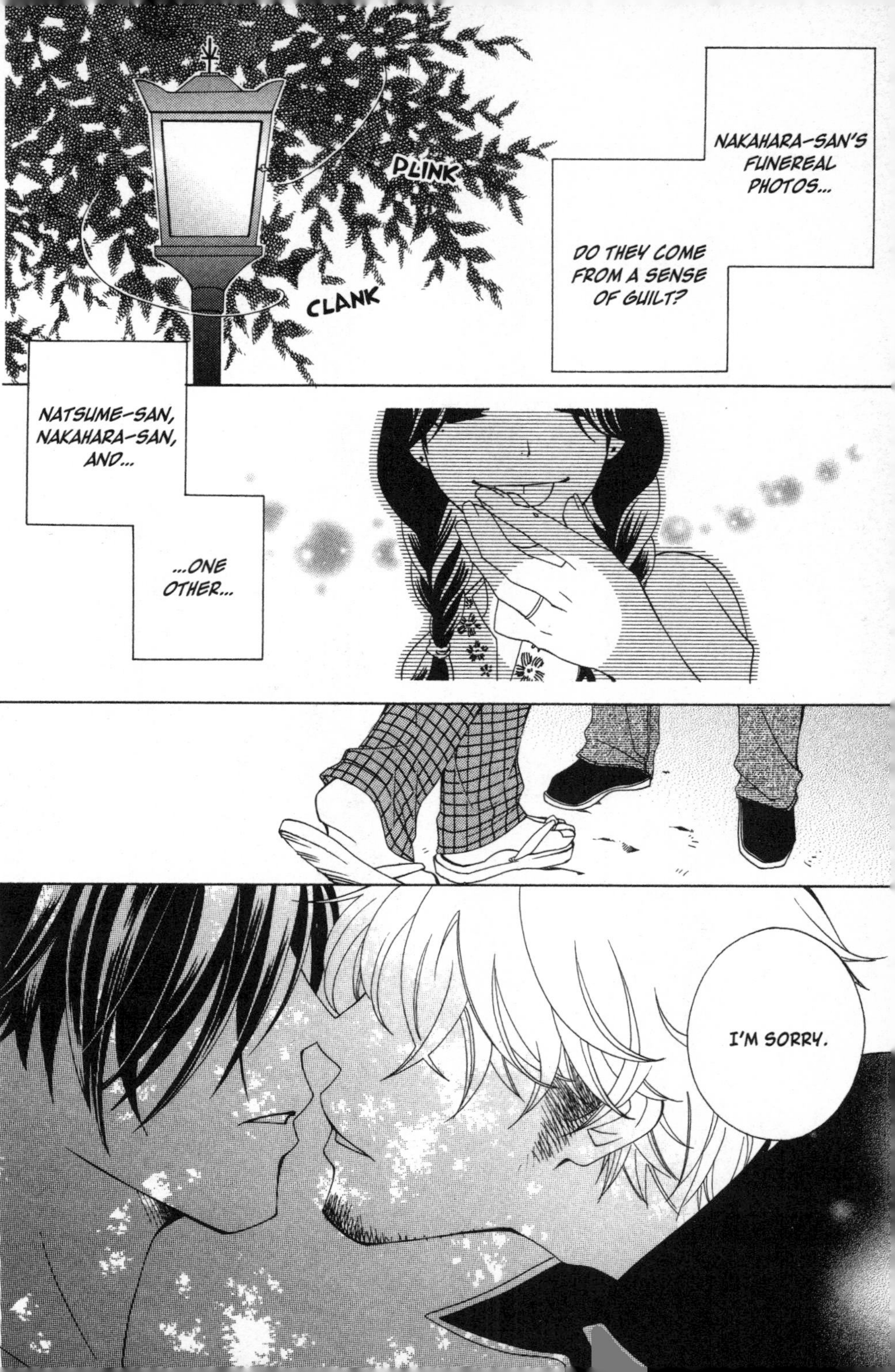
NAKAHARA-SAN'S FUNEREAL PHOTOS...
DO THEY COME FROM A SENSE OF GUILT?
PLINK
CLANK
NATSUME-SAN, NAKAHARA-SAN, AND...
...ONE OTHER...
I'M SORRY.

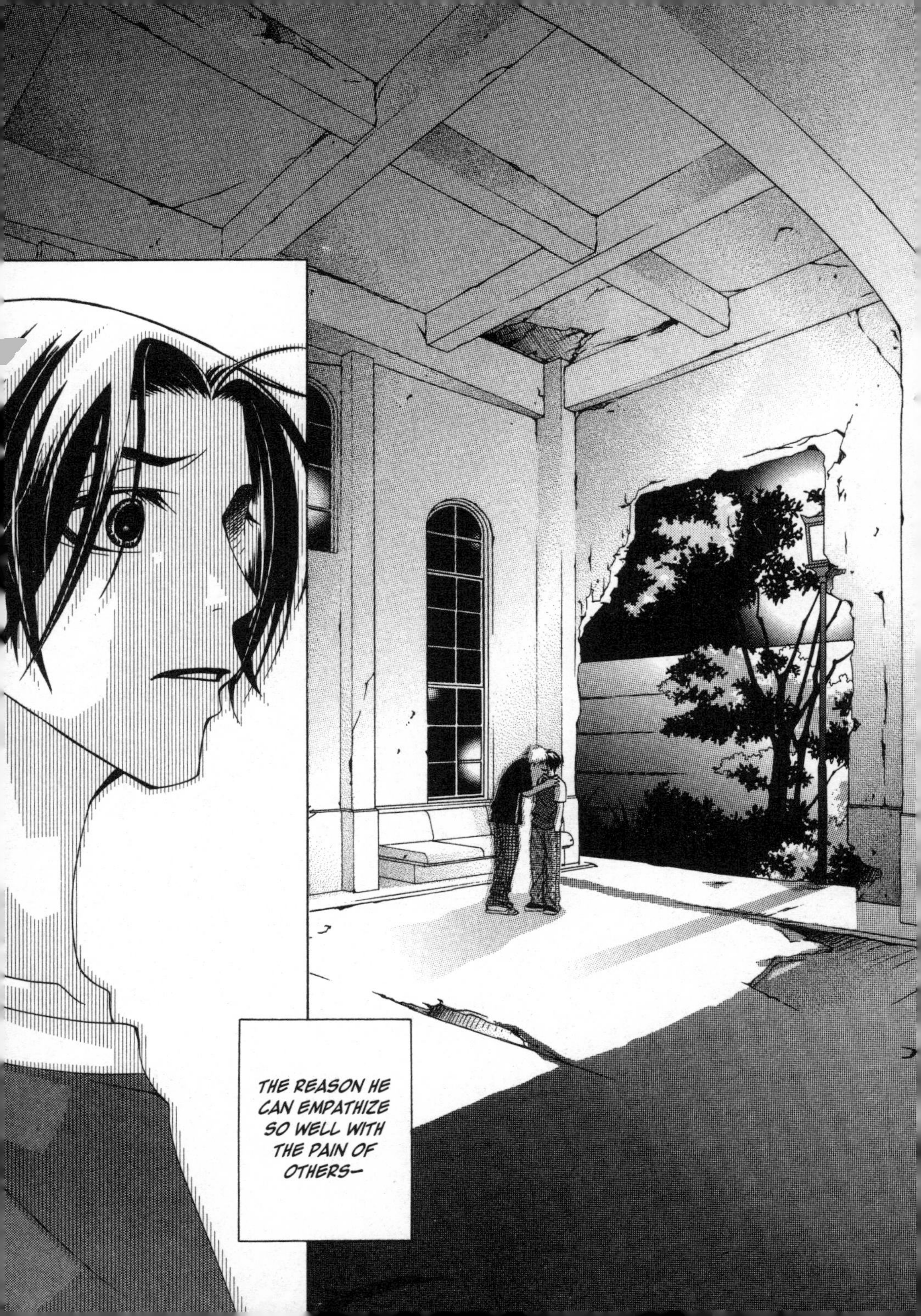
THE REASON HE CAN EMPATHIZE SO WELL WITH THE PAIN OF OTHERS—

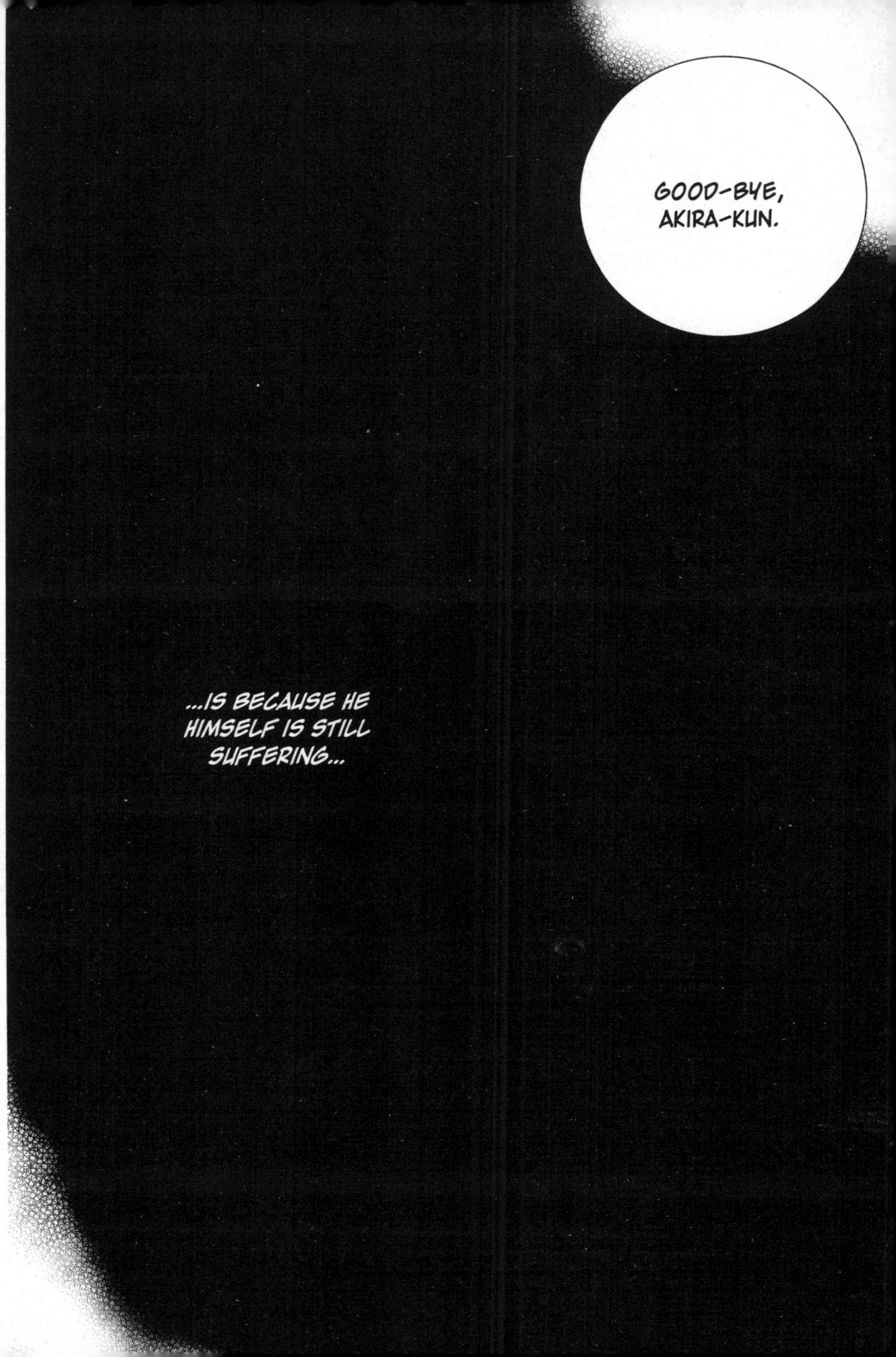
GOOD-BYE, AKIRA-KUN.
...IS BECAUSE HE HIMSELF IS STILL SUFFERING...

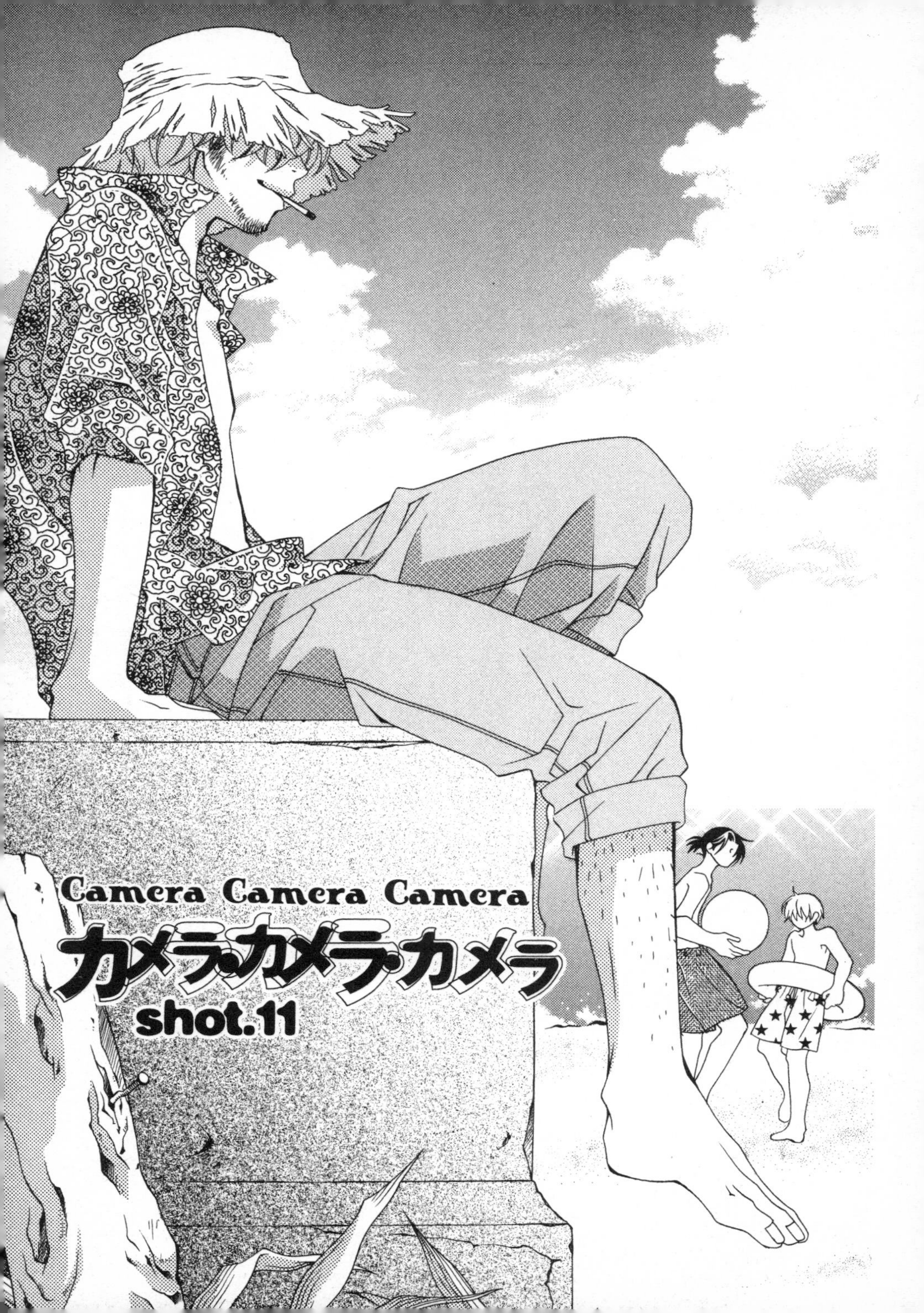
Camera Camera Camera
カメラ・カメラ・カメラ
shot.11

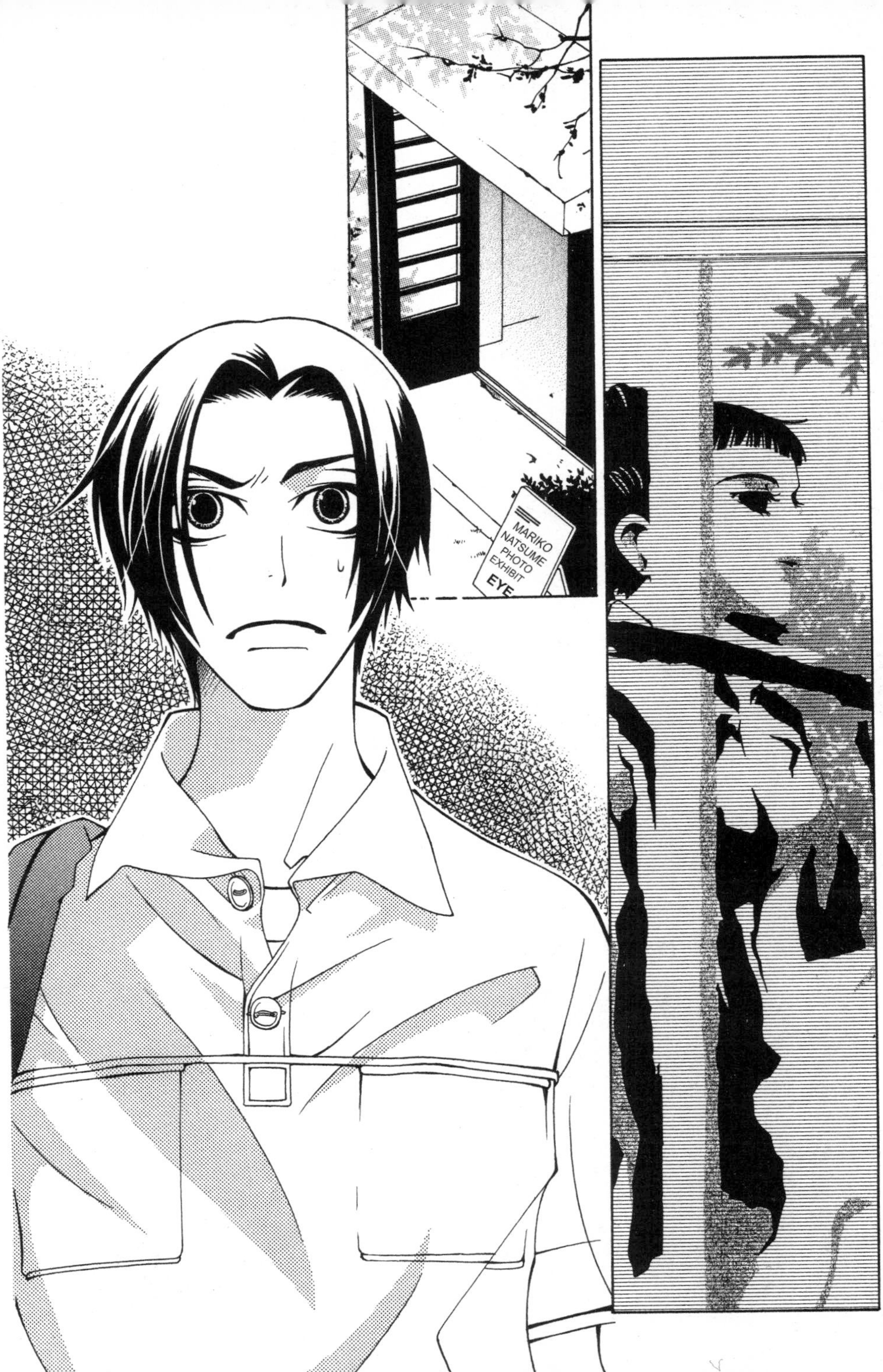
MARIKO NATSUME PHOTO EXHIBIT EYE

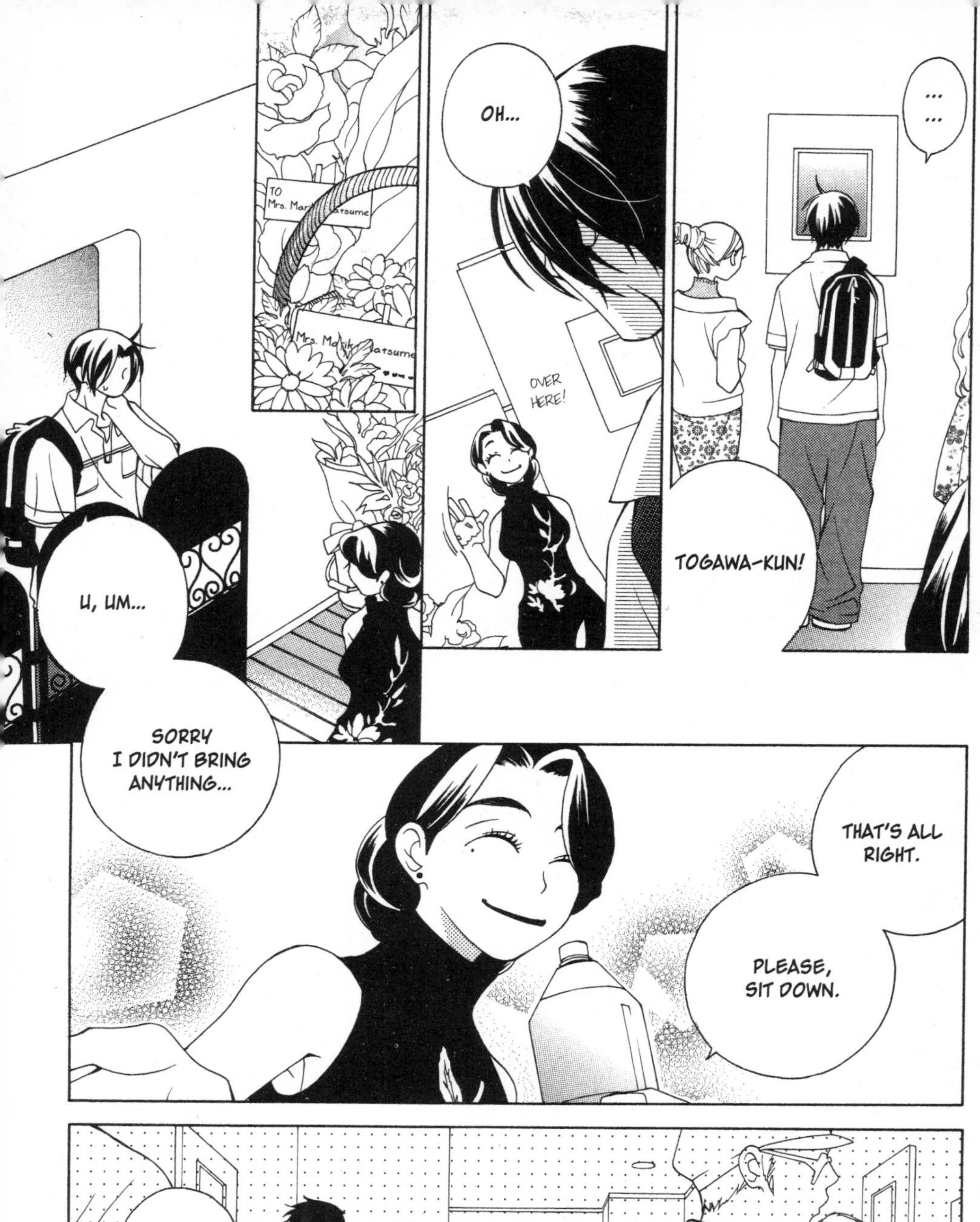

...
...
TOGAWA-KUN!
OH...
OVER HERE!
U, UM...
SORRY I DIDN'T BRING ANYTHING...
THAT'S ALL RIGHT.
PLEASE, SIT DOWN.
...OKAY...

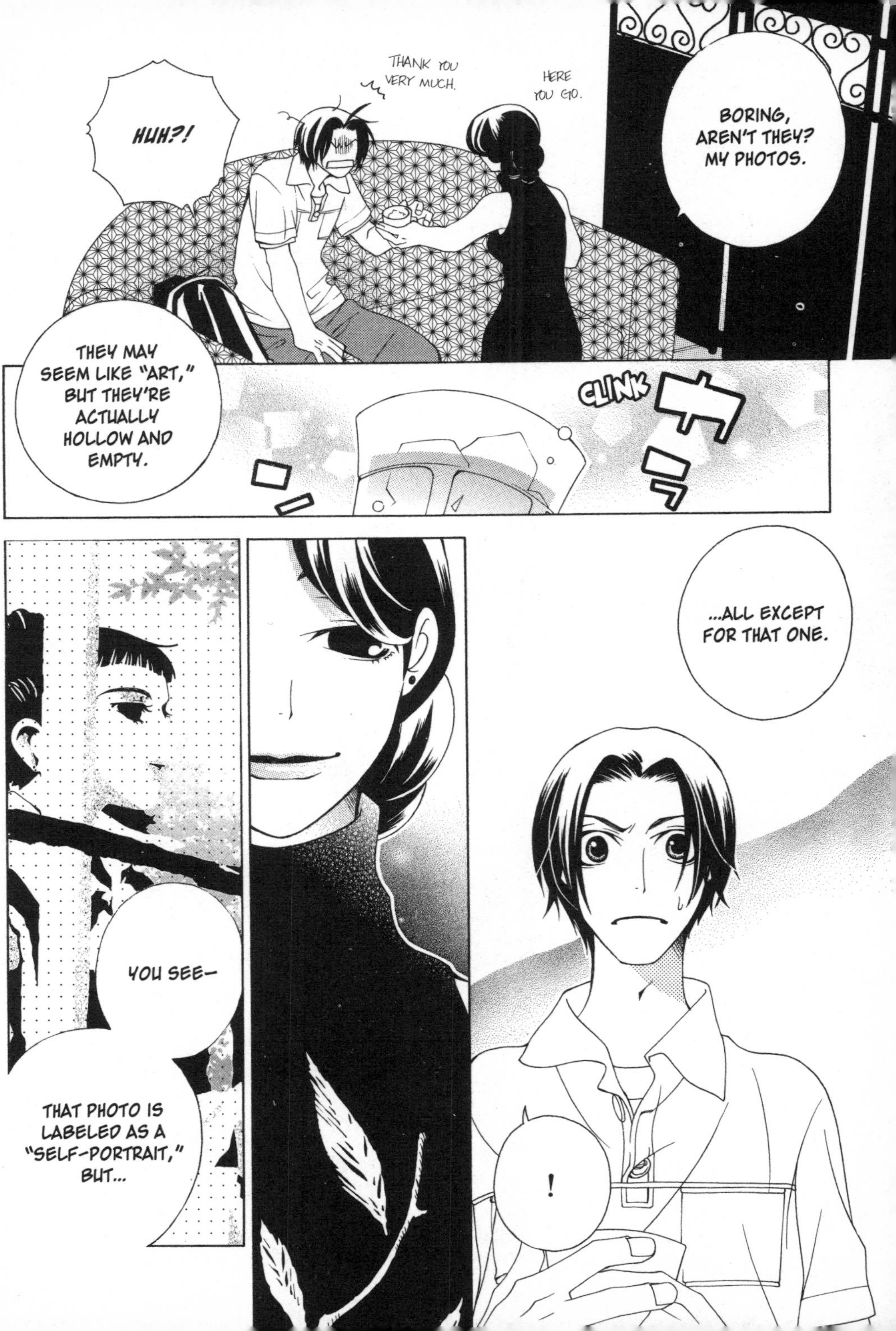
BORING, AREN'T THEY? MY PHOTOS.
HERE YOU GO.
THANK YOU VERY MUCH.
HUH?!
CLINK
THEY MAY SEEM LIKE "ART," BUT THEY'RE ACTUALLY HOLLOW AND EMPTY.
...ALL EXCEPT FOR THAT ONE.
!
YOU SEE—
THAT PHOTO IS LABELED AS A "SELF-PORTRAIT," BUT...

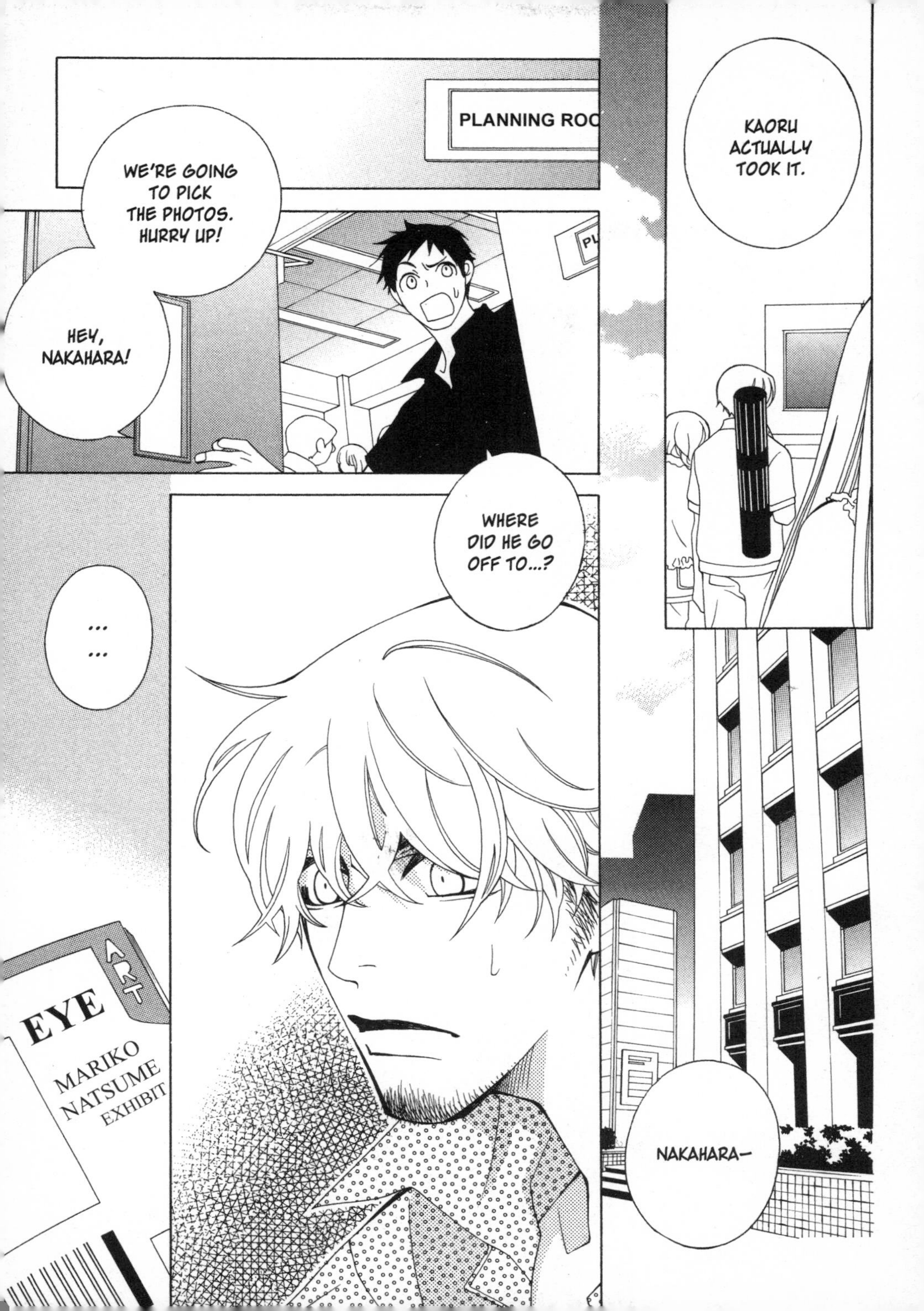
KAORU ACTUALLY TOOK IT.
NAKAHARA—
PLANNING RO
WE'RE GOING TO PICK THE PHOTOS. HURRY UP!
HEY, NAKAHARA!
WHERE DID HE GO OFF TO...?
... ...
ART
EYE
MARIKO NATSUME EXHIBIT

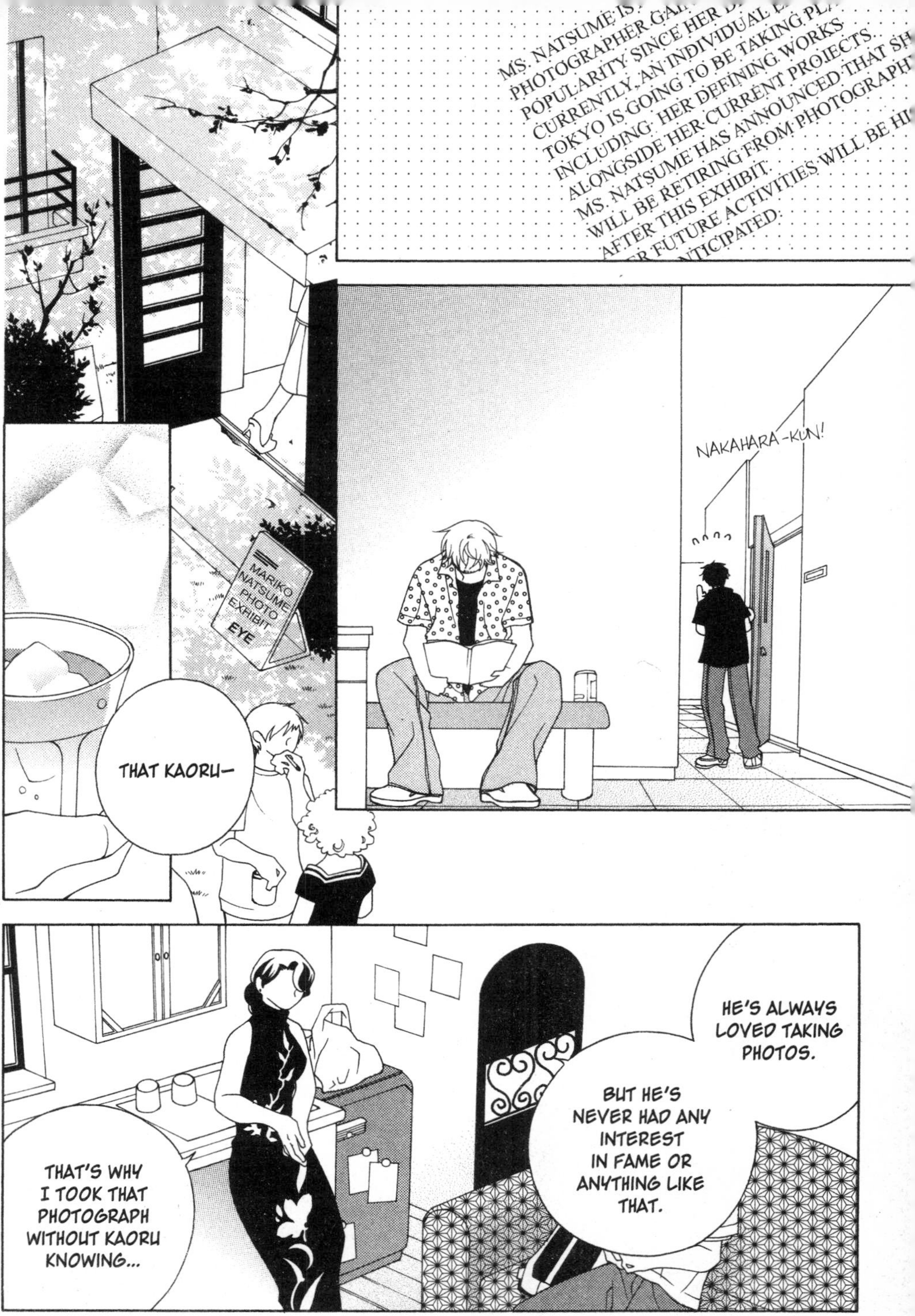
MS. NATSUME IS
PHOTOGRAPHER GAI
POPULARITY SINCE HER D
CURRENTLY, AN INDIVIDUAL E
TOKYO IS GOING TO BE TAKING PLA
INCLUDING HER DEFINING WORKS
ALONGSIDE HER CURRENT PROJECTS.
MS. NATSUME HAS ANNOUNCED THAT SH
WILL BE RETIRING FROM PHOTOGRAPH
AFTER THIS EXHIBIT.
ER FUTURE ACTIVITIES WILL BE HI
NTICIPATED.
NAKAHARA-KUN!
MARIKO NATSUME PHOTO EXHIBIT EYE
THAT KAORU—
HE'S ALWAYS LOVED TAKING PHOTOS.
BUT HE'S NEVER HAD ANY INTEREST IN FAME OR ANYTHING LIKE THAT.
THAT'S WHY I TOOK THAT PHOTOGRAPH WITHOUT KAORU KNOWING...

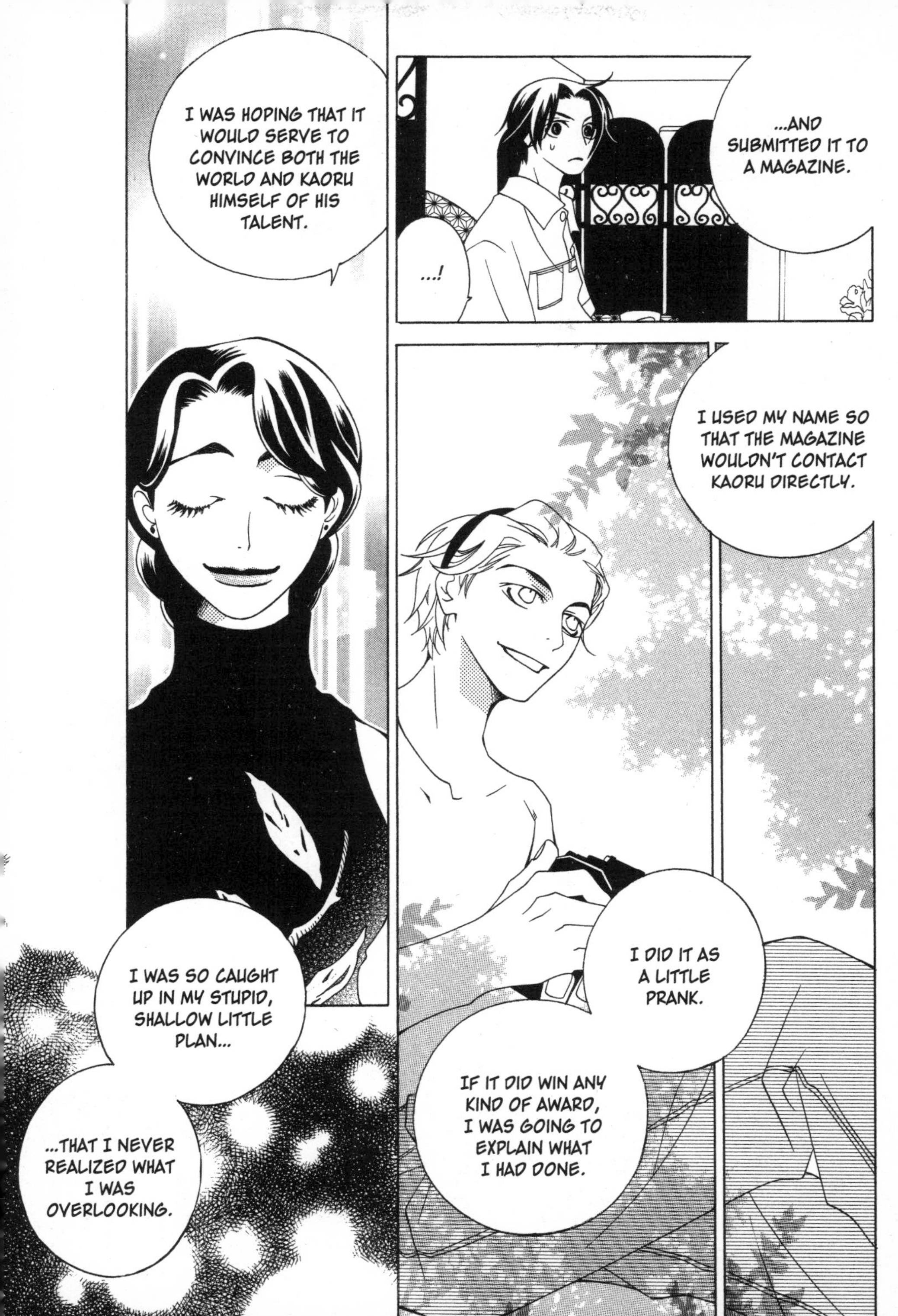
...AND SUBMITTED IT TO A MAGAZINE.
...!
I USED MY NAME SO THAT THE MAGAZINE WOULDN'T CONTACT KAORU DIRECTLY.
I DID IT AS A LITTLE PRANK.
IF IT DID WIN ANY KIND OF AWARD, I WAS GOING TO EXPLAIN WHAT I HAD DONE.
I WAS HOPING THAT IT WOULD SERVE TO CONVINCE BOTH THE WORLD AND KAORU HIMSELF OF HIS TALENT.
I WAS SO CAUGHT UP IN MY STUPID, SHALLOW LITTLE PLAN...
...THAT I NEVER REALIZED WHAT I WAS OVERLOOKING.

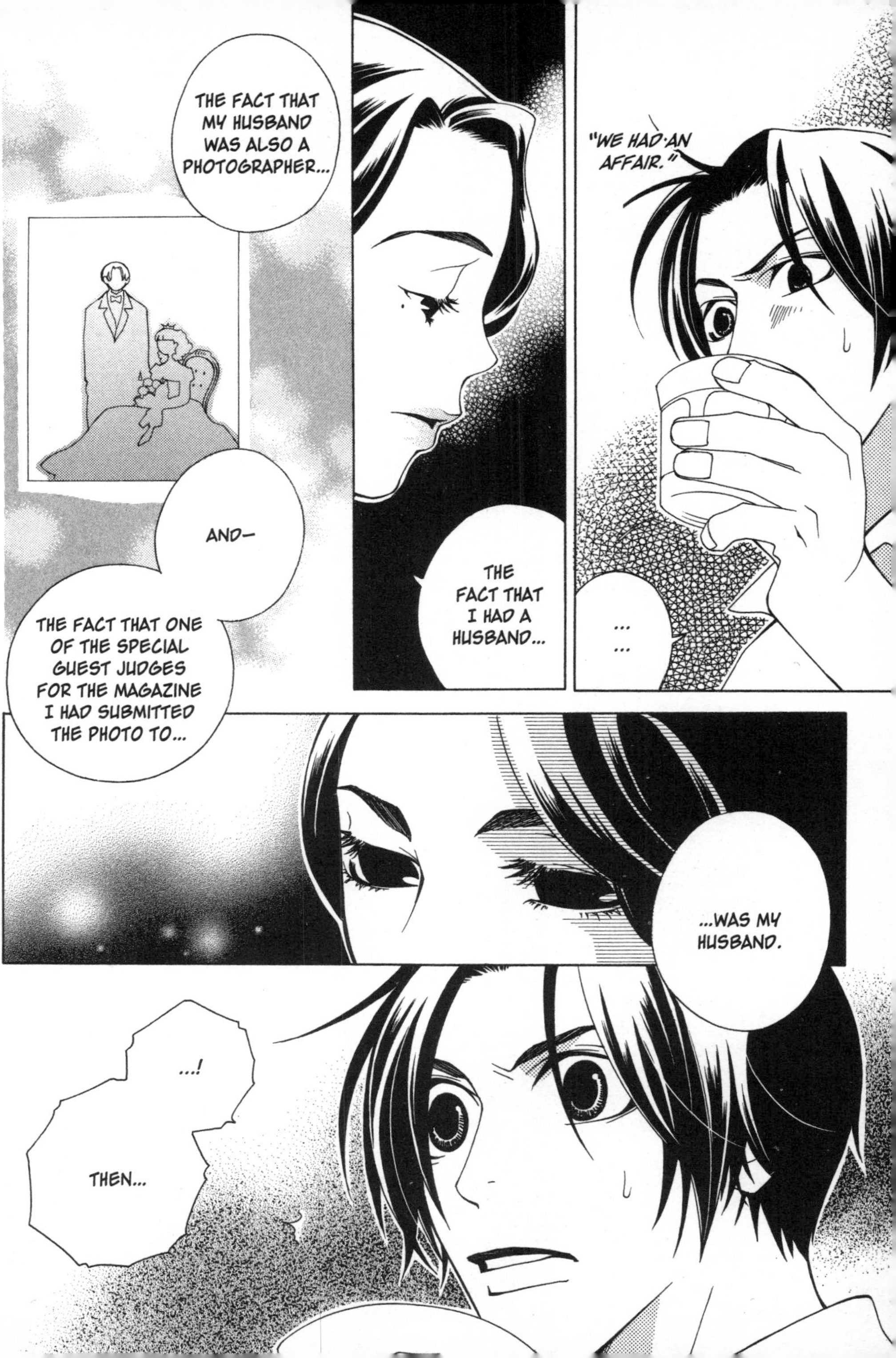
"WE HAD·AN AFFAIR."
......
THE FACT THAT I HAD A HUSBAND...
THE FACT THAT MY HUSBAND WAS ALSO A PHOTOGRAPHER...
AND—
THE FACT THAT ONE OF THE SPECIAL GUEST JUDGES FOR THE MAGAZINE I HAD SUBMITTED THE PHOTO TO...
...WAS MY HUSBAND.
...!
THEN...

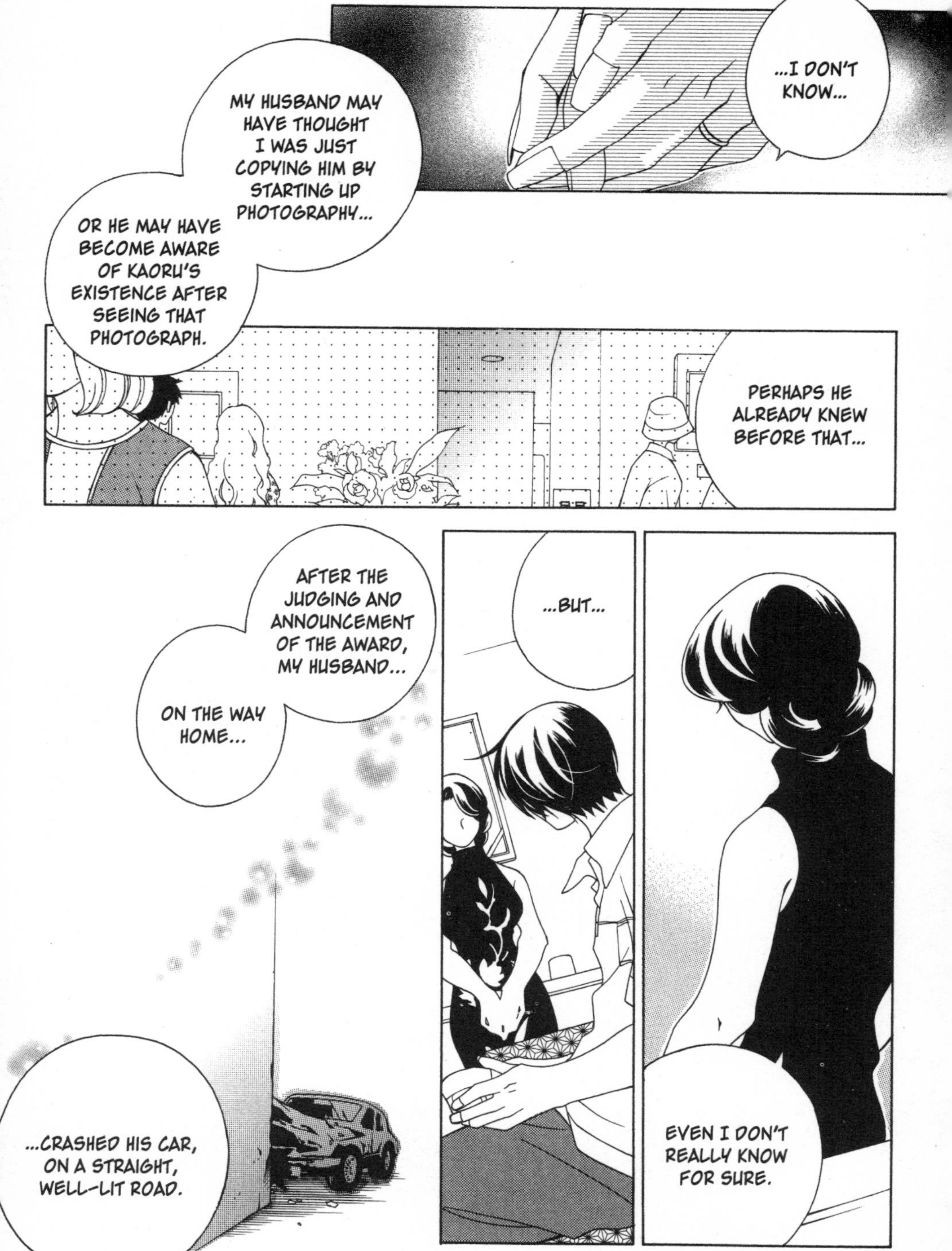
...I DON'T KNOW...
MY HUSBAND MAY HAVE THOUGHT I WAS JUST COPYING HIM BY STARTING UP PHOTOGRAPHY...
OR HE MAY HAVE BECOME AWARE OF KAORU'S EXISTENCE AFTER SEEING THAT PHOTOGRAPH.
PERHAPS HE ALREADY KNEW BEFORE THAT...
EVEN I DON'T REALLY KNOW FOR SURE.
...BUT...
AFTER THE JUDGING AND ANNOUNCEMENT OF THE AWARD, MY HUSBAND...
ON THE WAY HOME...
...CRASHED HIS CAR, ON A STRAIGHT, WELL-LIT ROAD.

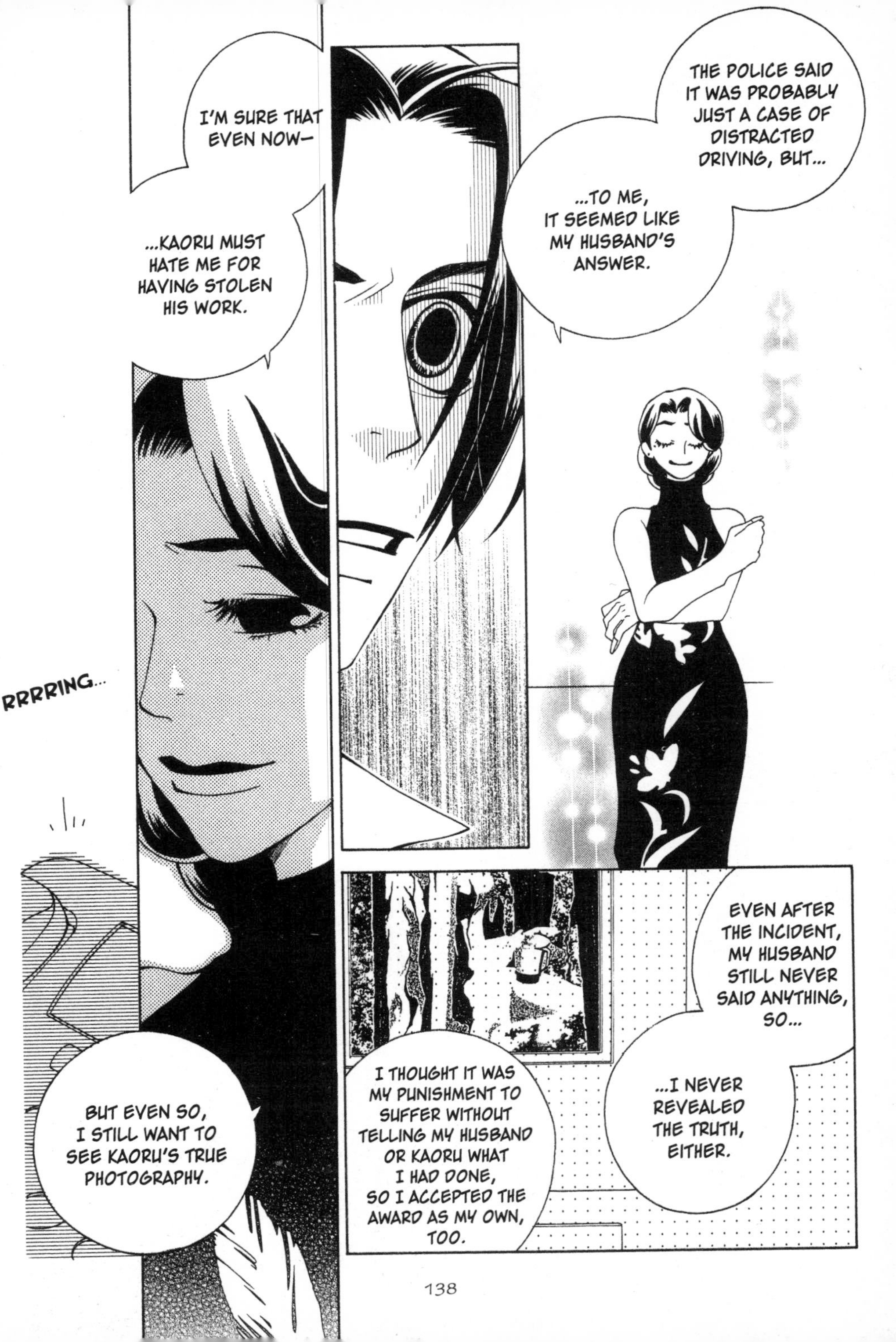
THE POLICE SAID IT WAS PROBABLY JUST A CASE OF DISTRACTED DRIVING, BUT...
...TO ME, IT SEEMED LIKE MY HUSBAND'S ANSWER.
EVEN AFTER THE INCIDENT, MY HUSBAND STILL NEVER SAID ANYTHING, SO...
...I NEVER REVEALED THE TRUTH, EITHER.
I THOUGHT IT WAS MY PUNISHMENT TO SUFFER WITHOUT TELLING MY HUSBAND OR KAORU WHAT I HAD DONE, SO I ACCEPTED THE AWARD AS MY OWN, TOO.
I'M SURE THAT EVEN NOW—
...KAORU MUST HATE ME FOR HAVING STOLEN HIS WORK.
RRRRING...
BUT EVEN SO, I STILL WANT TO SEE KAORU'S TRUE PHOTOGRAPHY.

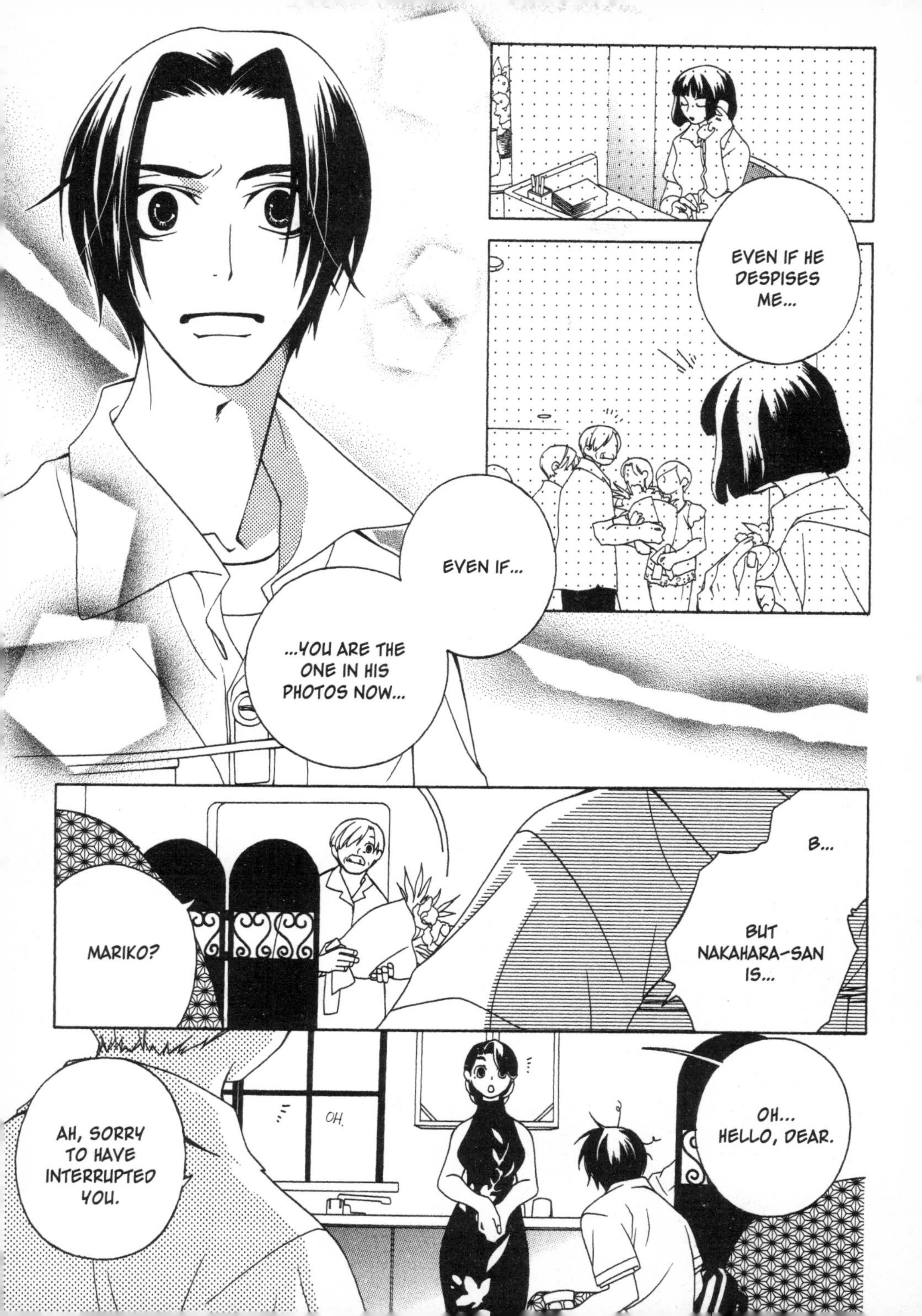
EVEN IF HE DESPISES ME...
EVEN IF...
...YOU ARE THE ONE IN HIS PHOTOS NOW...
B...
BUT NAKAHARA-SAN IS...
MARIKO?
OH... HELLO, DEAR.
OH.
AH, SORRY TO HAVE INTERRUPTED YOU.

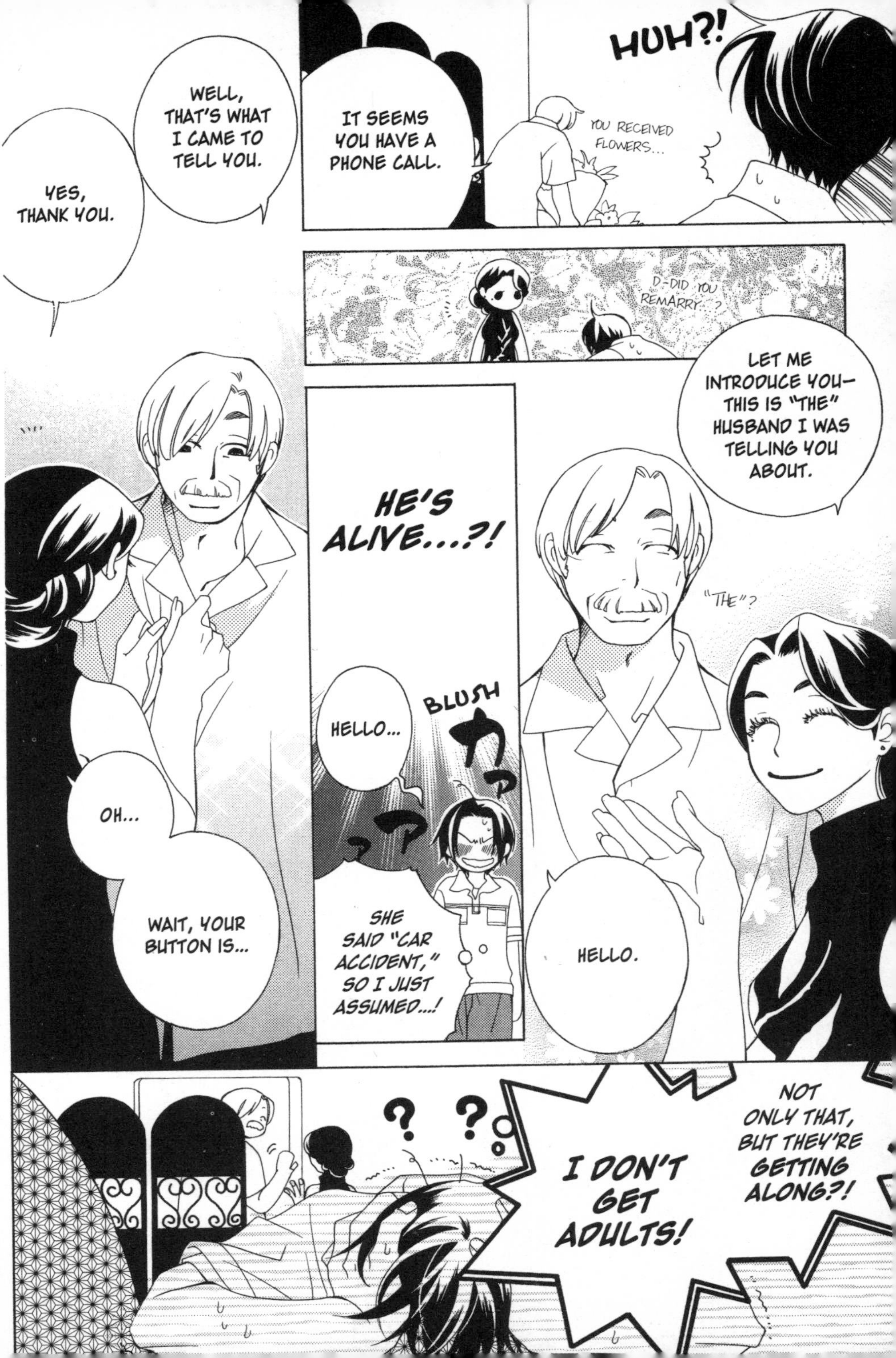
HUH?!
YOU RECEIVED FLOWERS...
IT SEEMS YOU HAVE A PHONE CALL.
D-DID YOU REMARRY...?
LET ME INTRODUCE YOU—THIS IS "THE" HUSBAND I WAS TELLING YOU ABOUT.
"THE"?
HELLO.
HE'S ALIVE...?!
BLUSH
HELLO...
SHE SAID "CAR ACCIDENT," SO I JUST ASSUMED...!
WELL, THAT'S WHAT I CAME TO TELL YOU.
YES, THANK YOU.
OH...
WAIT, YOUR BUTTON IS...
NOT ONLY THAT, BUT THEY'RE GETTING ALONG?!
I DON'T GET ADULTS!

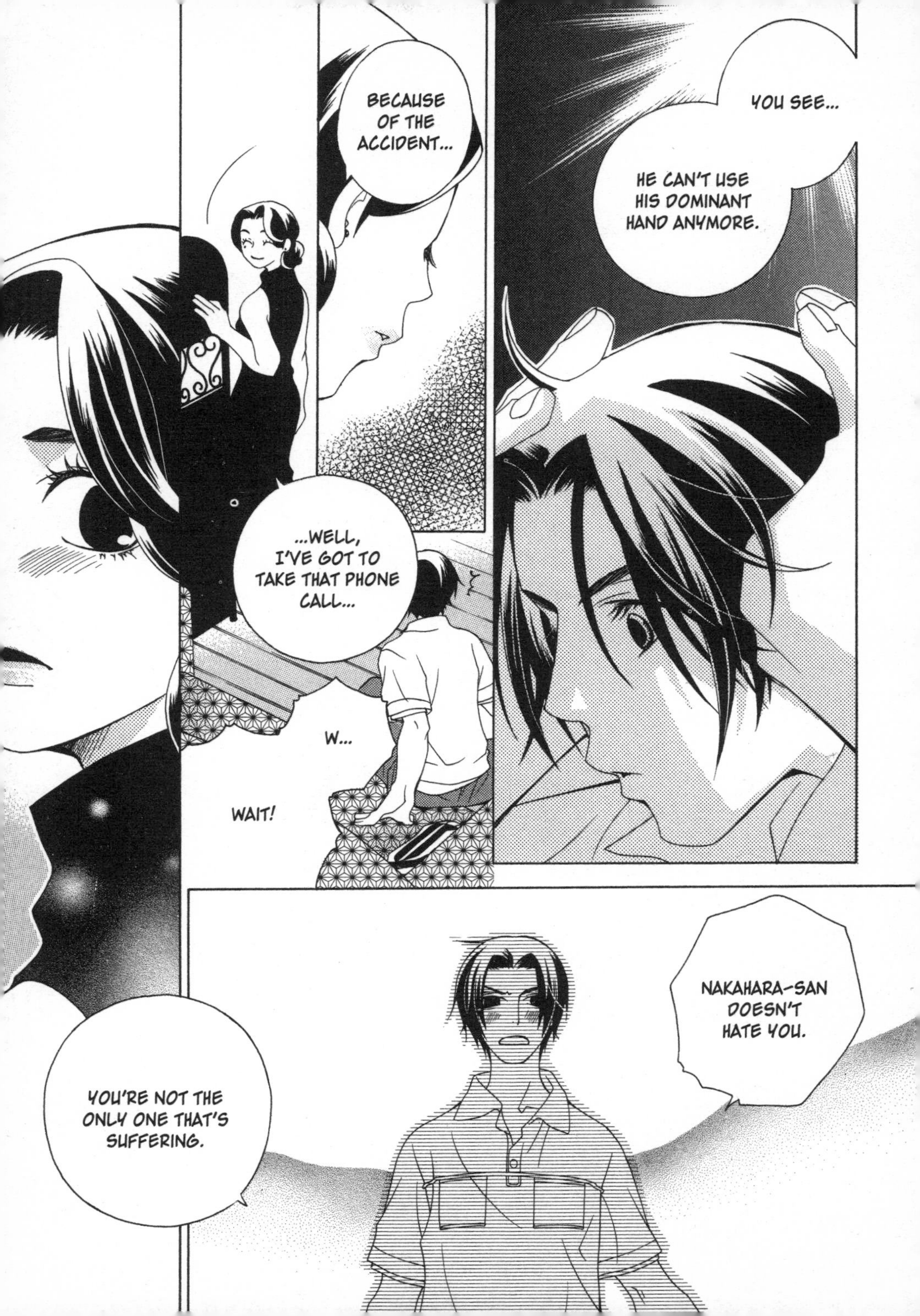
YOU SEE...
HE CAN'T USE HIS DOMINANT HAND ANYMORE.
BECAUSE OF THE ACCIDENT...
...WELL, I'VE GOT TO TAKE THAT PHONE CALL...
W...
WAIT!
NAKAHARA-SAN DOESN'T HATE YOU.
YOU'RE NOT THE ONLY ONE THAT'S SUFFERING.

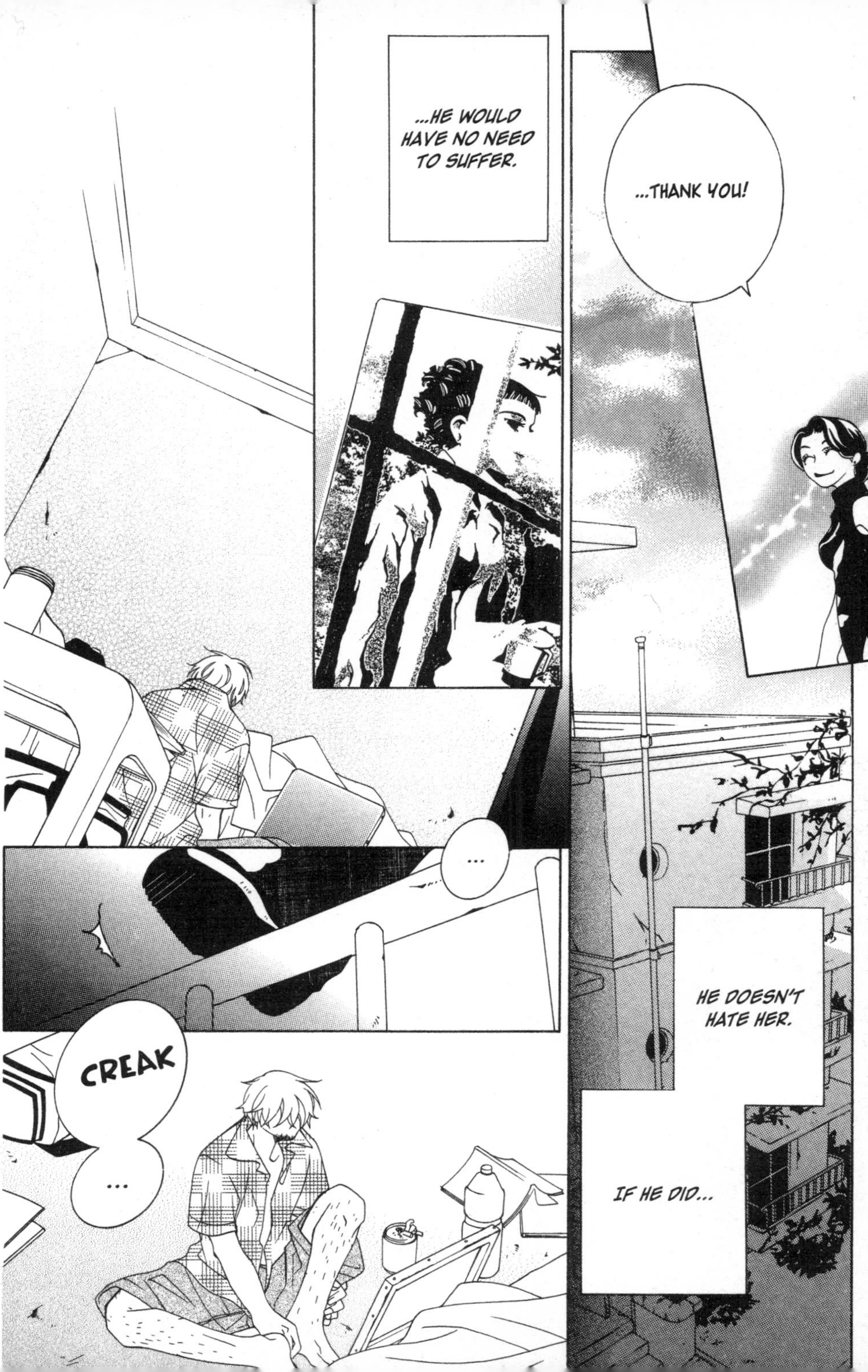
...THANK YOU!
HE DOESN'T HATE HER.
IF HE DID...
...HE WOULD HAVE NO NEED TO SUFFER.
...
CREAK
...

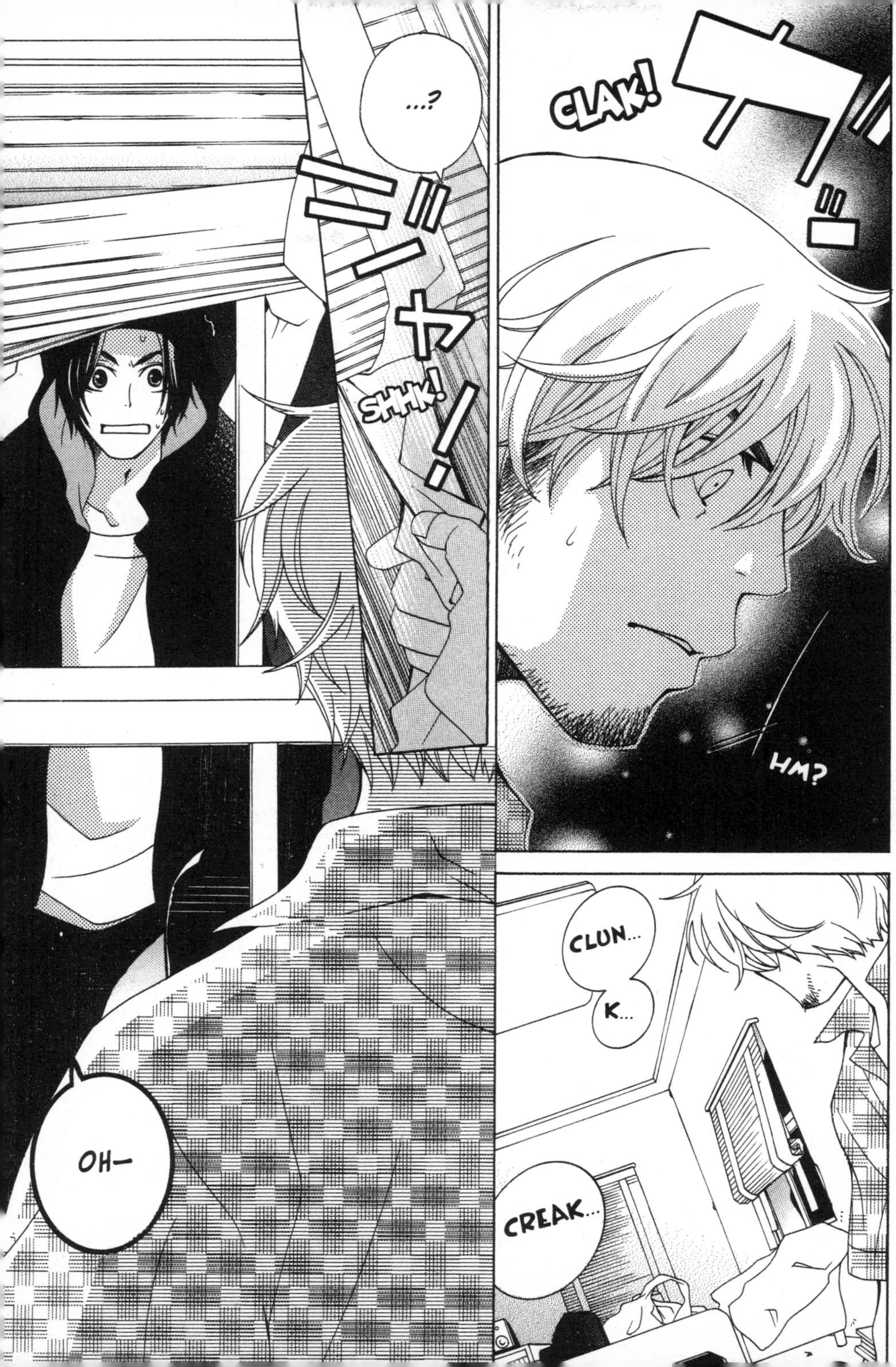
CLAK!
HM?
CLUN...
K...
CREAK...
...?
SHHK!
OH—

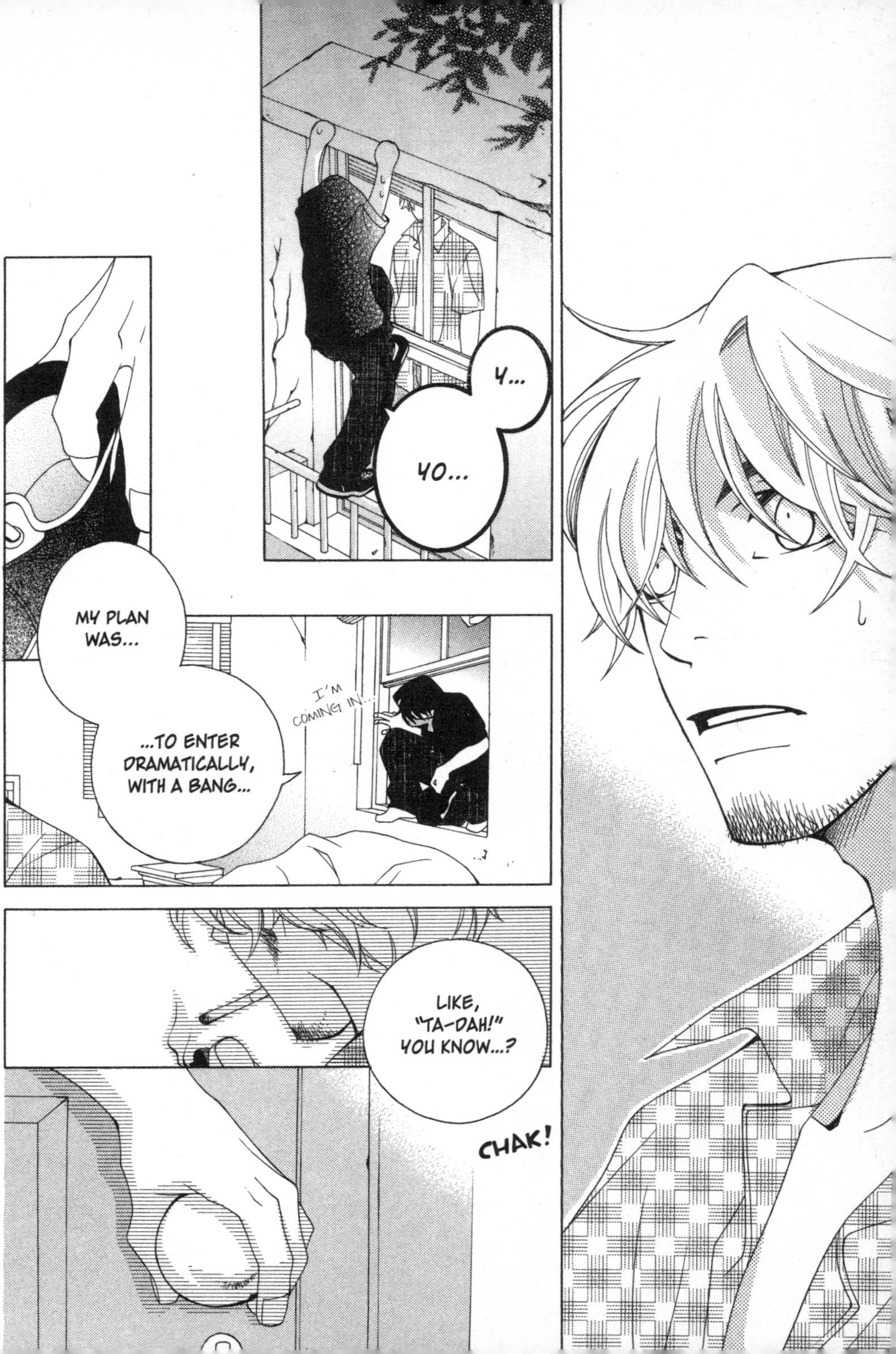
Y...
YO...
MY PLAN WAS...
I'M COMING IN...
...TO ENTER DRAMATICALLY, WITH A BANG...
LIKE, "TA-DAH!" YOU KNOW...?
CHAK!

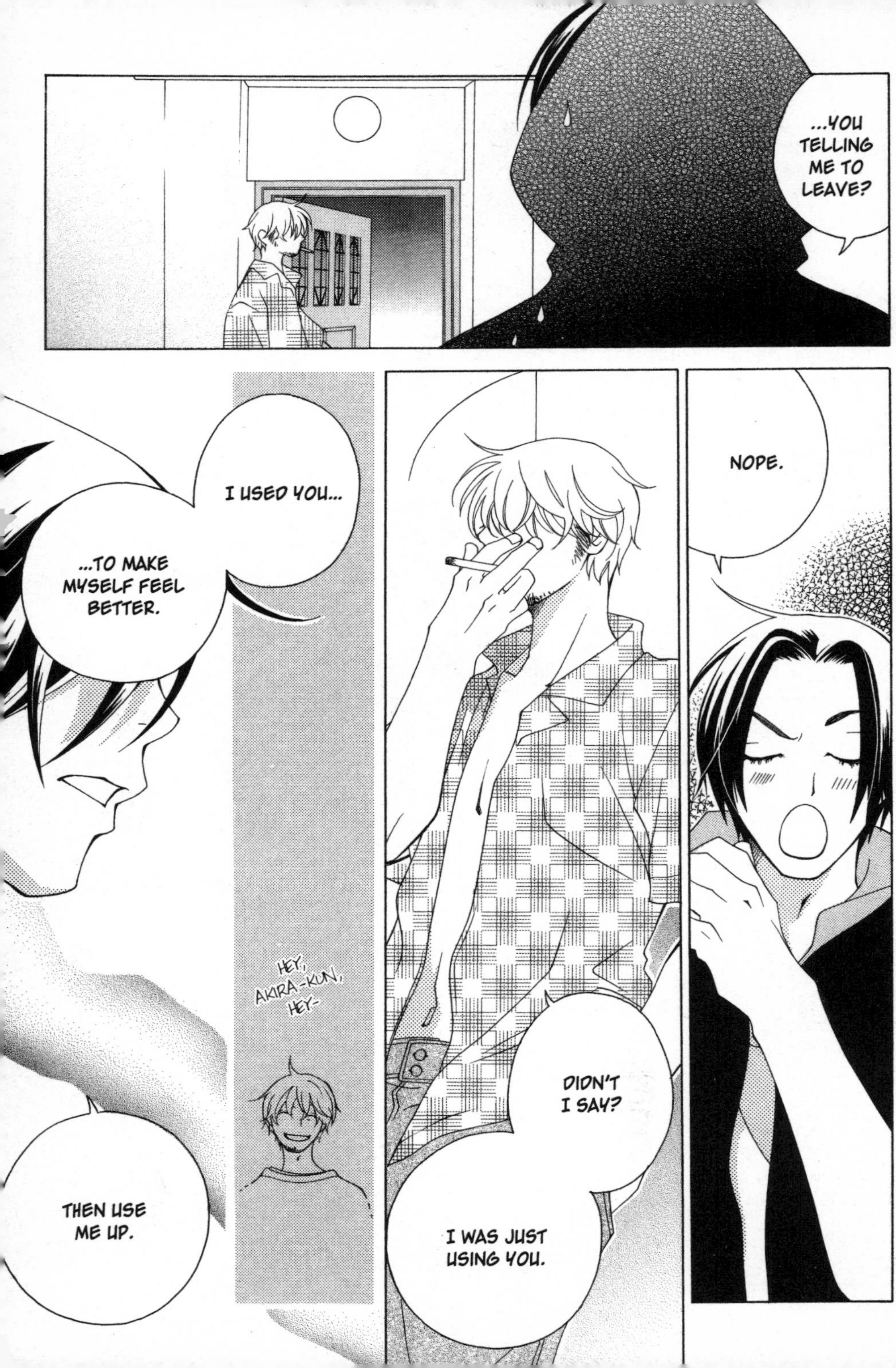
...YOU TELLING ME TO LEAVE?
NOPE.
DIDN'T I SAY?
I WAS JUST USING YOU.
I USED YOU...
...TO MAKE MYSELF FEEL BETTER.
HEY, AKIRA-KUN, HEY-
THEN USE ME UP.

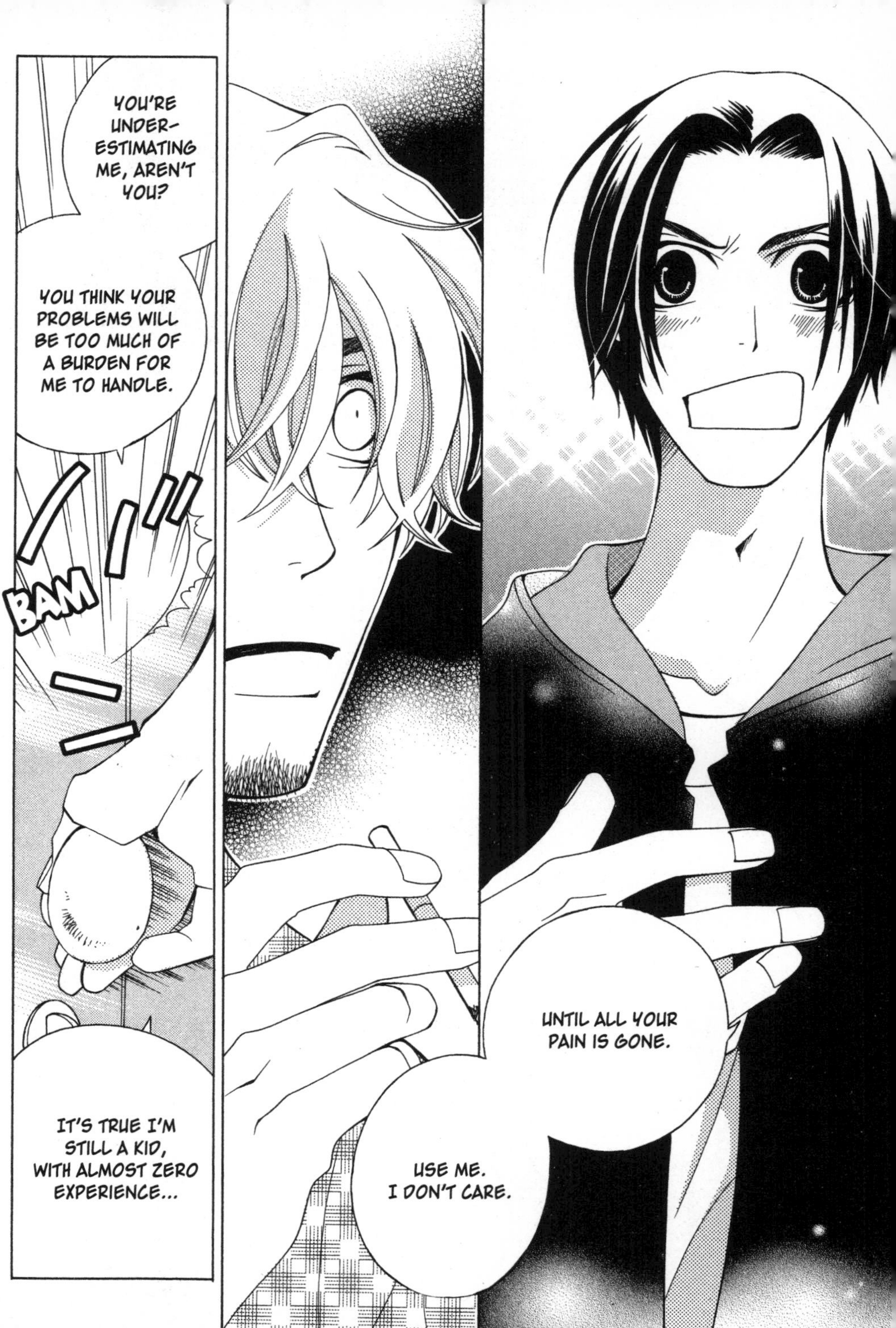
UNTIL ALL YOUR PAIN IS GONE.
USE ME. I DON'T CARE.
YOU'RE UNDER-ESTIMATING ME, AREN'T YOU?
YOU THINK YOUR PROBLEMS WILL BE TOO MUCH OF A BURDEN FOR ME TO HANDLE.
BAM
IT'S TRUE I'M STILL A KID, WITH ALMOST ZERO EXPERIENCE...

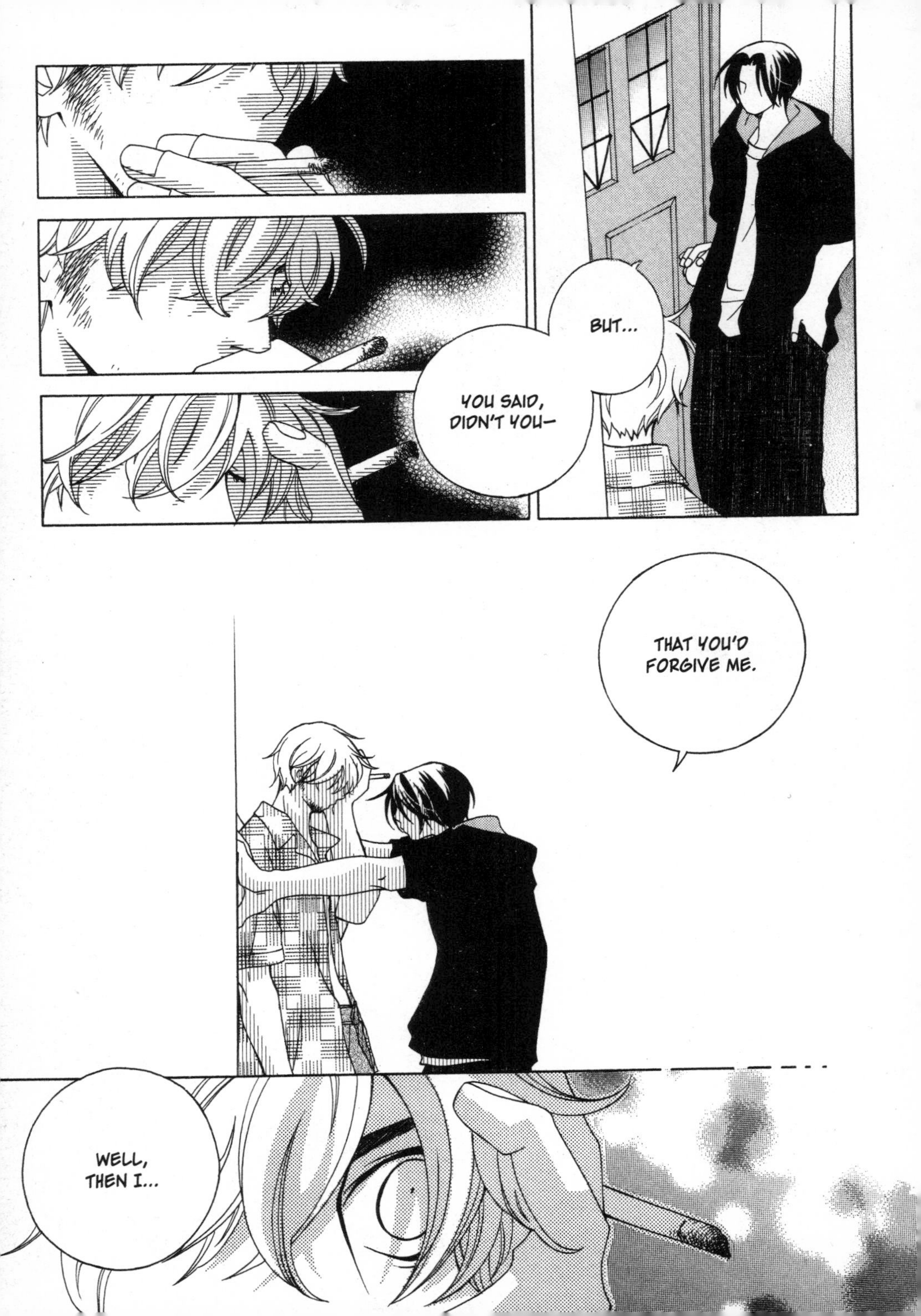
BUT...
YOU SAID, DIDN'T YOU—
THAT YOU'D FORGIVE ME.
WELL, THEN I...

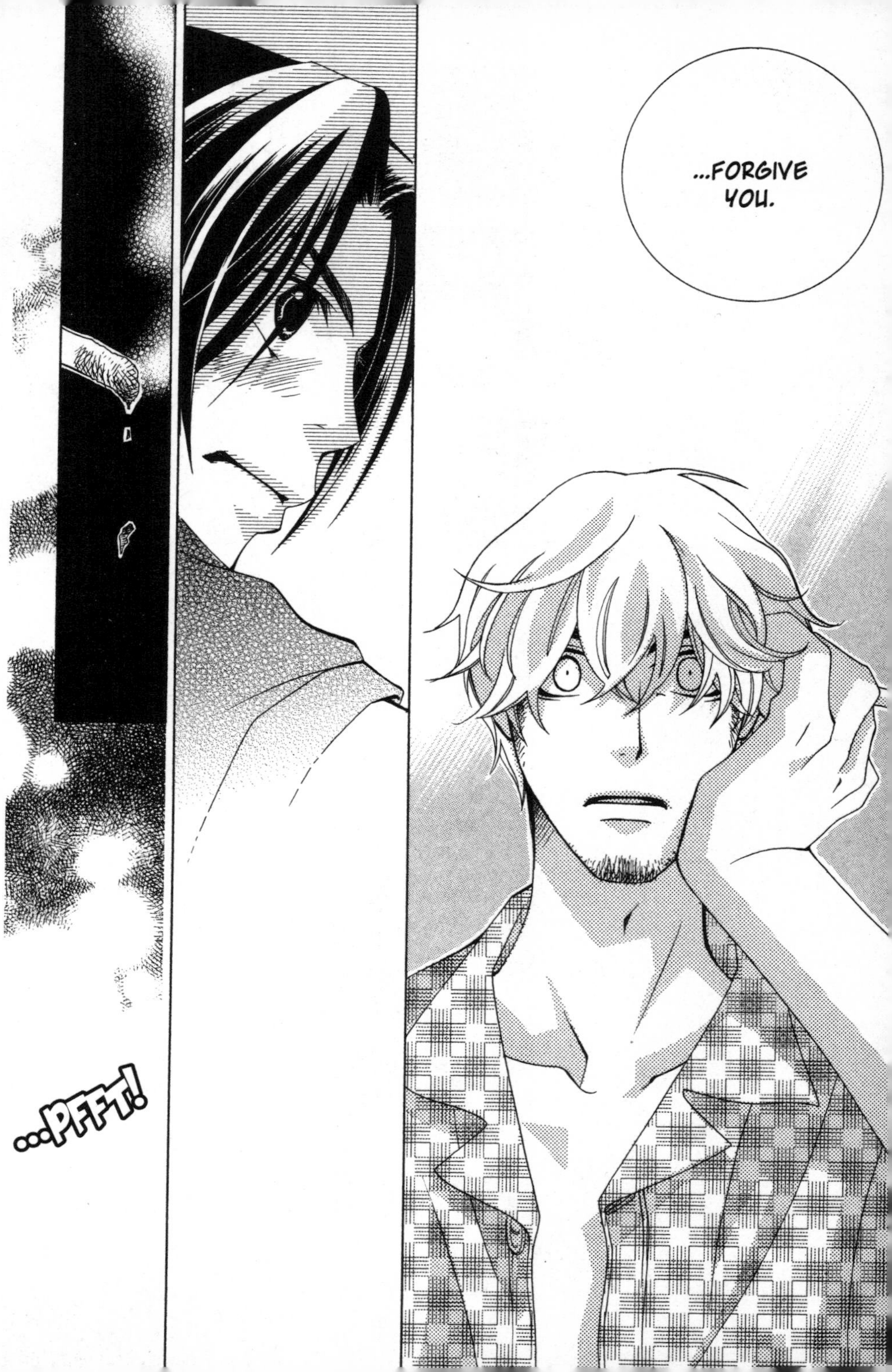
...FORGIVE YOU.
...PFFT!

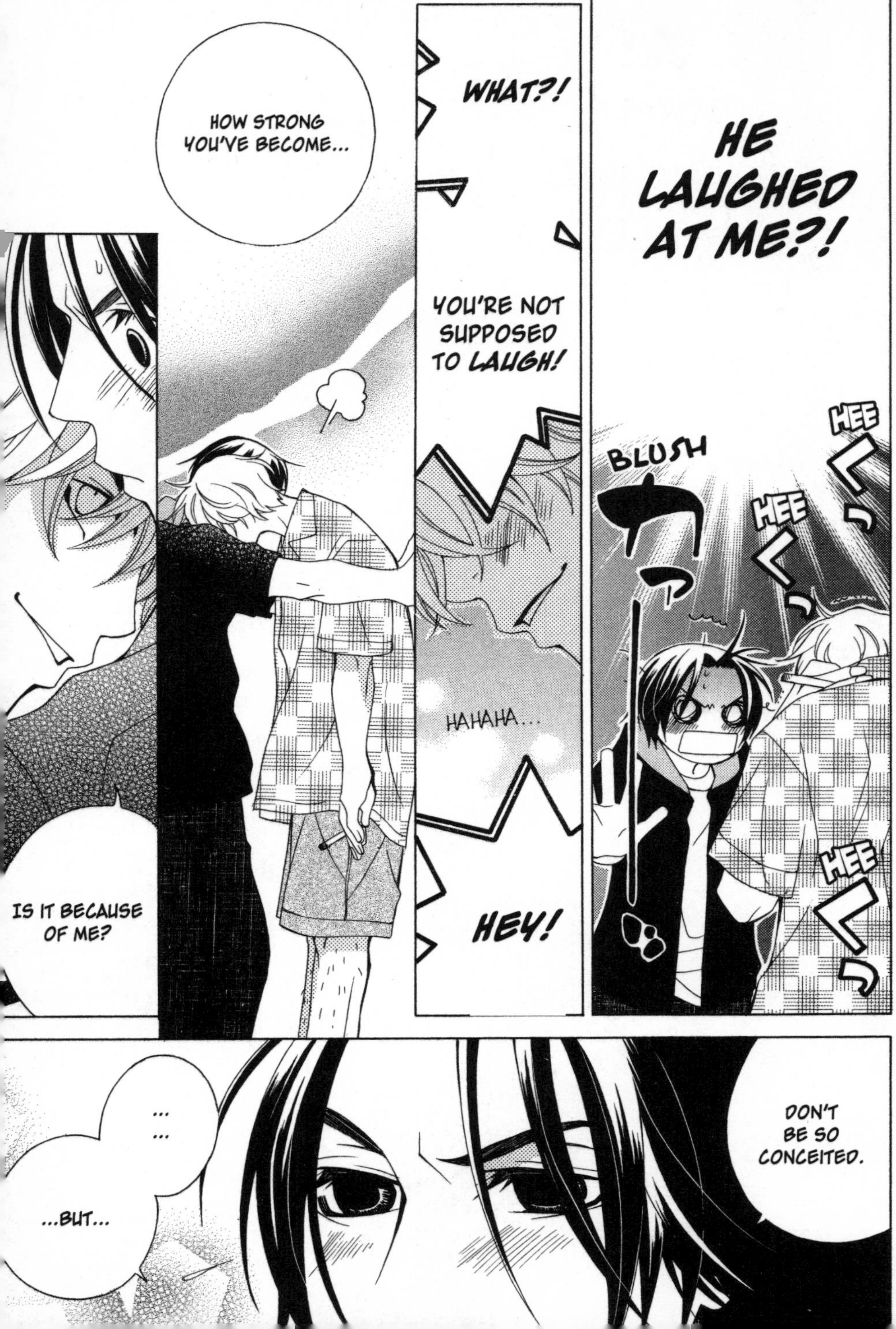
HE LAUGHED AT ME?!
HEE
HEE
BLUSH
HEE
WHAT?!
YOU'RE NOT SUPPOSED TO LAUGH!
HAHAHA...
HEY!
HOW STRONG YOU'VE BECOME...
IS IT BECAUSE OF ME?
DON'T BE SO CONCEITED.
...
...
...BUT...

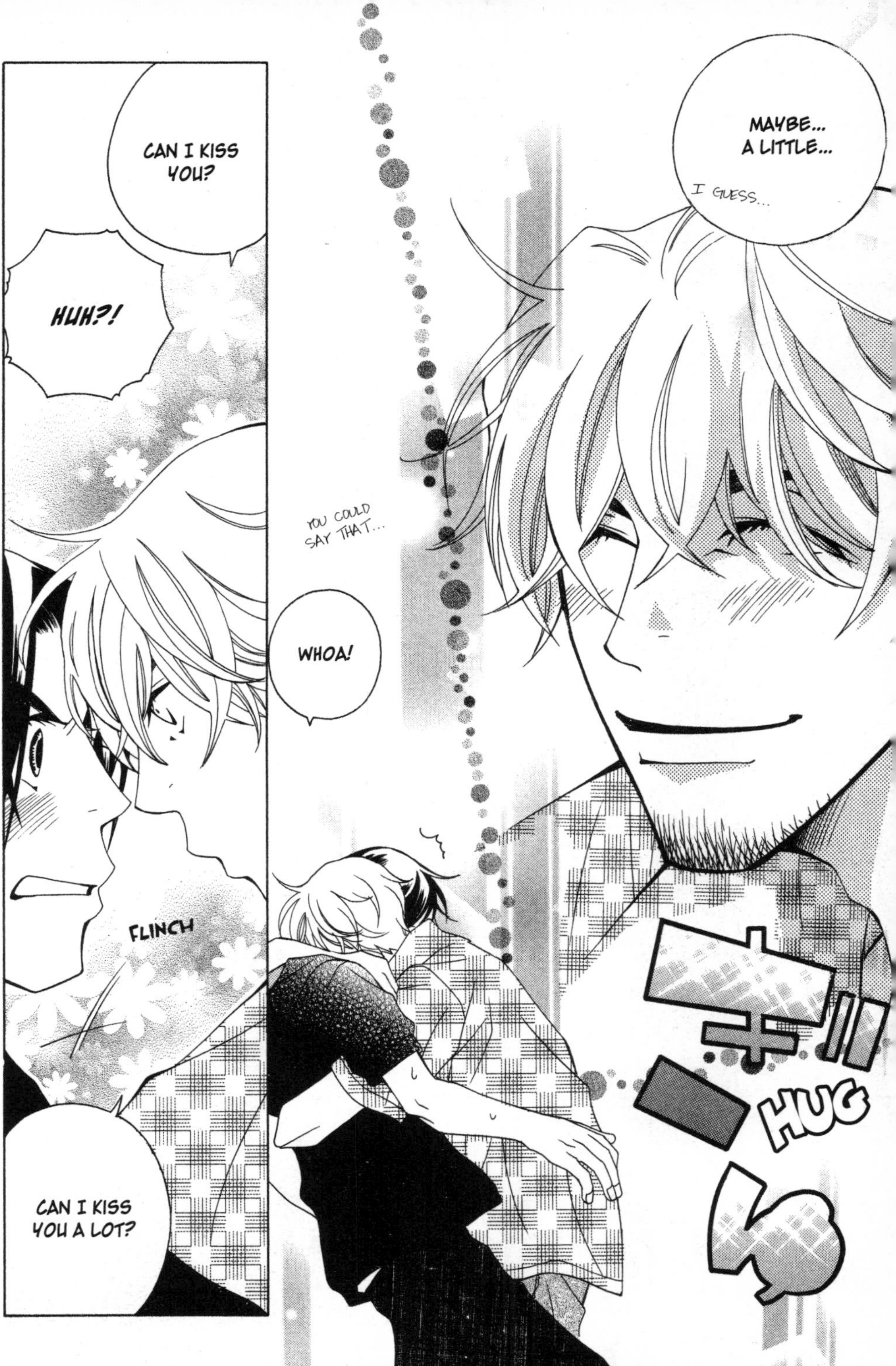
MAYBE... A LITTLE...
I GUESS...
YOU COULD SAY THAT...
WHOA!
HUG
CAN I KISS YOU?
HUH?!
FLINCH
CAN I KISS YOU A LOT?

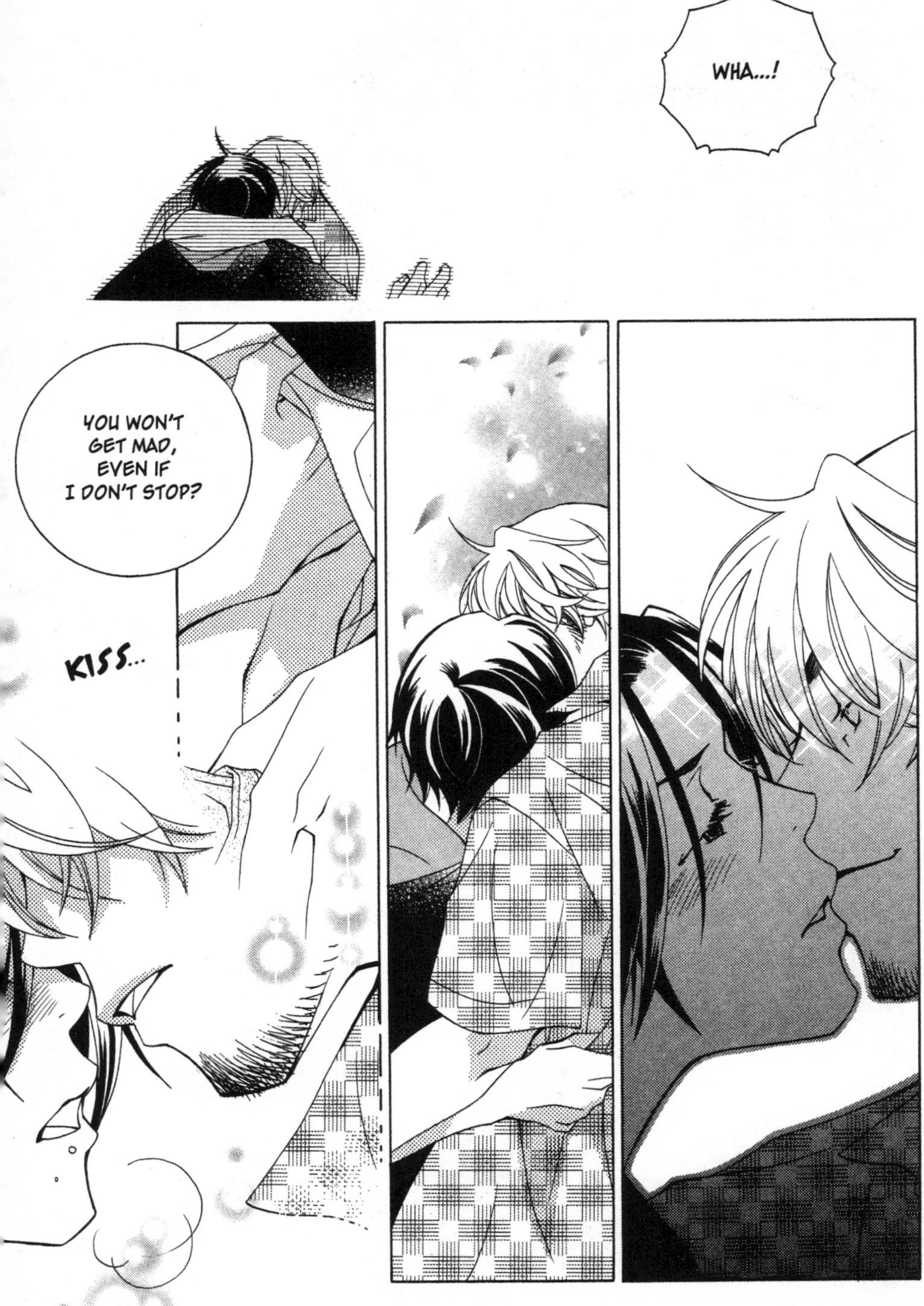
WHA...!
YOU WON'T GET MAD, EVEN IF I DON'T STOP?
KISS...

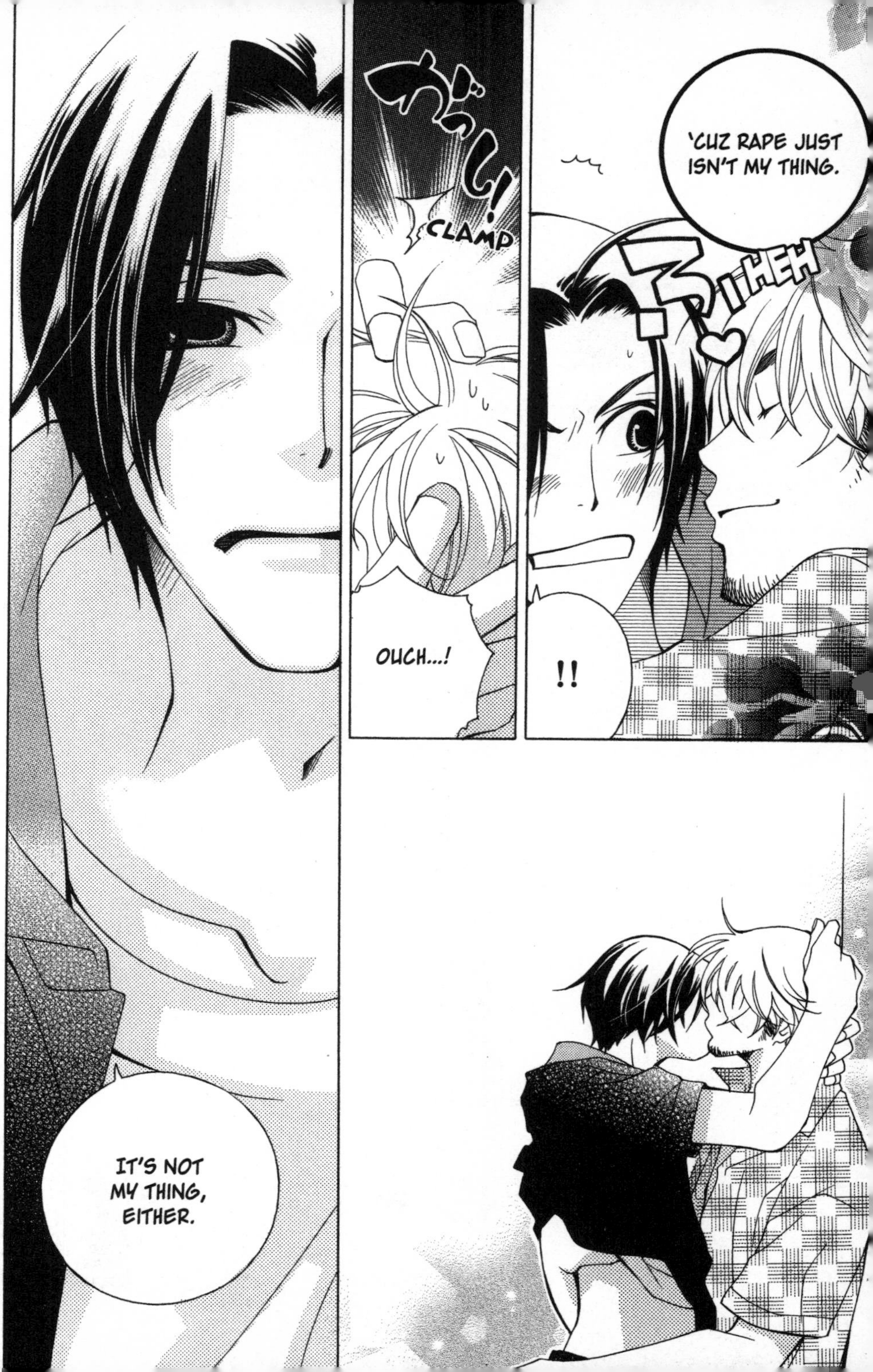
'CUZ RAPE JUST ISN'T MY THING.
HEH
!!
CLAMP
OUCH...!
IT'S NOT MY THING, EITHER.

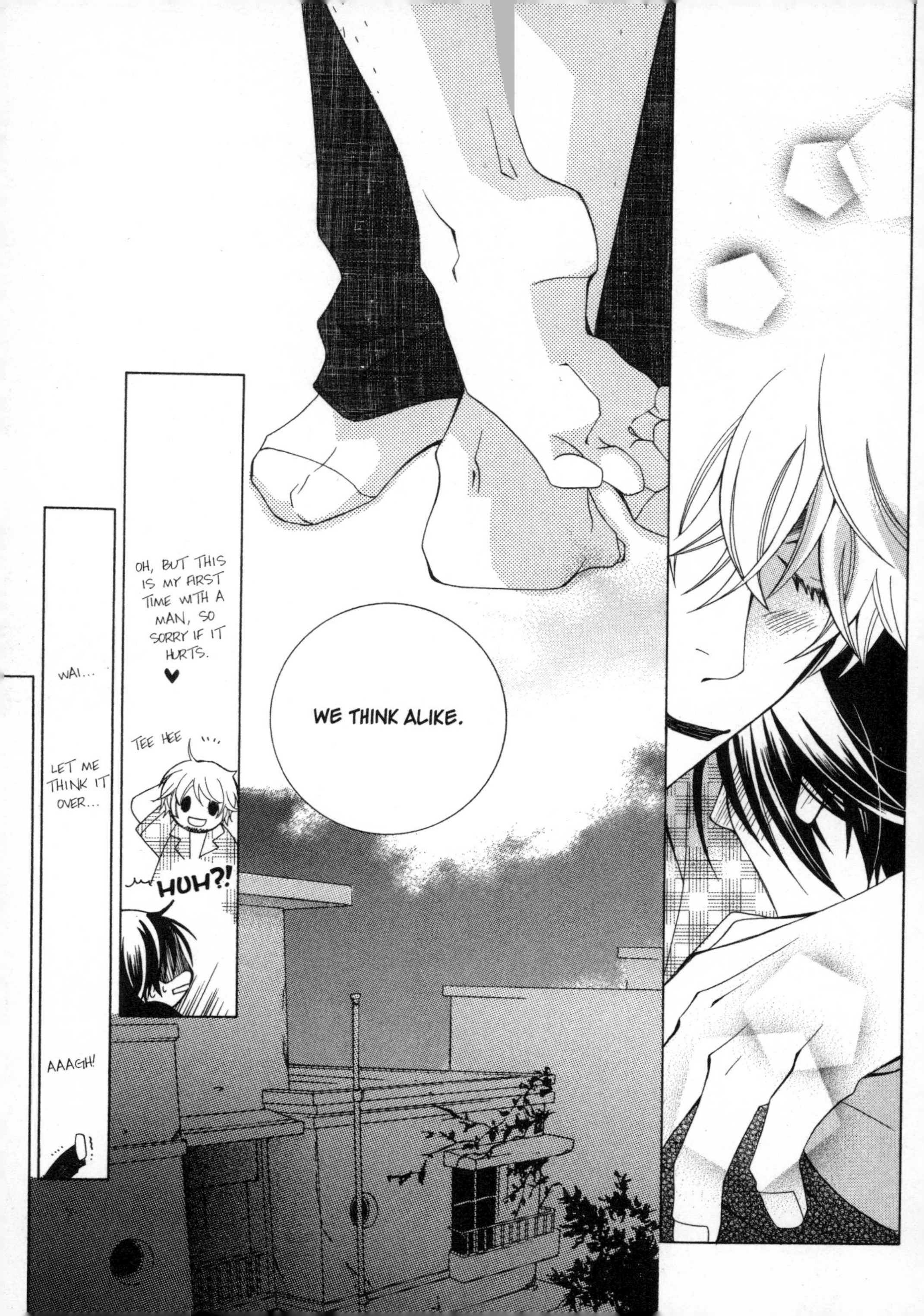
WE THINK ALIKE.
OH, BUT THIS IS MY FIRST TIME WITH A MAN, SO SORRY IF IT HURTS. ♥
TEE HEE
HUH?!
WAI...
LET ME THINK IT OVER...
AAAGH!

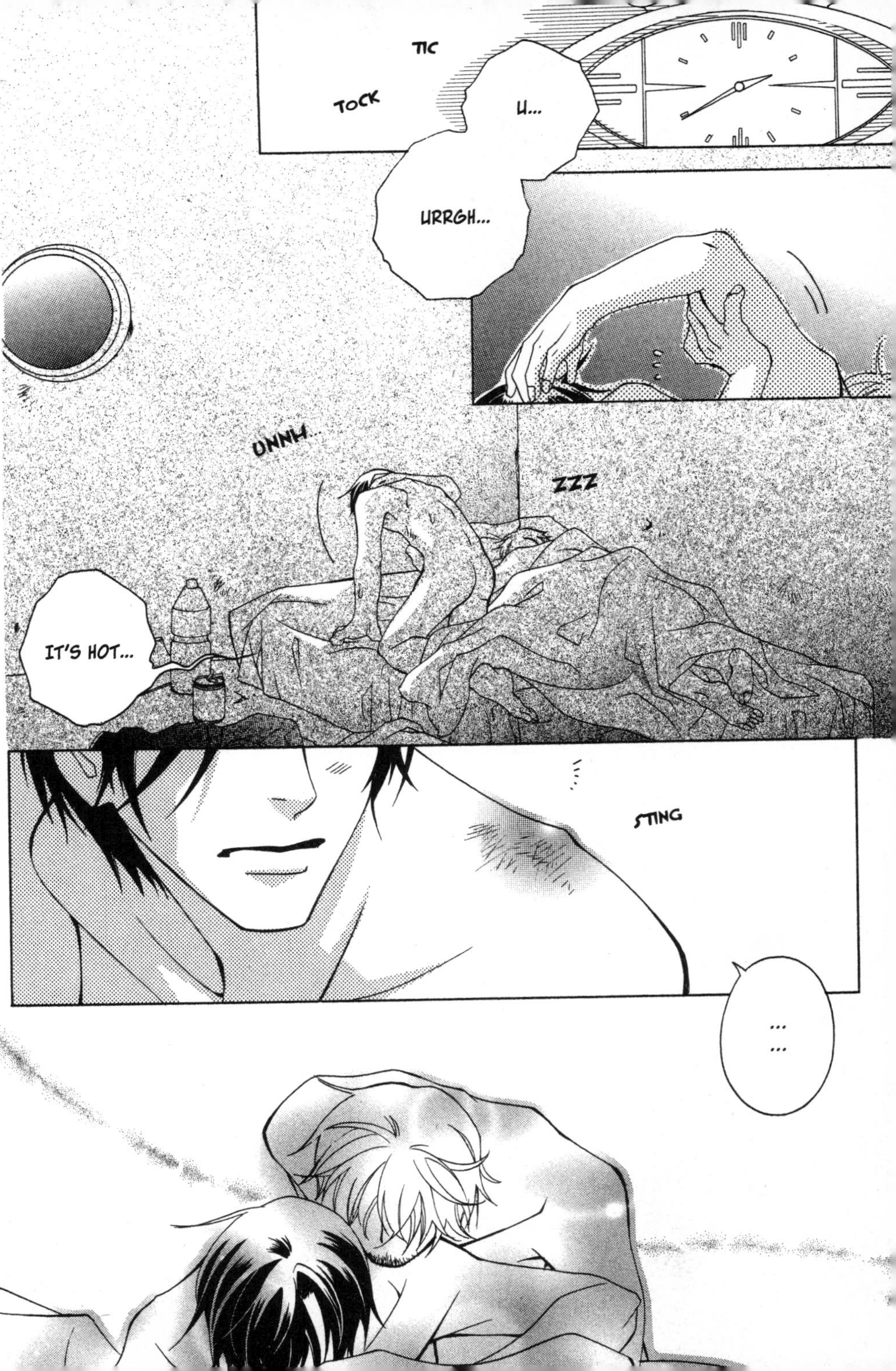
TIC
TOCK
U...
URRGH...
ZZZ
UNNH...
IT'S HOT...
STING
...
...

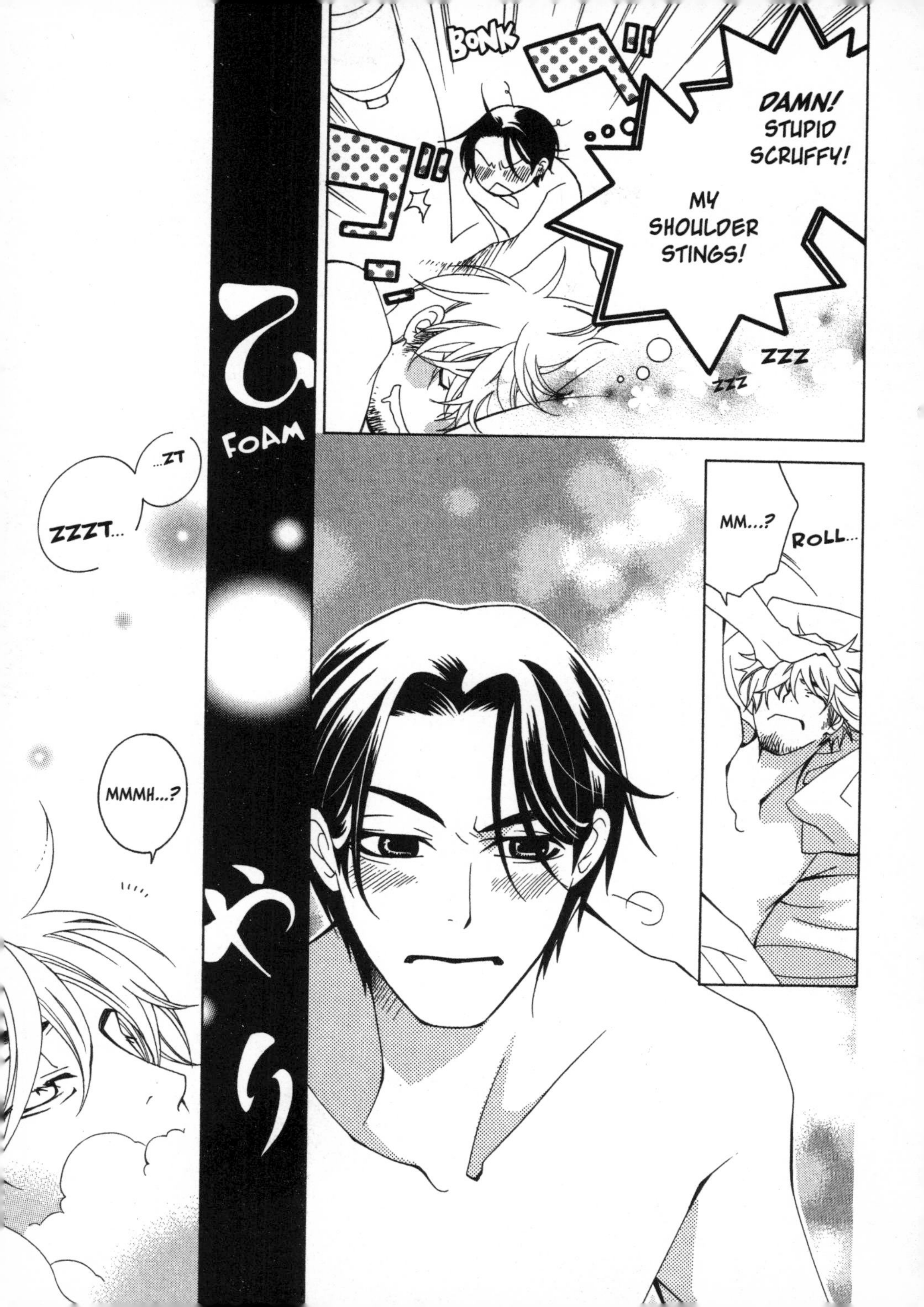
BONK
DAMN! STUPID SCRUFFY!
MY SHOULDER STINGS!
ZZZ
ZZZ
FOAM
MM...?
ROLL...
...ZT
ZZZT...
MMMH...?

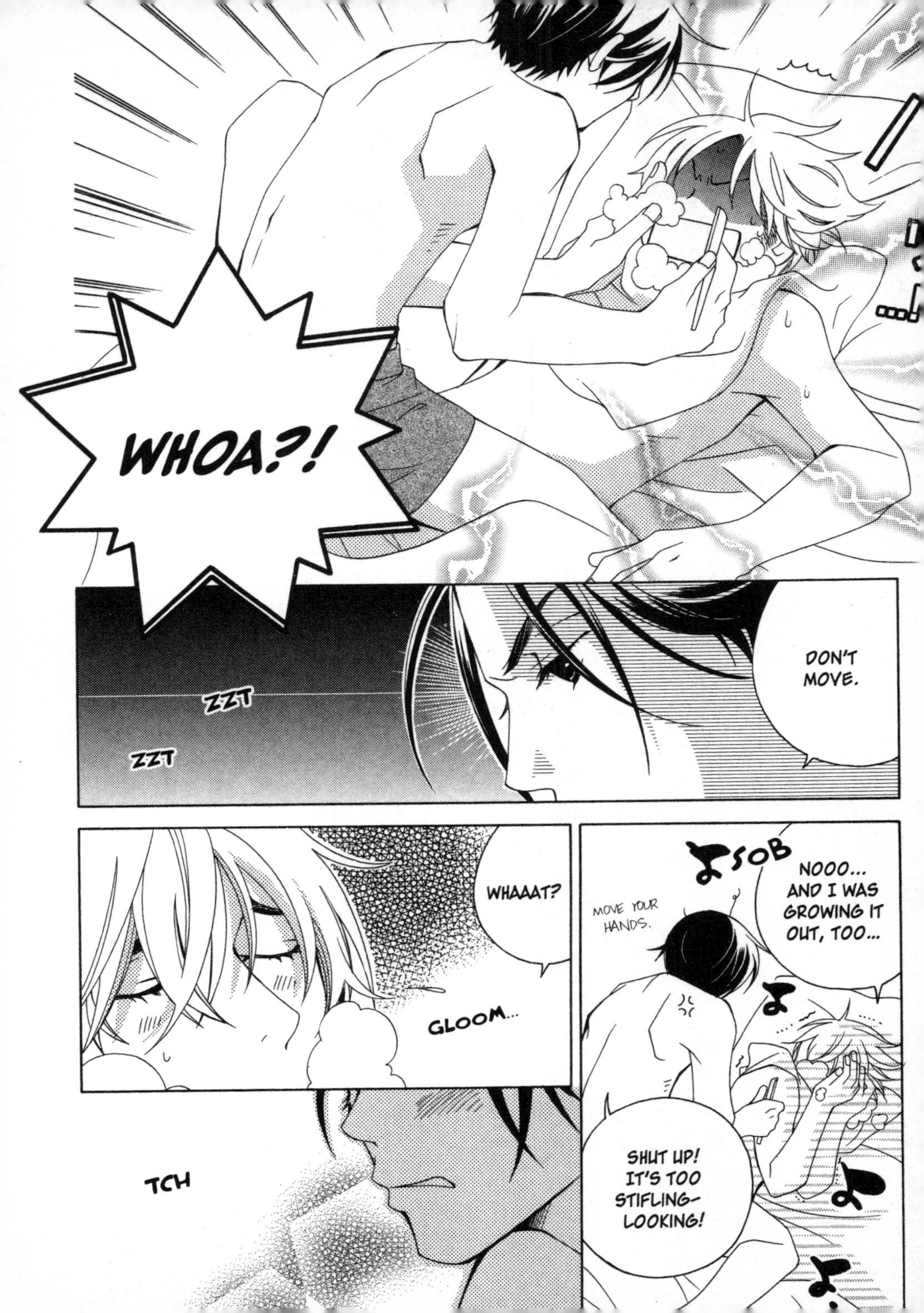
WHOA?!
DON'T MOVE.
ZZT
ZZT
よSOB
NOOO... AND I WAS GROWING IT OUT, TOO...
MOVE YOUR HANDS.
SHUT UP! IT'S TOO STIFLING-LOOKING!
WHAAAT?
GLOOM...
TCH

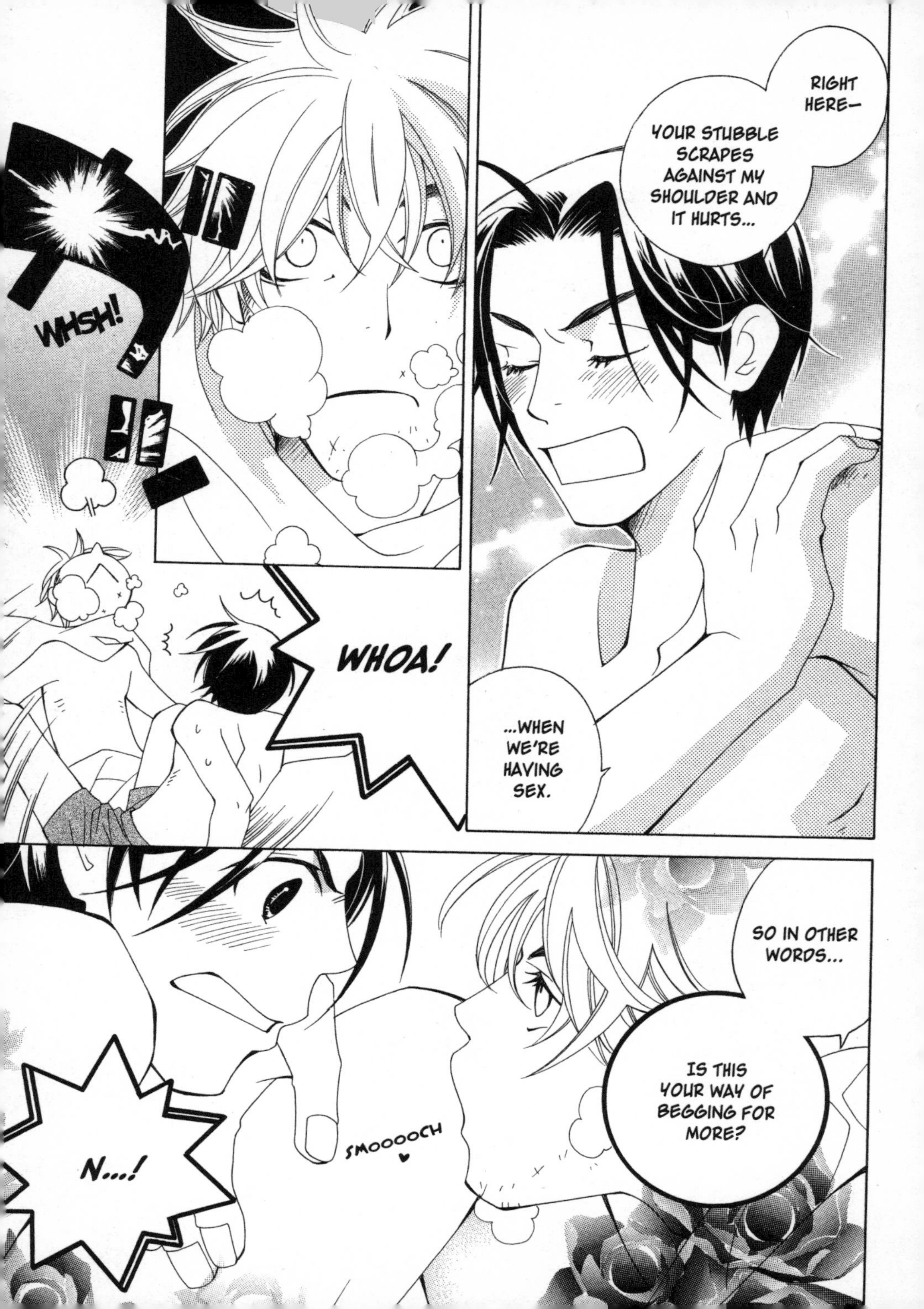
RIGHT HERE—
YOUR STUBBLE SCRAPES AGAINST MY SHOULDER AND IT HURTS...
...WHEN WE'RE HAVING SEX.
WHSH!
WHOA!
SO IN OTHER WORDS...
IS THIS YOUR WAY OF BEGGING FOR MORE?
SMOOOOCH
N...!

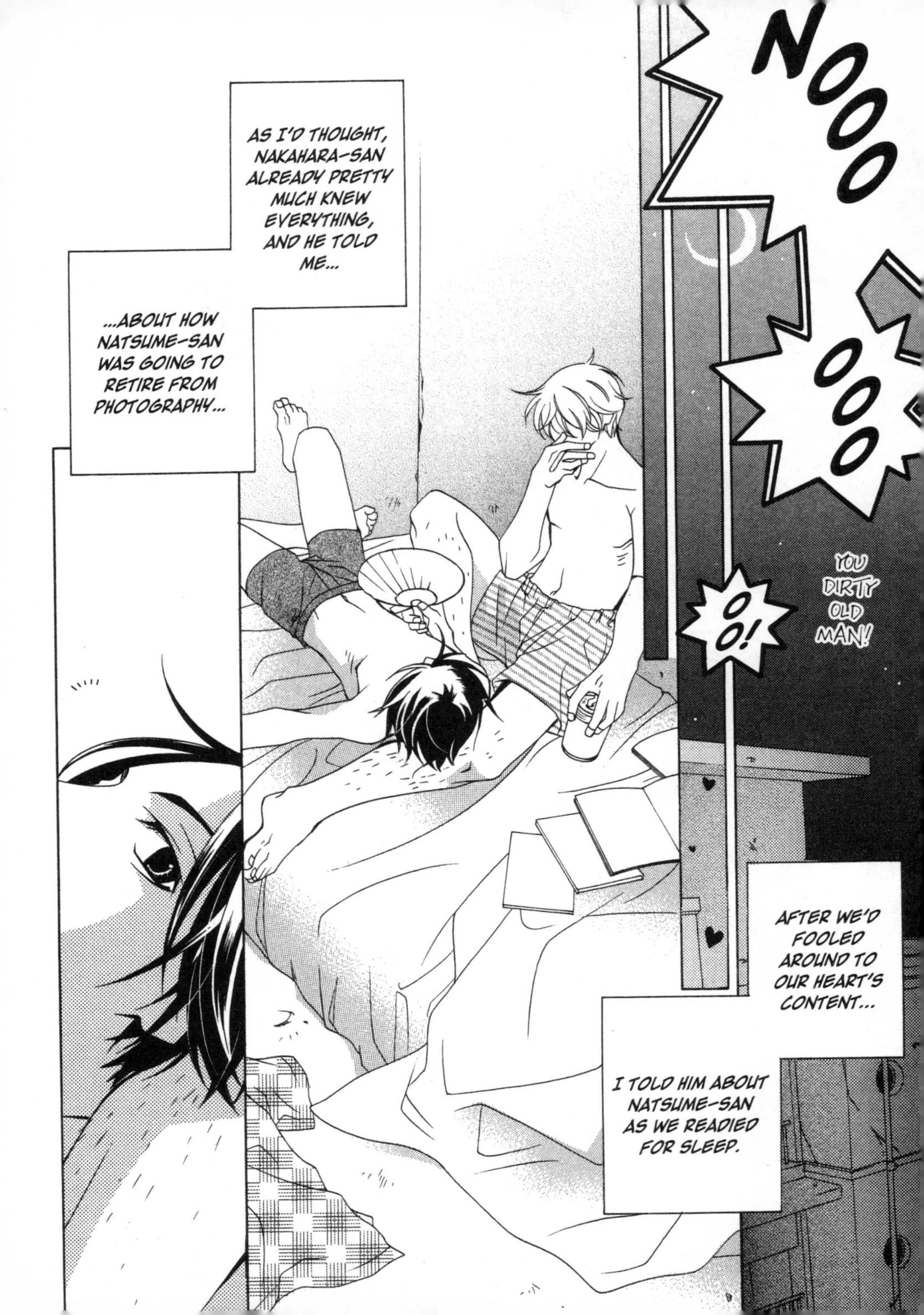
NOOOOOOOO
OO!
YOU DIRTY OLD MAN!
AFTER WE'D FOOLED AROUND TO OUR HEART'S CONTENT...
I TOLD HIM ABOUT NATSUME-SAN AS WE READIED FOR SLEEP.
AS I'D THOUGHT, NAKAHARA-SAN ALREADY PRETTY MUCH KNEW EVERYTHING, AND HE TOLD ME...
...ABOUT HOW NATSUME-SAN WAS GOING TO RETIRE FROM PHOTOGRAPHY...

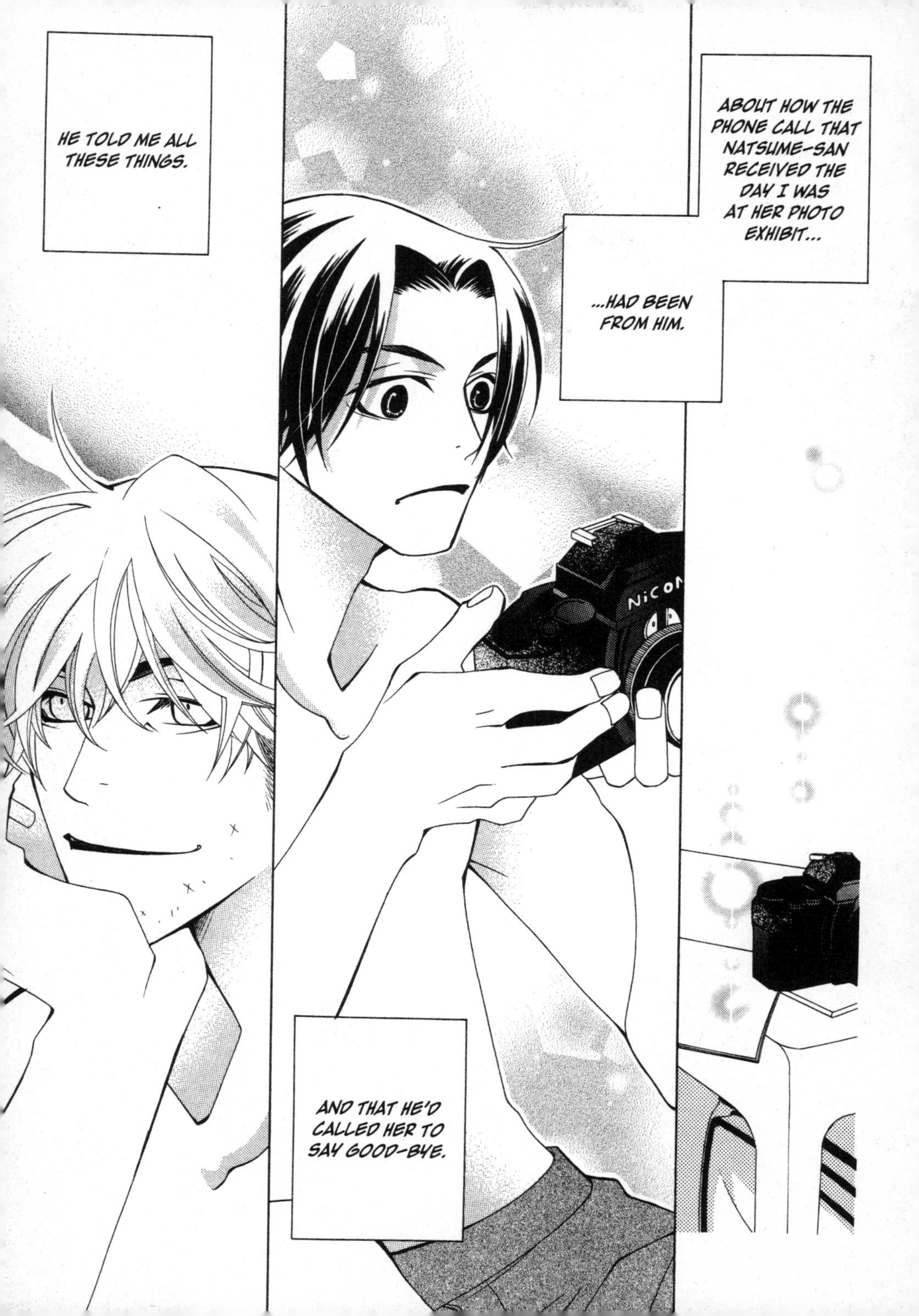
ABOUT HOW THE PHONE CALL THAT NATSUME-SAN RECEIVED THE DAY I WAS AT HER PHOTO EXHIBIT...
...HAD BEEN FROM HIM.
NiCON
AND THAT HE'D CALLED HER TO SAY GOOD-BYE.
HE TOLD ME ALL THESE THINGS.

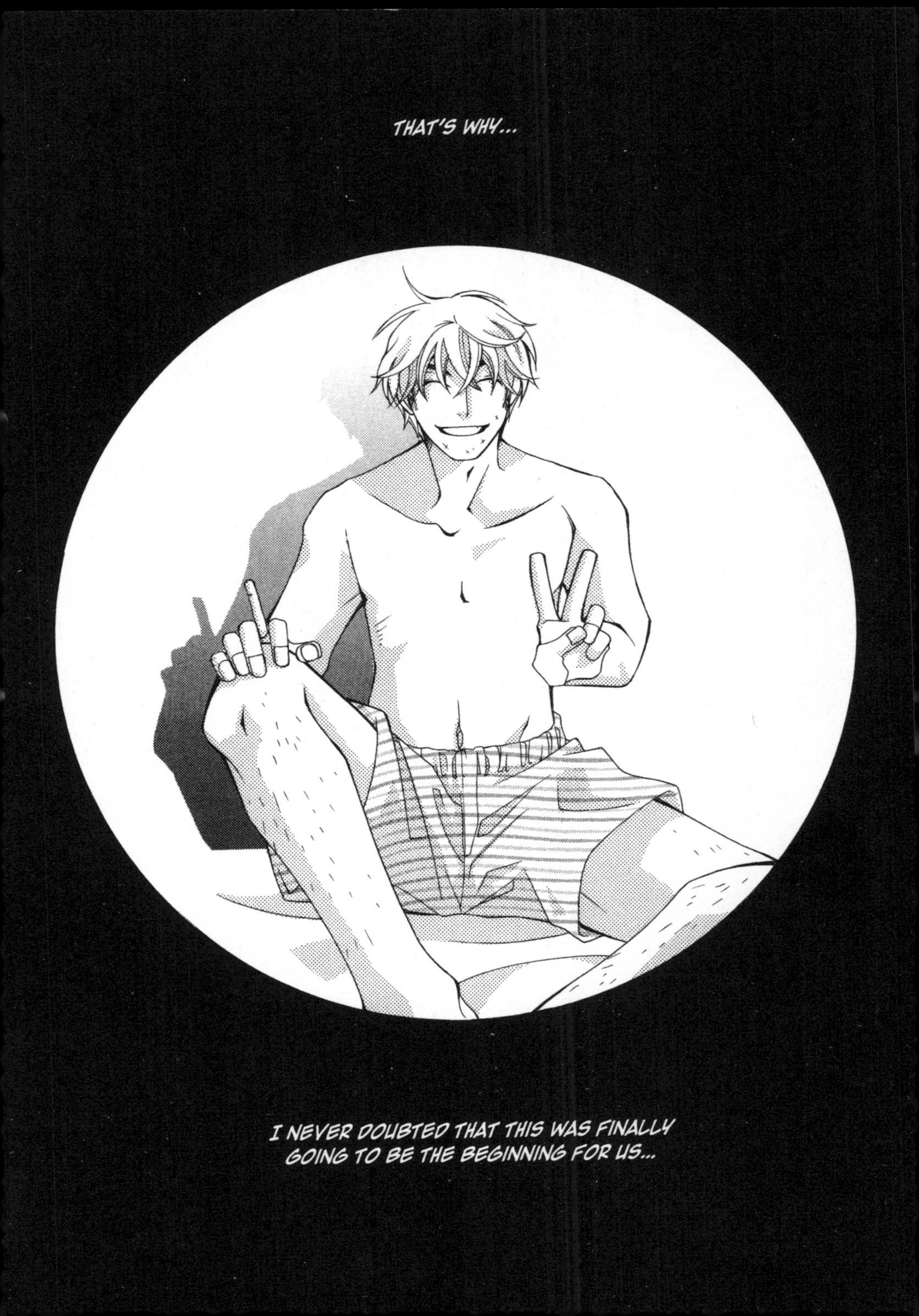
THAT'S WHY...
I NEVER DOUBTED THAT THIS WAS FINALLY GOING TO BE THE BEGINNING FOR US...

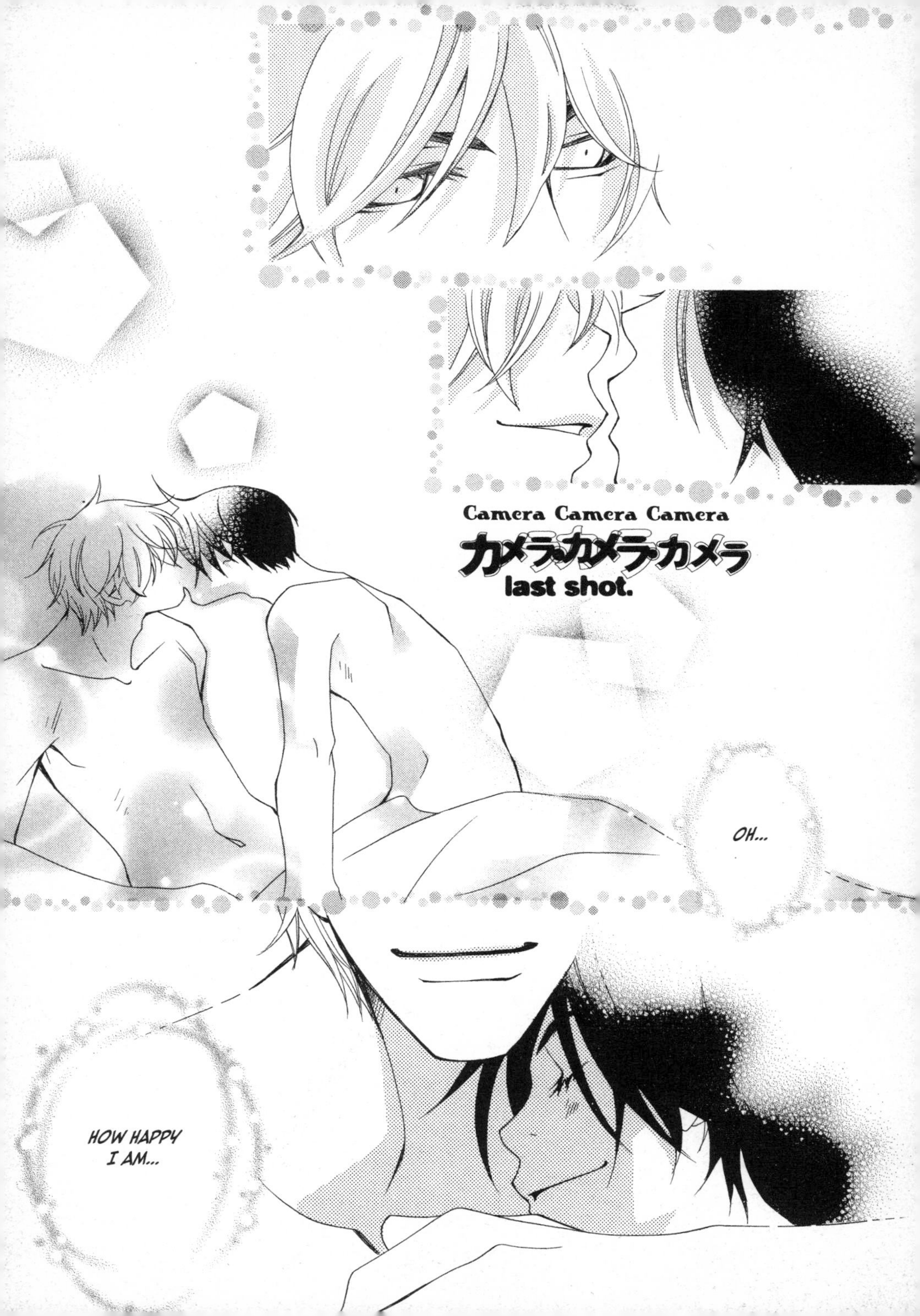
Camera Camera Camera
カメラ・カメラ・カメラ
last shot.
OH...
HOW HAPPY I AM...

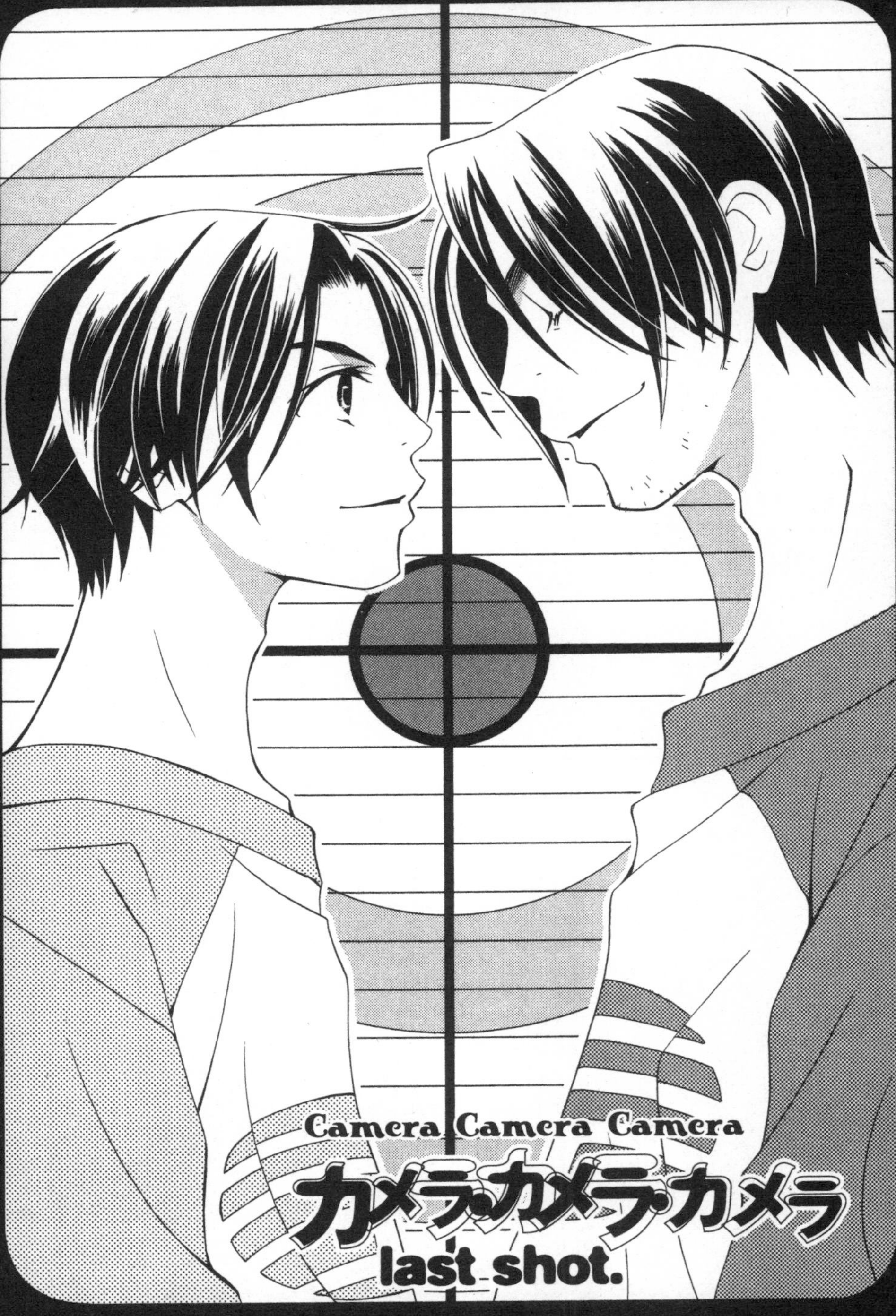
Camera Camera Camera
カメラ・カメラ・カメラ
last shot.

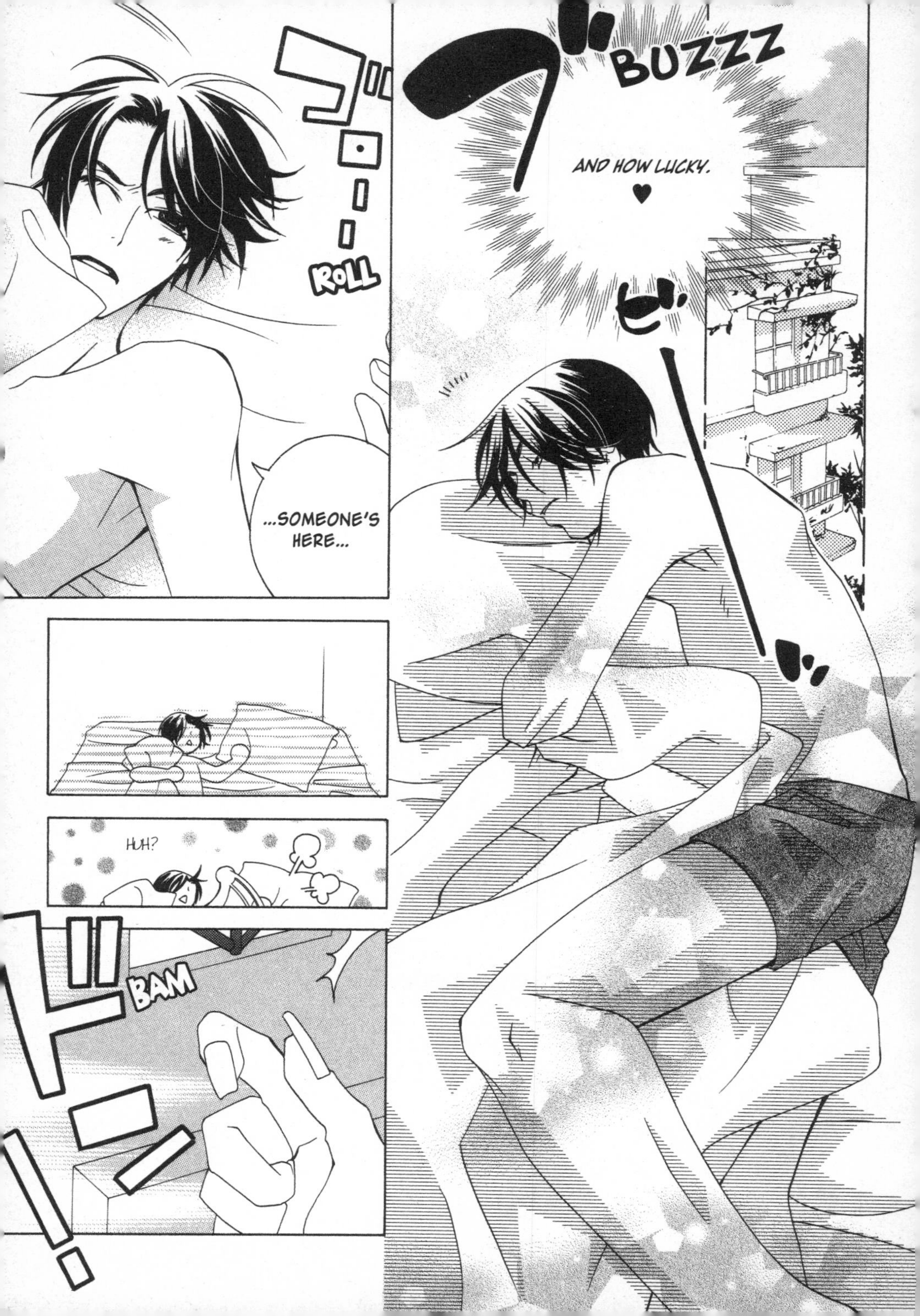
BUZZZ
AND HOW LUCKY. ♥
ROLL
...SOMEONE'S HERE...
HUH?
BAM

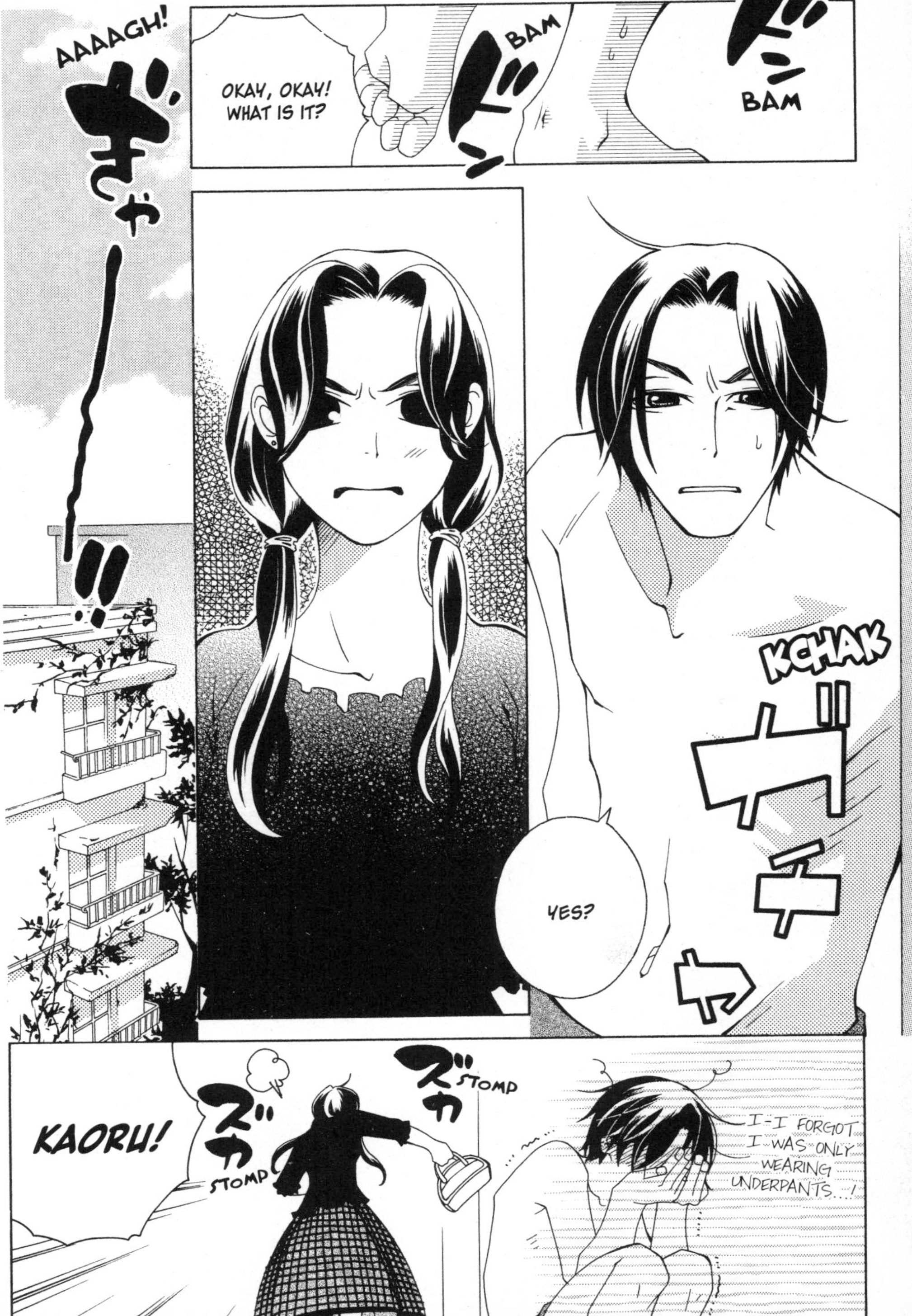
BAM
BAM
OKAY, OKAY! WHAT IS IT?
KCHAK
YES?
AAAAGH!
I-I FORGOT I WAS ONLY WEARING UNDERPANTS...!
STOMP
STOMP
KAORU!

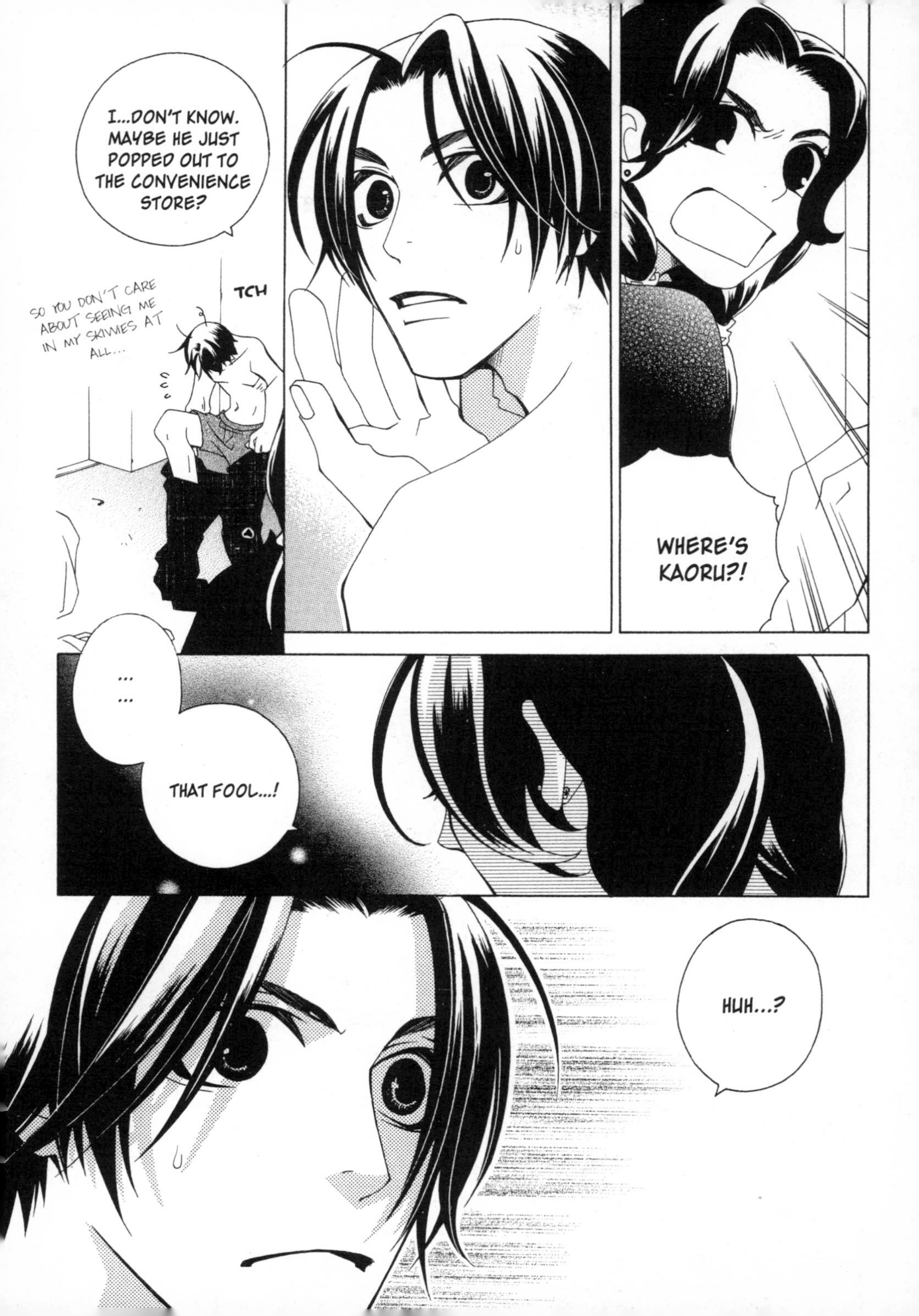
WHERE'S KAORU?!
I...DON'T KNOW. MAYBE HE JUST POPPED OUT TO THE CONVENIENCE STORE?
TCH
SO YOU DON'T CARE ABOUT SEEING ME IN MY SKIVVIES AT ALL...
...
...
THAT FOOL...!
HUH...?

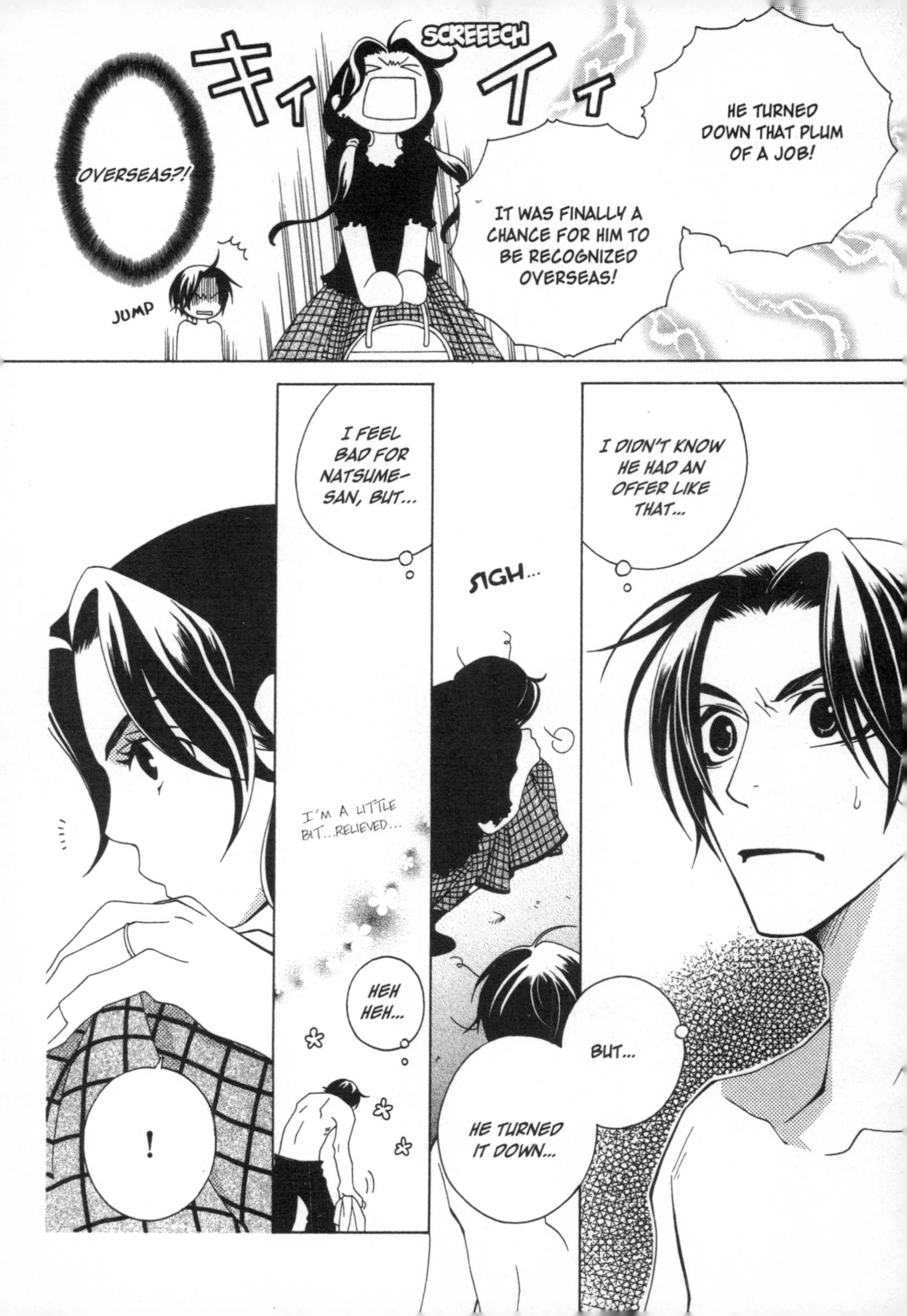
HE TURNED DOWN THAT PLUM OF A JOB!
IT WAS FINALLY A CHANCE FOR HIM TO BE RECOGNIZED OVERSEAS!
SCREEECH
キィイィ
OVERSEAS?!
JUMP
I DIDN'T KNOW HE HAD AN OFFER LIKE THAT...
BUT...
HE TURNED IT DOWN...
I FEEL BAD FOR NATSUME-SAN, BUT...
SIGH...
I'M A LITTLE BIT...RELIEVED...
HEH HEH...
!

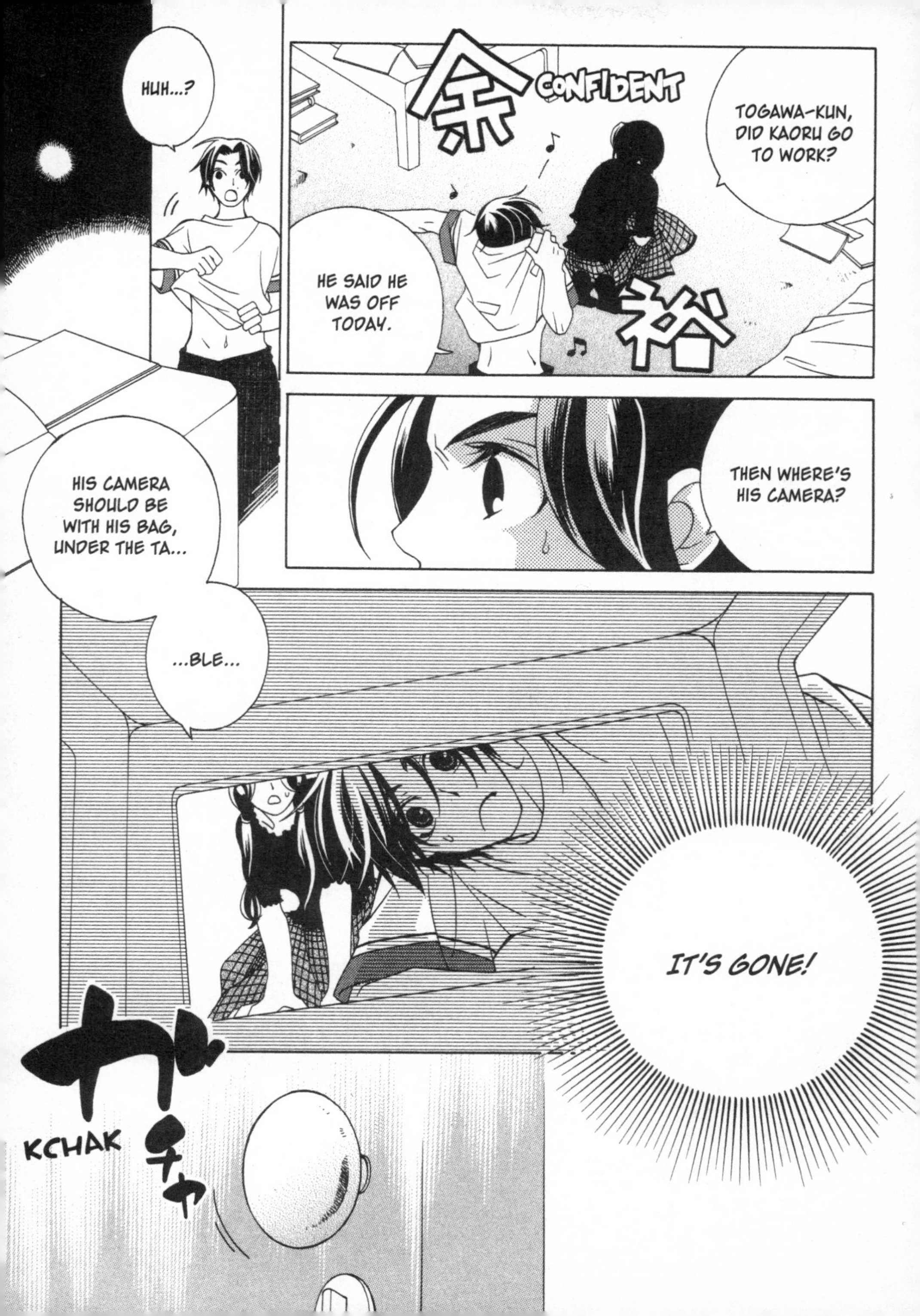
TOGAWA-KUN, DID KAORU GO TO WORK?
CONFIDENT
HE SAID HE WAS OFF TODAY.
THEN WHERE'S HIS CAMERA?
HUH...?
HIS CAMERA SHOULD BE WITH HIS BAG, UNDER THE TA...
...BLE...
IT'S GONE!
KCHAK

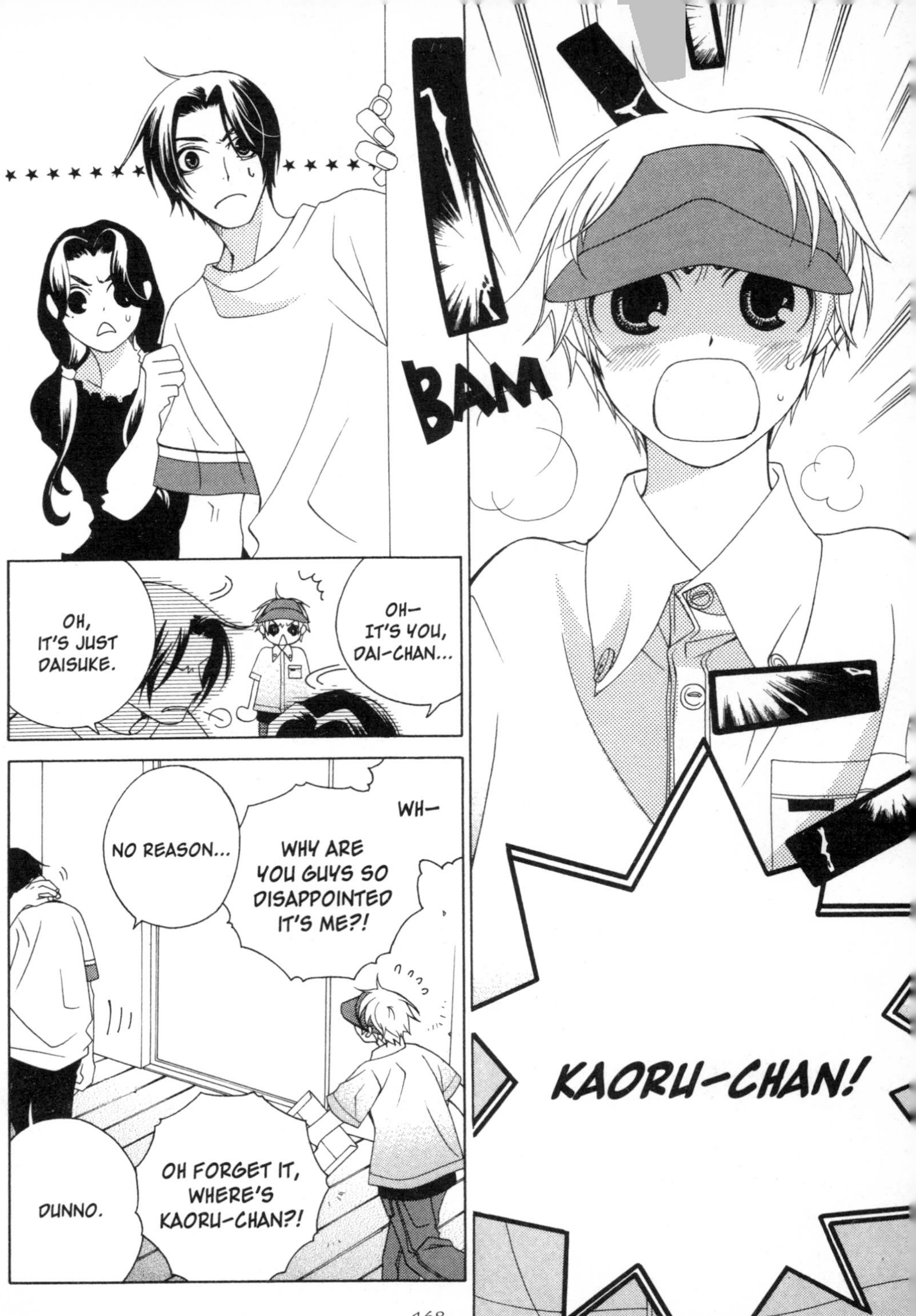
BAM
KAORU-CHAN!
OH— IT'S YOU, DAI-CHAN...
OH, IT'S JUST DAISUKE.
WH—
WHY ARE YOU GUYS SO DISAPPOINTED IT'S ME?!
NO REASON...
OH FORGET IT, WHERE'S KAORU-CHAN?!
DUNNO.

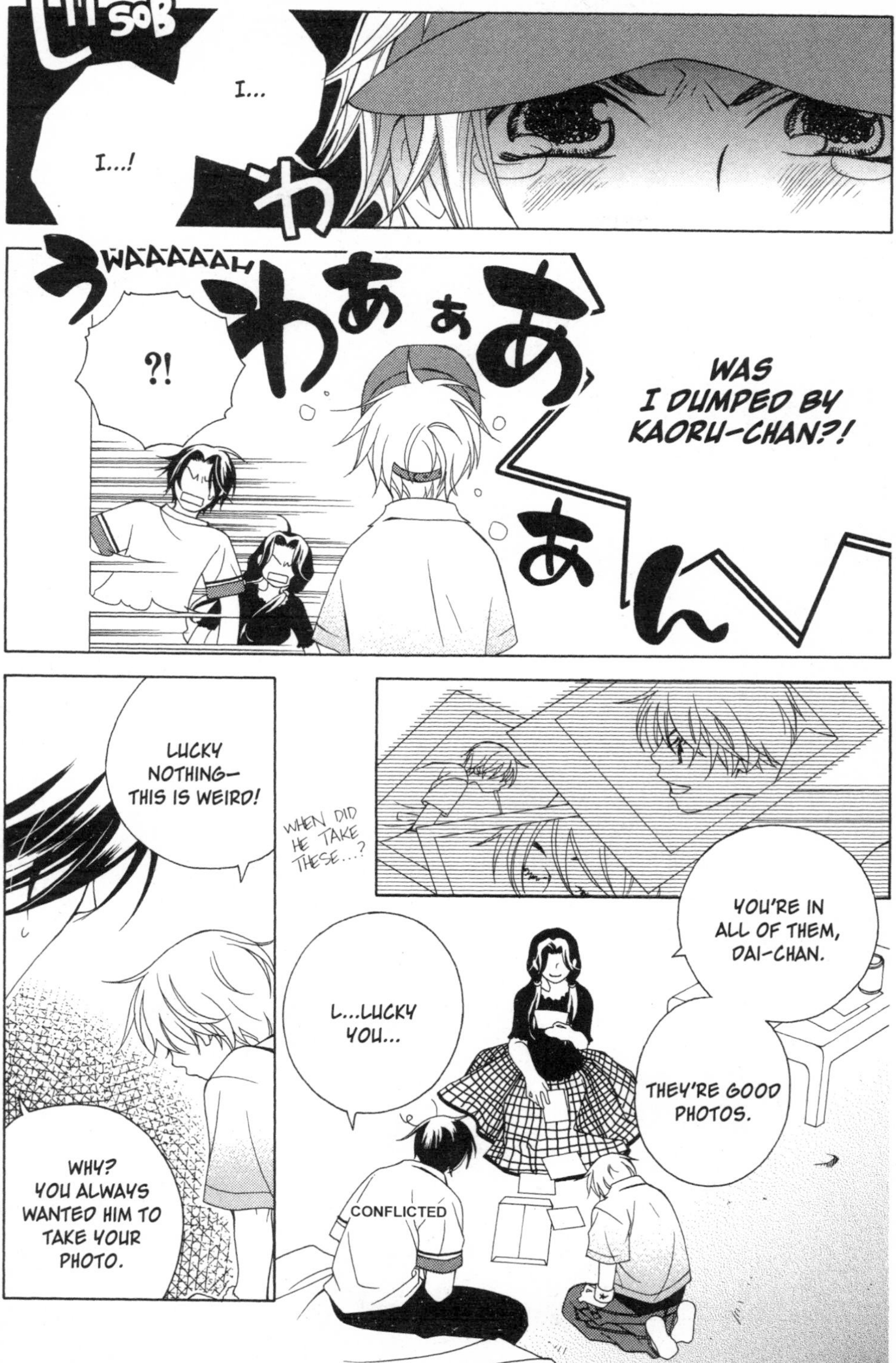
SOB
I...
I...!
わ
WAAAAAH
うわあぁああん
?!
WAS I DUMPED BY KAORU-CHAN?!
YOU'RE IN ALL OF THEM, DAI-CHAN.
THEY'RE GOOD PHOTOS.
L...LUCKY YOU...
CONFLICTED
LUCKY NOTHING— THIS IS WEIRD!
WHEN DID HE TAKE THESE...?
WHY? YOU ALWAYS WANTED HIM TO TAKE YOUR PHOTO.

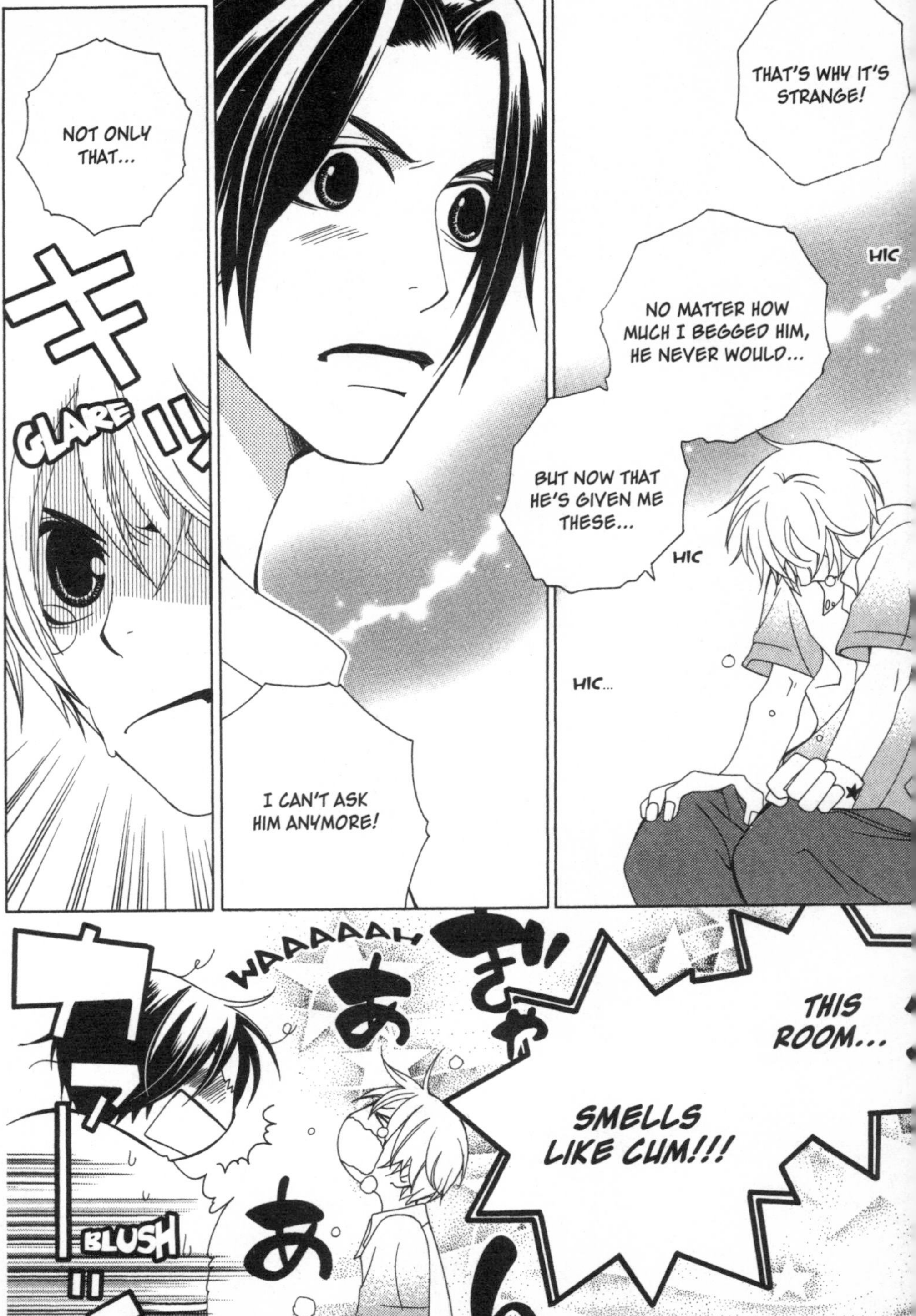
THAT'S WHY IT'S STRANGE!
HIC
NO MATTER HOW MUCH I BEGGED HIM, HE NEVER WOULD...
BUT NOW THAT HE'S GIVEN ME THESE...
HIC
HIC...
I CAN'T ASK HIM ANYMORE!
NOT ONLY THAT...
キ
GLARE
!!
THIS ROOM...
SMELLS LIKE CUM!!!
ぎゃあああん
WAAAAAH
カァ
BLUSH
!!

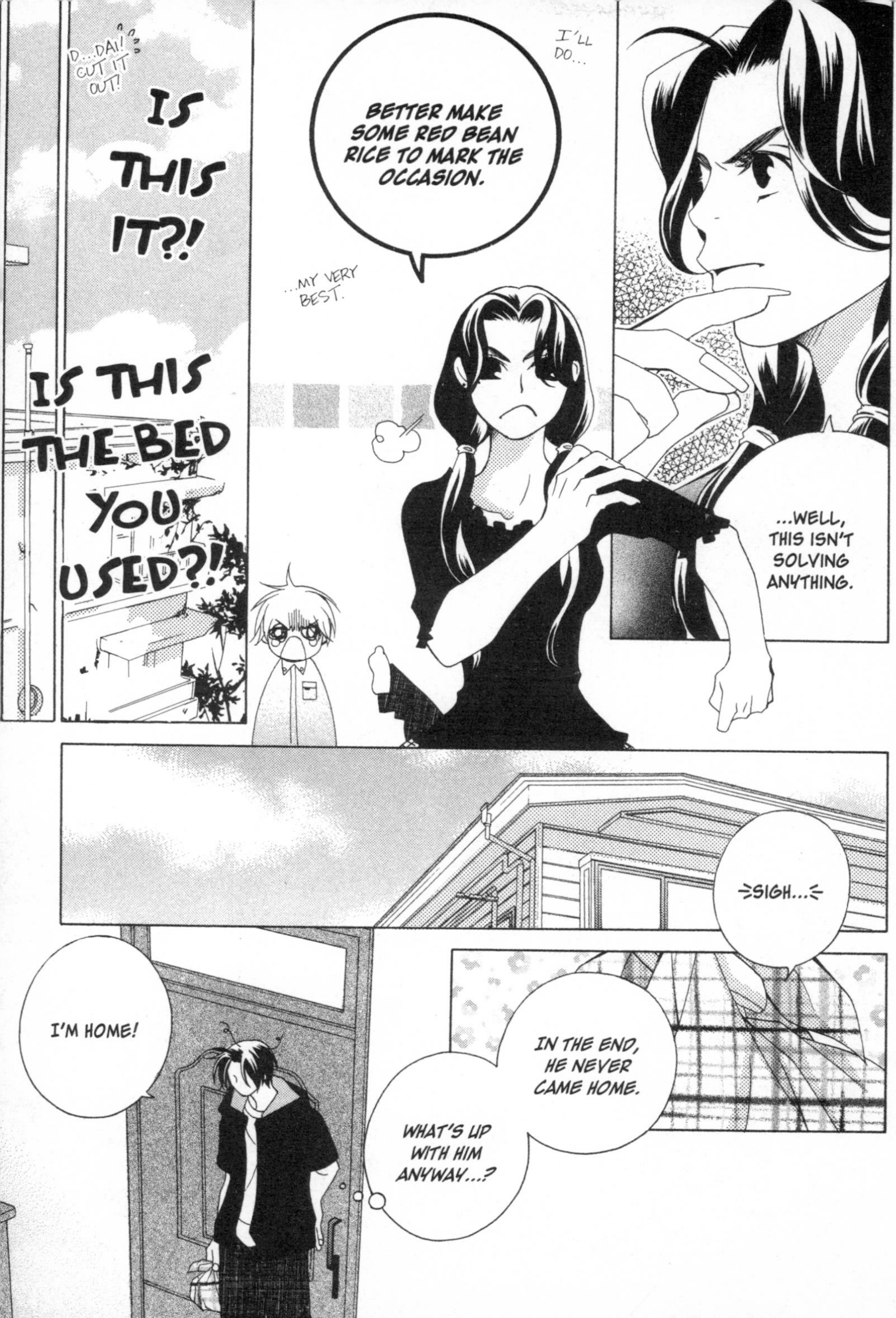
...WELL, THIS ISN'T SOLVING ANYTHING.
I'LL DO...
BETTER MAKE SOME RED BEAN RICE TO MARK THE OCCASION.
...MY VERY BEST.
IS THIS IT?!
IS THIS THE BED YOU USED?!
D...DAI! CUT IT OUT!
SIGH...
IN THE END, HE NEVER CAME HOME.
WHAT'S UP WITH HIM ANYWAY...?
I'M HOME!

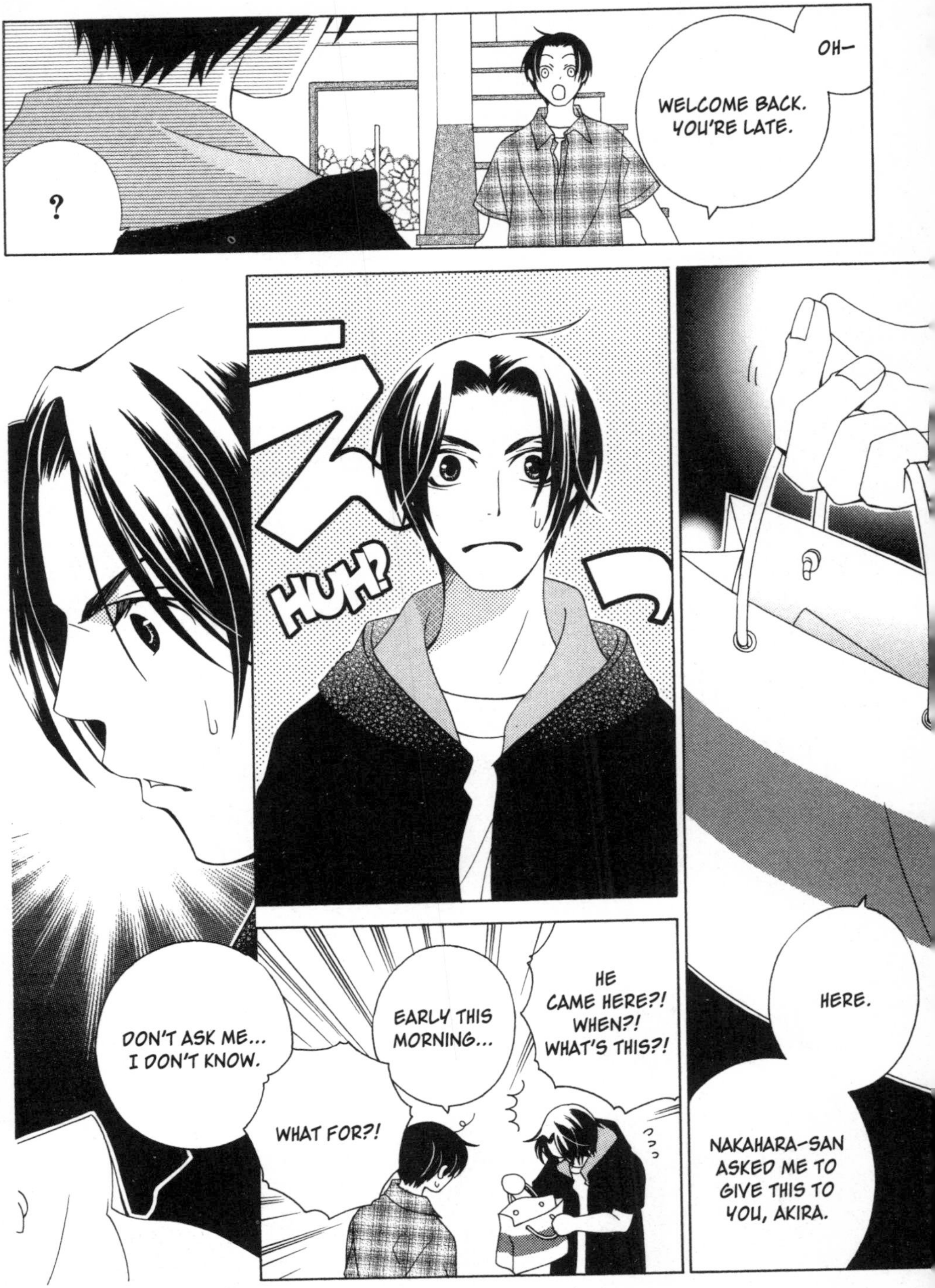
OH—
WELCOME BACK. YOU'RE LATE.
?
HERE.
NAKAHARA-SAN ASKED ME TO GIVE THIS TO YOU, AKIRA.
HUH?
HE CAME HERE?! WHEN?! WHAT'S THIS?!
EARLY THIS MORNING...
WHAT FOR?!
DON'T ASK ME... I DON'T KNOW.

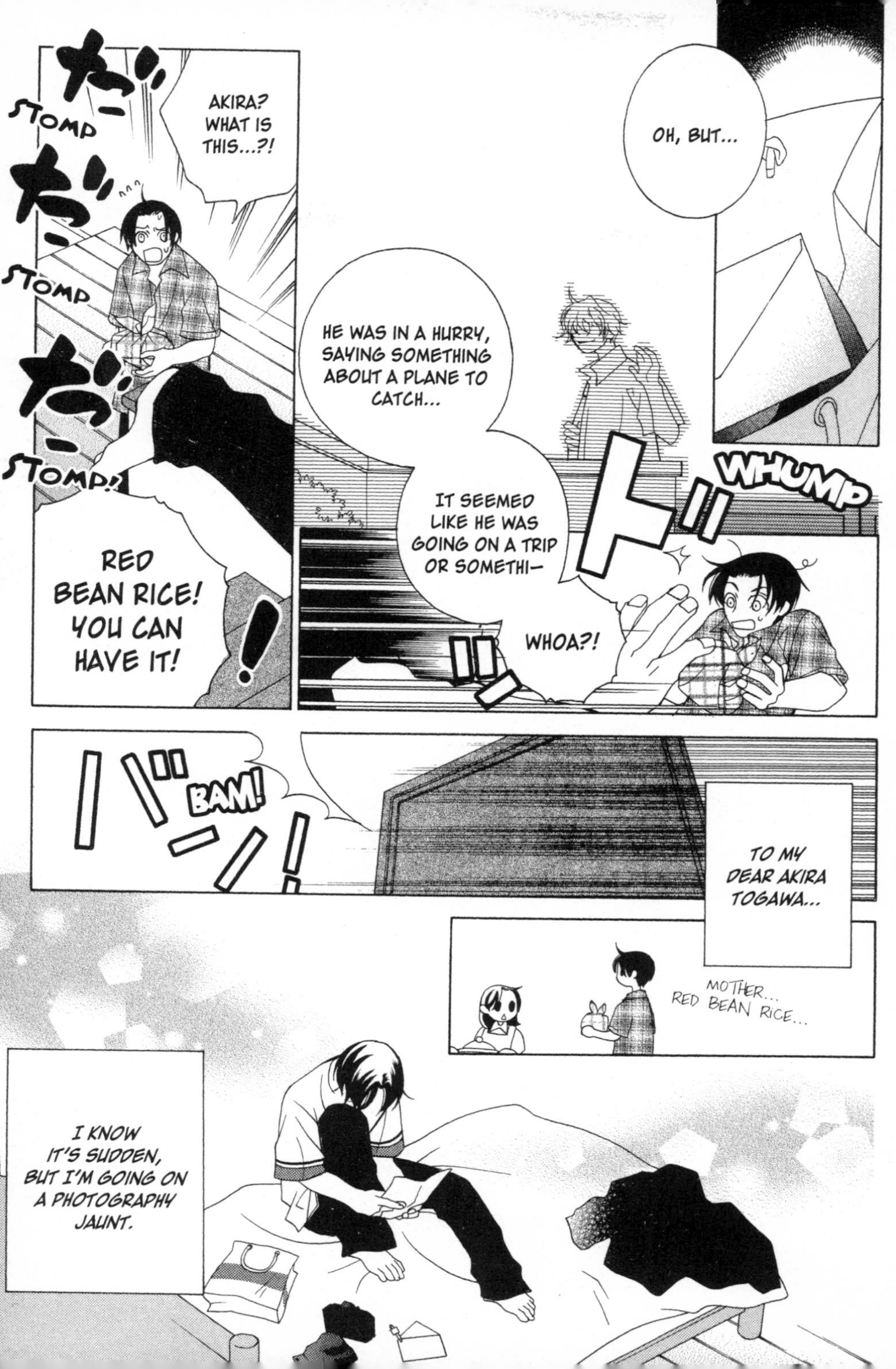
OH, BUT...
HE WAS IN A HURRY, SAYING SOMETHING ABOUT A PLANE TO CATCH...
IT SEEMED LIKE HE WAS GOING ON A TRIP OR SOMETHI—
WHUMP
WHOA?!
STOMP
STOMP
STOMP!
AKIRA? WHAT IS THIS...?!
RED BEAN RICE! YOU CAN HAVE IT!
BAM!
TO MY DEAR AKIRA TOGAWA...
MOTHER... RED BEAN RICE...
I KNOW IT'S SUDDEN, BUT I'M GOING ON A PHOTOGRAPHY JAUNT.

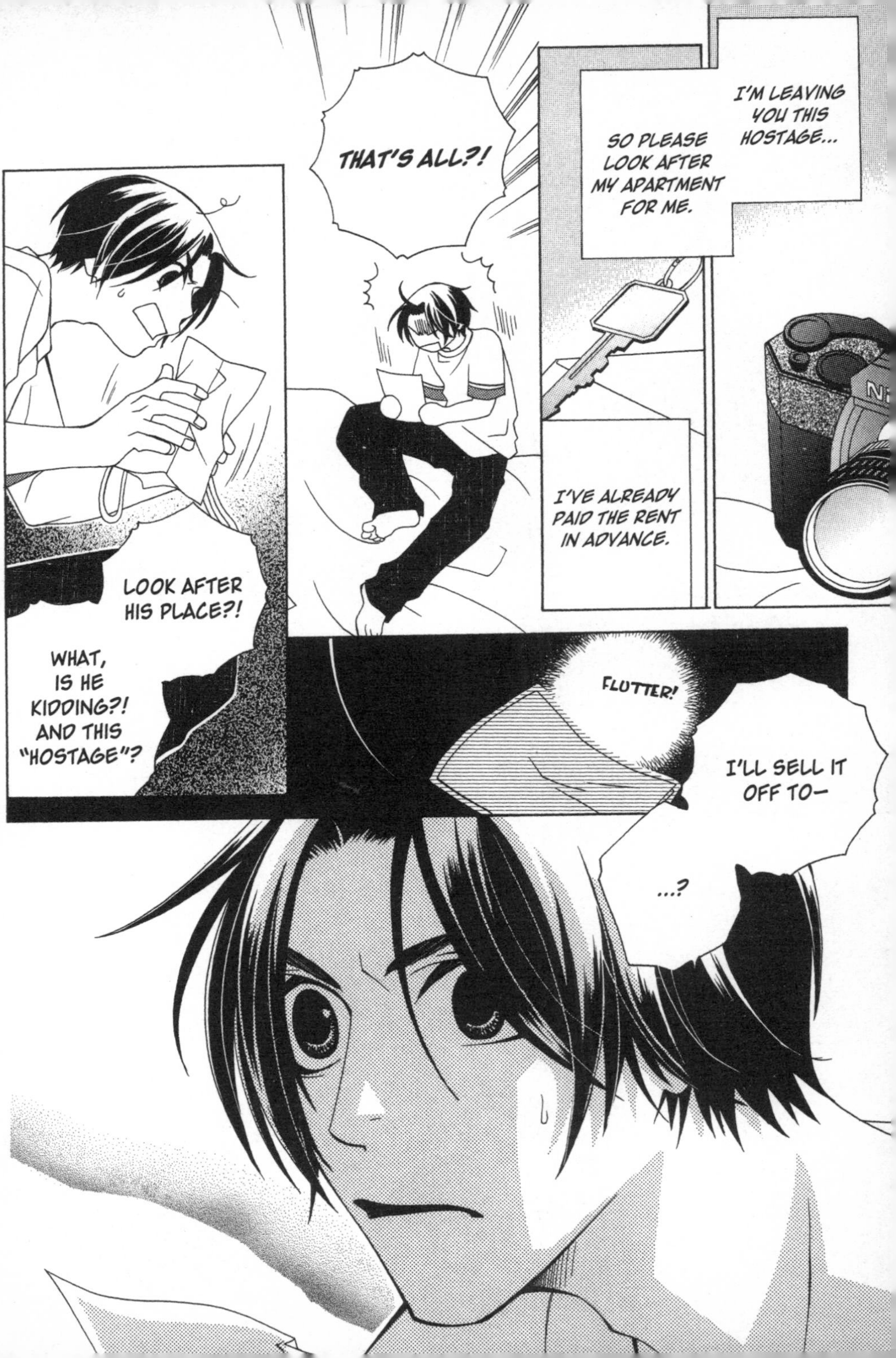
I'M LEAVING YOU THIS HOSTAGE...
SO PLEASE LOOK AFTER MY APARTMENT FOR ME.
I'VE ALREADY PAID THE RENT IN ADVANCE.
THAT'S ALL?!
LOOK AFTER HIS PLACE?!
WHAT, IS HE KIDDING?! AND THIS "HOSTAGE"?
FLUTTER!
I'LL SELL IT OFF TO—
...?

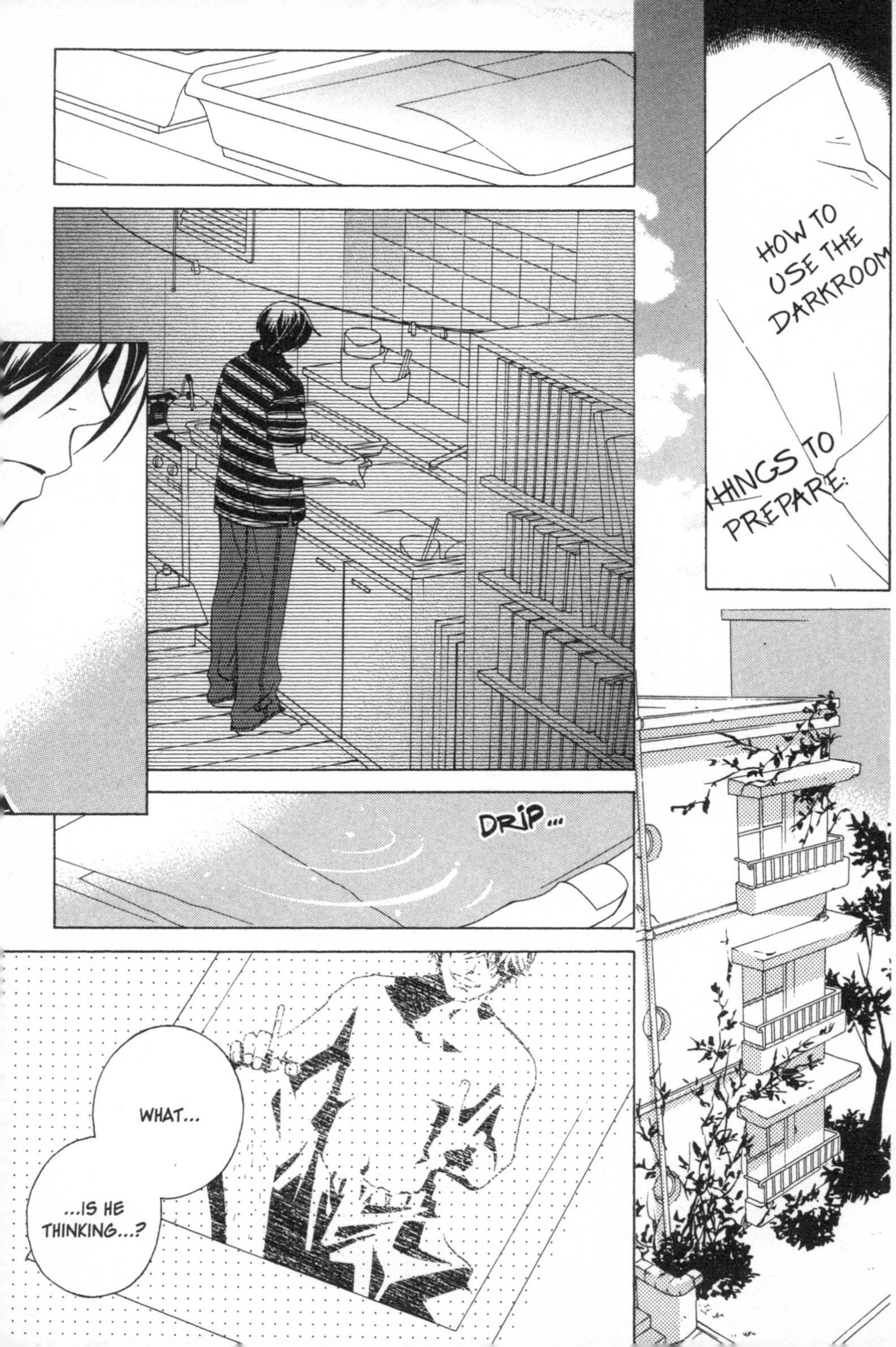
HOW TO USE THE DARKROOM
THINGS TO PREPARE:
DRIP...
WHAT...
...IS HE THINKING...?

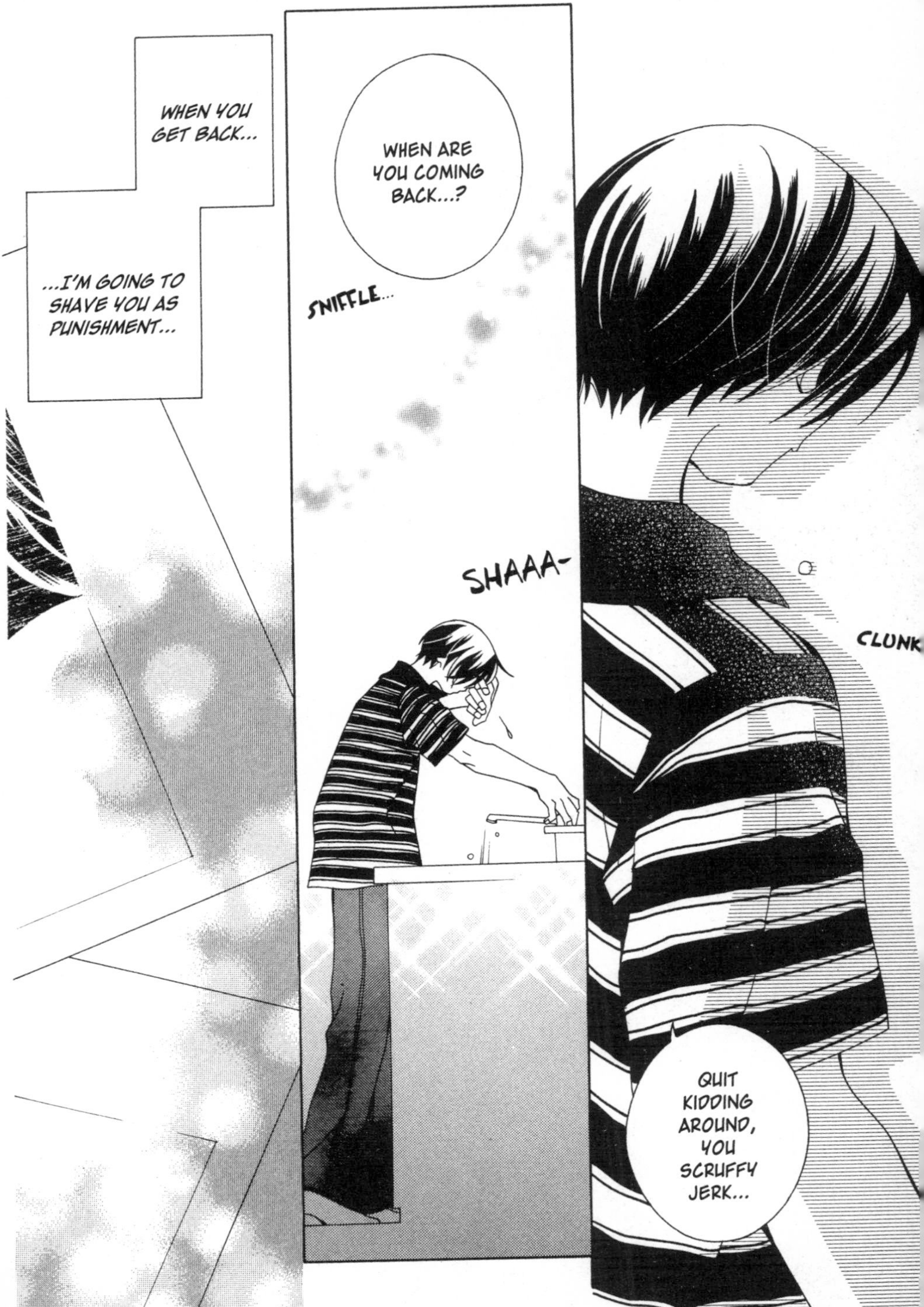
CLUNK
QUIT KIDDING AROUND, YOU SCRUFFY JERK...
WHEN ARE YOU COMING BACK...?
SNIFFLE...
SHAAA-
WHEN YOU GET BACK...
...I'M GOING TO SHAVE YOU AS PUNISHMENT...

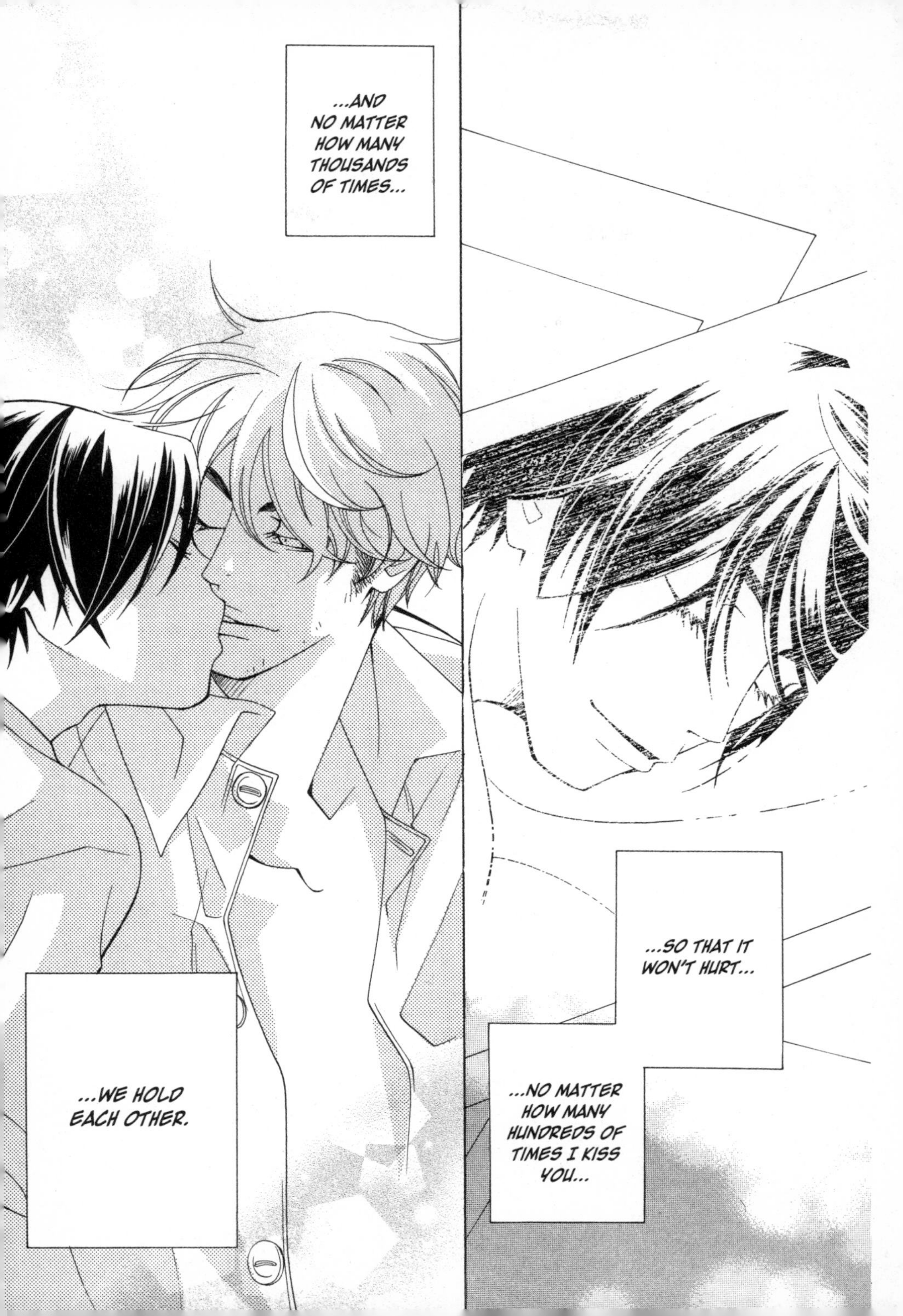
...SO THAT IT WON'T HURT...
...NO MATTER HOW MANY HUNDREDS OF TIMES I KISS YOU...
...AND NO MATTER HOW MANY THOUSANDS OF TIMES...
...WE HOLD EACH OTHER.

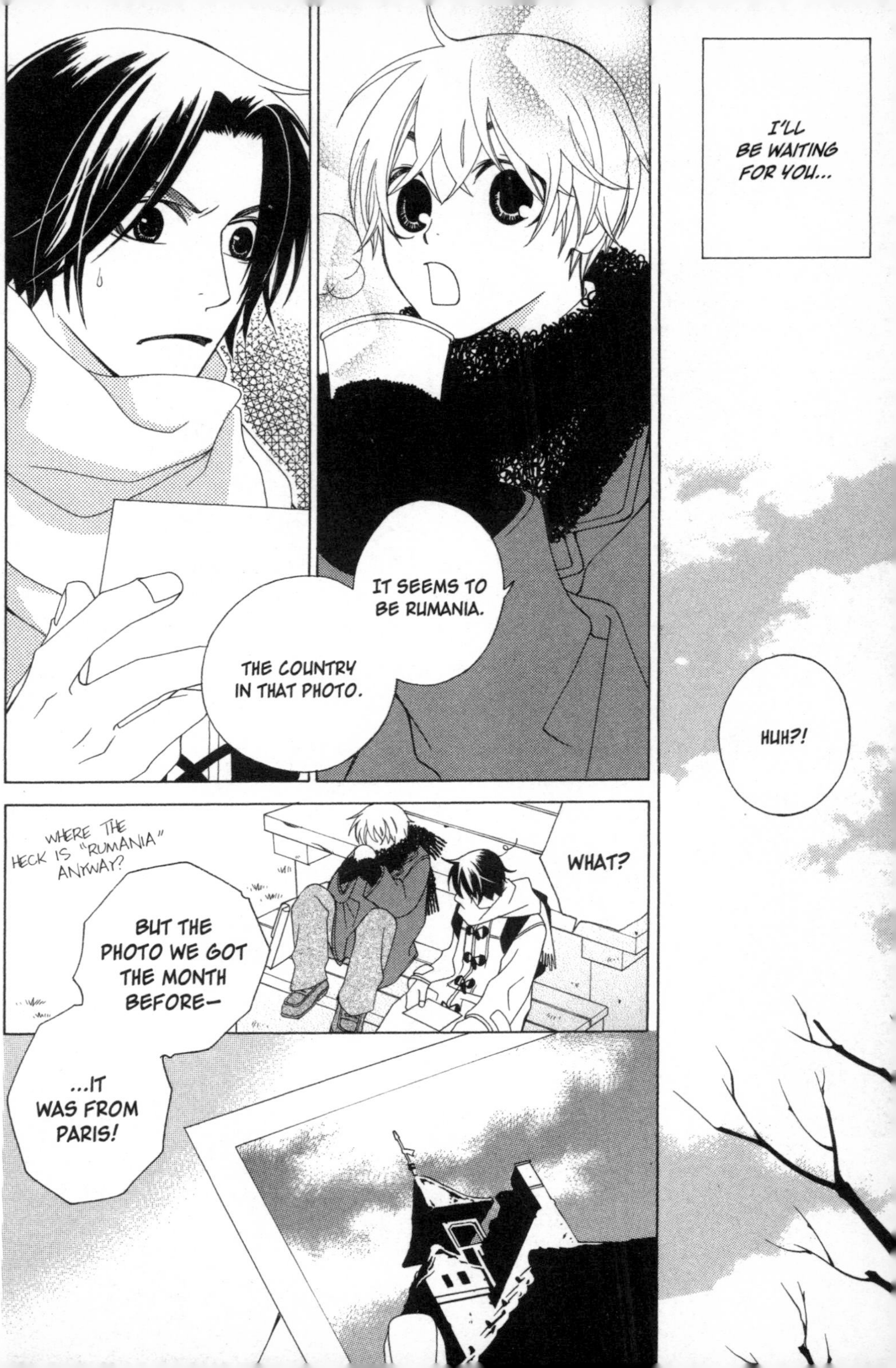
I'LL BE WAITING FOR YOU...
HUH?!
IT SEEMS TO BE RUMANIA.
THE COUNTRY IN THAT PHOTO.
WHAT?
WHERE THE HECK IS "RUMANIA" ANYWAY?
BUT THE PHOTO WE GOT THE MONTH BEFORE—
...IT WAS FROM PARIS!

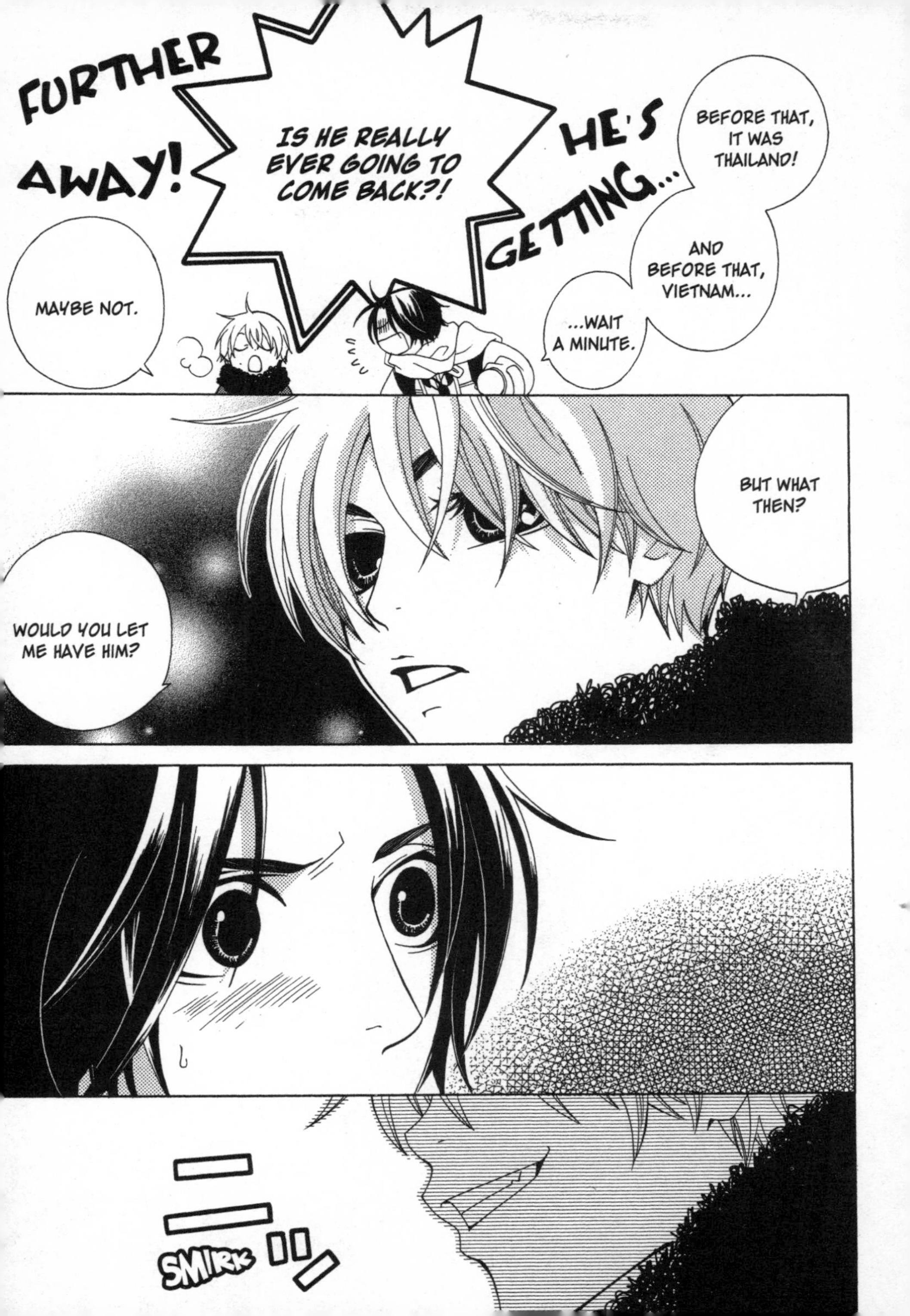
BEFORE THAT, IT WAS THAILAND!
AND BEFORE THAT, VIETNAM...
HE'S GETTING... FURTHER AWAY!
IS HE REALLY EVER GOING TO COME BACK?!
...WAIT A MINUTE.
MAYBE NOT.
BUT WHAT THEN?
WOULD YOU LET ME HAVE HIM?
SMIRK

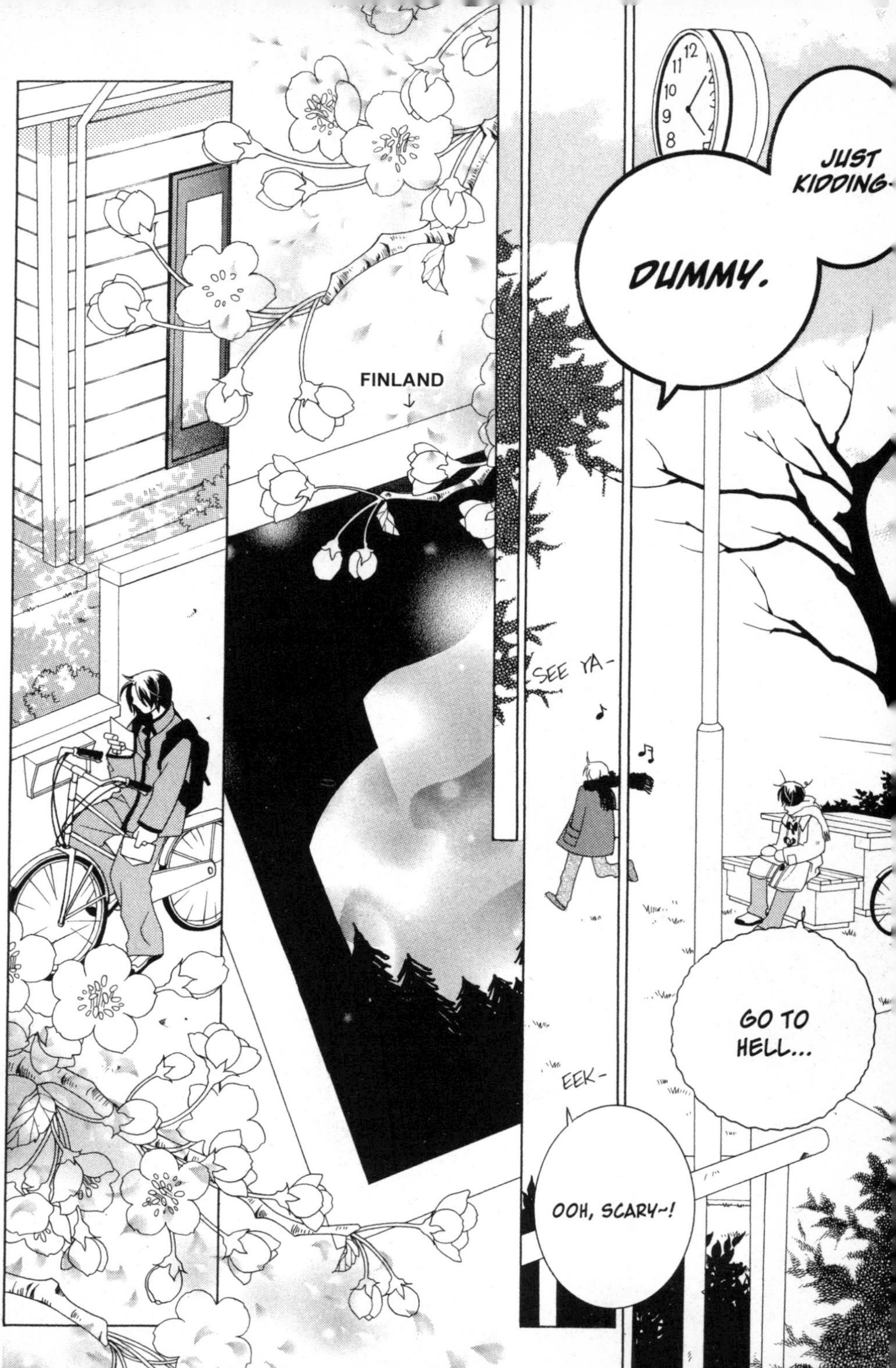
JUST KIDDING-
DUMMY.
SEE YA-
GO TO HELL...
EEK-
OOH, SCARY~!
FINLAND

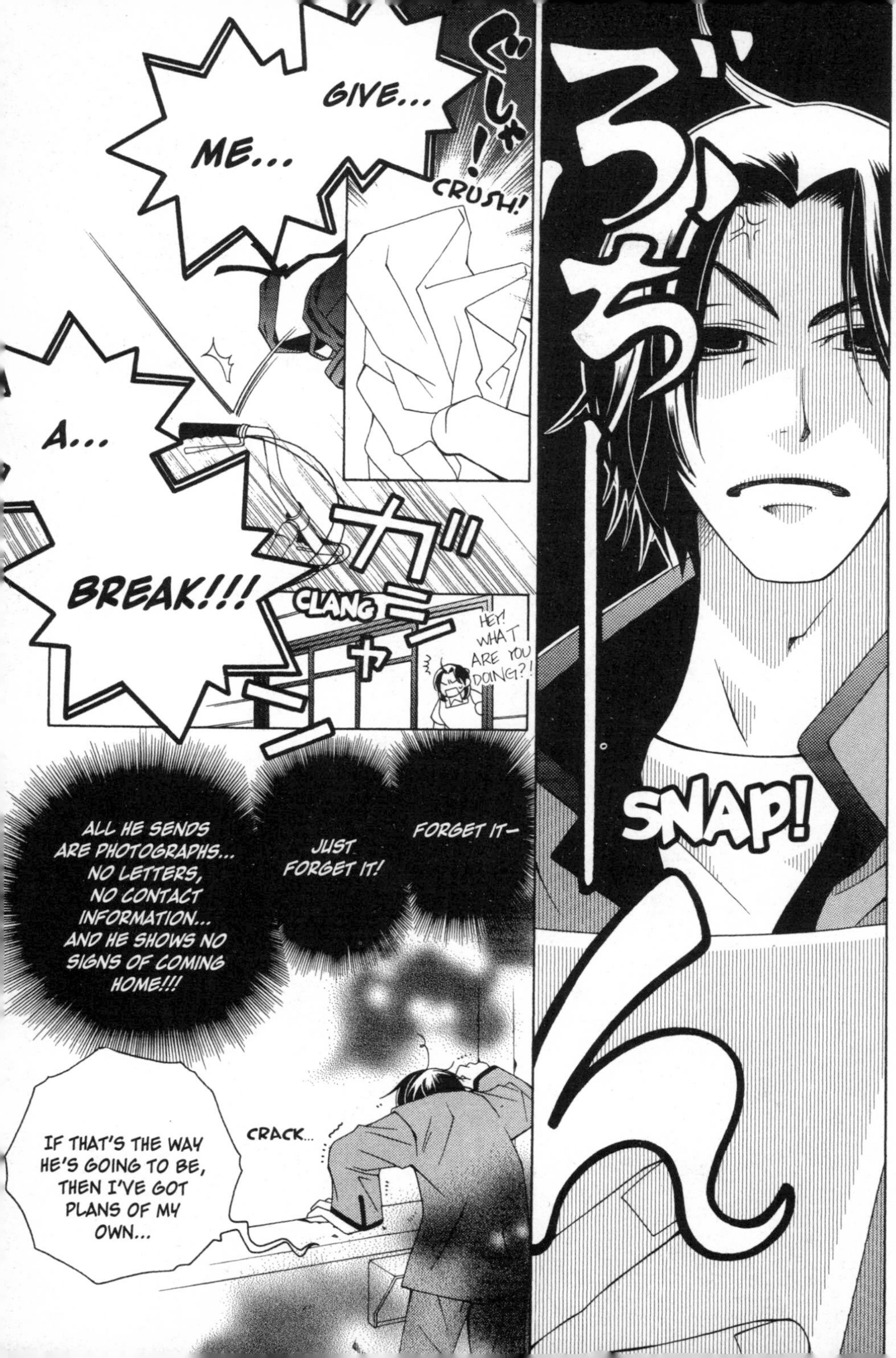
SNAP!
GIVE...
ME...
CRUSH!
A...
BREAK!!!
CLANG
HEY! WHAT ARE YOU DOING?!
FORGET IT—
JUST FORGET IT!
ALL HE SENDS ARE PHOTOGRAPHS... NO LETTERS, NO CONTACT INFORMATION... AND HE SHOWS NO SIGNS OF COMING HOME!!!
CRACK...
IF THAT'S THE WAY HE'S GOING TO BE, THEN I'VE GOT PLANS OF MY OWN...

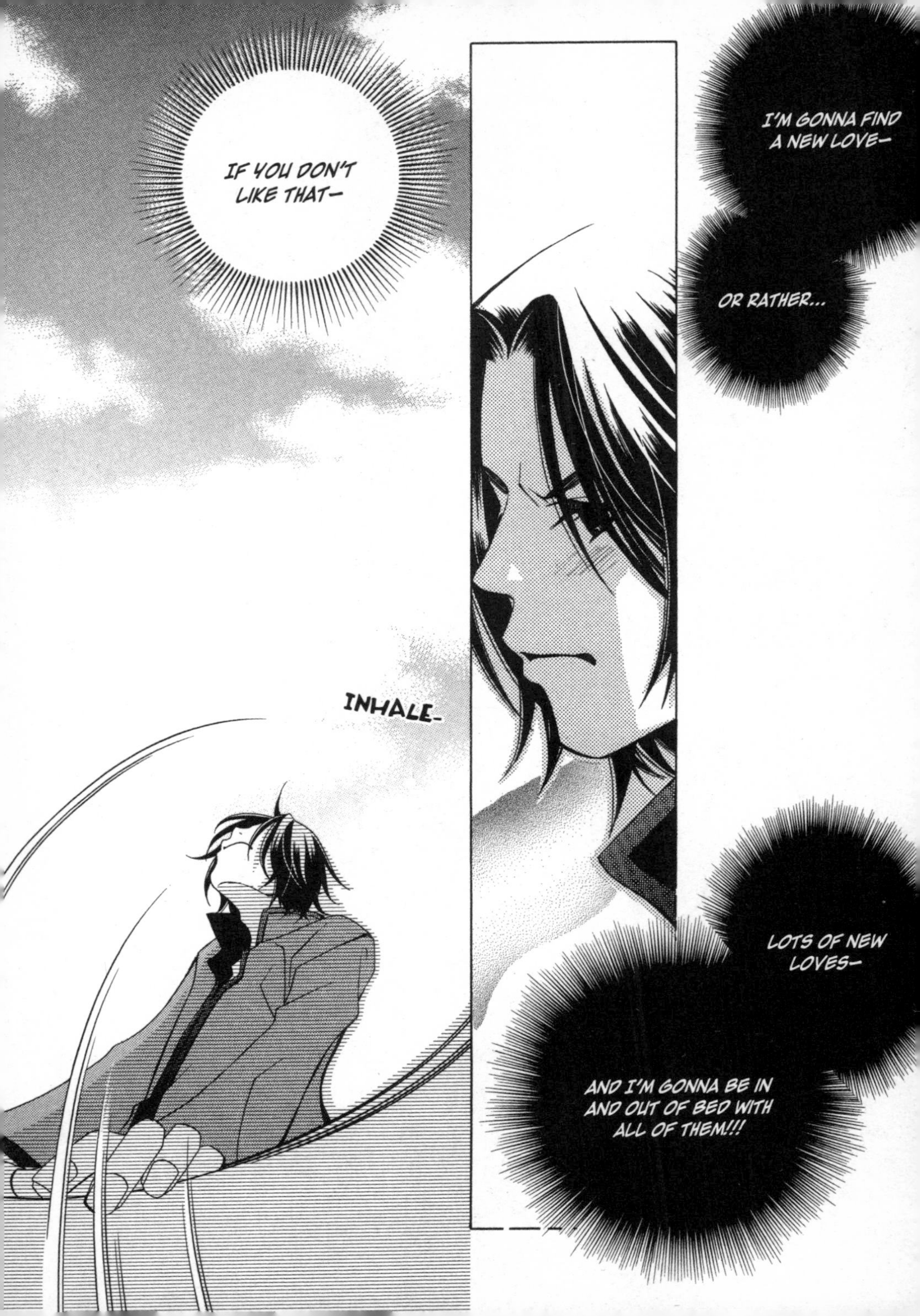
I'M GONNA FIND A NEW LOVE–
OR RATHER...
LOTS OF NEW LOVES–
AND I'M GONNA BE IN AND OUT OF BED WITH ALL OF THEM!!!
IF YOU DON'T LIKE THAT–
INHALE-

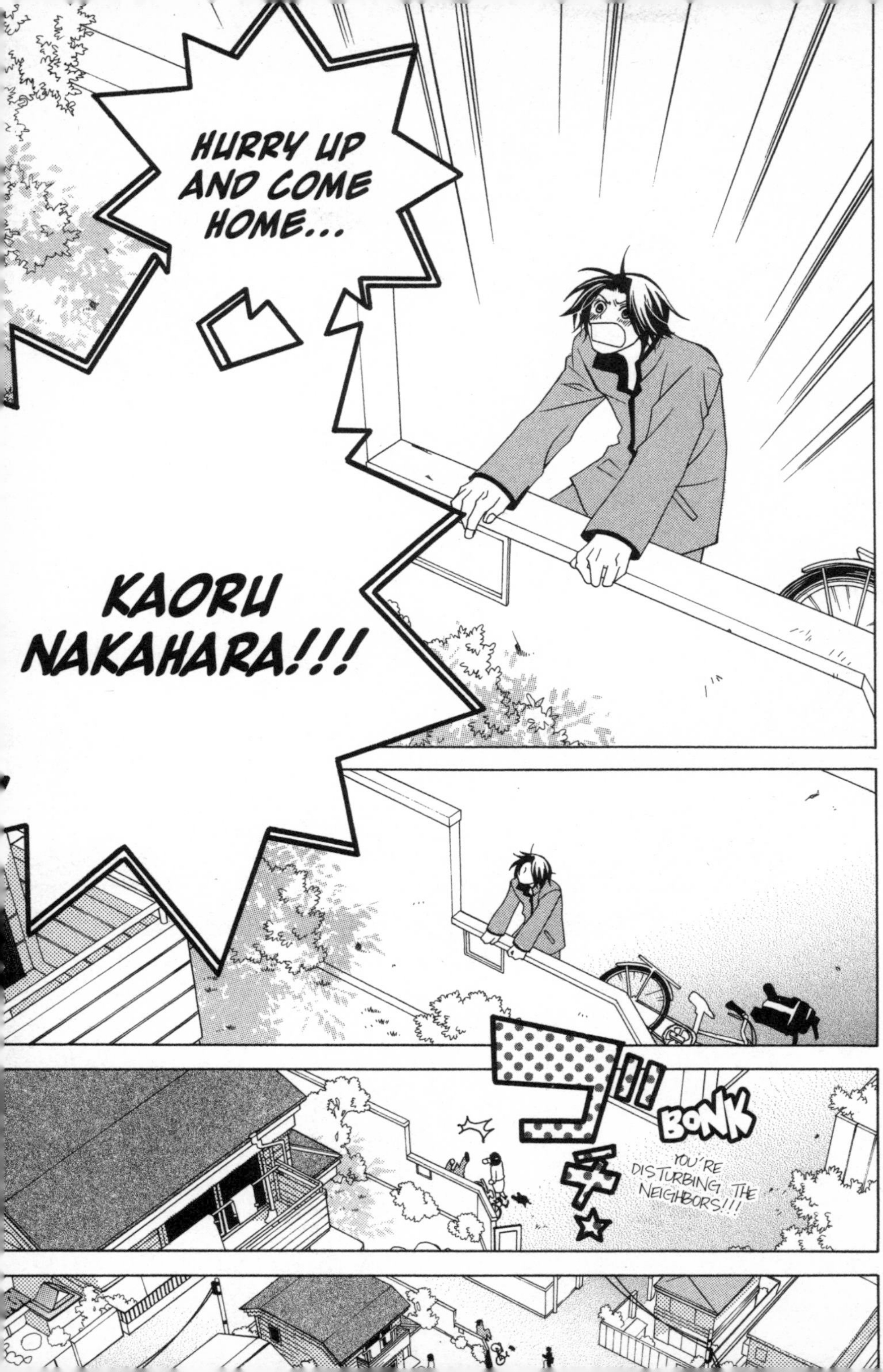
HURRY UP AND COME HOME...
KAORU NAKAHARA!!!
BONK
YOU'RE DISTURBING THE NEIGHBORS!!!

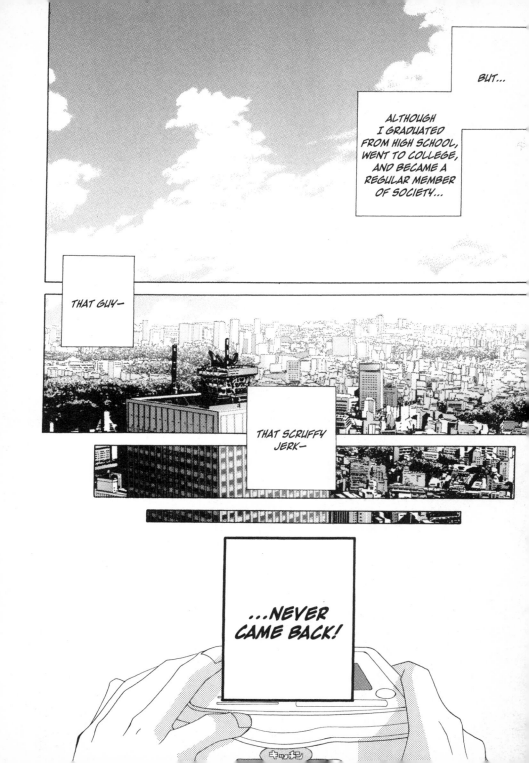

BUT...

ALTHOUGH
I GRADUATED
FROM HIGH SCHOOL,
WENT TO COLLEGE,
AND BECAME A
REGULAR MEMBER
OF SOCIETY...

THAT GUY—

THAT SCRUFFY
JERK—

...NEVER
CAME BACK!

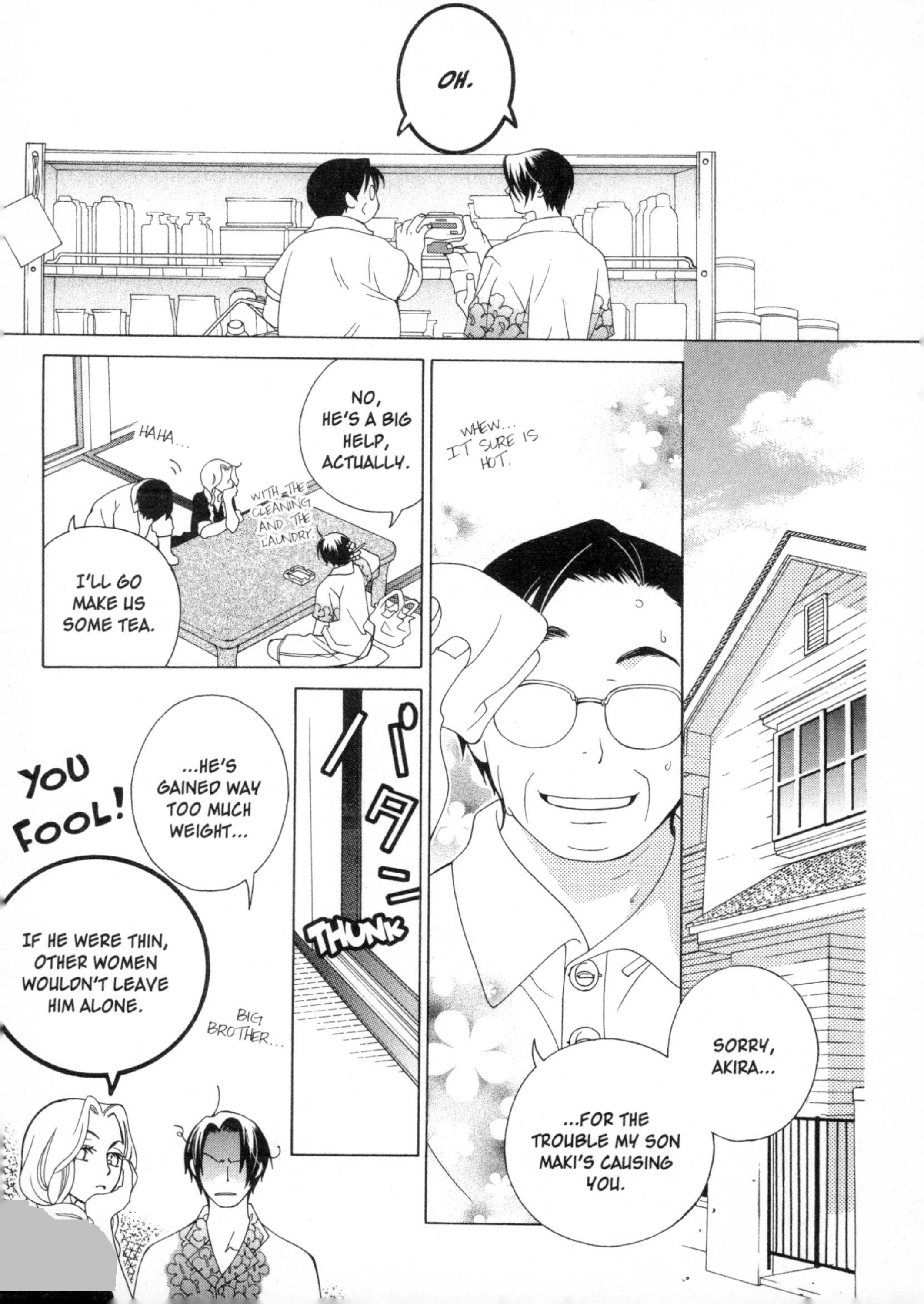
OH.
WHEW... IT SURE IS HOT.
SORRY, AKIRA...
...FOR THE TROUBLE MY SON MAKI'S CAUSING YOU.
NO, HE'S A BIG HELP, ACTUALLY.
WITH THE CLEANING AND THE LAUNDRY.
HAHA...
I'LL GO MAKE US SOME TEA.
パタン
THUNK
...HE'S GAINED WAY TOO MUCH WEIGHT...
YOU FOOL!
IF HE WERE THIN, OTHER WOMEN WOULDN'T LEAVE HIM ALONE.
BIG BROTHER...

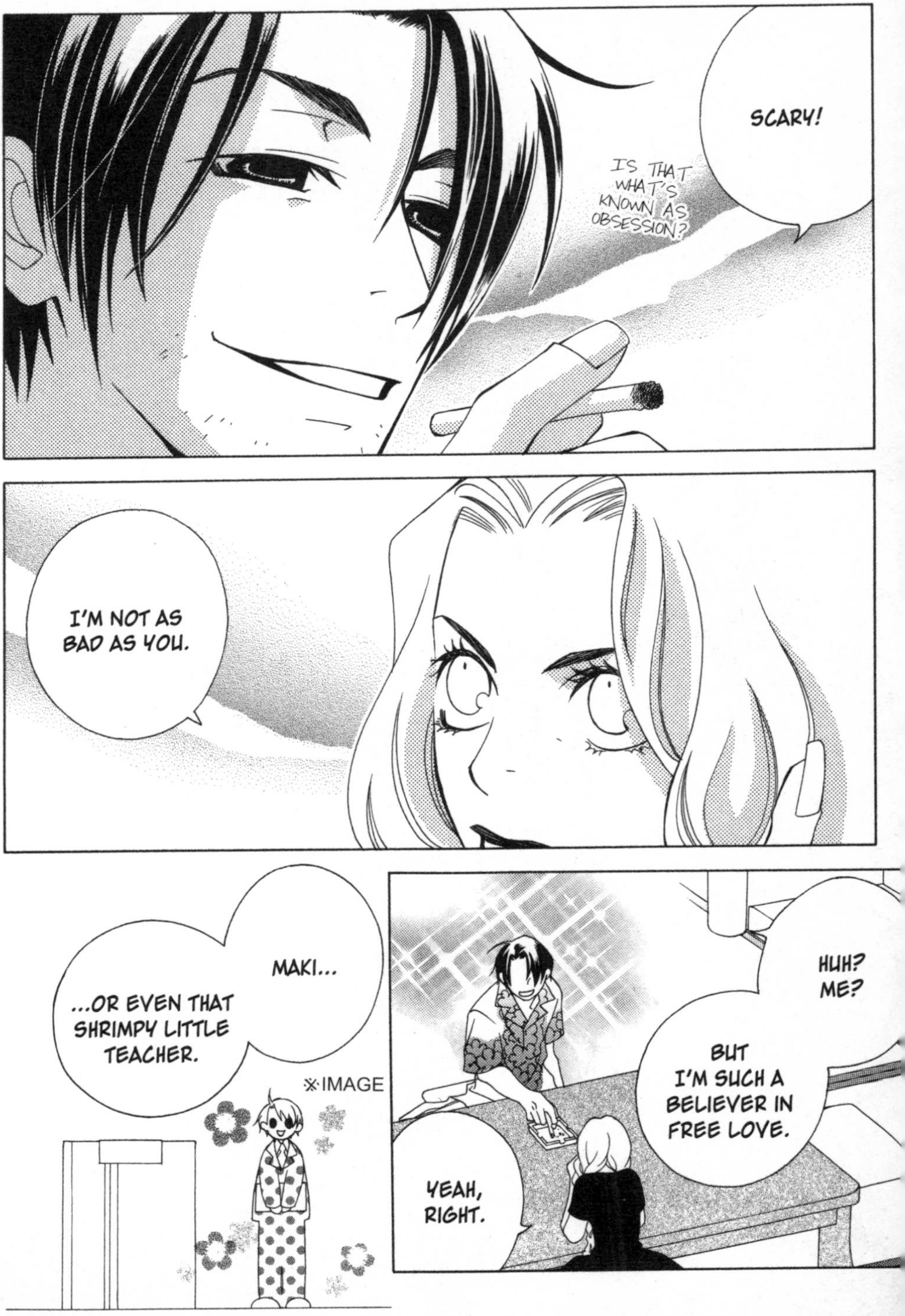
SCARY!
IS THAT WHAT'S KNOWN AS OBSESSION?
I'M NOT AS BAD AS YOU.
HUH? ME?
BUT I'M SUCH A BELIEVER IN FREE LOVE.
YEAH, RIGHT.
MAKI...
...OR EVEN THAT SHRIMPY LITTLE TEACHER.
※IMAGE

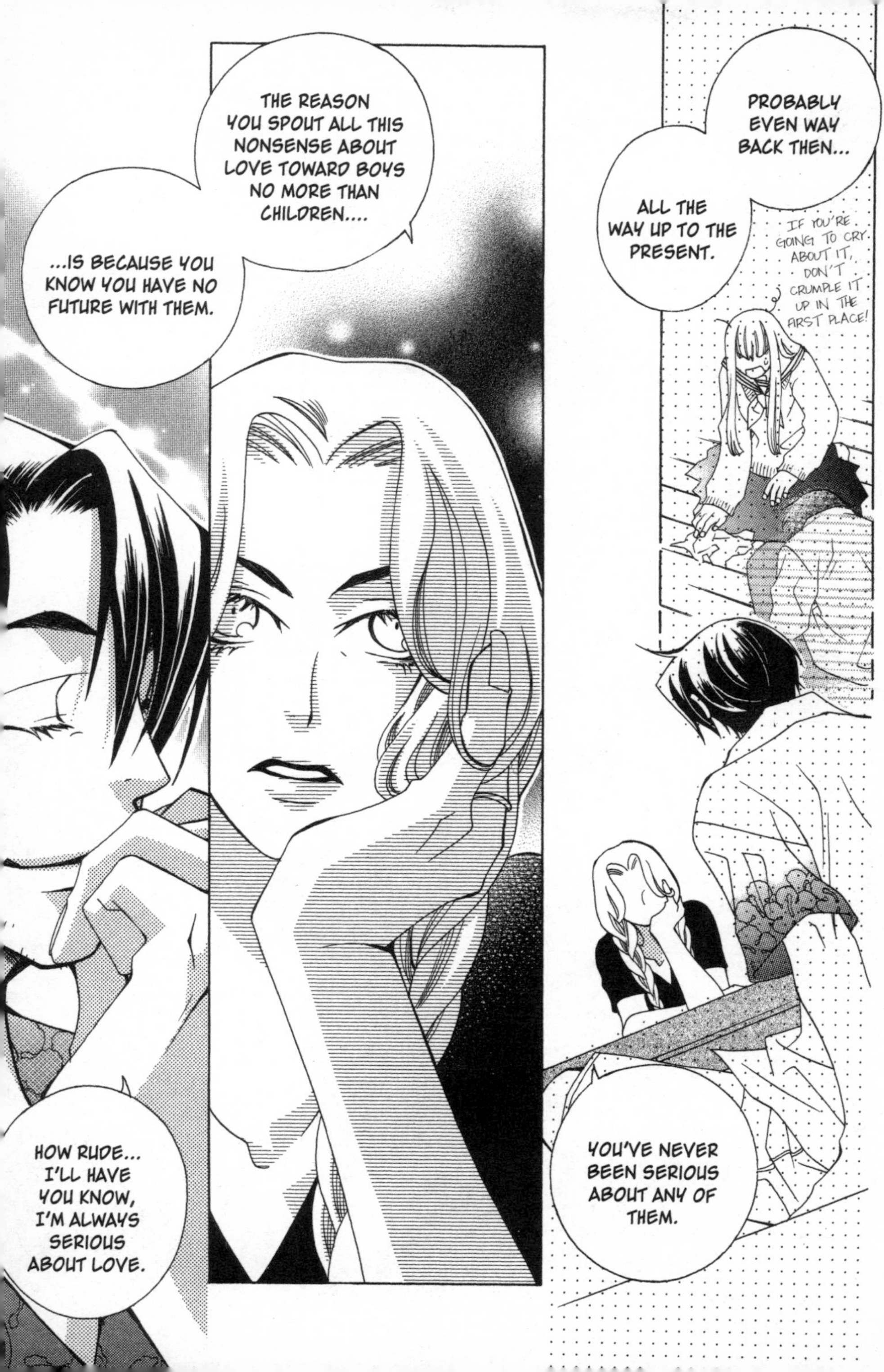
PROBABLY EVEN WAY BACK THEN...
ALL THE WAY UP TO THE PRESENT.
IF YOU'RE GOING TO CRY ABOUT IT, DON'T CRUMPLE IT UP IN THE FIRST PLACE!
YOU'VE NEVER BEEN SERIOUS ABOUT ANY OF THEM.
THE REASON YOU SPOUT ALL THIS NONSENSE ABOUT LOVE TOWARD BOYS NO MORE THAN CHILDREN....
...IS BECAUSE YOU KNOW YOU HAVE NO FUTURE WITH THEM.
HOW RUDE... I'LL HAVE YOU KNOW, I'M ALWAYS SERIOUS ABOUT LOVE.

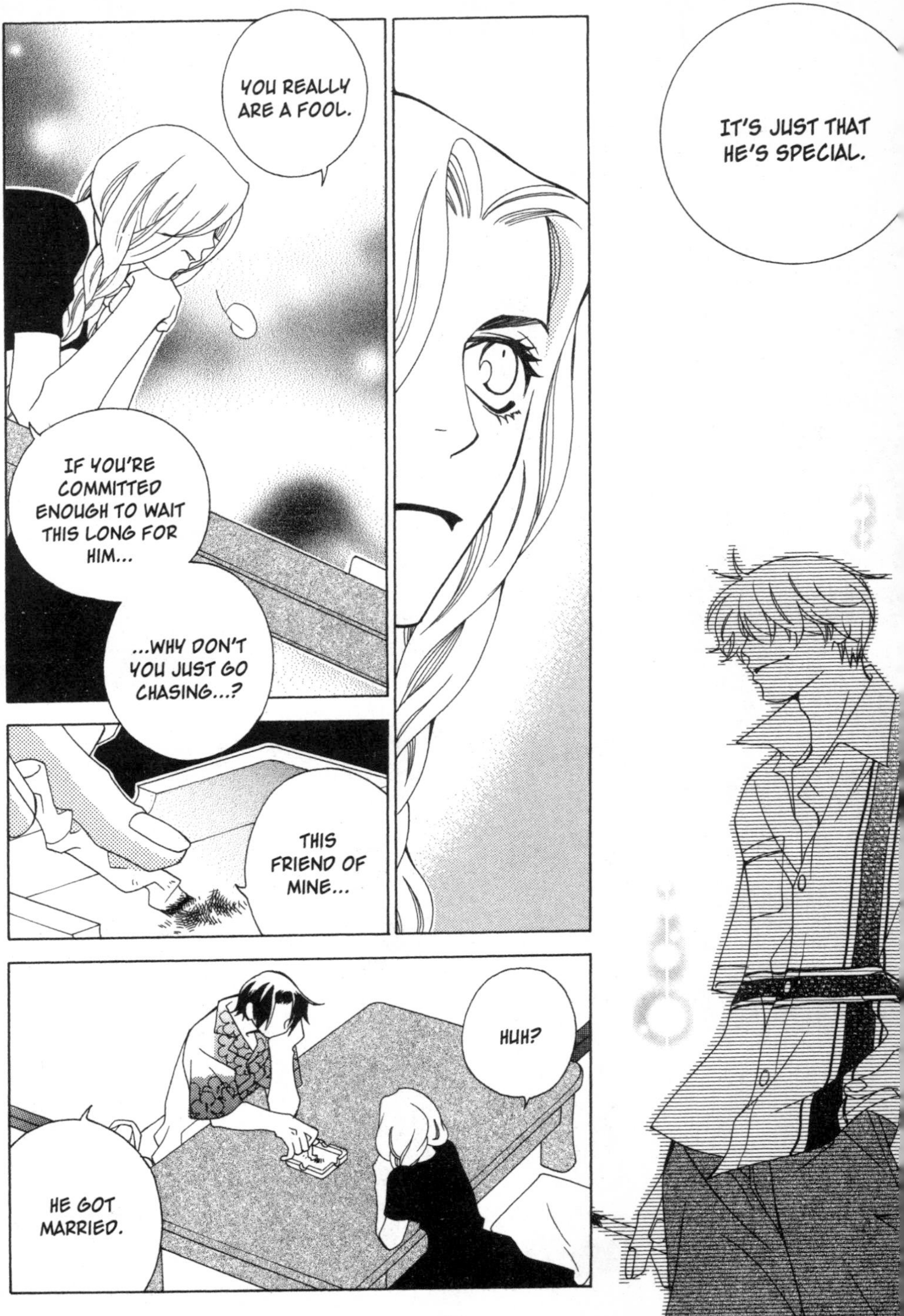
IT'S JUST THAT HE'S SPECIAL.
YOU REALLY ARE A FOOL.
IF YOU'RE COMMITTED ENOUGH TO WAIT THIS LONG FOR HIM...
...WHY DON'T YOU JUST GO CHASING...?
THIS FRIEND OF MINE...
HUH?
HE GOT MARRIED.

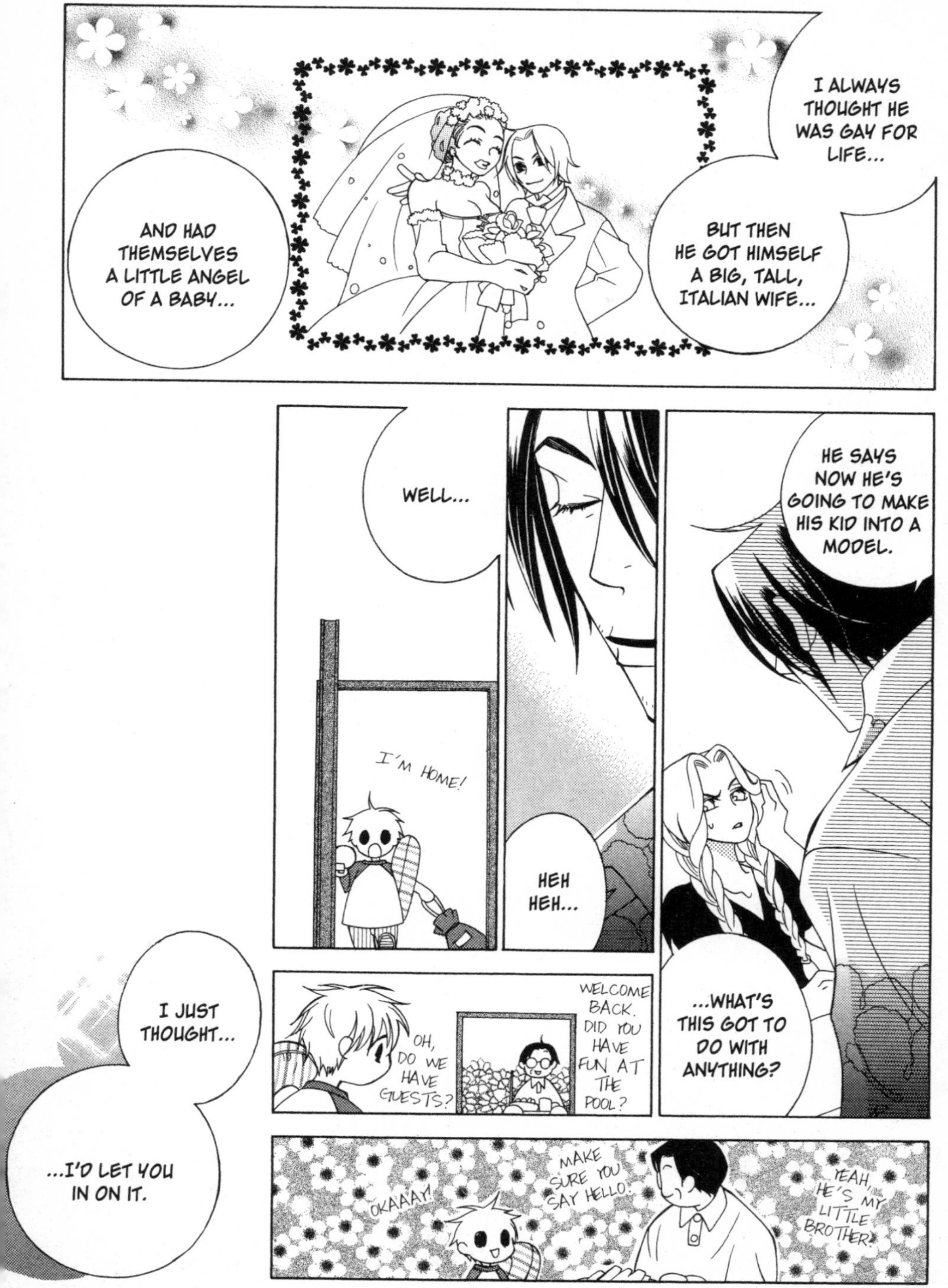
I ALWAYS THOUGHT HE WAS GAY FOR LIFE...
BUT THEN HE GOT HIMSELF A BIG, TALL, ITALIAN WIFE...
AND HAD THEMSELVES A LITTLE ANGEL OF A BABY...
HE SAYS NOW HE'S GOING TO MAKE HIS KID INTO A MODEL.
...WHAT'S THIS GOT TO DO WITH ANYTHING?
HEH HEH...
WELL...
I'M HOME!
WELCOME BACK. DID YOU HAVE FUN AT THE POOL?
OH, DO WE HAVE GUESTS?
I JUST THOUGHT...
YEAH, HE'S MY LITTLE BROTHER!
MAKE SURE YOU SAY HELLO.
OKAAAY!
...I'D LET YOU IN ON IT.

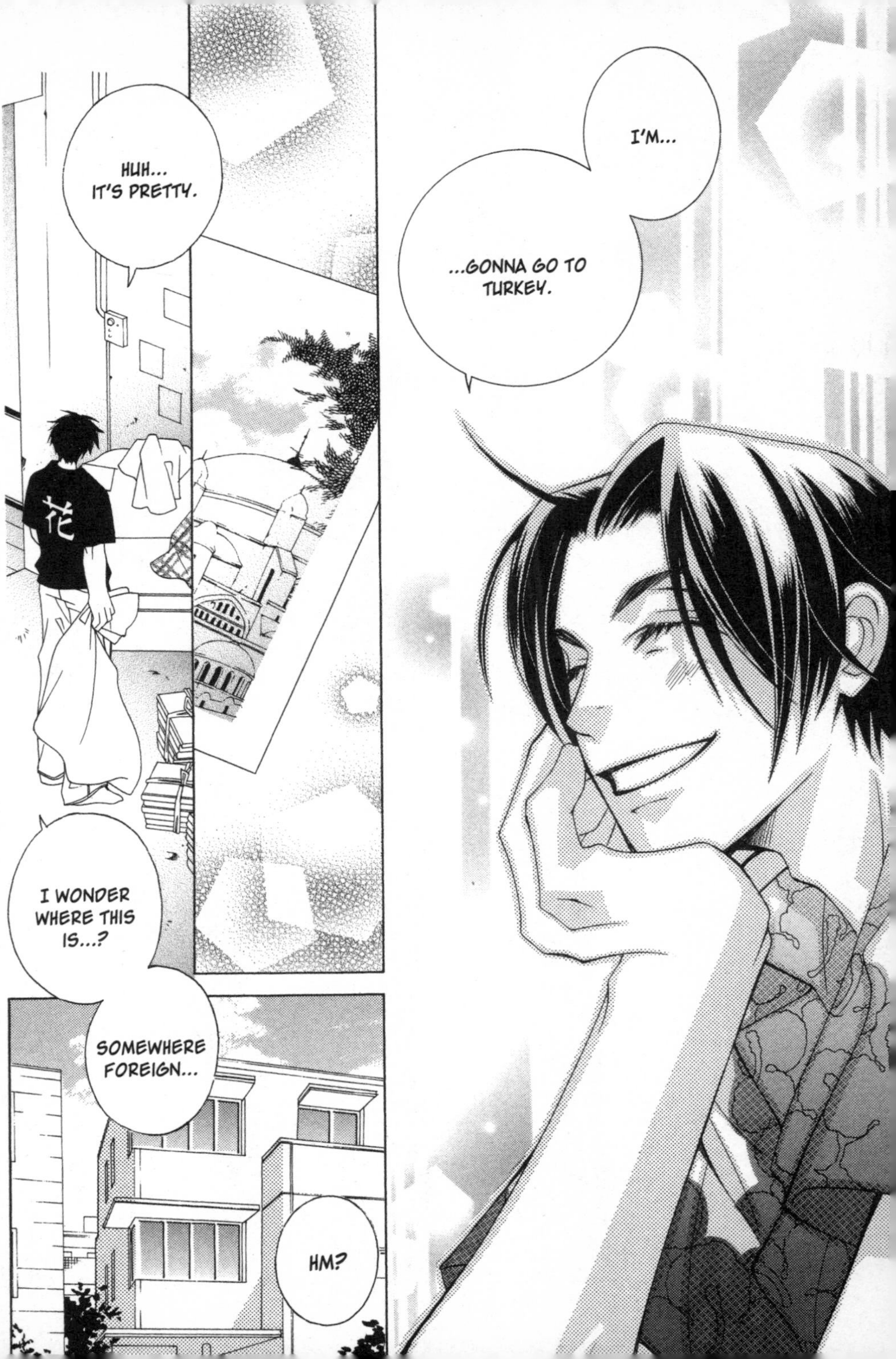

I'M...
...GONNA GO TO TURKEY.
HUH... IT'S PRETTY.
花
I WONDER WHERE THIS IS...?
SOMEWHERE FOREIGN...
HM?

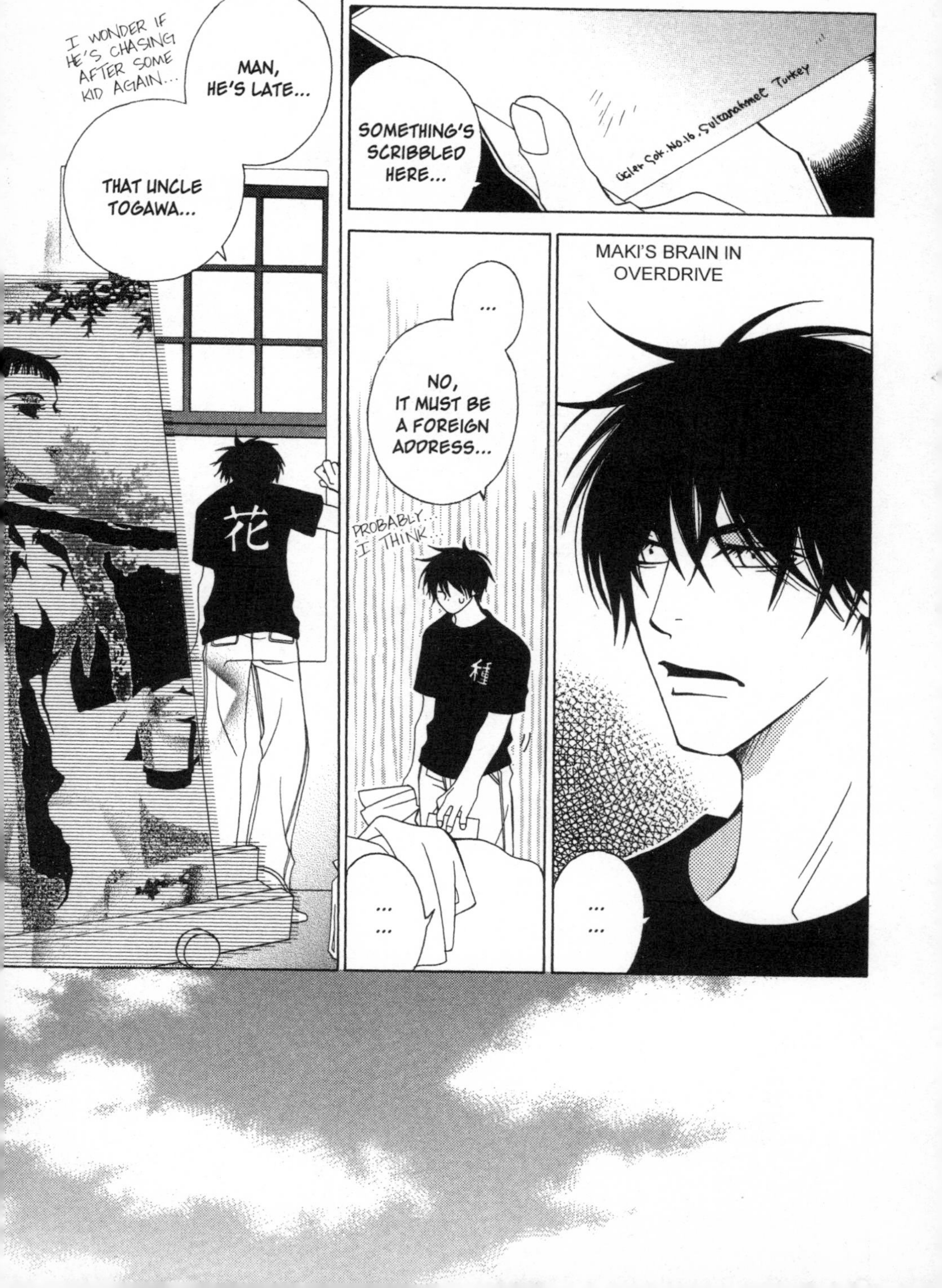
SOMETHING'S SCRIBBLED HERE...
Üçler Sok. No.16, Sultanahmet Turkey
MAKI'S BRAIN IN OVERDRIVE
... ...
...
NO, IT MUST BE A FOREIGN ADDRESS...
PROBABLY... I THINK...
... ...
MAN, HE'S LATE...
I WONDER IF HE'S CHASING AFTER SOME KID AGAIN...
THAT UNCLE TOGAWA...

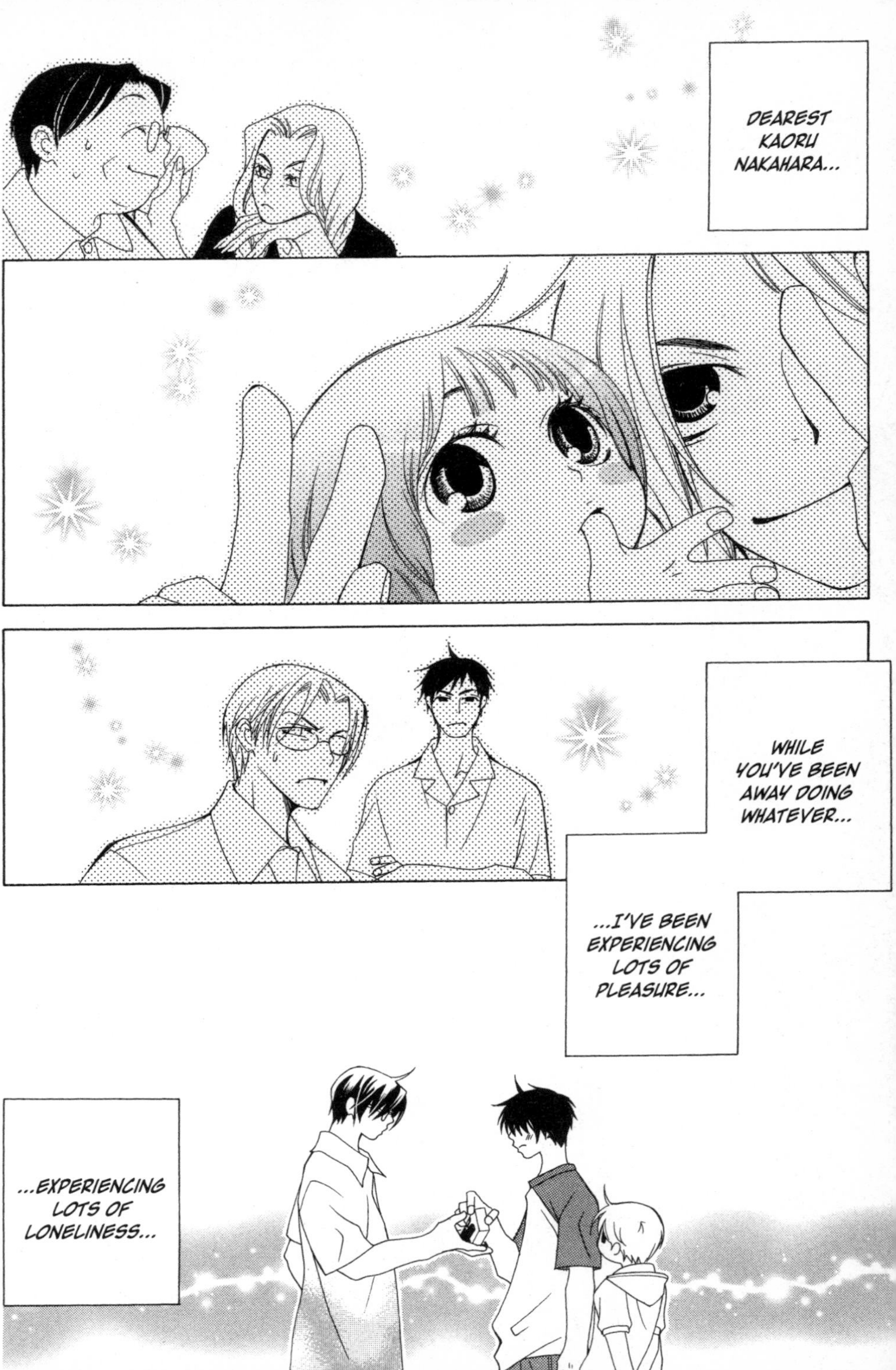
DEAREST KAORU NAKAHARA...
WHILE YOU'VE BEEN AWAY DOING WHATEVER...
...I'VE BEEN EXPERIENCING LOTS OF PLEASURE...
...EXPERIENCING LOTS OF LONELINESS...

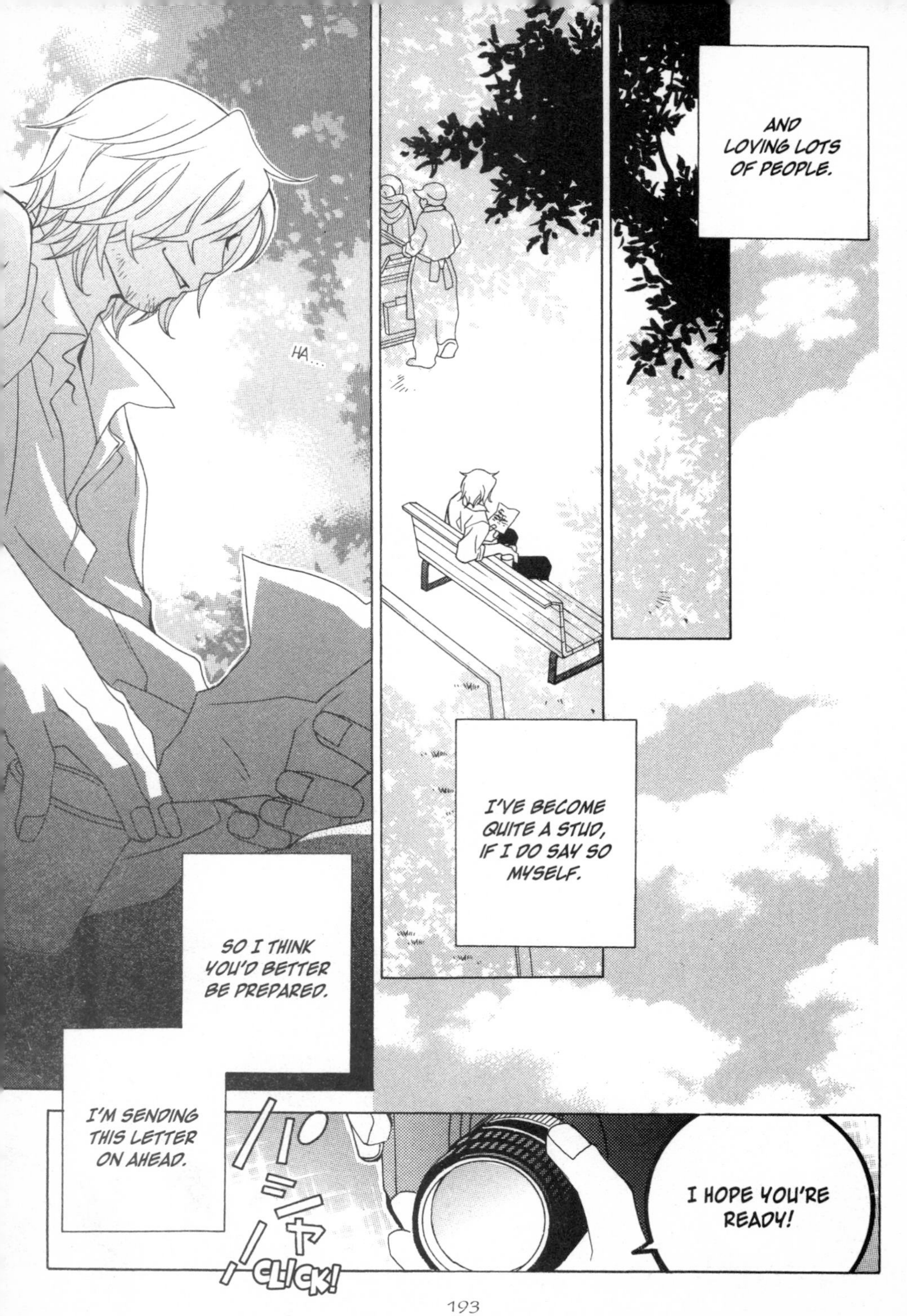
AND LOVING LOTS OF PEOPLE.
I'VE BECOME QUITE A STUD, IF I DO SAY SO MYSELF.
HA...
SO I THINK YOU'D BETTER BE PREPARED.
I'M SENDING THIS LETTER ON AHEAD.
I HOPE YOU'RE READY!
CLICK!

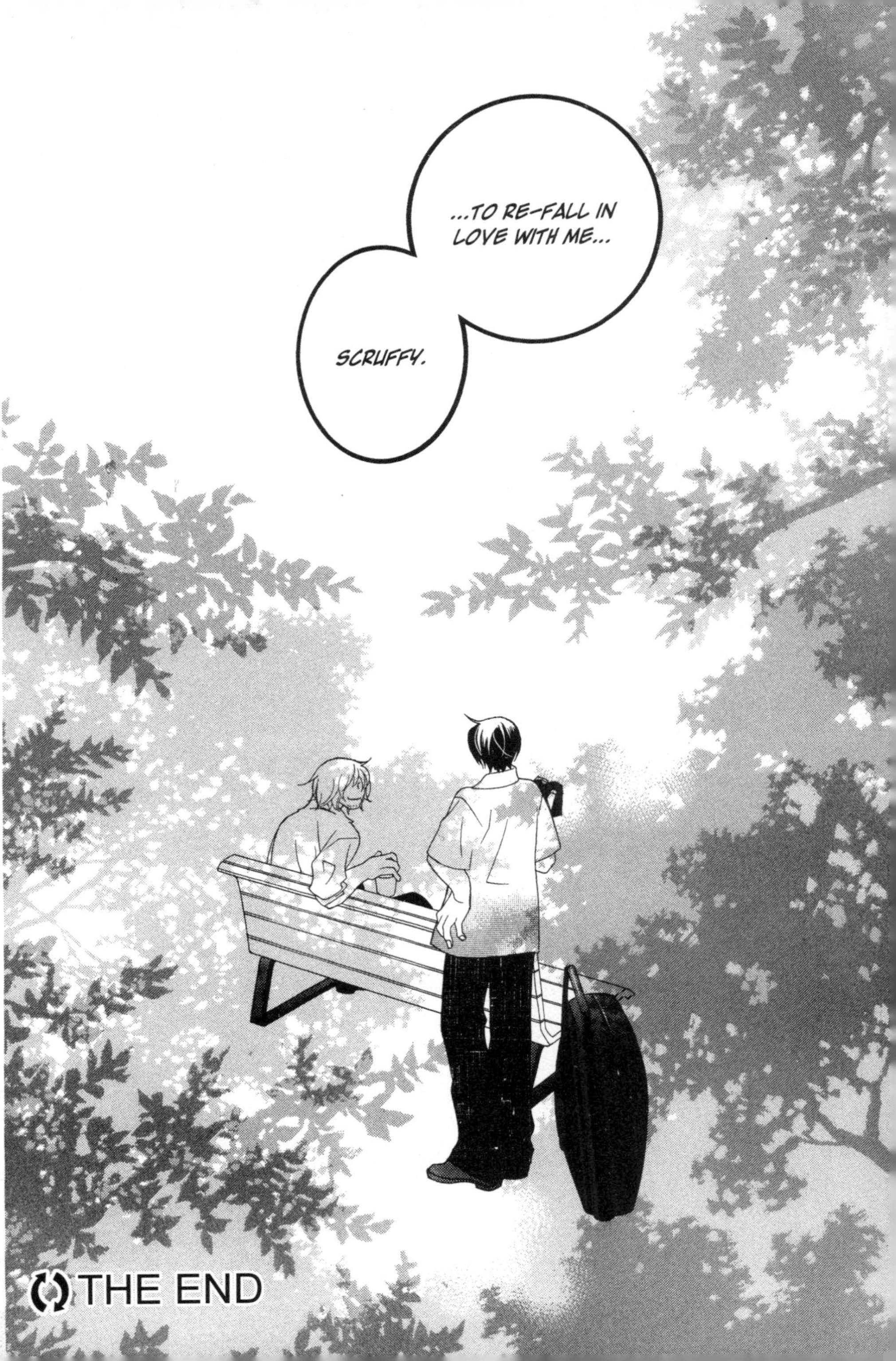
...TO RE-FALL IN LOVE WITH ME...
SCRUFFY.
THE END

EPILOGUE MANGA

End Shot.

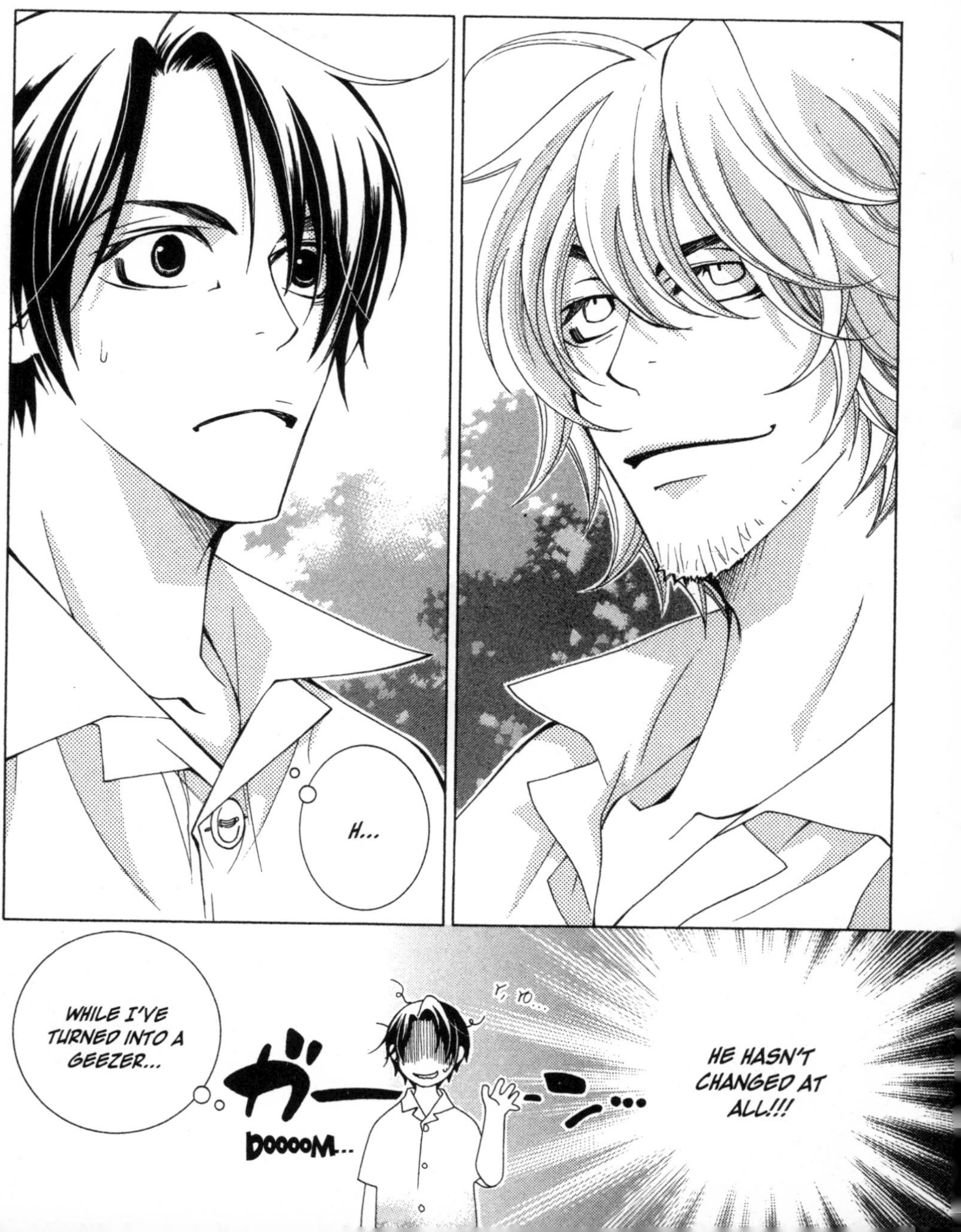
H...
HE HASN'T CHANGED AT ALL!!!
Y, YO...
ガーン...
DOOOOM...
WHILE I'VE TURNED INTO A GEEZER...

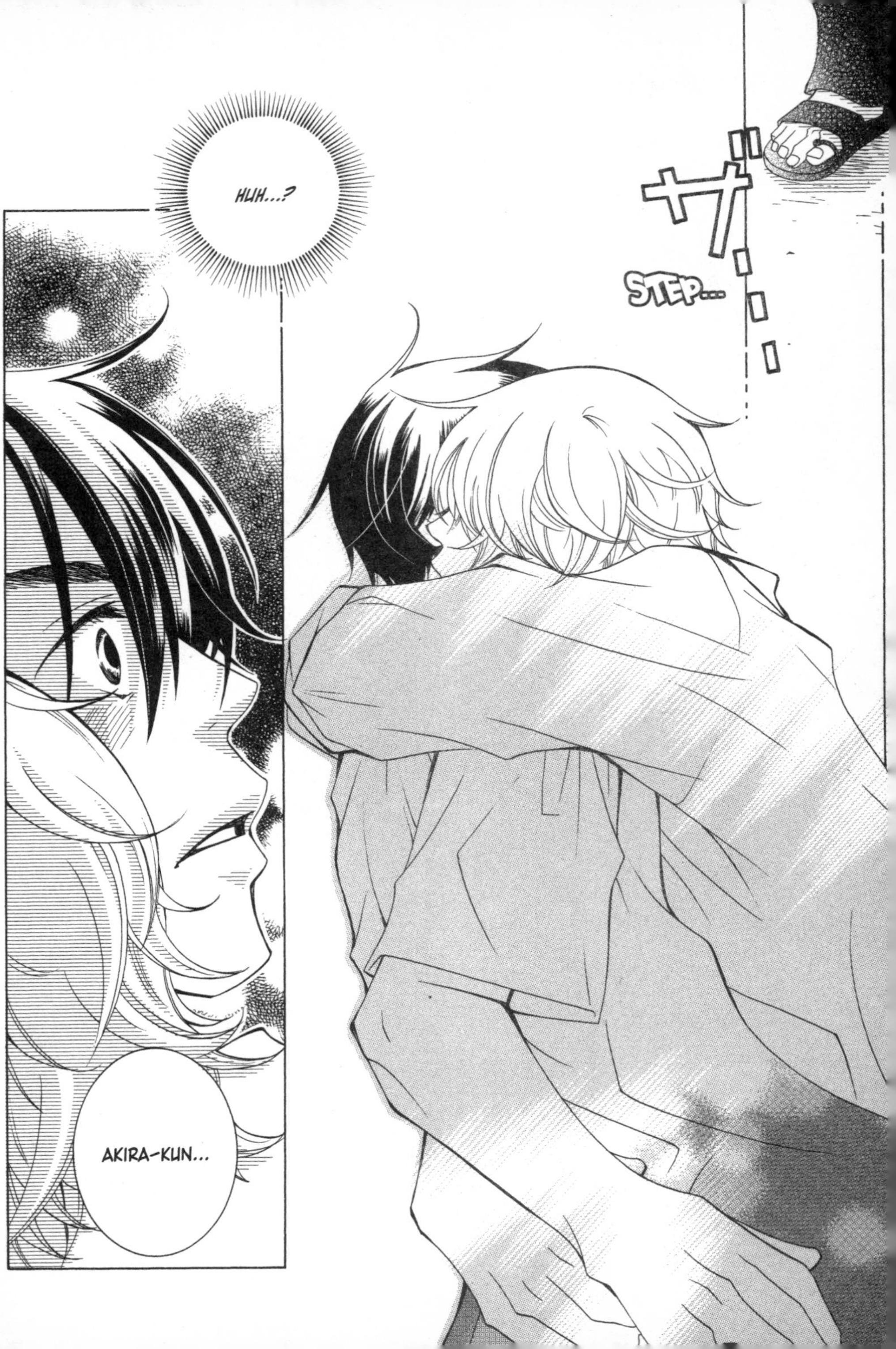
ザ
STEP...
HUH...?
AKIRA-KUN...

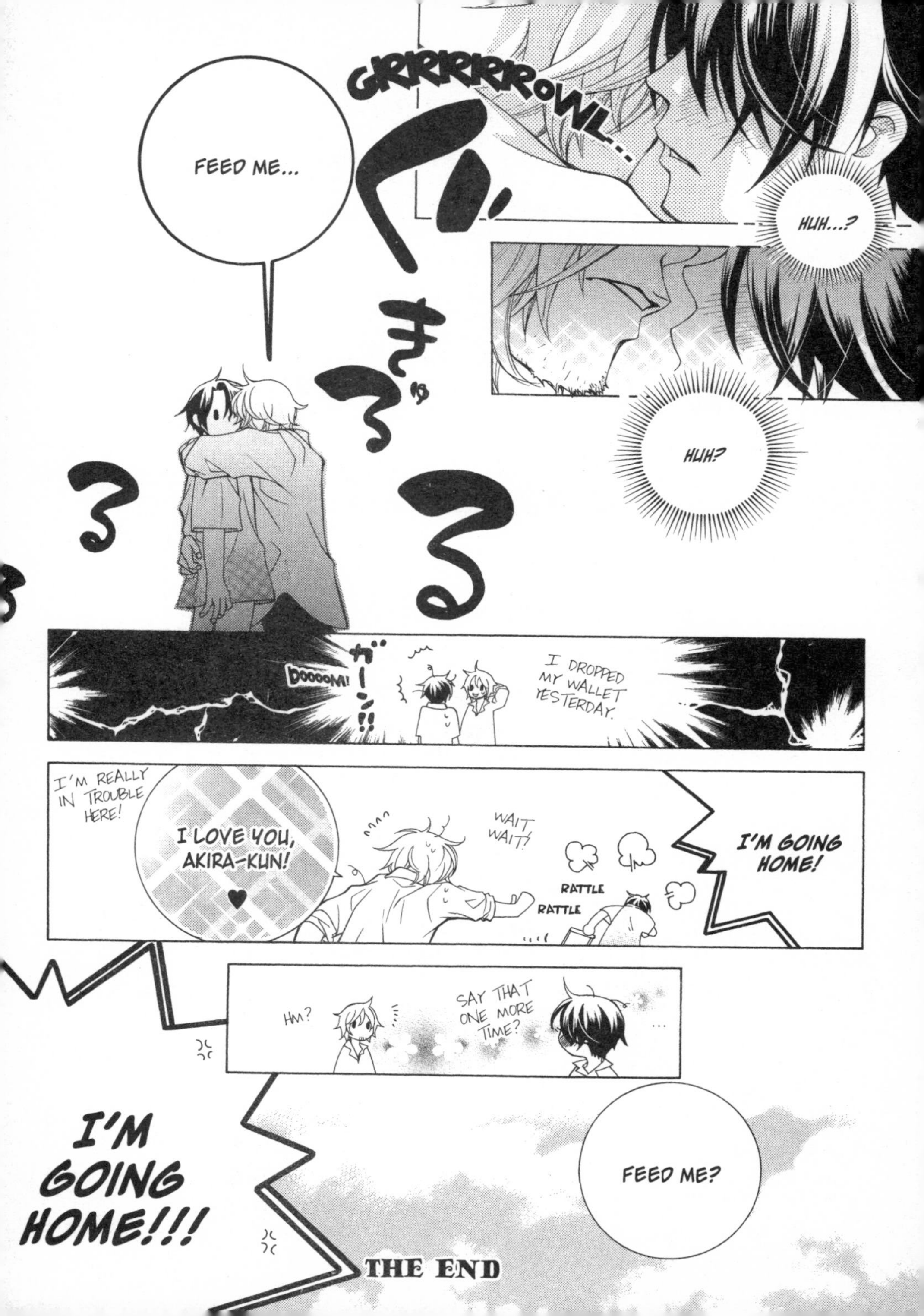
GRRRRRROWL...
HUH...?
HUH?
FEED ME...
I DROPPED MY WALLET YESTERDAY.
DOOOOM!
I'M GOING HOME!
RATTLE
RATTLE
WAIT, WAIT!
I LOVE YOU, AKIRA-KUN!
I'M REALLY IN TROUBLE HERE!
...
SAY THAT ONE MORE TIME?
HM?
FEED ME?
I'M GOING HOME!!!
THE END

Afterword

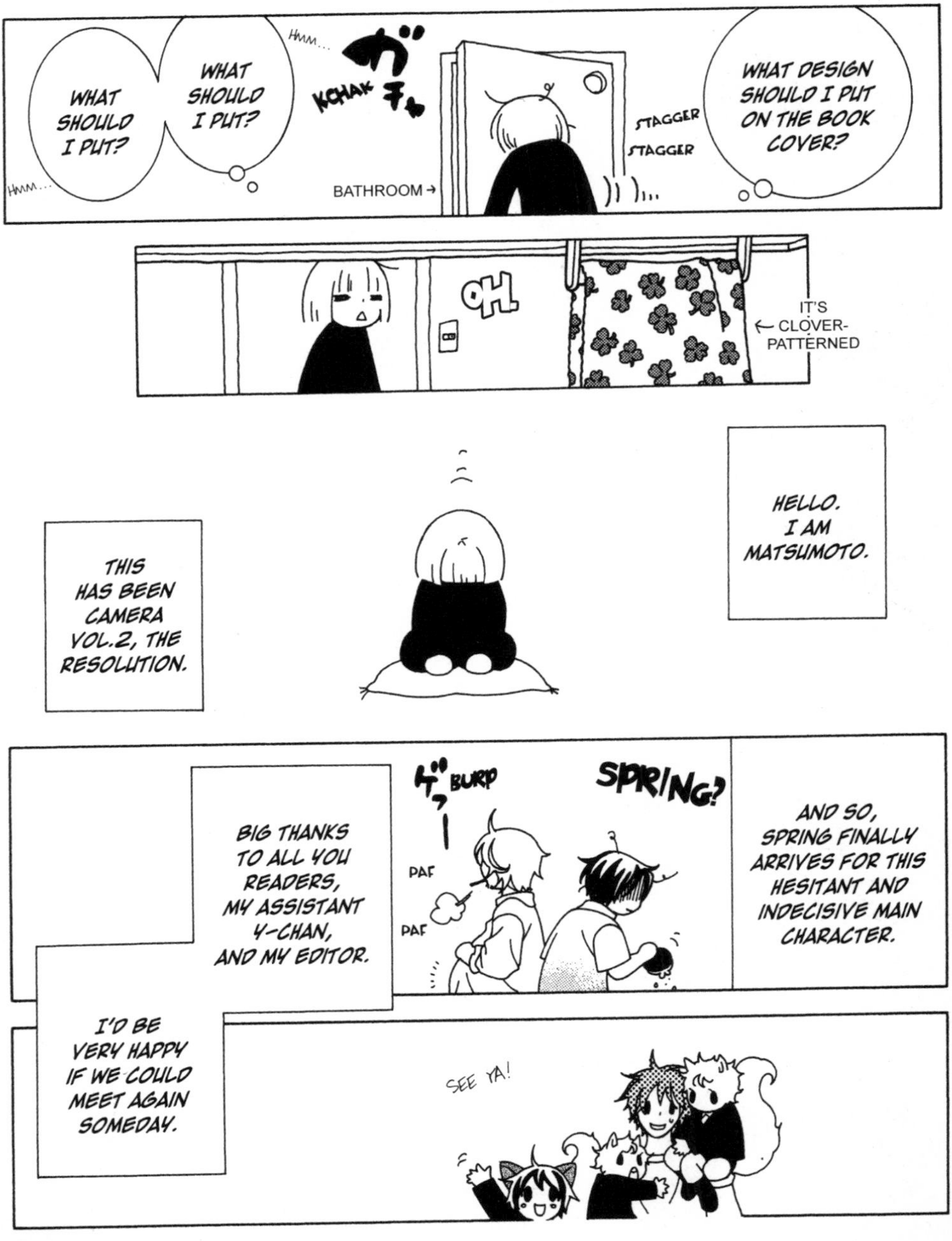
WHAT DESIGN SHOULD I PUT ON THE BOOK COVER?
STAGGER
STAGGER
BATHROOM →
KCHAK
HMM...
WHAT SHOULD I PUT?
WHAT SHOULD I PUT?
HMM...
IT'S ← CLOVER-PATTERNED
OH.
HELLO. I AM MATSUMOTO.
THIS HAS BEEN CAMERA VOL.2, THE RESOLUTION.
AND SO, SPRING FINALLY ARRIVES FOR THIS HESITANT AND INDECISIVE MAIN CHARACTER.
SPRING?
BURP
PAF
PAF
BIG THANKS TO ALL YOU READERS, MY ASSISTANT Y-CHAN, AND MY EDITOR.
I'D BE VERY HAPPY IF WE COULD MEET AGAIN SOMEDAY.
SEE YA!

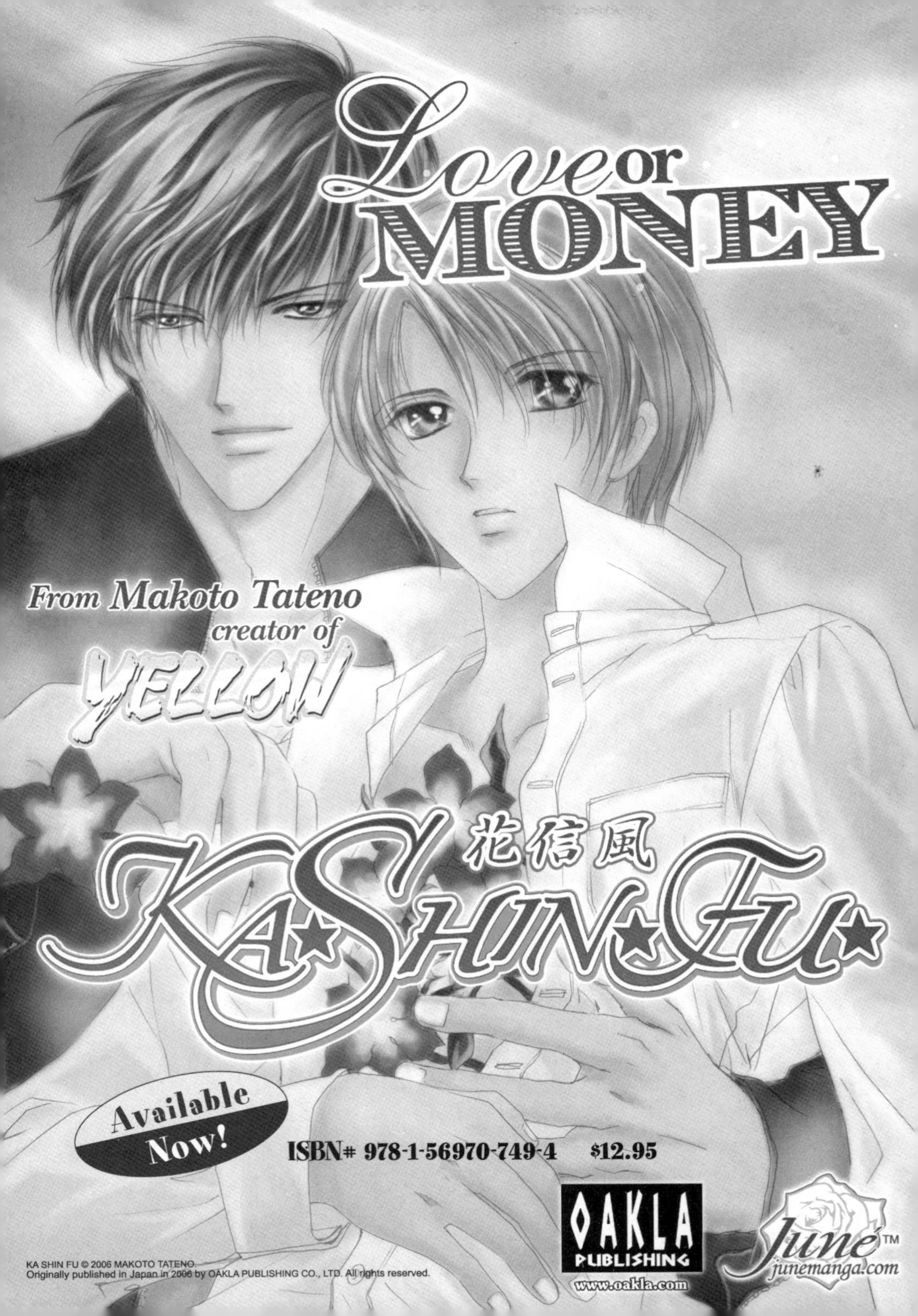

Love or MONEY
From Makoto Tateno creator of
YELLOW
花信風
KA★SHIN★FU★
Available Now!
ISBN# 978-1-56970-749-4
$12.95
OAKLA PUBLISHING
www.oakla.com
June™
junemanga.com
KA SHIN FU © 2006 MAKOTO TATENO.
Originally published in Japan in 2006 by OAKLA PUBLISHING CO., LTD. All rights reserved.

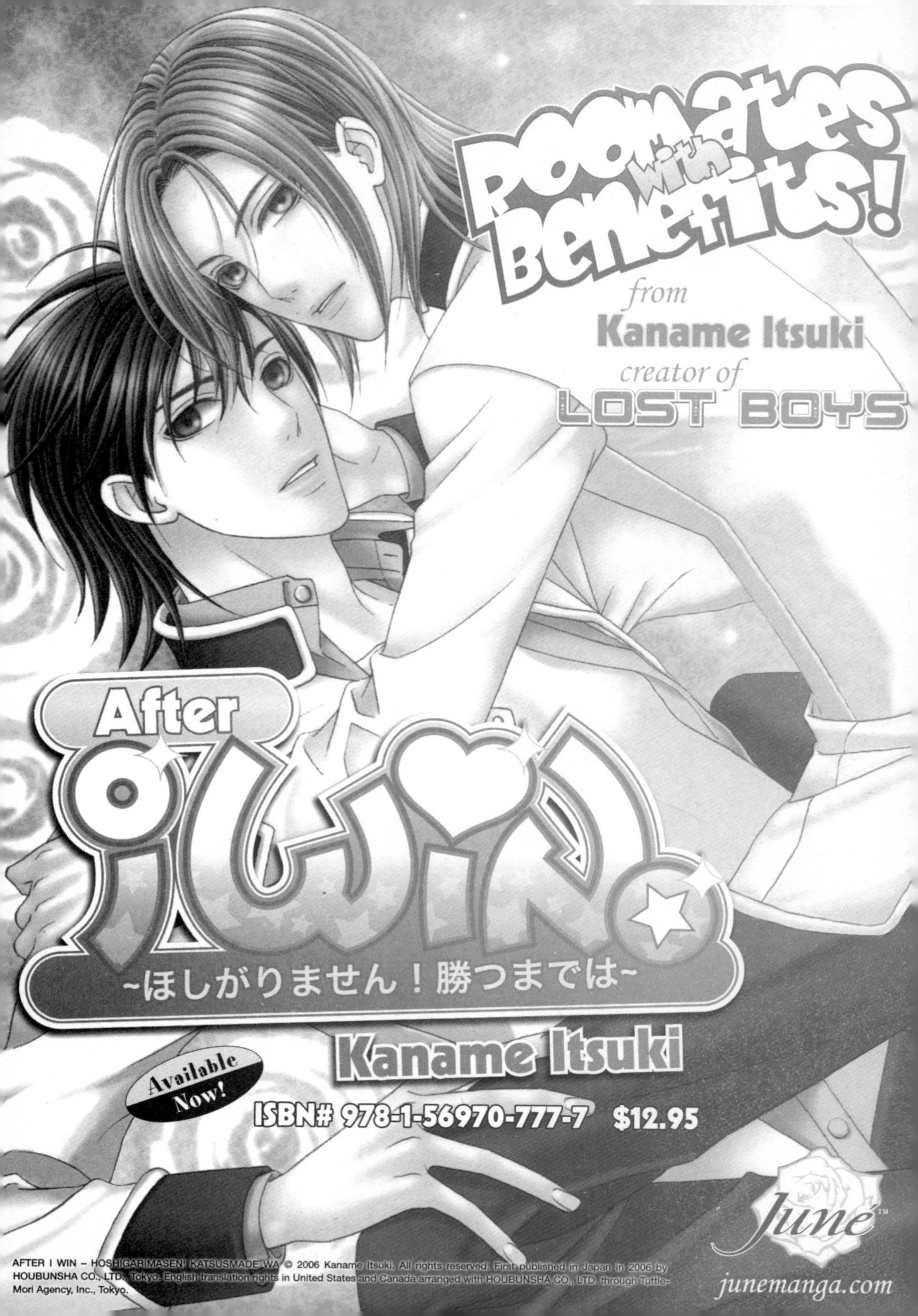
Roommates with Benefits!
from
Kaname Itsuki
creator of
LOST BOYS
After I Win
~ほしがりません！勝つまでは~
Kaname Itsuki
Available Now!
ISBN# 978-1-56970-777-7 $12.95
June™
junemanga.com
AFTER I WIN – HOSHIGARIMASEN! KATSUSMADE WA © 2006 Kaname Itsuki. All rights reserved. First published in Japan in 2006 by HOUBUNSHA CO., LTD., Tokyo. English translation rights in United States and Canada arranged with HOUBUNSHA CO., LTD. through Tuttle-Mori Agency, Inc., Tokyo.

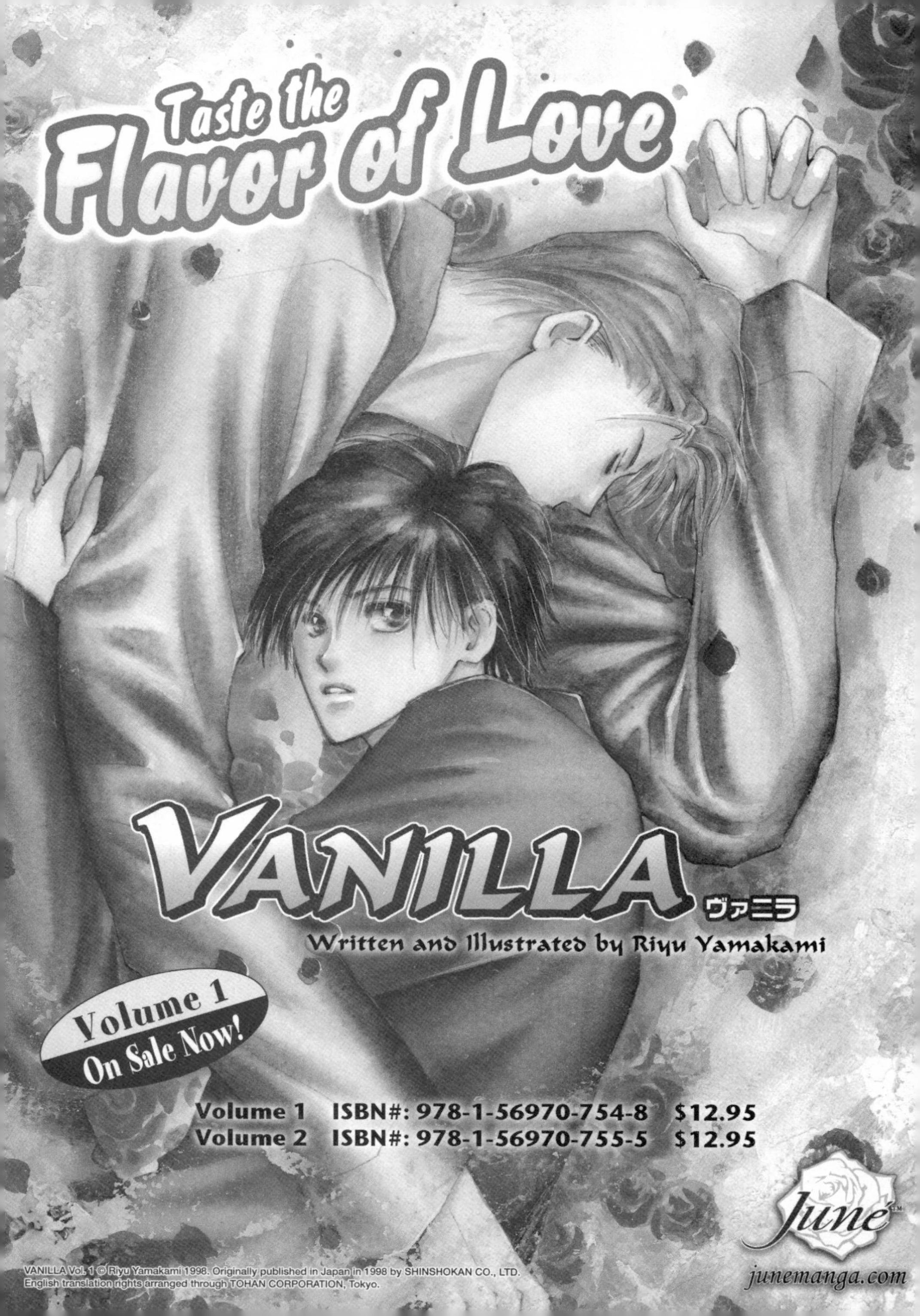

Taste the Flavor of Love

VANILLA
ヴァニラ

Written and Illustrated by Riyu Yamakami

Volume 1
On Sale Now!

Volume 1   ISBN#: 978-1-56970-754-8 $12.95
Volume 2   ISBN#: 978-1-56970-755-5 $12.95

June™

junemanga.com

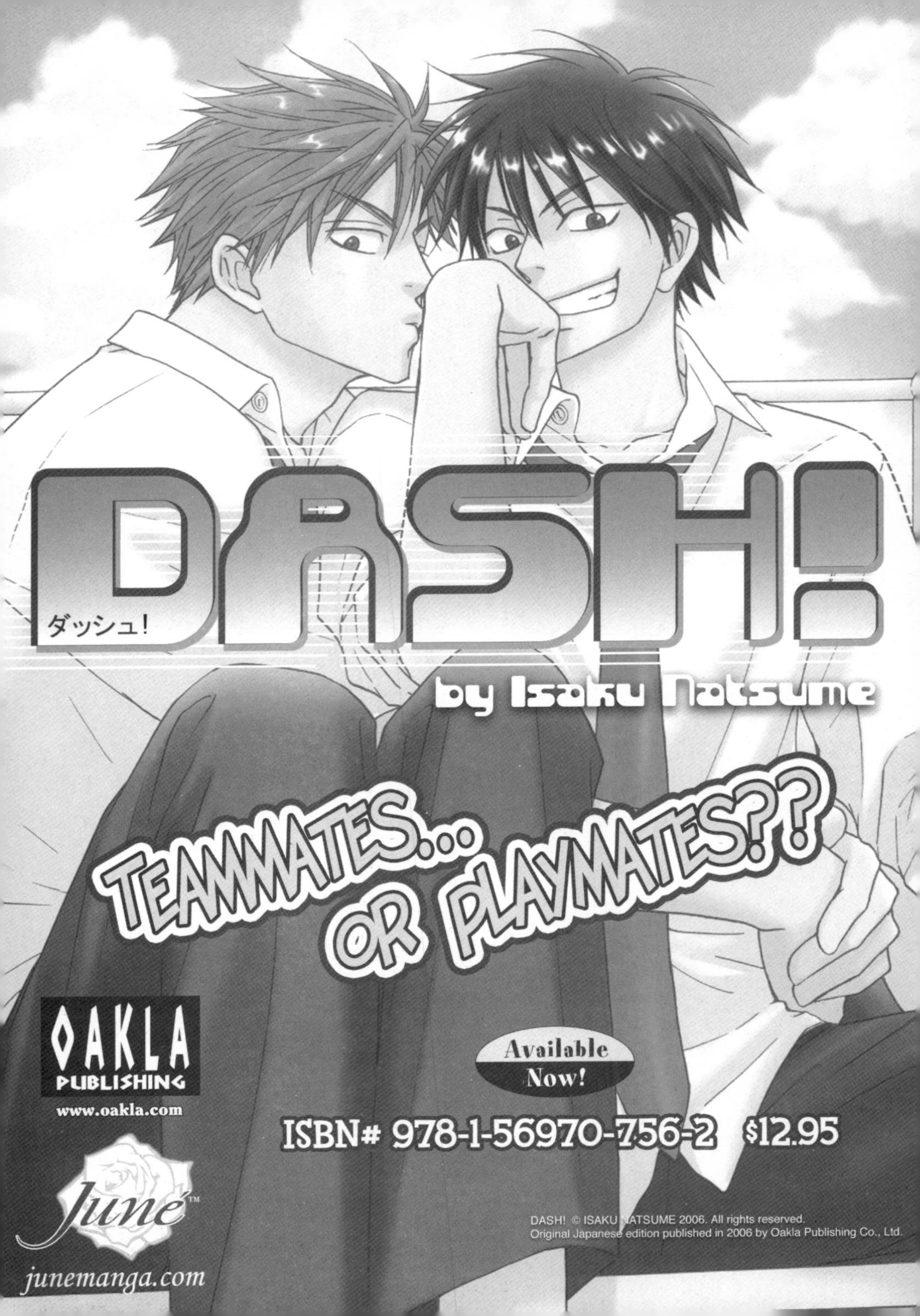
DASH!
ダッシュ!
by Isaku Natsume
TEAMMATES... OR PLAYMATES??
OAKLA PUBLISHING
www.oakla.com
Available Now!
ISBN# 978-1-56970-756-2 $12.95
June™
junemanga.com
DASH! © ISAKU NATSUME 2006. All rights reserved.
Original Japanese edition published in 2006 by Oakla Publishing Co., Ltd.

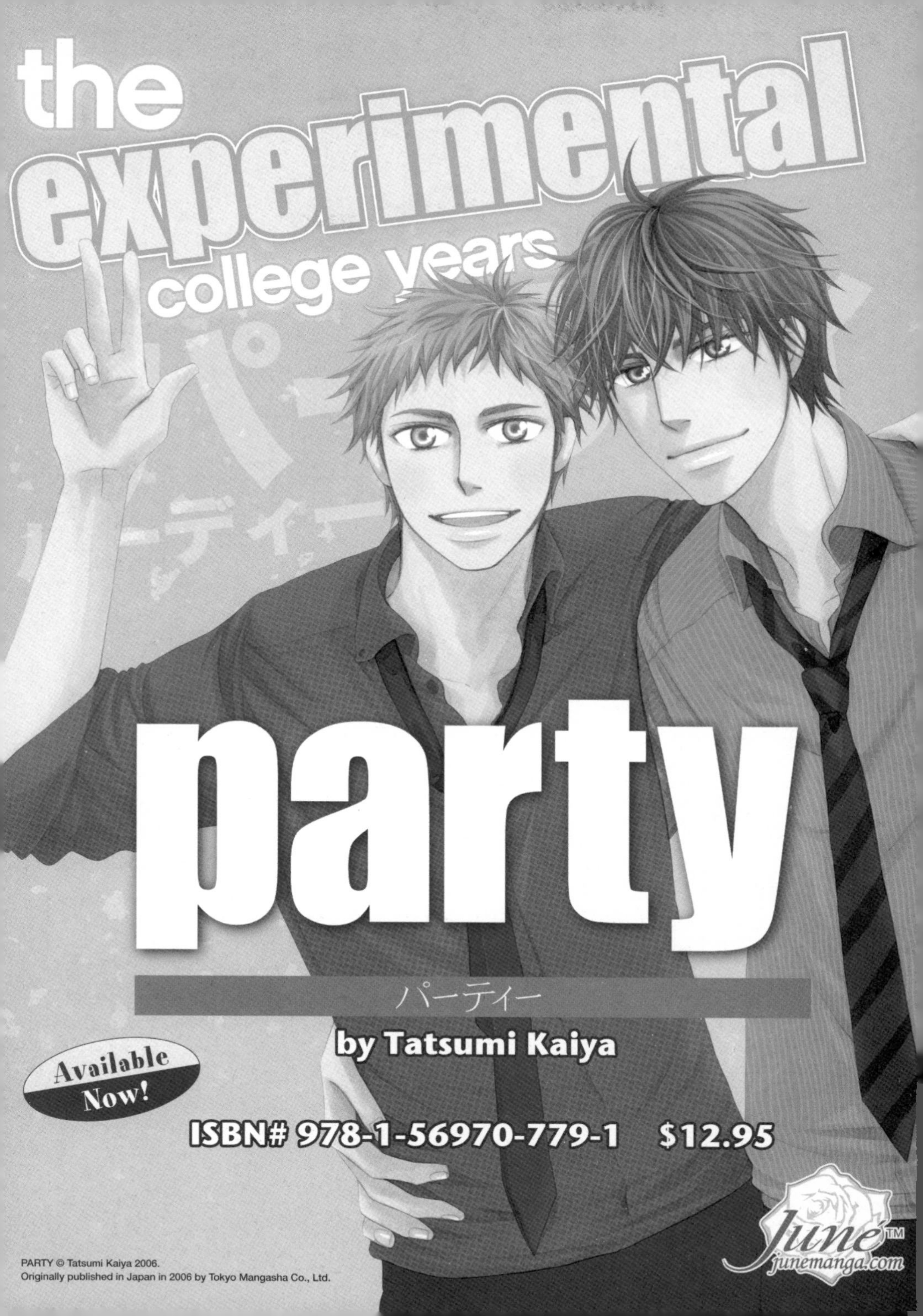
the experimental college years
パーティー
party
パーティー
by Tatsumi Kaiya
Available Now!
ISBN# 978-1-56970-779-1 $12.95
Juné™
junemanga.com
PARTY © Tatsumi Kaiya 2006.
Originally published in Japan in 2006 by Tokyo Mangasha Co., Ltd.

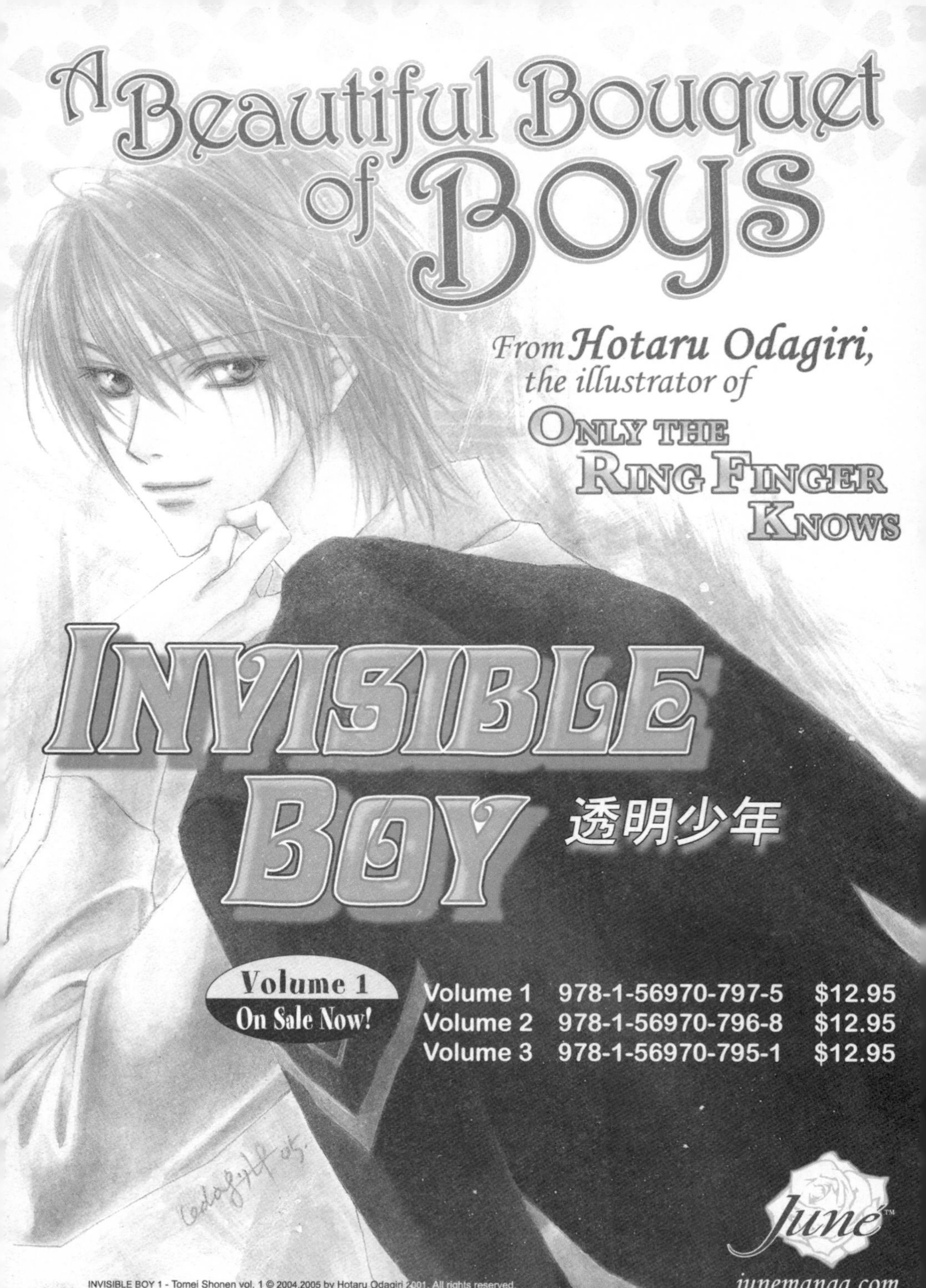
A Beautiful Bouquet of BOYS
From Hotaru Odagiri, the illustrator of
ONLY THE RING FINGER KNOWS
INVISIBLE BOY
透明少年
Volume 1
On Sale Now!
Volume 1 978-1-56970-797-5 $12.95
Volume 2 978-1-56970-796-8 $12.95
Volume 3 978-1-56970-795-1 $12.95
Juné™
junemanga.com

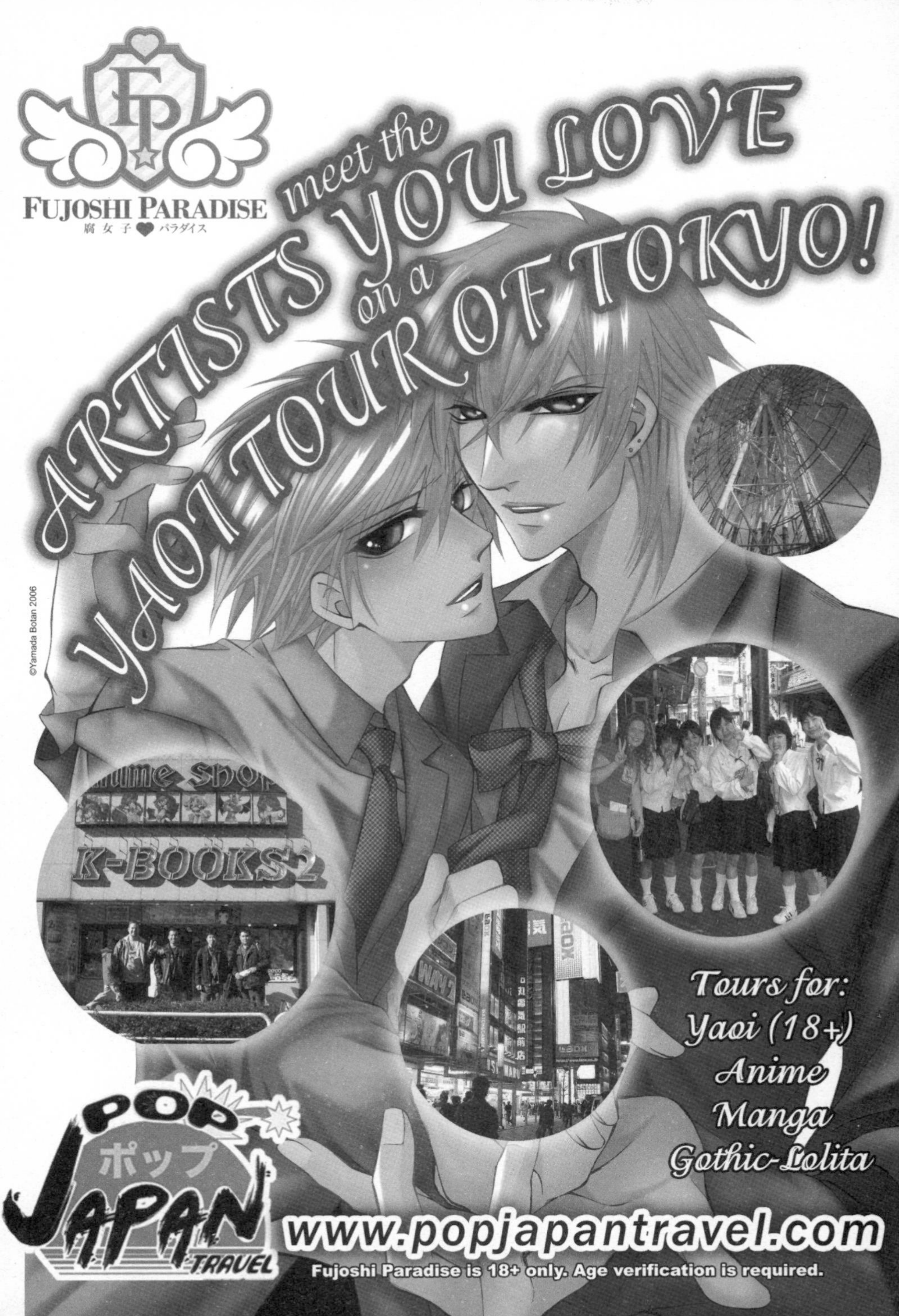

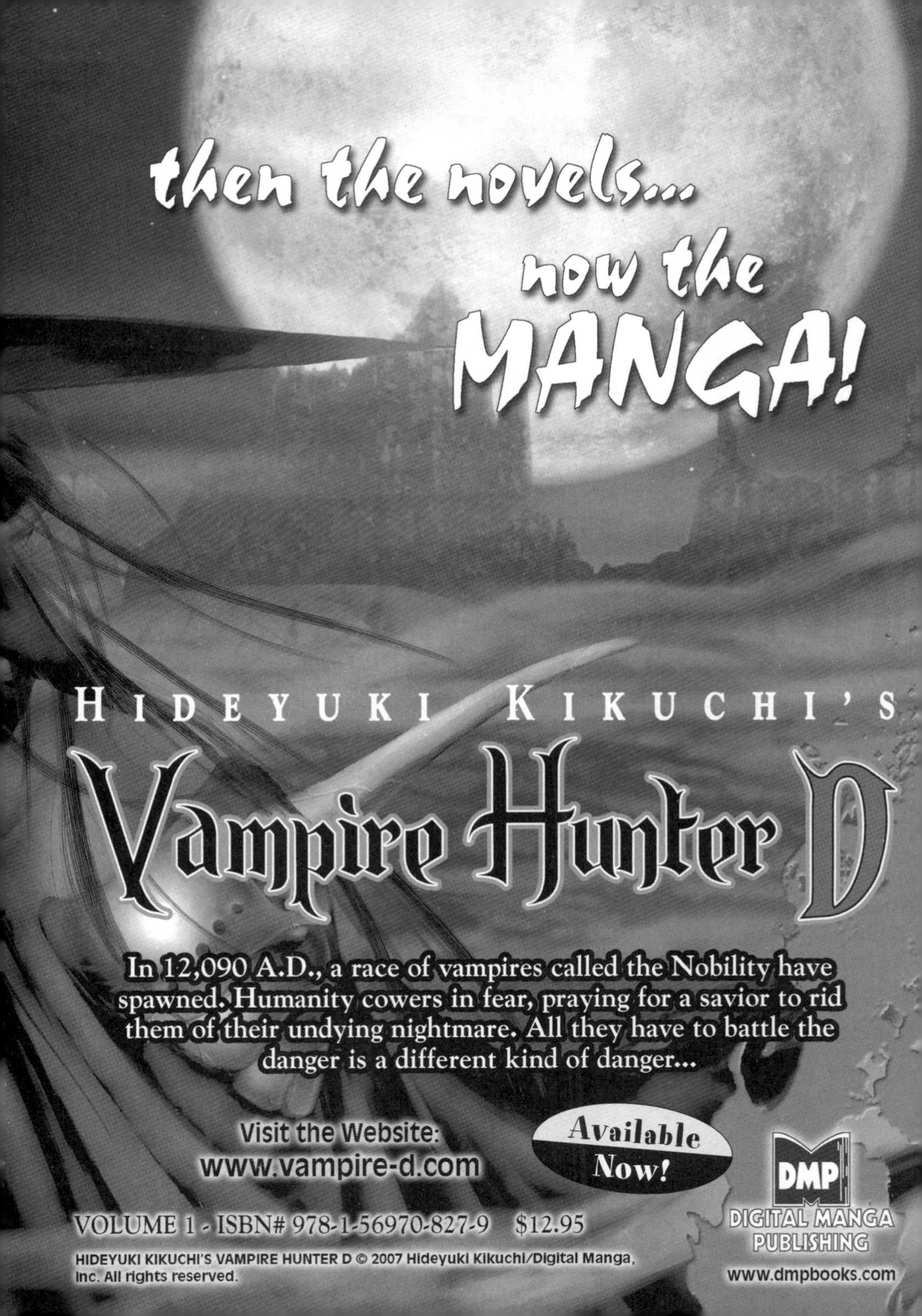
then the novels...
now the MANGA!
HIDEYUKI KIKUCHI'S
Vampire Hunter D
In 12,090 A.D., a race of vampires called the Nobility have spawned. Humanity cowers in fear, praying for a savior to rid them of their undying nightmare. All they have to battle the danger is a different kind of danger...
Visit the Website:
www.vampire-d.com
Available Now!
DMP
DIGITAL MANGA PUBLISHING
VOLUME 1 - ISBN# 978-1-56970-827-9 $12.95
HIDEYUKI KIKUCHI'S VAMPIRE HUNTER D © 2007 Hideyuki Kikuchi/Digital Manga, Inc. All rights reserved.
www.dmpbooks.com

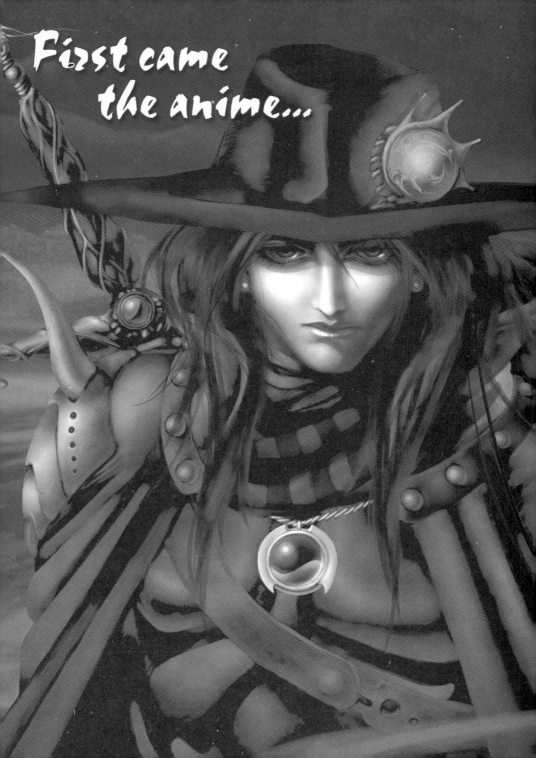

First came
the anime...

STOP

This is the back of the book! Start from the other side.

NATIVE MANGA
readers read manga from *right to left*.

1
2
1
3
2
3
5
4
4
6
5
5
8
7
6

If you run into our ***Native Manga*** *logo on any of our books... you'll know that this manga is published in it's true original native Japanese right to left reading format, as it was intended. Turn to the other side of the book and start reading from right to left, top to bottom.*

Follow the diagram to see how its done.
Surf's Up!

NATIVE MANGA
READ RIGHT TO LEFT